Super
Ocean
Weekend

CHARACTERS

ORNI is a platypus who knows an amazing island where he loves to go swimming among the sea creatures and watch them play.

CASTOR is a beaver who loves to ask lots of questions. She's super excited to be spending a weekend by the ocean!

SQUEAK is a rat who can't get enough of the sky and the stars. But the ocean isn't really his thing.

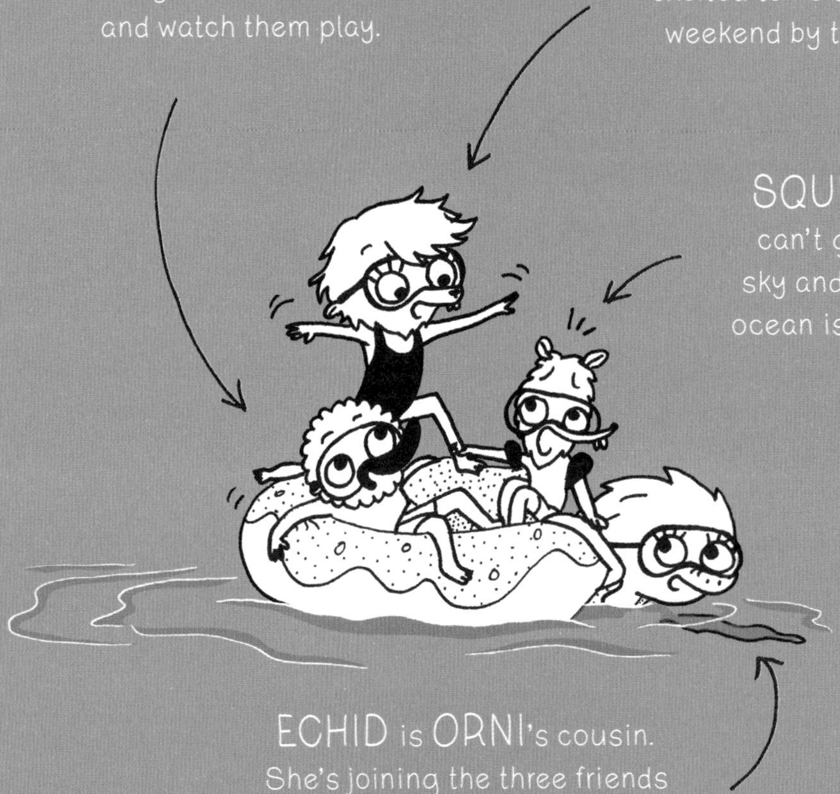

ECHID is ORNI's cousin. She's joining the three friends on a super adventure for the first time! Echid is an echidna, a spiny anteater from Australia who has lots to teach them about the ocean and the creatures that live there.

SUPER OCEAN WEEKEND

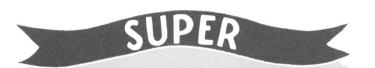

Gaëlle Alméras

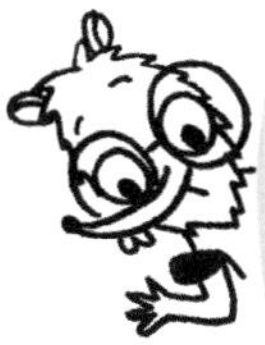

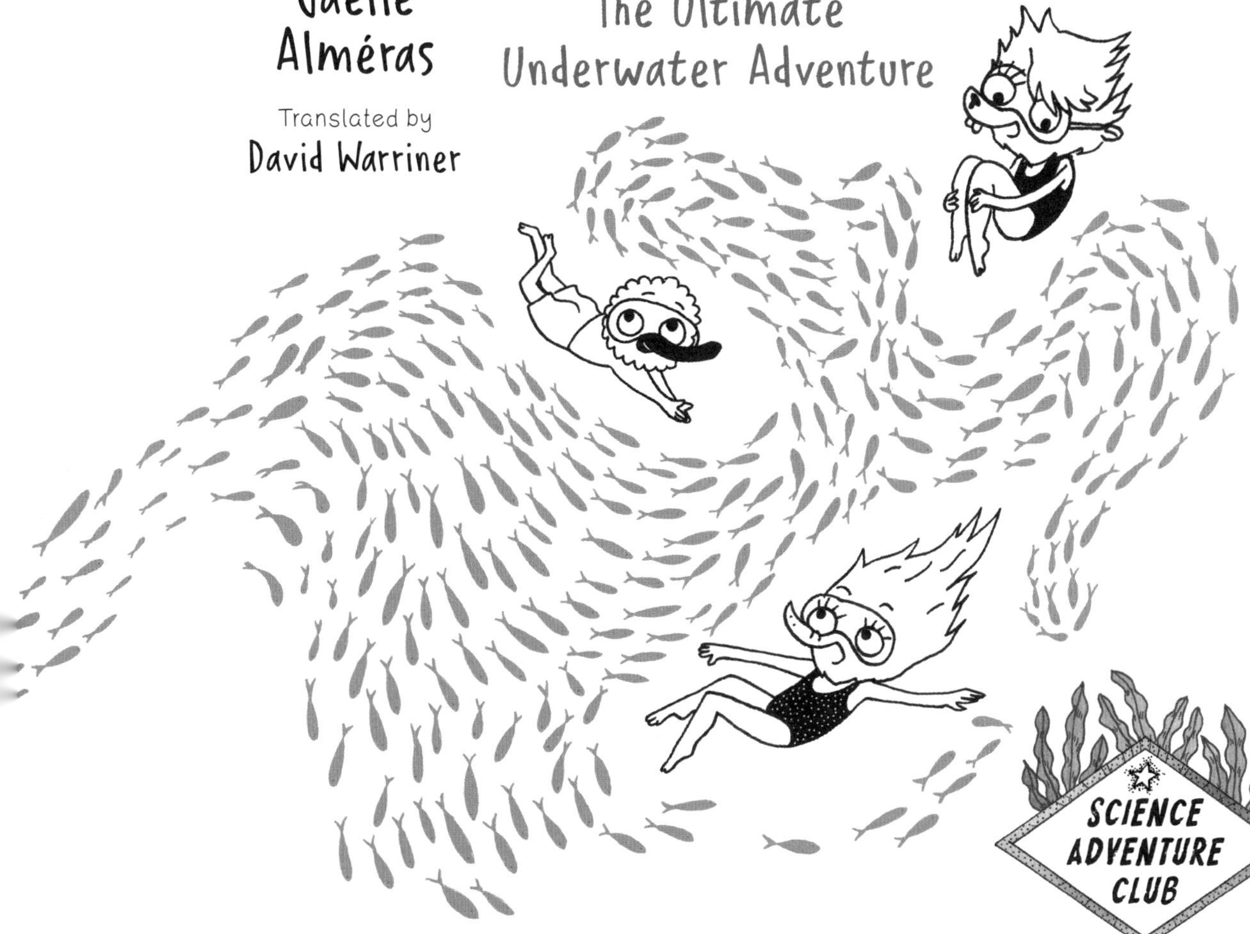

The Ultimate Underwater Adventure

Translated by David Warriner

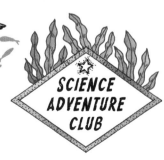

SCIENCE ADVENTURE CLUB

DAVID SUZUKI INSTITUTE

GREYSTONE KIDS

GREYSTONE BOOKS • VANCOUVER/BERKELEY/LONDON

CONTENTS

ARE YOU READY FOR AN AMAZING JOURNEY?

The ocean is such a vast, complex place that it's impossible to cram all its treasures into just one book. But we can push the door open a crack, enough to catch a glimpse of some of the marine life and riches it holds and let us dream a little.

This book is an invitation from the author and her endearing, enjoyable characters to discover the world's wonderful ocean playground!

Every scientific exploration is first and foremost a great human adventure, and now YOU get to be a part of the expedition. So, come dip your toes in the water with Orni, Echid, Castor, and Squeak.

Together, we can preserve and protect our planet's most precious resource—the all-powerful yet ever-fragile ocean.

Fair winds, young ocean adventurers!

MARJOLAINE MATABOS
Deep-sea ecology researcher at the Ifremer Biology and Ecology of Deep Marine Ecosystems Laboratory

INTRODUCTION

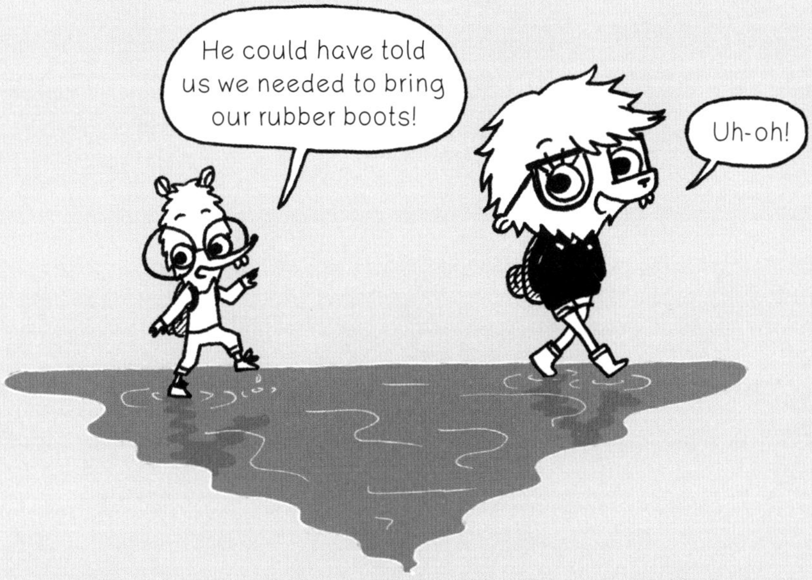
He could have told us we needed to bring our rubber boots!
Uh-oh!

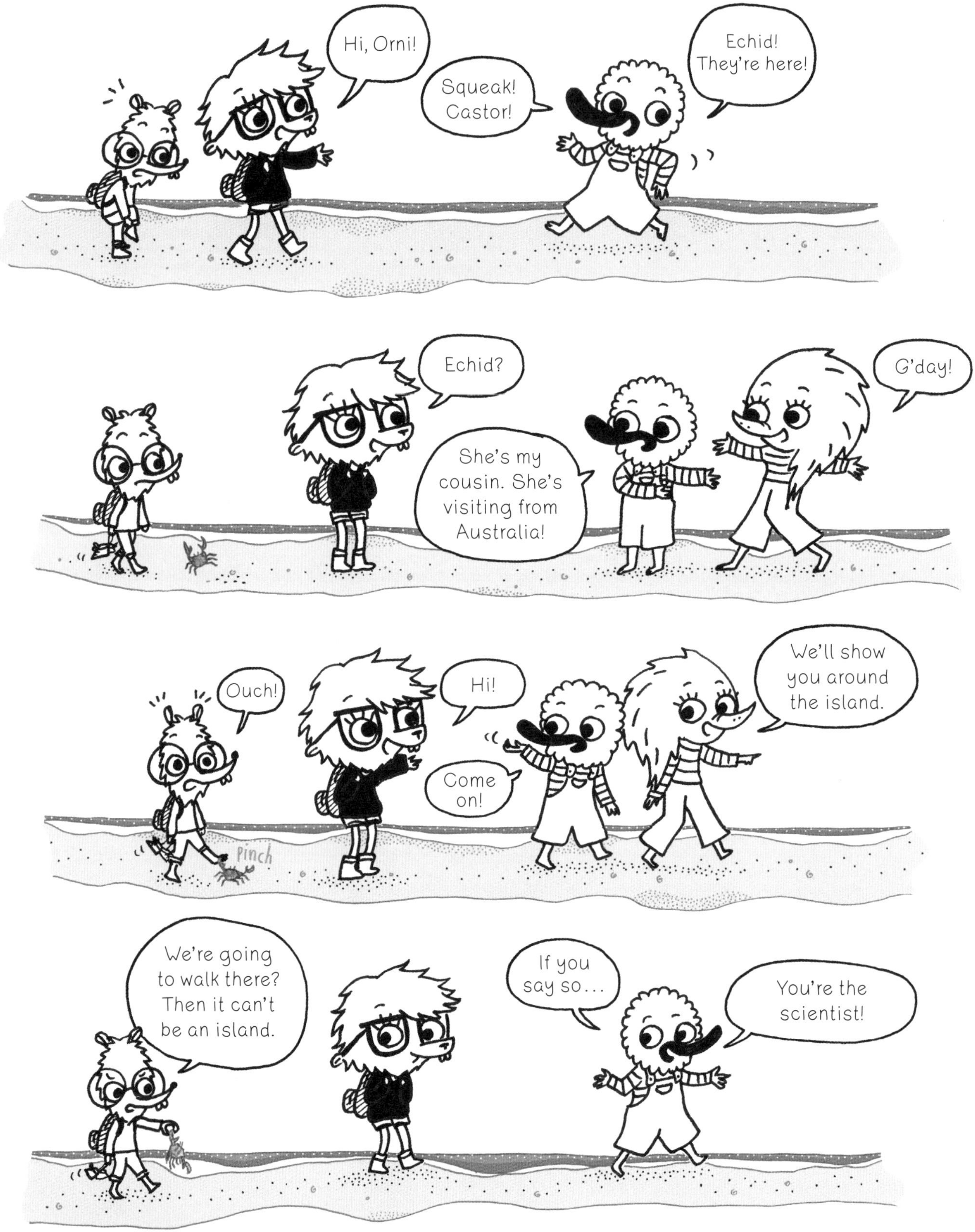
Hi, Orni!
Squeak! Castor!
Echid! They're here!
Echid?
She's my cousin. She's visiting from Australia!
G'day!
Ouch!
Hi!
Come on!
We'll show you around the island.
Pinch
We're going to walk there? Then it can't be an island.
If you say so…
You're the scientist!

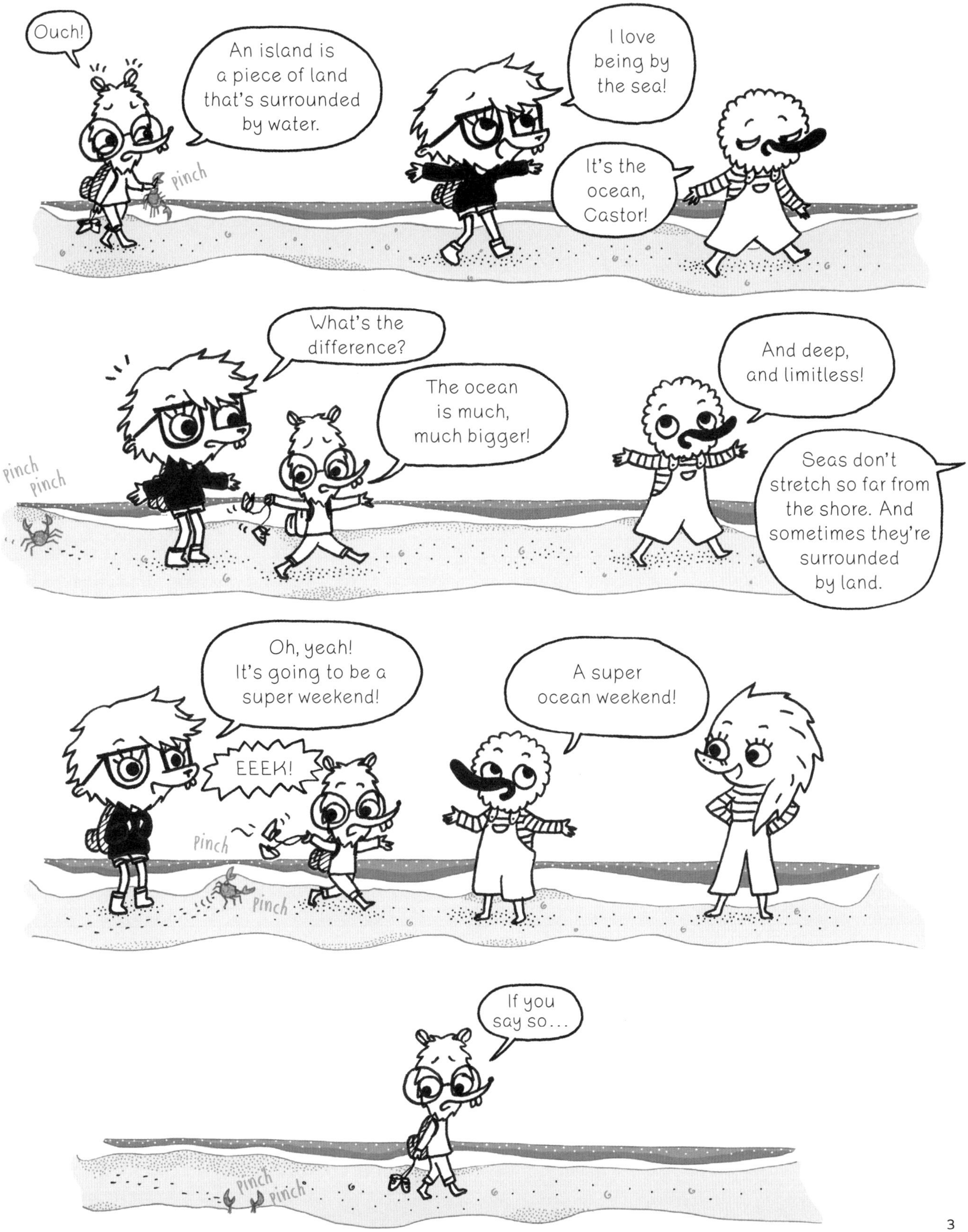
Ouch!
pinch
An island is a piece of land that's surrounded by water.
I love being by the sea!
It's the ocean, Castor!
pinch
pinch
What's the difference?
The ocean is much, much bigger!
And deep, and limitless!
Seas don't stretch so far from the shore. And sometimes they're surrounded by land.
Oh, yeah! It's going to be a super weekend!
EEEK!
Pinch
Pinch
A super ocean weekend!
If you say so...
Pinch
pinch

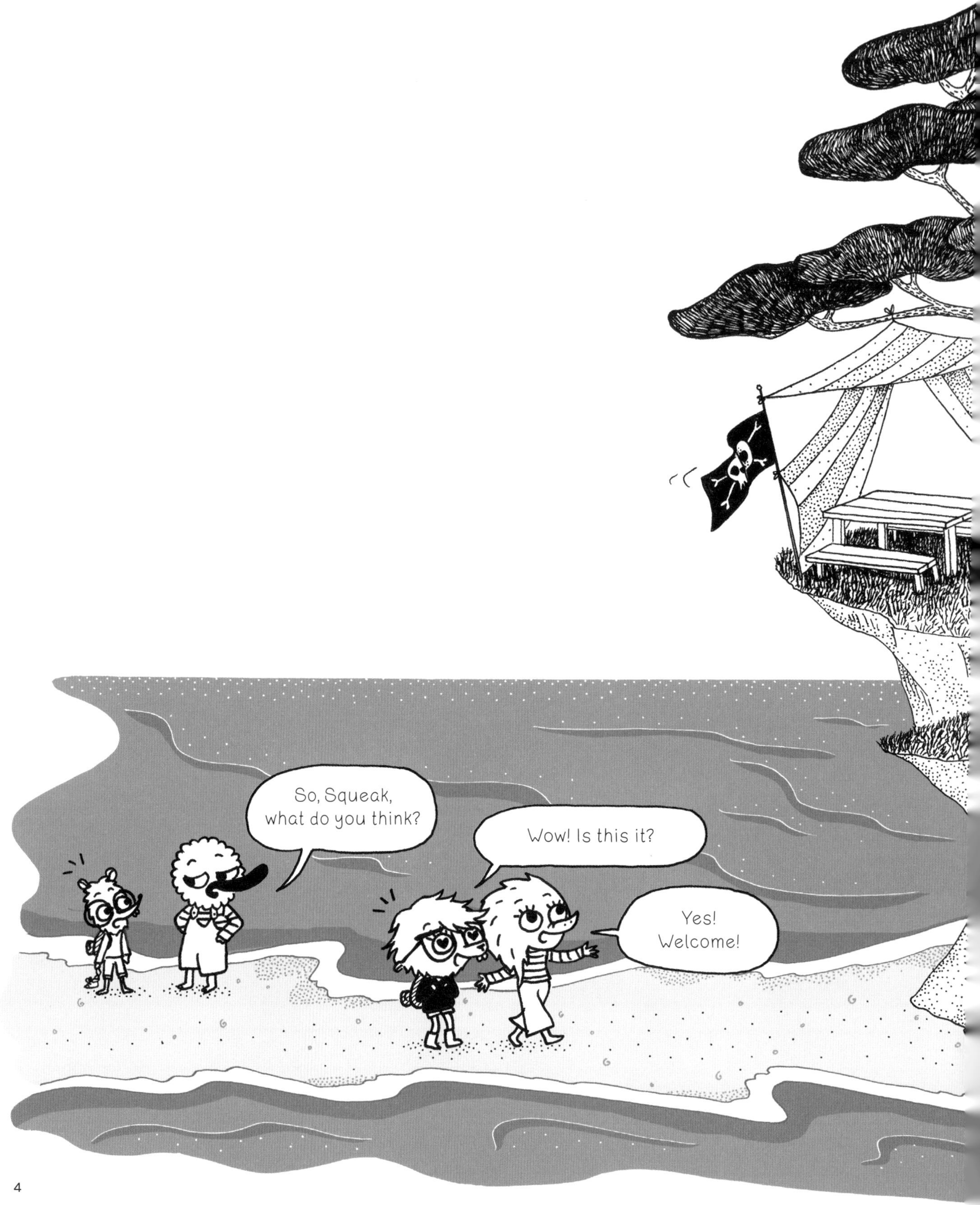
So, Squeak, what do you think?
Wow! Is this it?
Yes! Welcome!

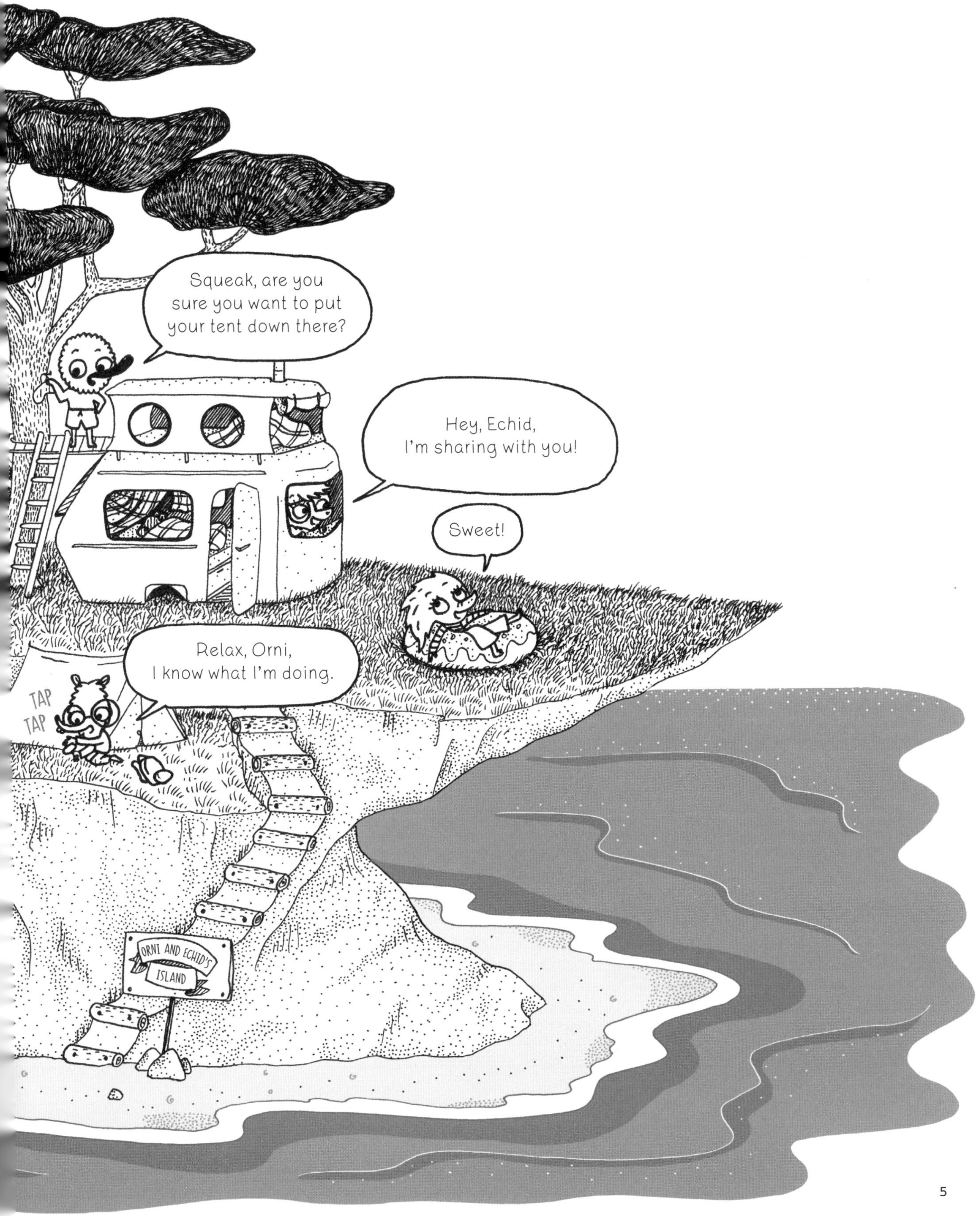
Squeak, are you sure you want to put your tent down there?
Hey, Echid, I'm sharing with you!
Sweet!
Relax, Orni, I know what I'm doing.
TAP TAP
ORNI AND ECHID'S ISLAND

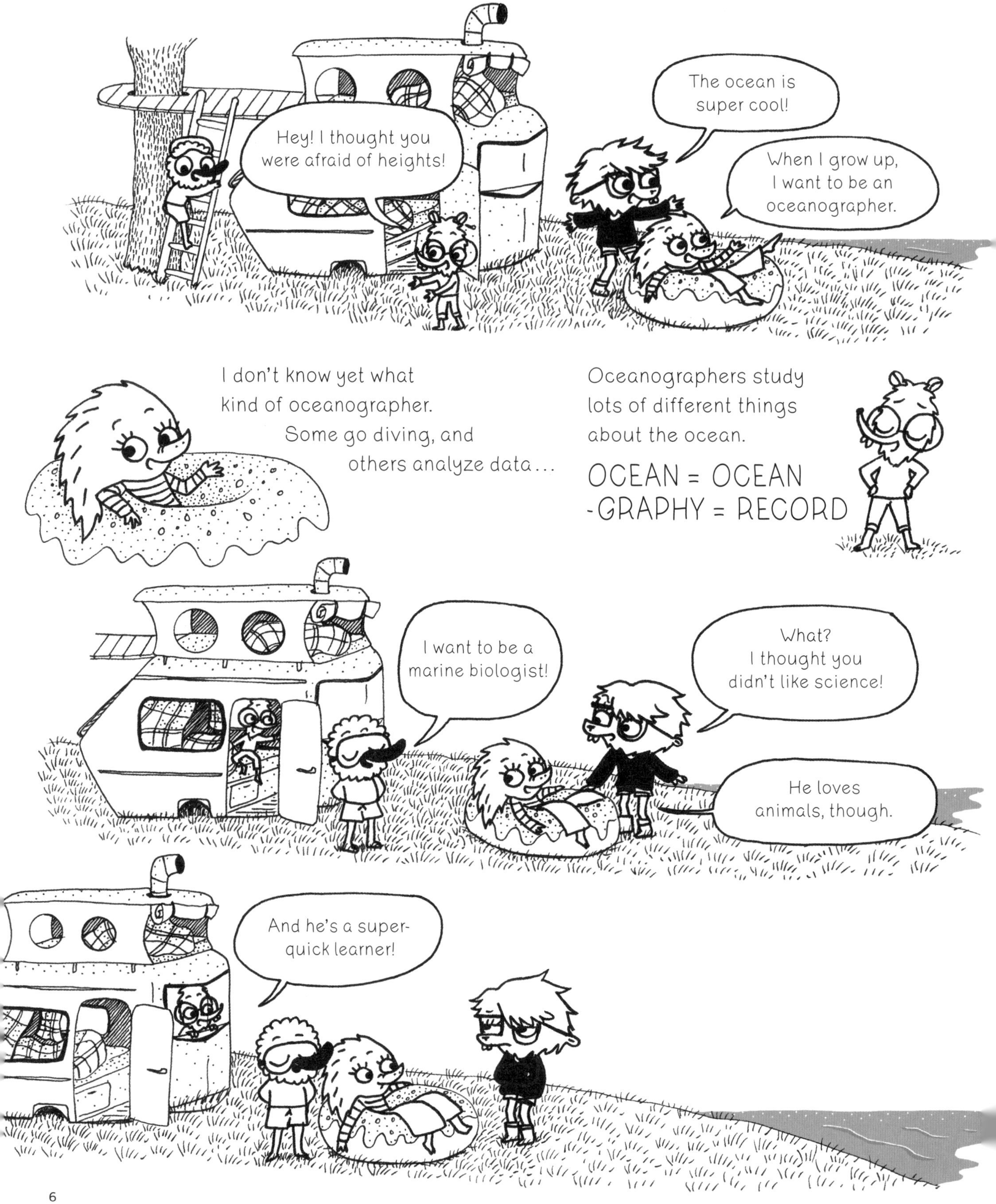
Hey! I thought you were afraid of heights!
The ocean is super cool!
When I grow up, I want to be an oceanographer.
I don't know yet what kind of oceanographer. Some go diving, and others analyze data . . .
Oceanographers study lots of different things about the ocean.
OCEAN = OCEAN
-GRAPHY = RECORD
I want to be a marine biologist!
What? I thought you didn't like science!
He loves animals, though.
And he's a super-quick learner!

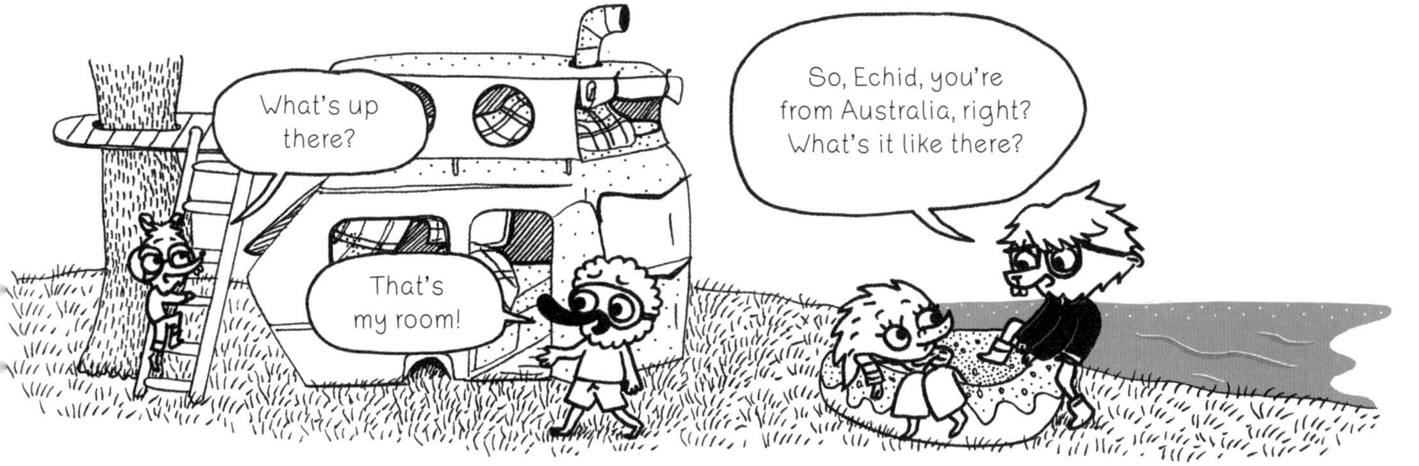
What's up there?
That's my room!
So, Echid, you're from Australia, right? What's it like there?

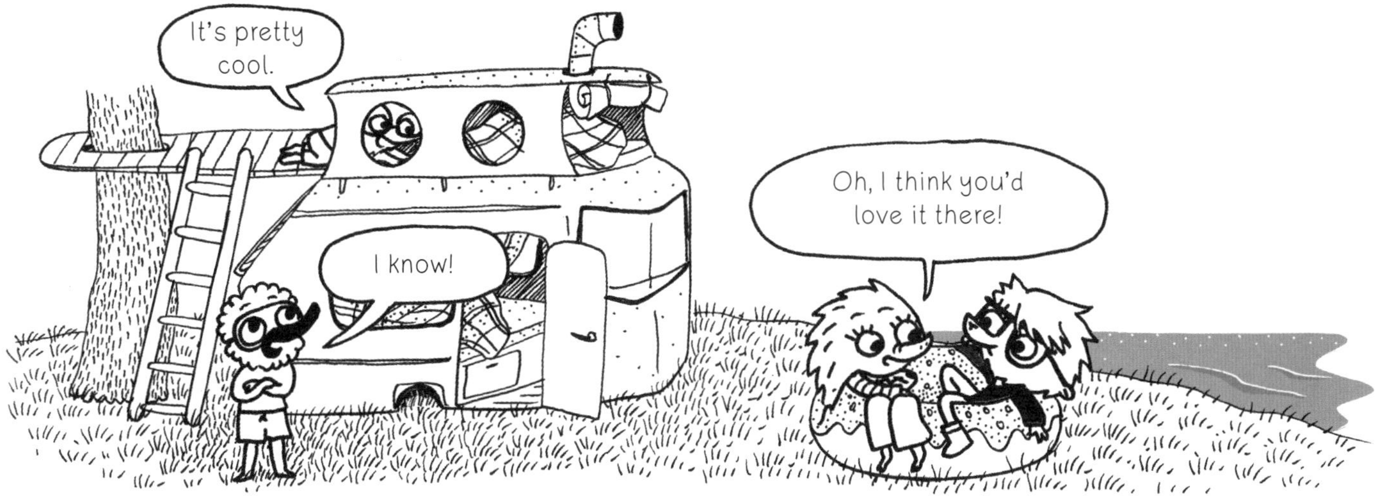
It's pretty cool.
I know!
Oh, I think you'd love it there!

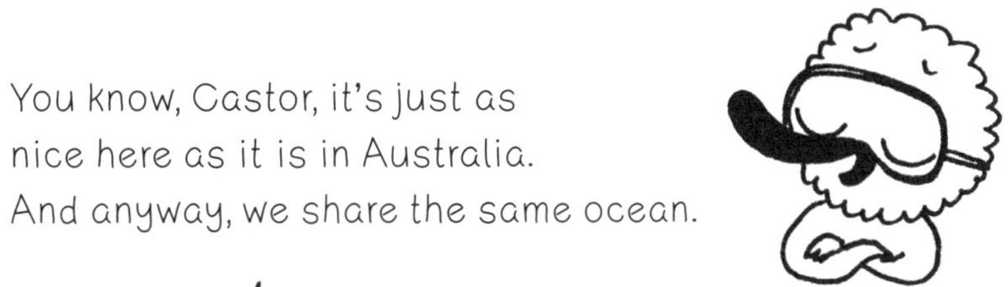
You know, Castor, it's just as nice here as it is in Australia. And anyway, we share the same ocean.

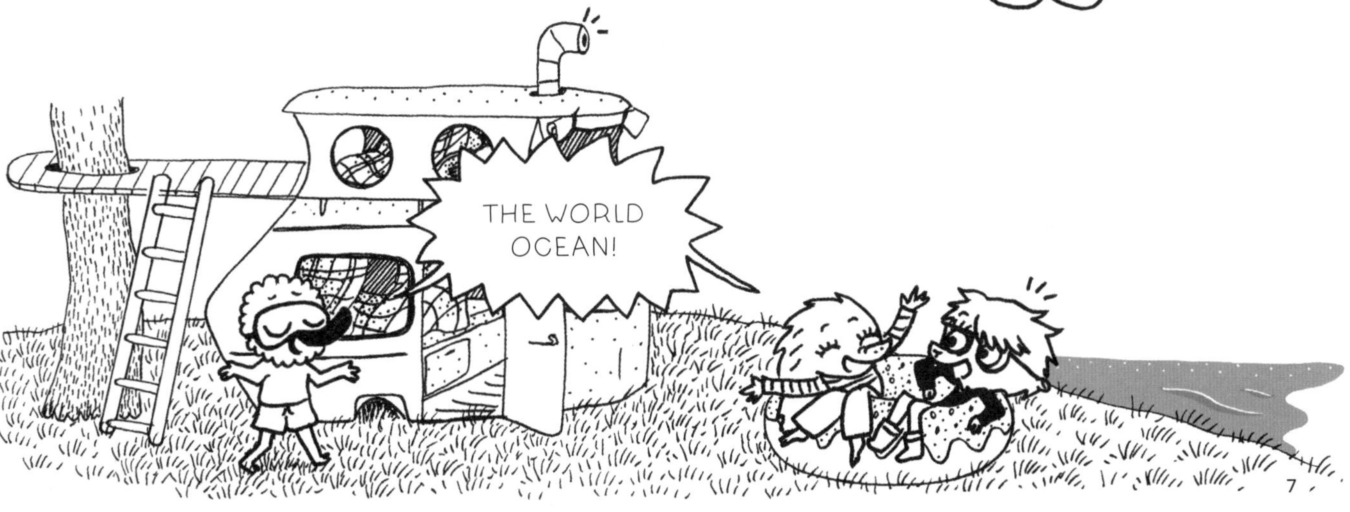
THE WORLD OCEAN!

1 THE OCEAN OF ALL OCEANS

THE WORLD OCEAN

covers 71% of the Earth's surface. It's one giant ocean made up of five smaller oceans, and those are made up of even smaller seas, bays, and gulfs.

THE ARCTIC OCEAN

is around the North Pole. It's the smallest of the world's oceans, and it's often covered in ice.

THE PACIFIC OCEAN

is the biggest and the deepest of all. This is where the highest underwater mountains are!

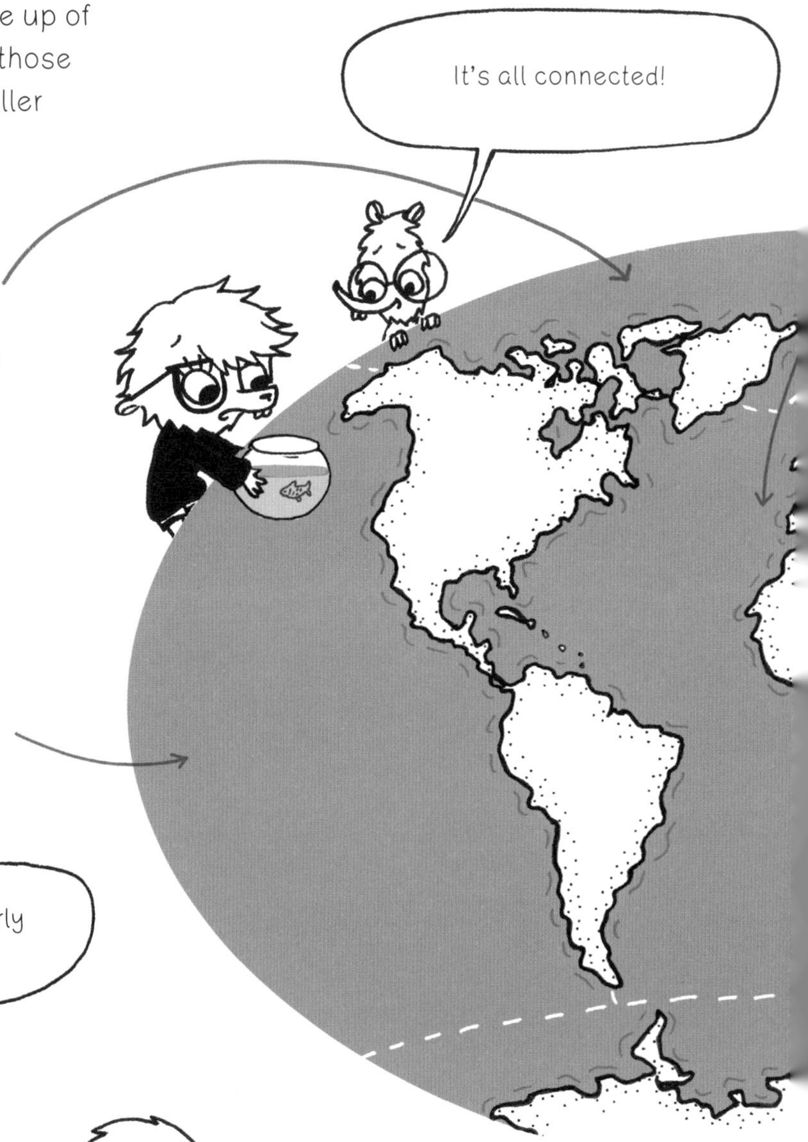
It's all connected!

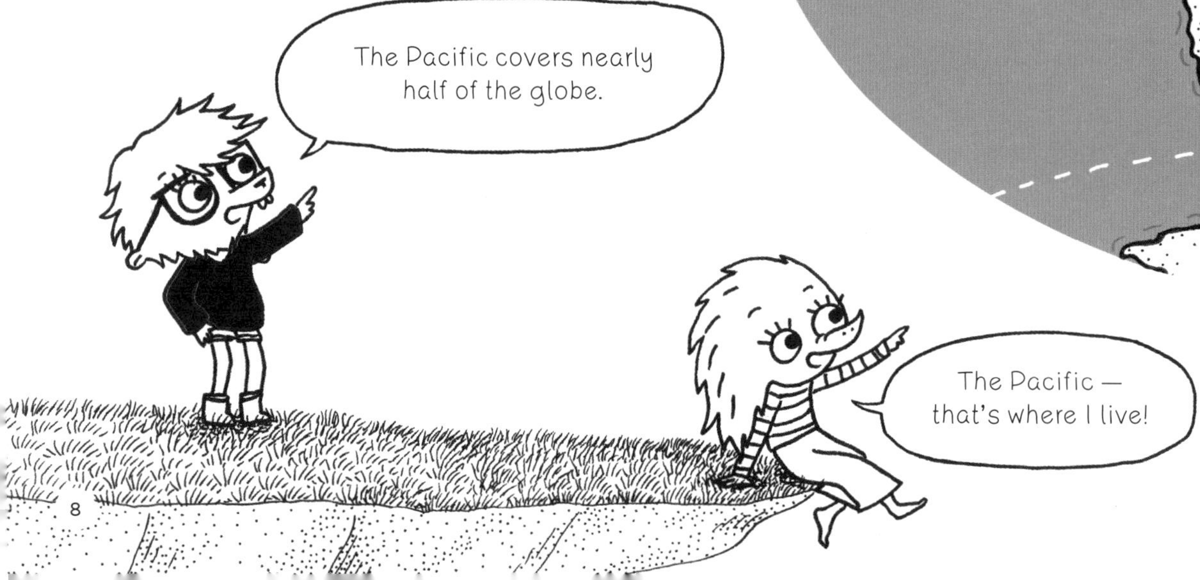
The Pacific covers nearly half of the globe.
The Pacific — that's where I live!

THE ATLANTIC OCEAN

stretches west from Europe and Africa. If you cross it, you'll end up in the Americas.

THE INDIAN OCEAN

covers the area between Africa, India, and Australia.

THE SOUTHERN OCEAN

is around the South Pole. Its boundaries were only defined in the year 2000.

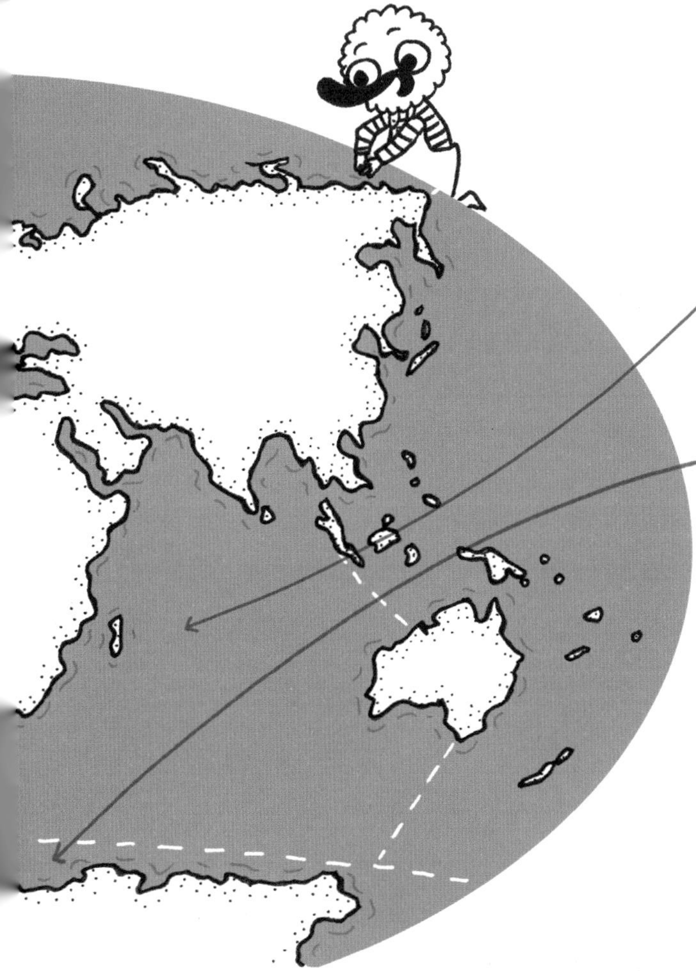

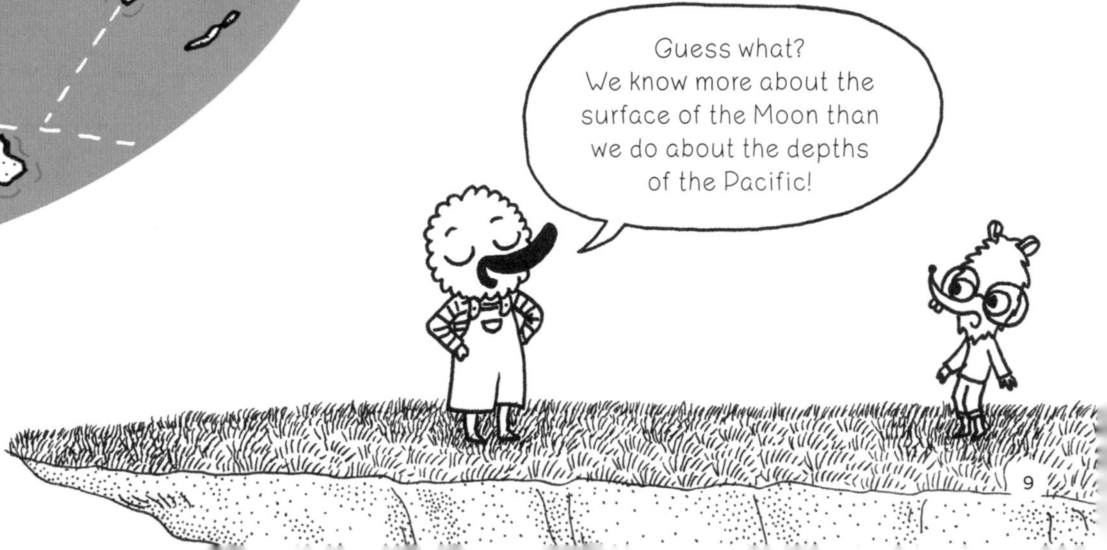
Guess what?
We know more about the surface of the Moon than we do about the depths of the Pacific!

HOW THE FIVE OCEANS FORMED

The World Ocean was born soon after the Earth itself, some 3.8 billion years ago. After some very heavy rains, the Earth was flooded with water.

The ridge system is like a puzzle made of different plates that move around on top of molten magma!

The line that looks like stitches is called the mid-ocean ridge system!

These plates are moving all the time. So much that, every year, the Atlantic gets a little bigger and the Pacific gets a little smaller!

This movement is what can cause earthquakes.

That's what we call plate tectonics!

CONTINENTAL PLATE

OCEANIC PLATE

Oceanic plates slide underneath continental plates.

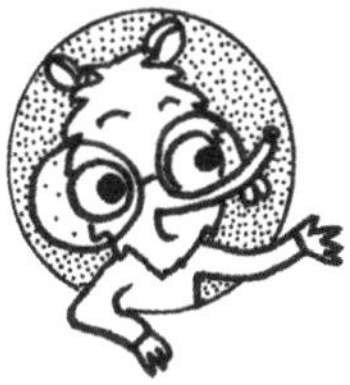

The Earth hasn't always been the way we know it today...

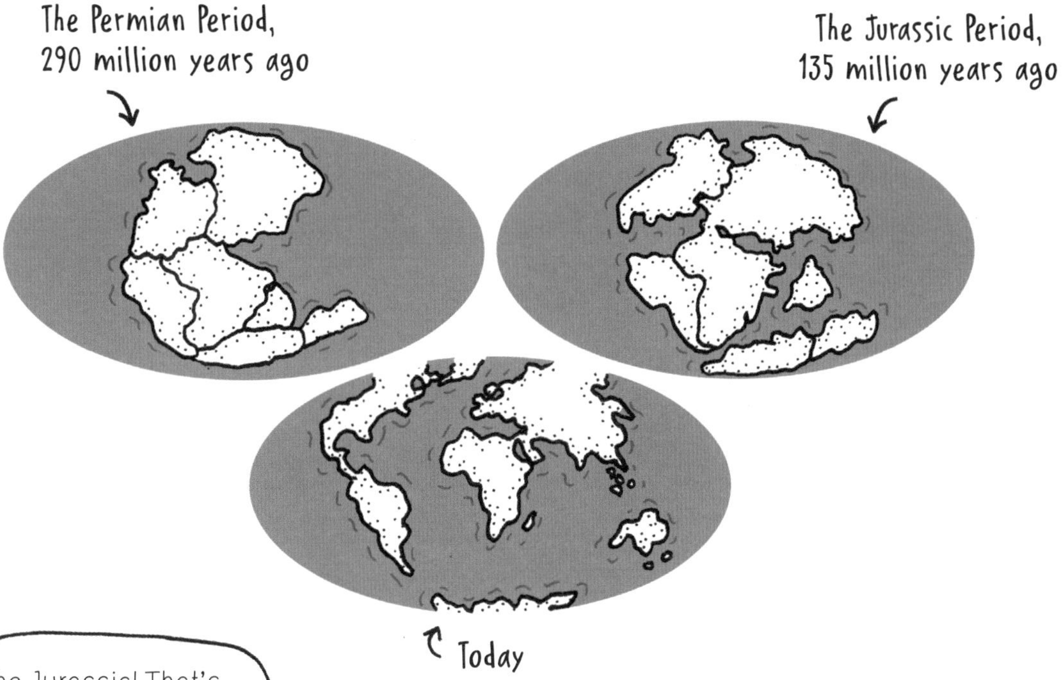

The Permian Period,
290 million years ago
The Jurassic Period,
135 million years ago
Today

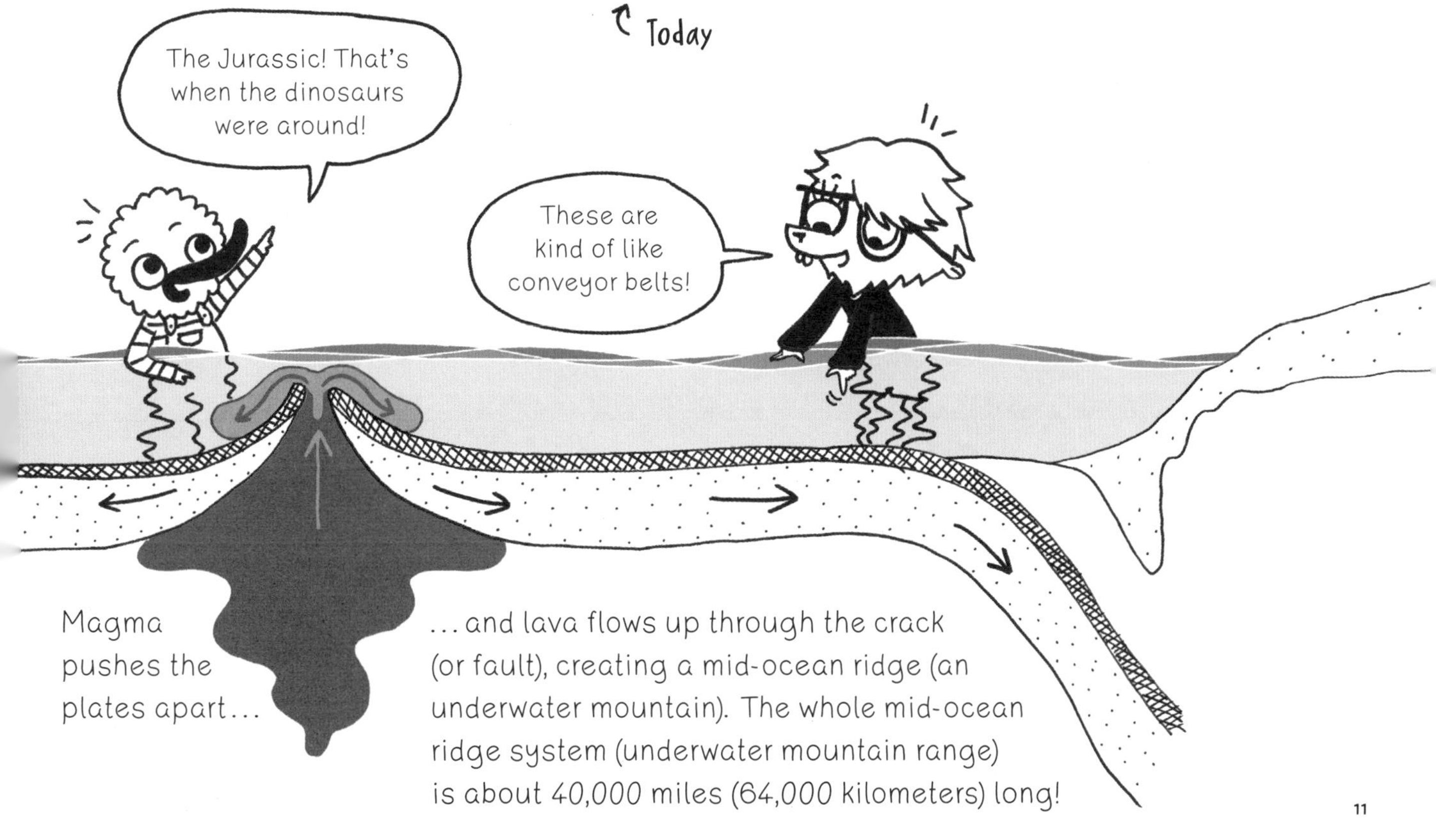

The Jurassic! That's when the dinosaurs were around!
These are kind of like conveyor belts!

Magma pushes the plates apart...

...and lava flows up through the crack (or fault), creating a mid-ocean ridge (an underwater mountain). The whole mid-ocean ridge system (underwater mountain range) is about 40,000 miles (64,000 kilometers) long!

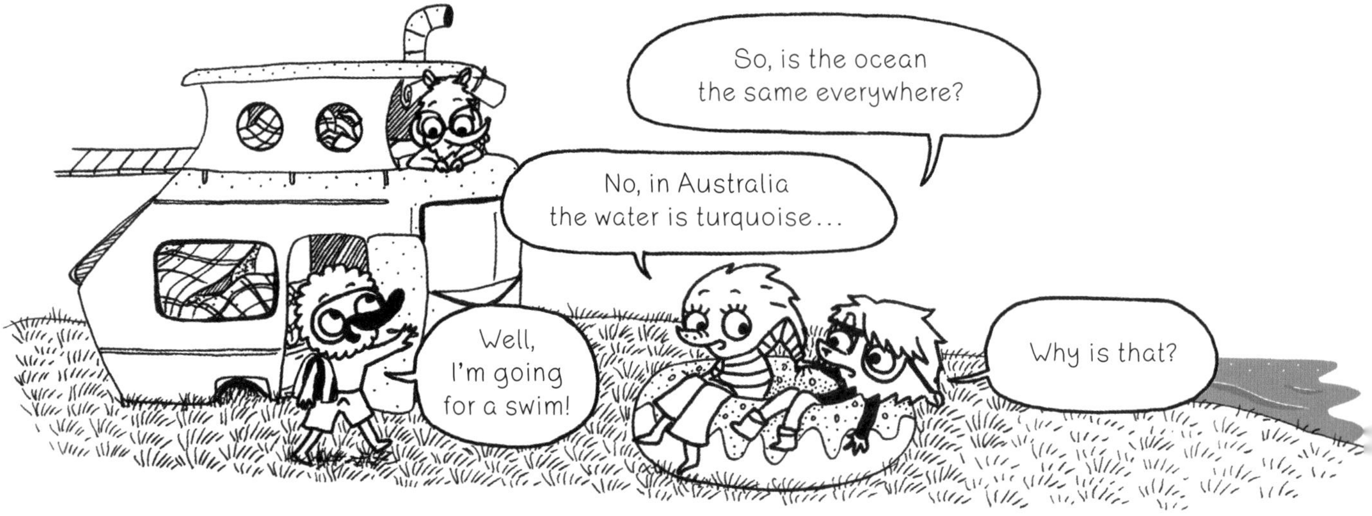
So, is the ocean the same everywhere?
No, in Australia the water is turquoise...
Well, I'm going for a swim!
Why is that?

Close to the shore, the color of the water depends on the nature of the land.

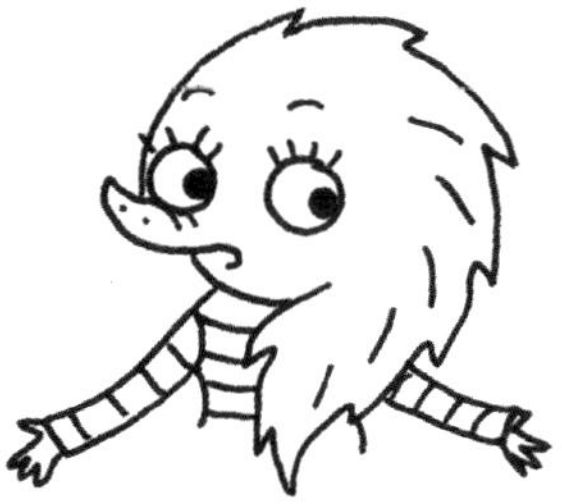

Away from the shore, it depends on the composition of the water, too, and the nutrients it contains!

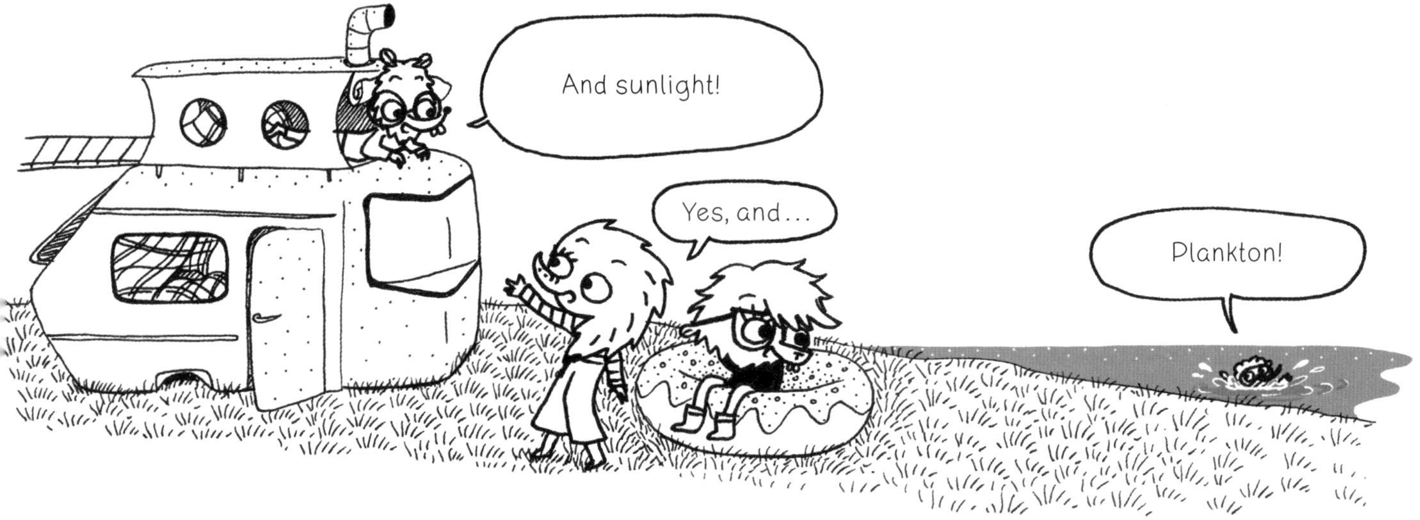
And sunlight!
Yes, and...
Plankton!

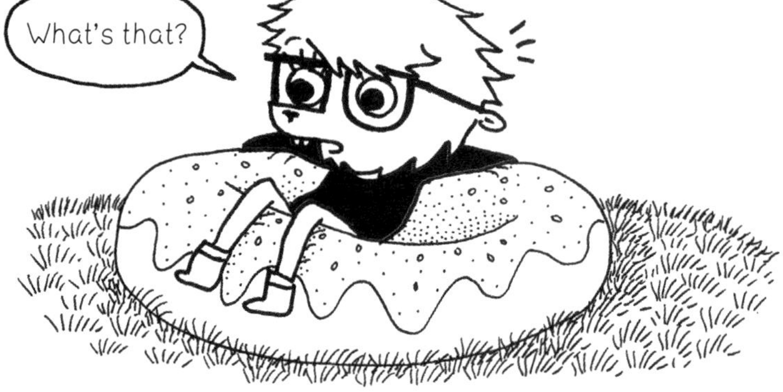
What's that?

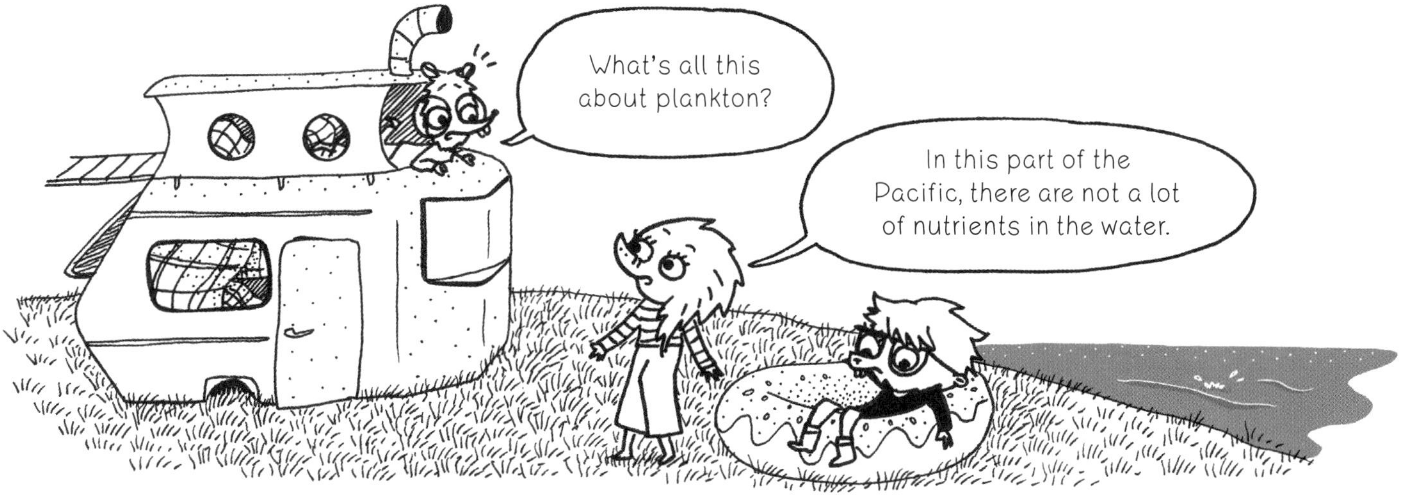
What's all this about plankton?
In this part of the Pacific, there are not a lot of nutrients in the water.

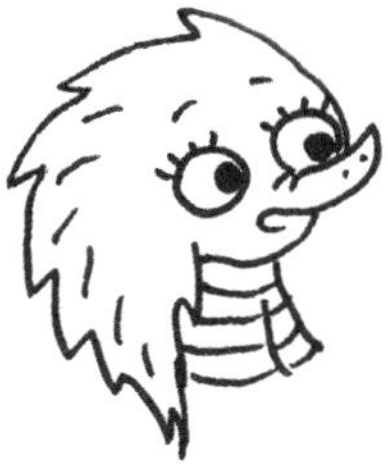

Nutrients are substances found in food that allow organisms to live, grow, and heal. Protein, minerals, fiber, and trace elements are all examples of nutrients.

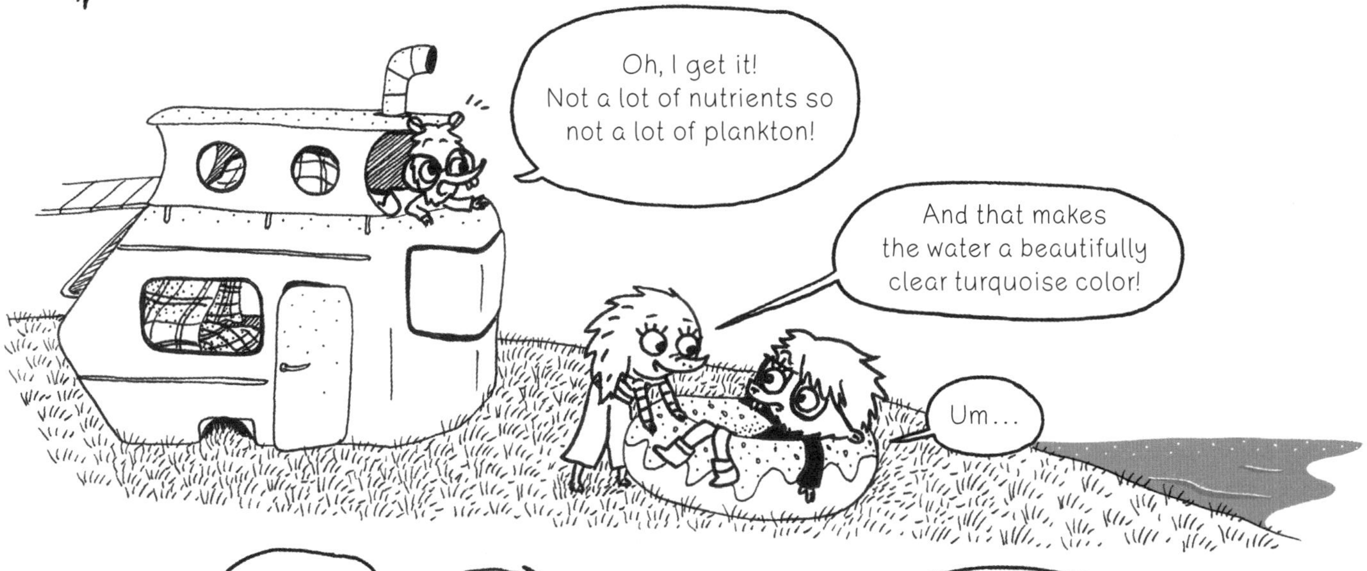
Oh, I get it!
Not a lot of nutrients so not a lot of plankton!
And that makes the water a beautifully clear turquoise color!
Um...

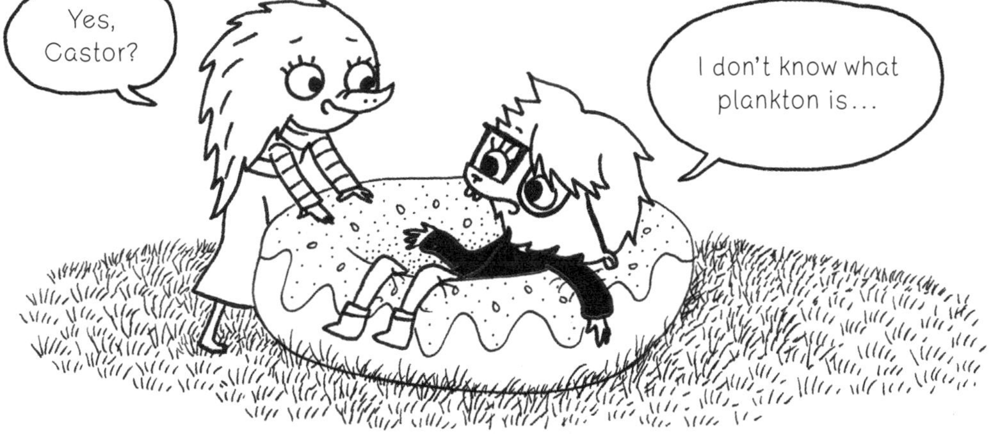
Yes, Castor?
I don't know what plankton is...

2 PLANKTON PARTY!

Plankton is the name for all the plant and animal organisms that drift on the ocean currents. Sometimes, they can develop really fast and create giant colorful "clouds" called blooms.

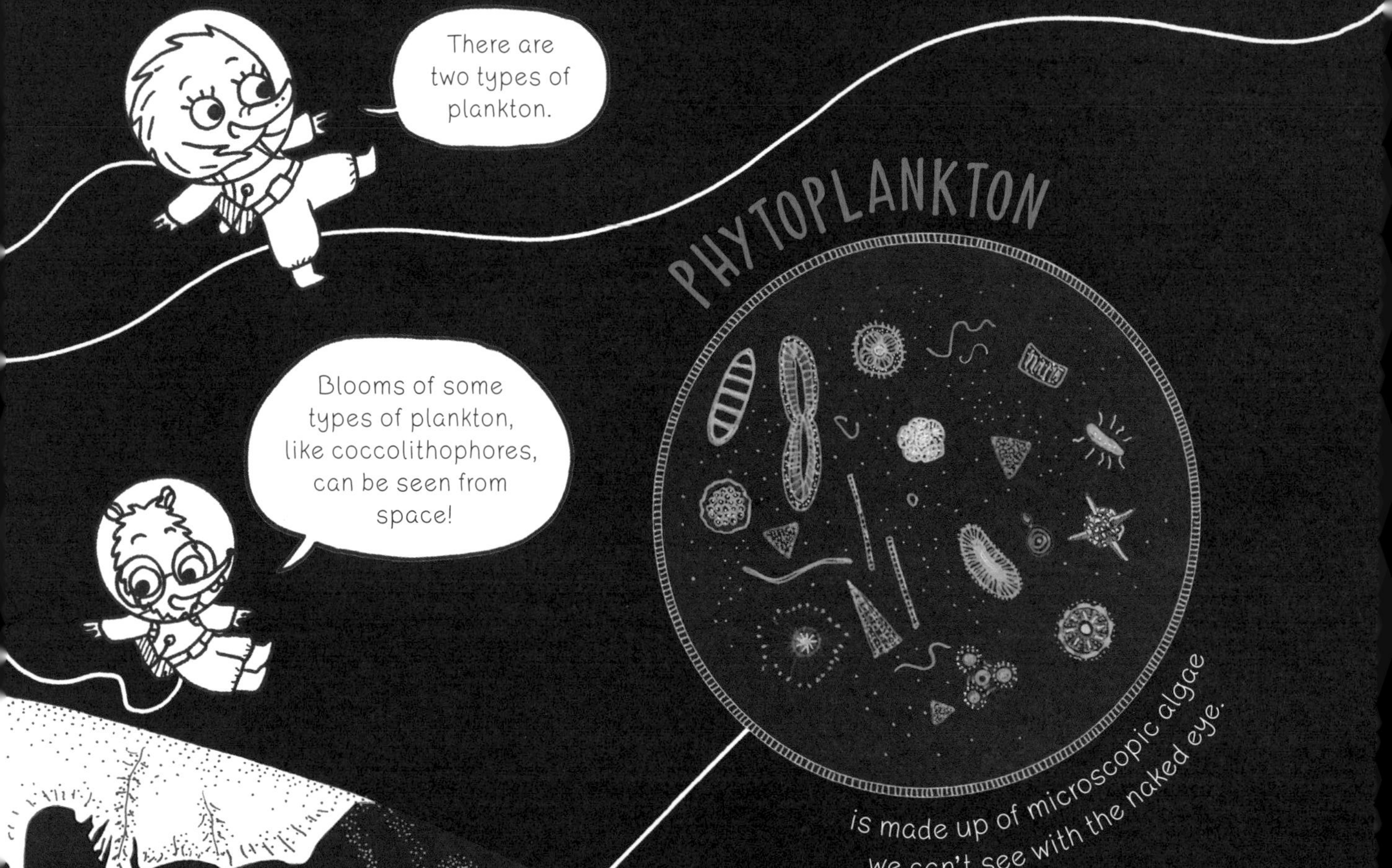

There are two types of plankton.
Blooms of some types of plankton, like coccolithophores, can be seen from space!
PHYTOPLANKTON
is made up of microscopic algae we can't see with the naked eye.

Like trees, phytoplankton absorbs sunlight, carbon dioxide, and water, and produces oxygen. This process is called photosynthesis.

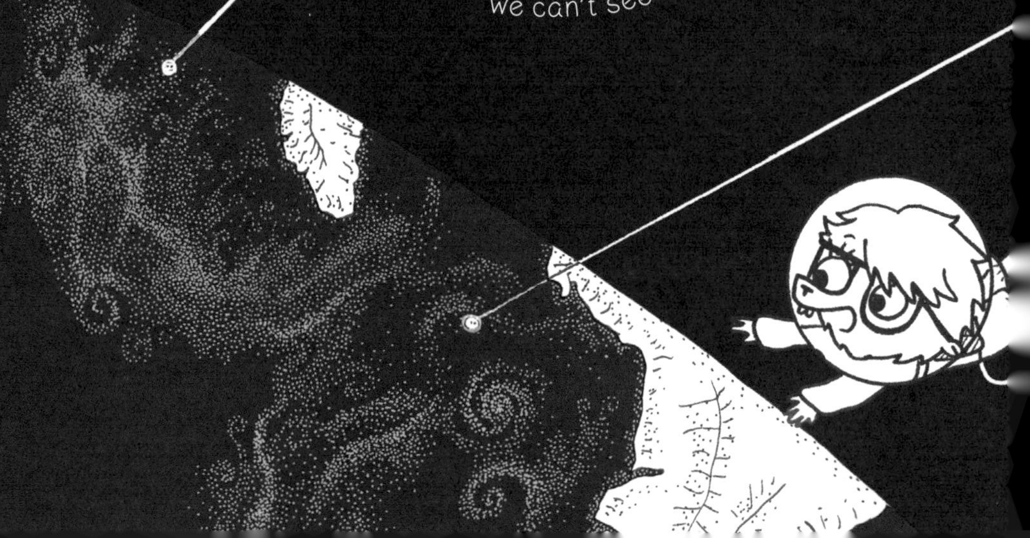

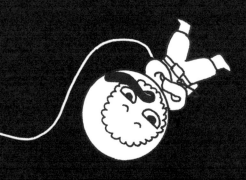

ZOOPLANKTON

is made up of animals and larvae that have a very limited range of movement.

Zooplankton can be much bigger than phytoplankton— sometimes up to 36 inches (1 meter) in size.

Some kinds of plankton even glow at night!

Even though most plankton is microscopically small, it's essential for life on Earth.

15

That's right! In the very beginning, plankton was the only life on Earth: blue algae and bacteria.

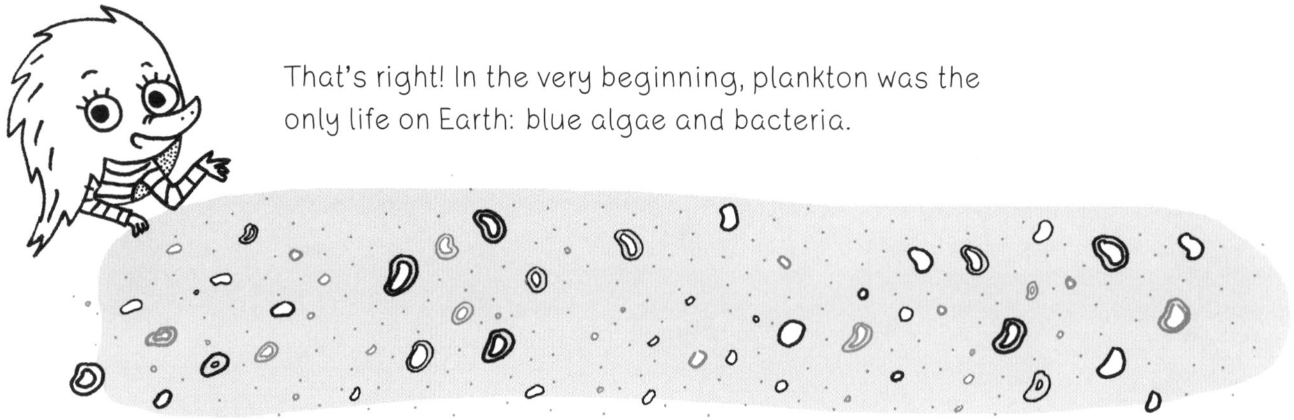

Over several billion years, they evolved. And around 500 million years ago, the Biological Big Bang happened!

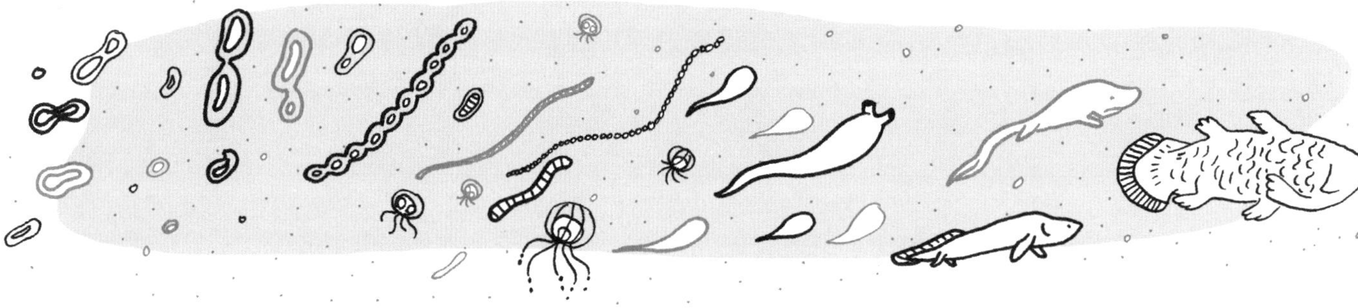

That's when fish, amphibians, dinosaurs, mammals, and birds first began to develop. Life-forms under the water kept on evolving, too, and they started to look very different as well!

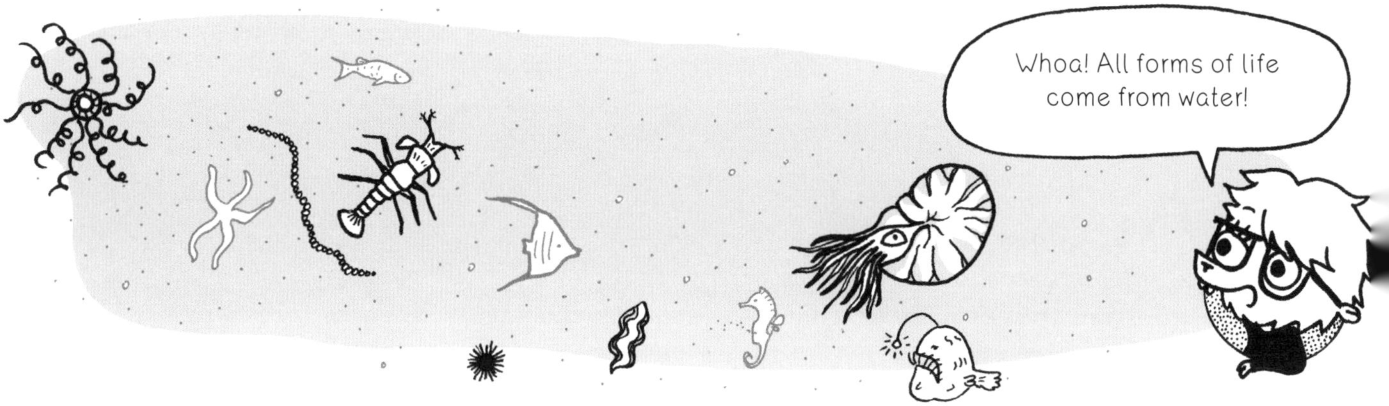
Whoa! All forms of life come from water!

Some animals, called marine mammals, evolved on land before they went to live in the ocean. They swim underwater and come back to the surface to breathe. Dolphins are marine mammals!

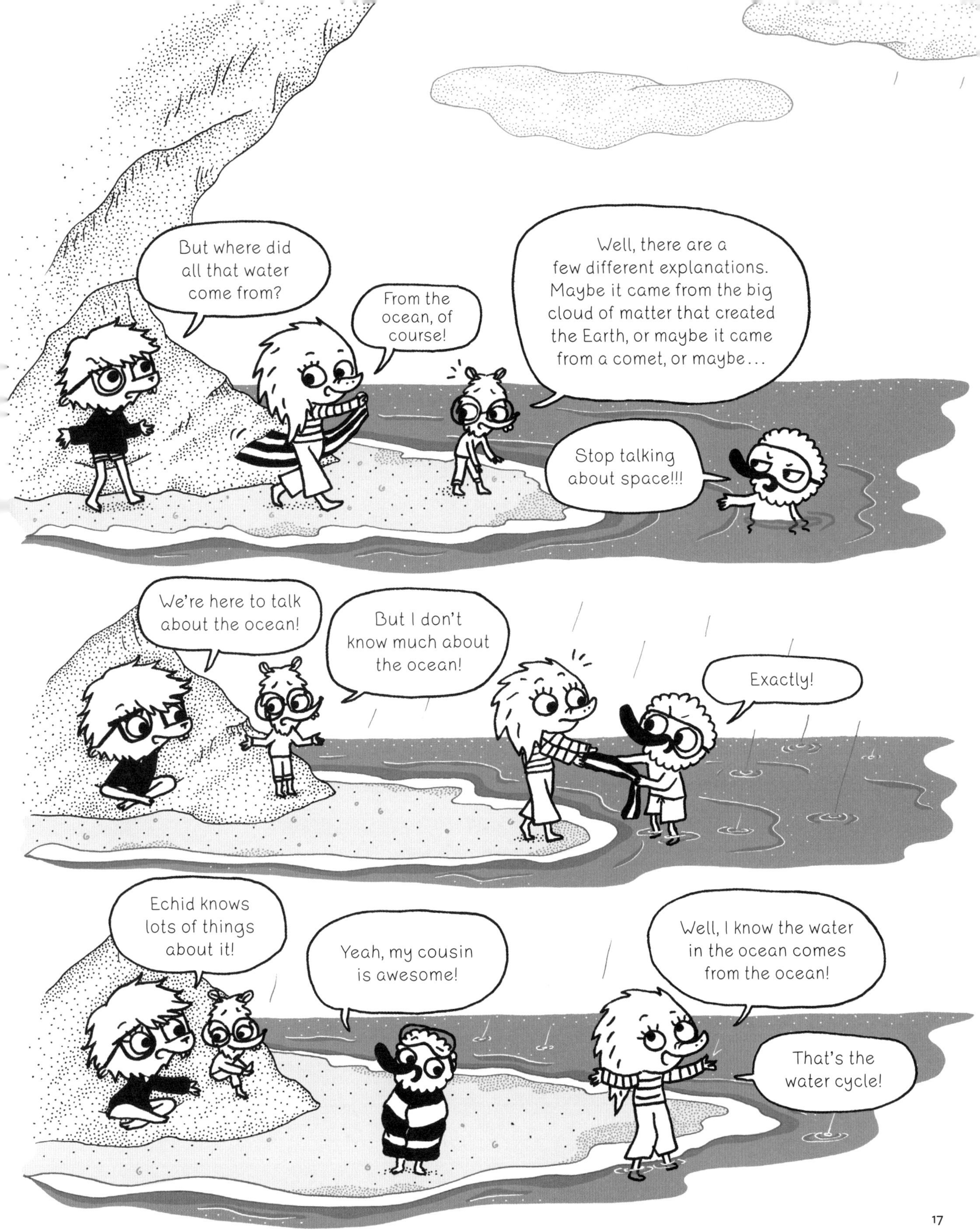
But where did all that water come from?
From the ocean, of course!
Well, there are a few different explanations. Maybe it came from the big cloud of matter that created the Earth, or maybe it came from a comet, or maybe...
Stop talking about space!!!
We're here to talk about the ocean!
But I don't know much about the ocean!
Exactly!
Echid knows lots of things about it!
Yeah, my cousin is awesome!
Well, I know the water in the ocean comes from the ocean!
That's the water cycle!

3 THE NEVER-ENDING CYCLE

On Earth, water exists in three states: liquid, solid, and gas. All three are present in the natural water cycle.

CONDENSATION

As it rises, the water vapor cools and turns into droplets. Together, these droplets form clouds.

EVAPORATION

The heat of the sun turns water on the Earth's surface into water vapor.

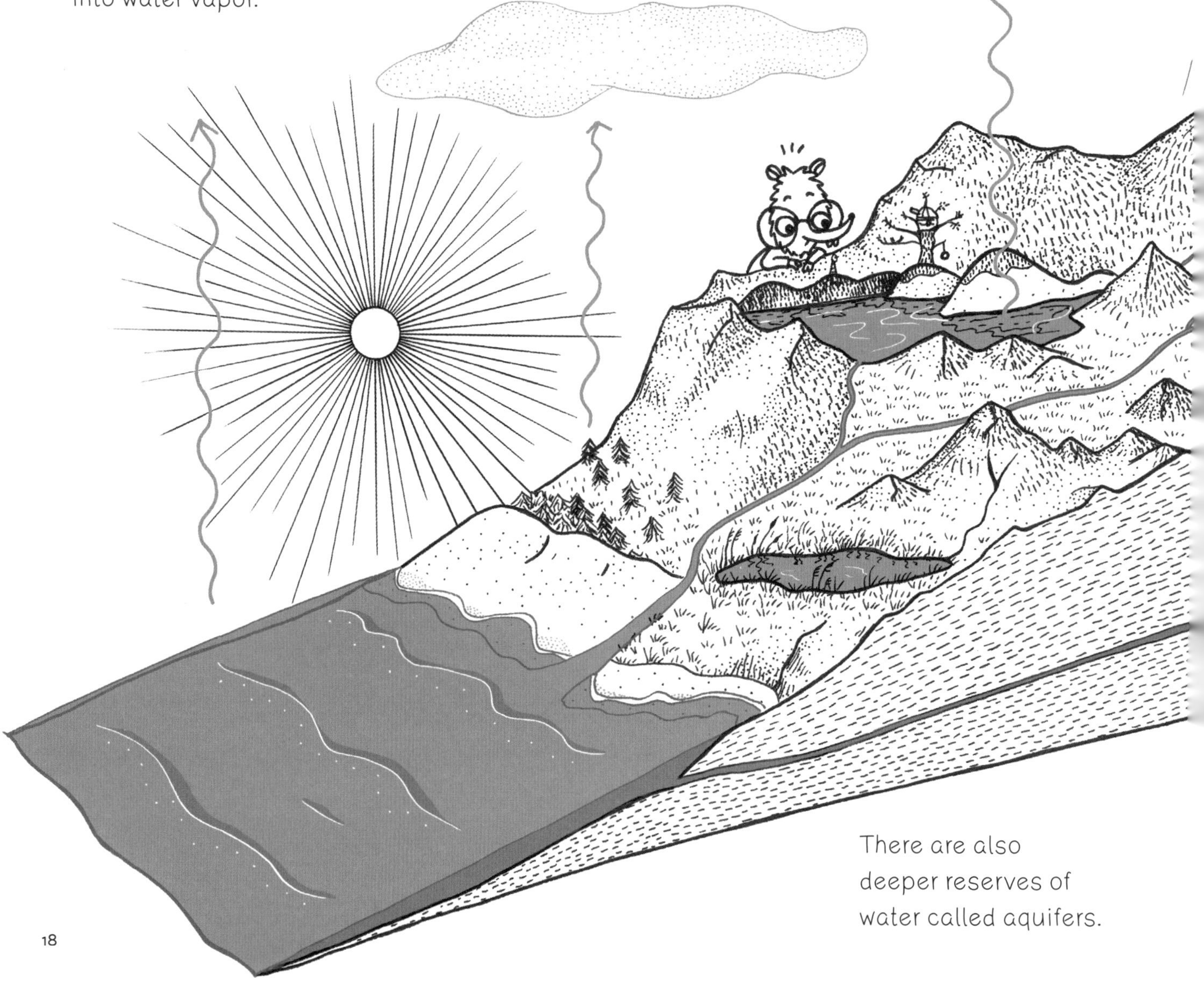

There are also deeper reserves of water called aquifers.

PRECIPITATION

The droplets stick to one another, and when they get too heavy, they fall and it rains.

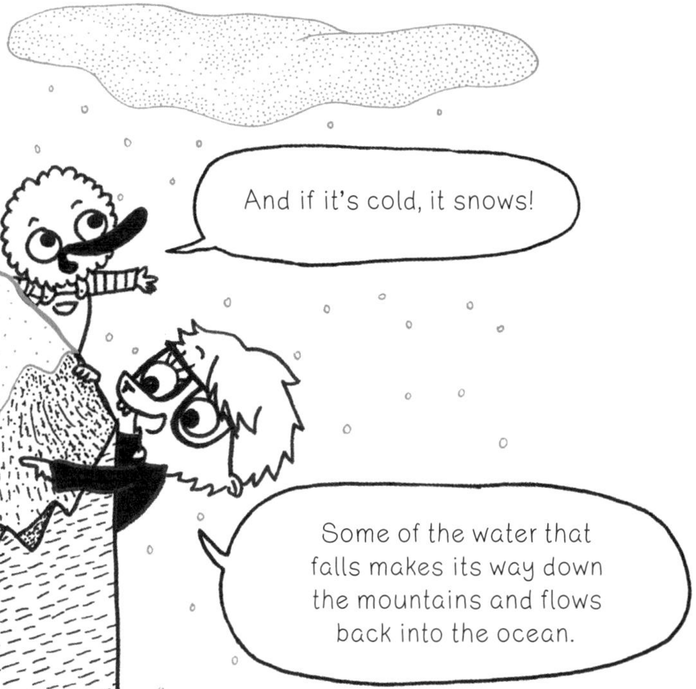
And if it's cold, it snows!
Some of the water that falls makes its way down the mountains and flows back into the ocean.

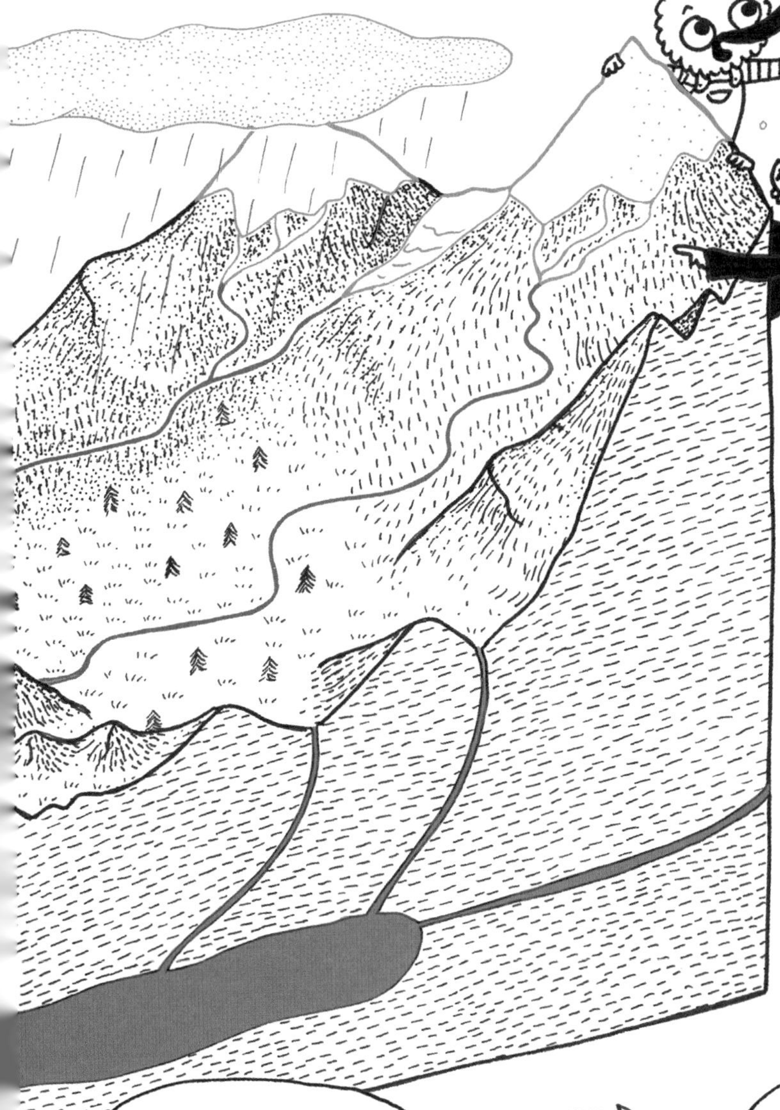

INFILTRATION

Some water flows into the water table. That's the name for pools of water, or reserves, that form underground. This is where well water, and spring water, comes from.

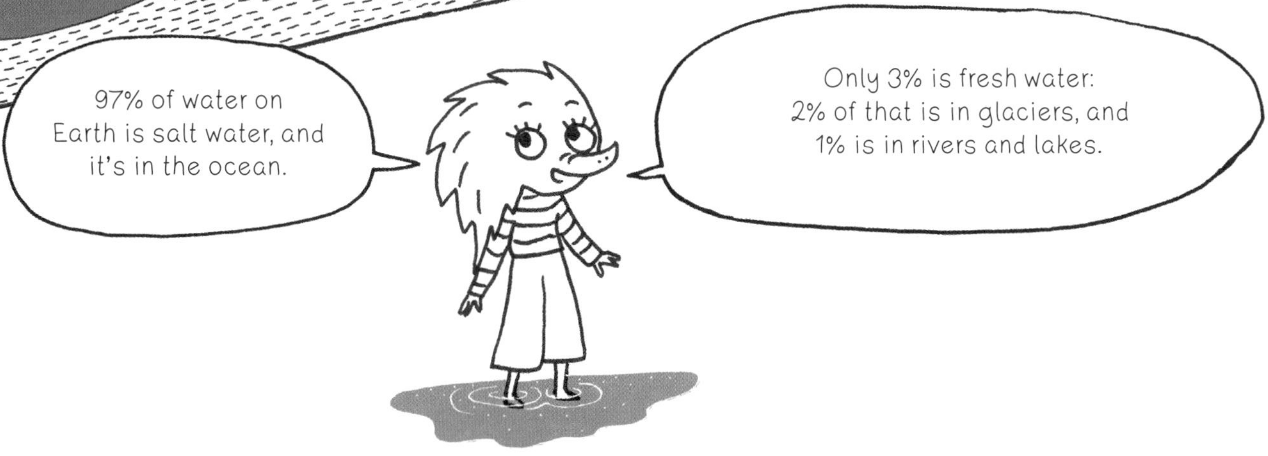
97% of water on Earth is salt water, and it's in the ocean.
Only 3% is fresh water: 2% of that is in glaciers, and 1% is in rivers and lakes.

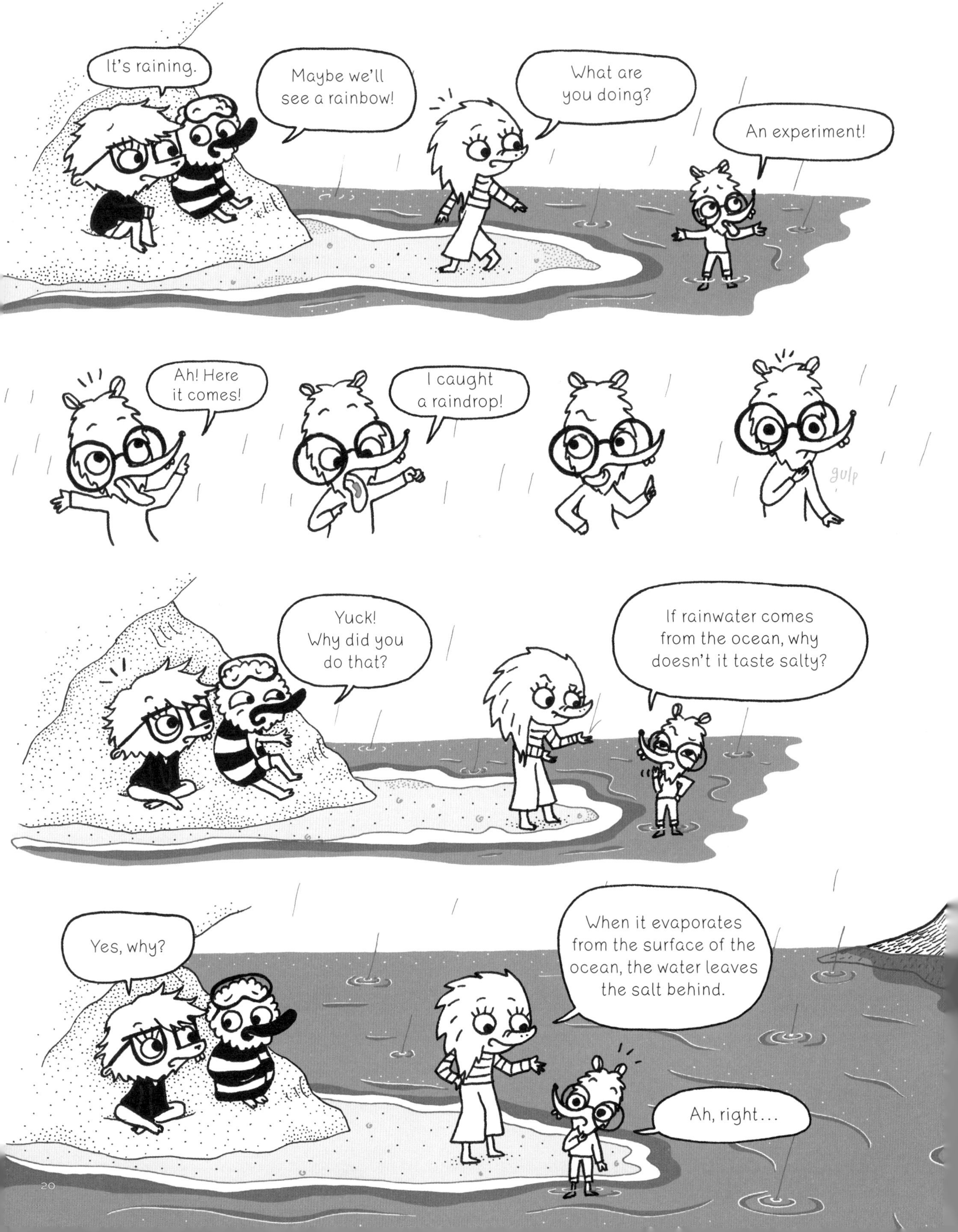
It's raining.
Maybe we'll see a rainbow!
What are you doing?
An experiment!
Ah! Here it comes!
I caught a raindrop!
gulp
Yuck! Why did you do that?
If rainwater comes from the ocean, why doesn't it taste salty?
Yes, why?
When it evaporates from the surface of the ocean, the water leaves the salt behind.
Ah, right...

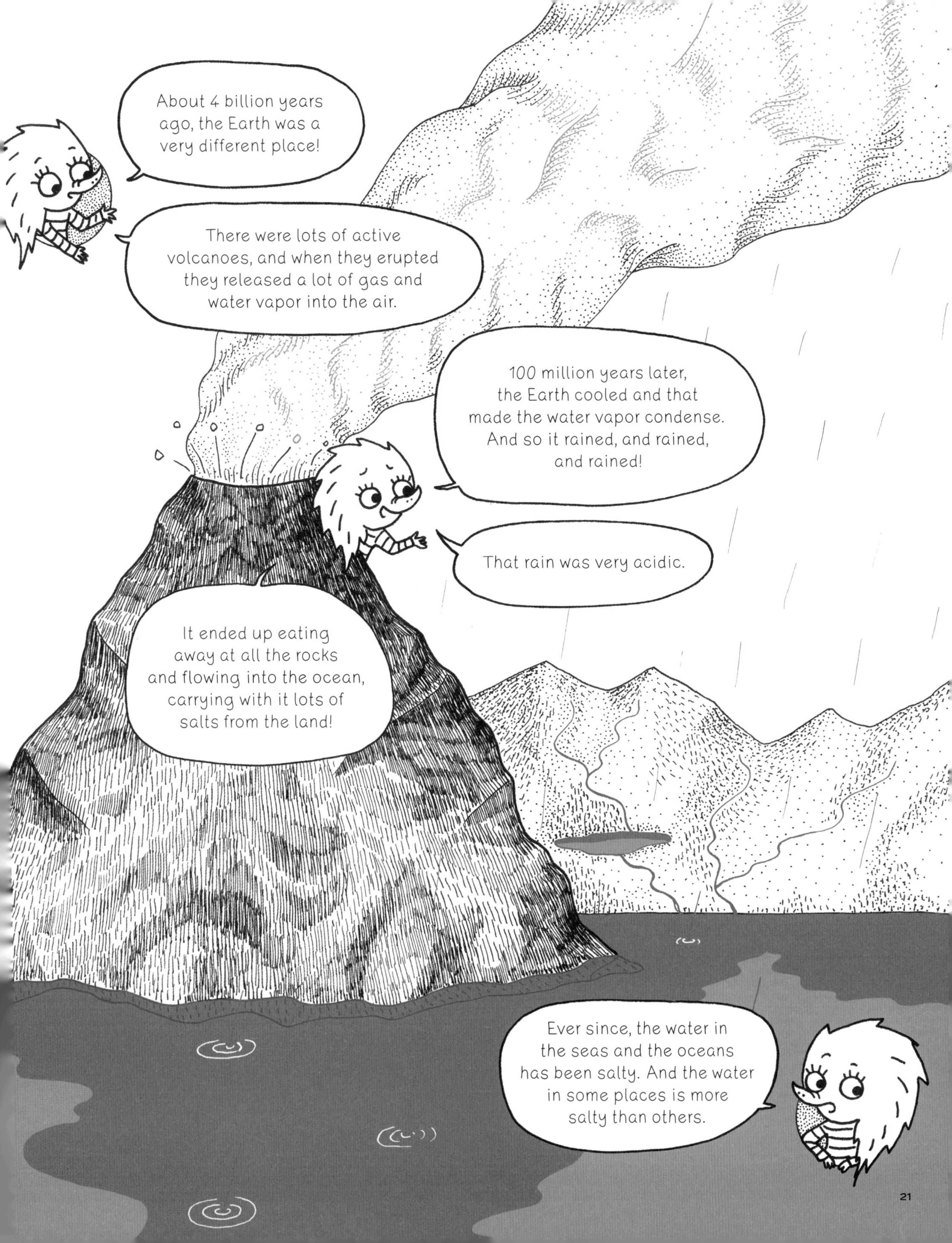
About 4 billion years ago, the Earth was a very different place!
There were lots of active volcanoes, and when they erupted they released a lot of gas and water vapor into the air.
100 million years later, the Earth cooled and that made the water vapor condense. And so it rained, and rained, and rained!
That rain was very acidic.
It ended up eating away at all the rocks and flowing into the ocean, carrying with it lots of salts from the land!
Ever since, the water in the seas and the oceans has been salty. And the water in some places is more salty than others.

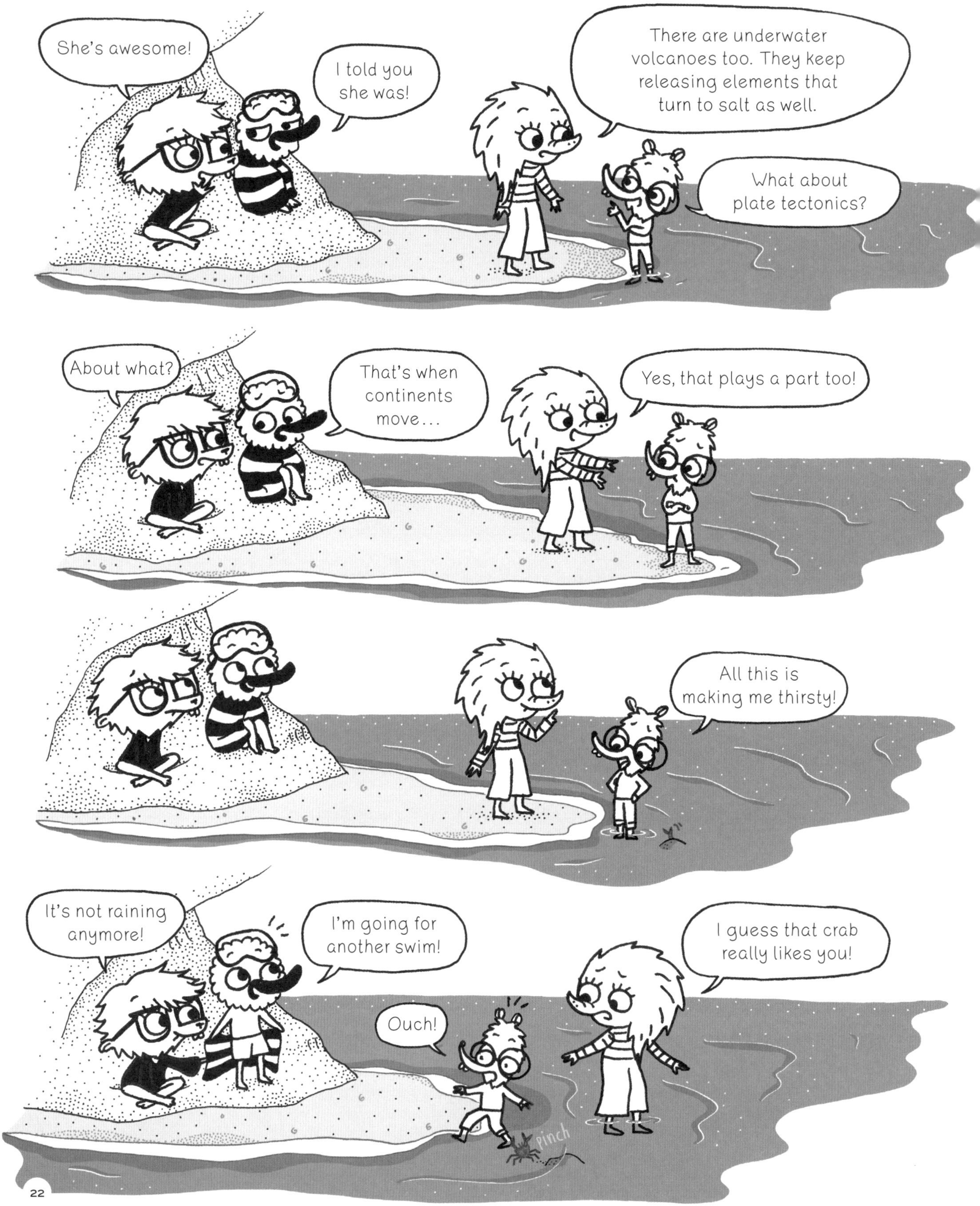
She's awesome!
I told you she was!
There are underwater volcanoes too. They keep releasing elements that turn to salt as well.
What about plate tectonics?
About what?
That's when continents move...
Yes, that plays a part too!
All this is making me thirsty!
It's not raining anymore!
I'm going for another swim!
I guess that crab really likes you!
Ouch!
Pinch

4 GO WITH THE FLOW

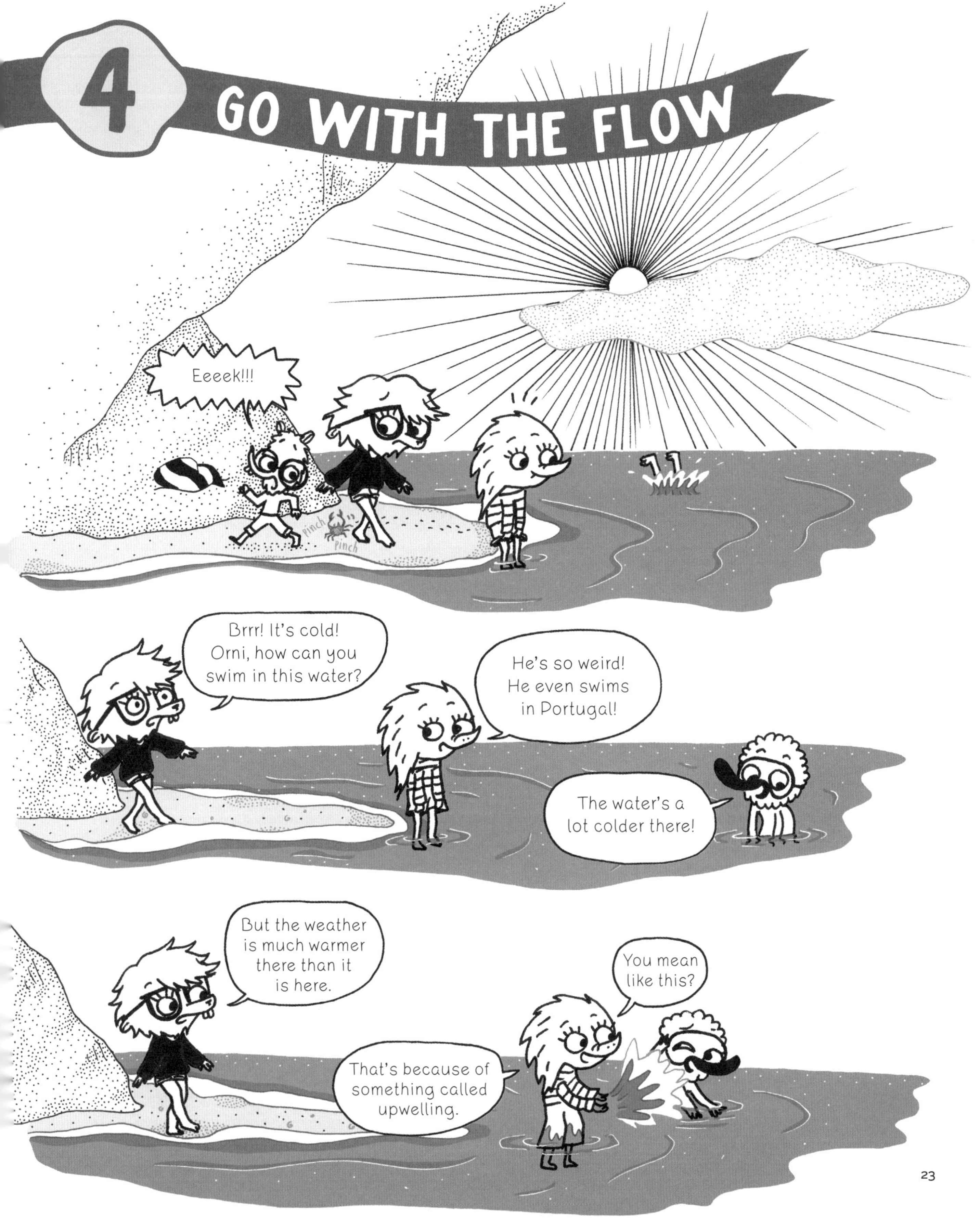
Eeeek!!!
Pinch
Pinch
Brrr! It's cold! Orni, how can you swim in this water?
He's so weird! He even swims in Portugal!
The water's a lot colder there!
But the weather is much warmer there than it is here.
That's because of something called upwelling.
You mean like this?

Upwelling is a very common phenomenon. It's caused by wind blowing over water!

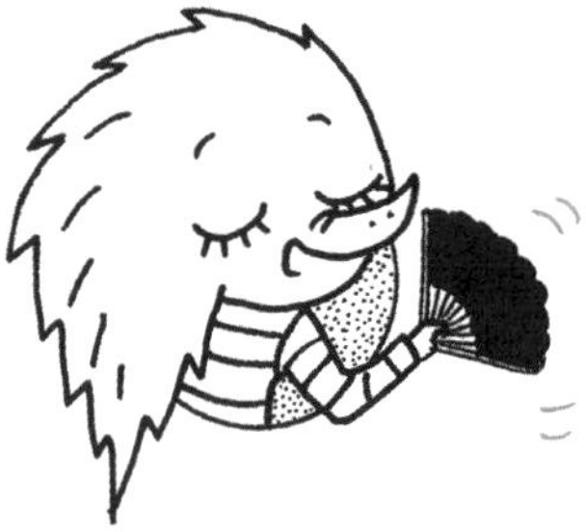

Wind is basically just air that's moving.

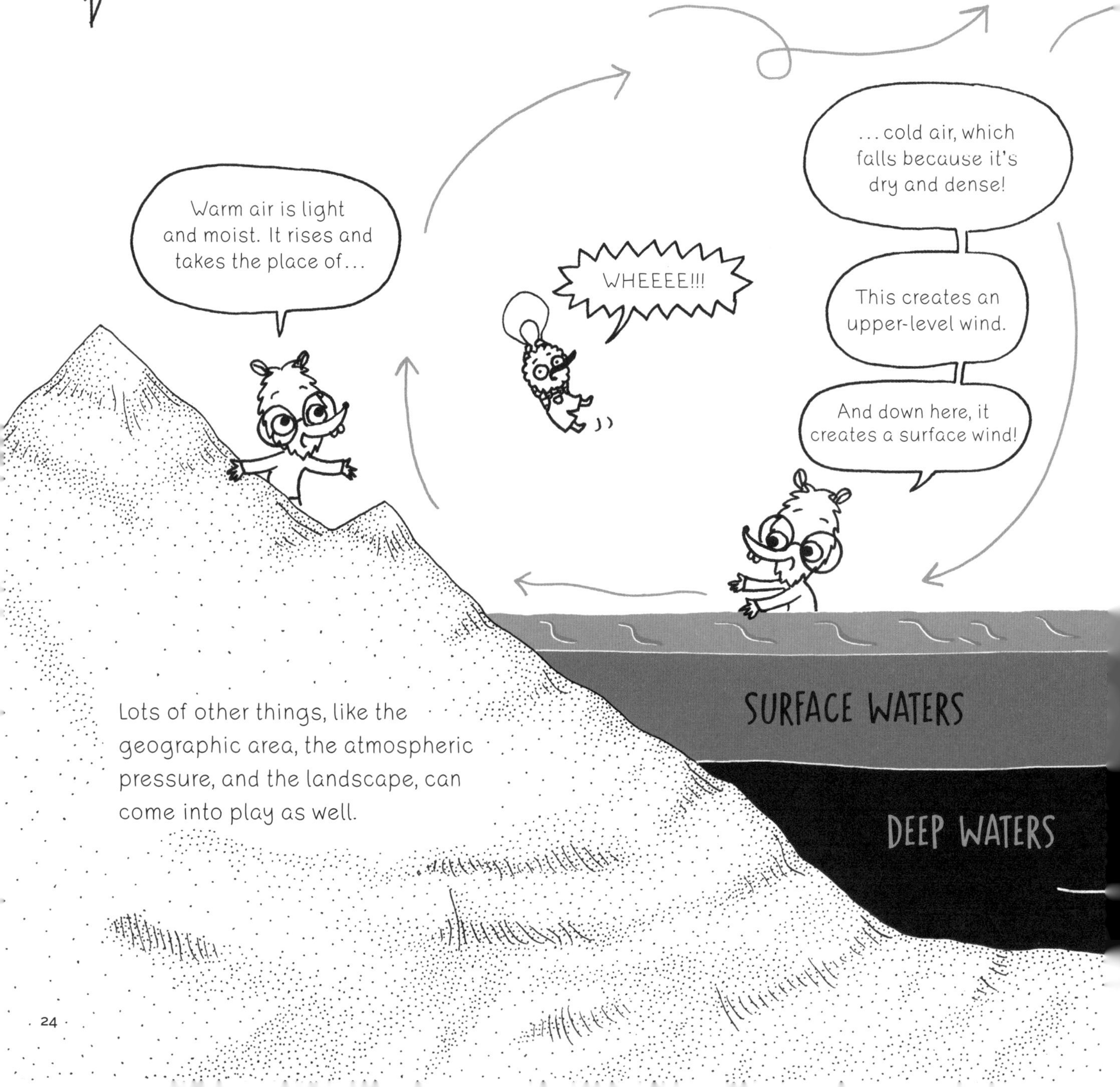

Warm air is light and moist. It rises and takes the place of...
WHEEEE!!!
...cold air, which falls because it's dry and dense!
This creates an upper-level wind.
And down here, it creates a surface wind!
SURFACE WATERS
DEEP WATERS

Lots of other things, like the geographic area, the atmospheric pressure, and the landscape, can come into play as well.

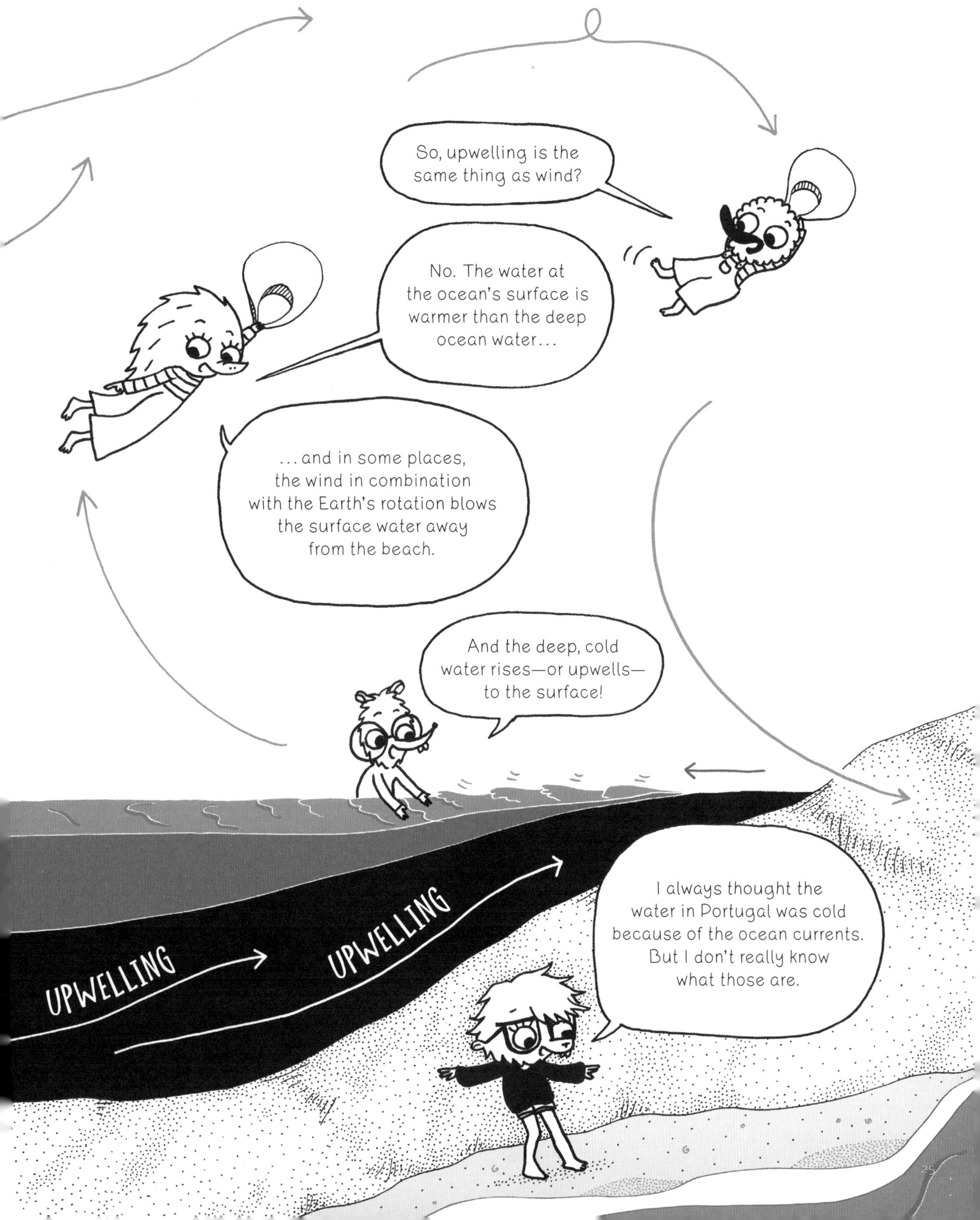

So, upwelling is the same thing as wind?
No. The water at the ocean's surface is warmer than the deep ocean water...
... and in some places, the wind in combination with the Earth's rotation blows the surface water away from the beach.
And the deep, cold water rises—or upwells— to the surface!
UPWELLING
UPWELLING
I always thought the water in Portugal was cold because of the ocean currents. But I don't really know what those are.

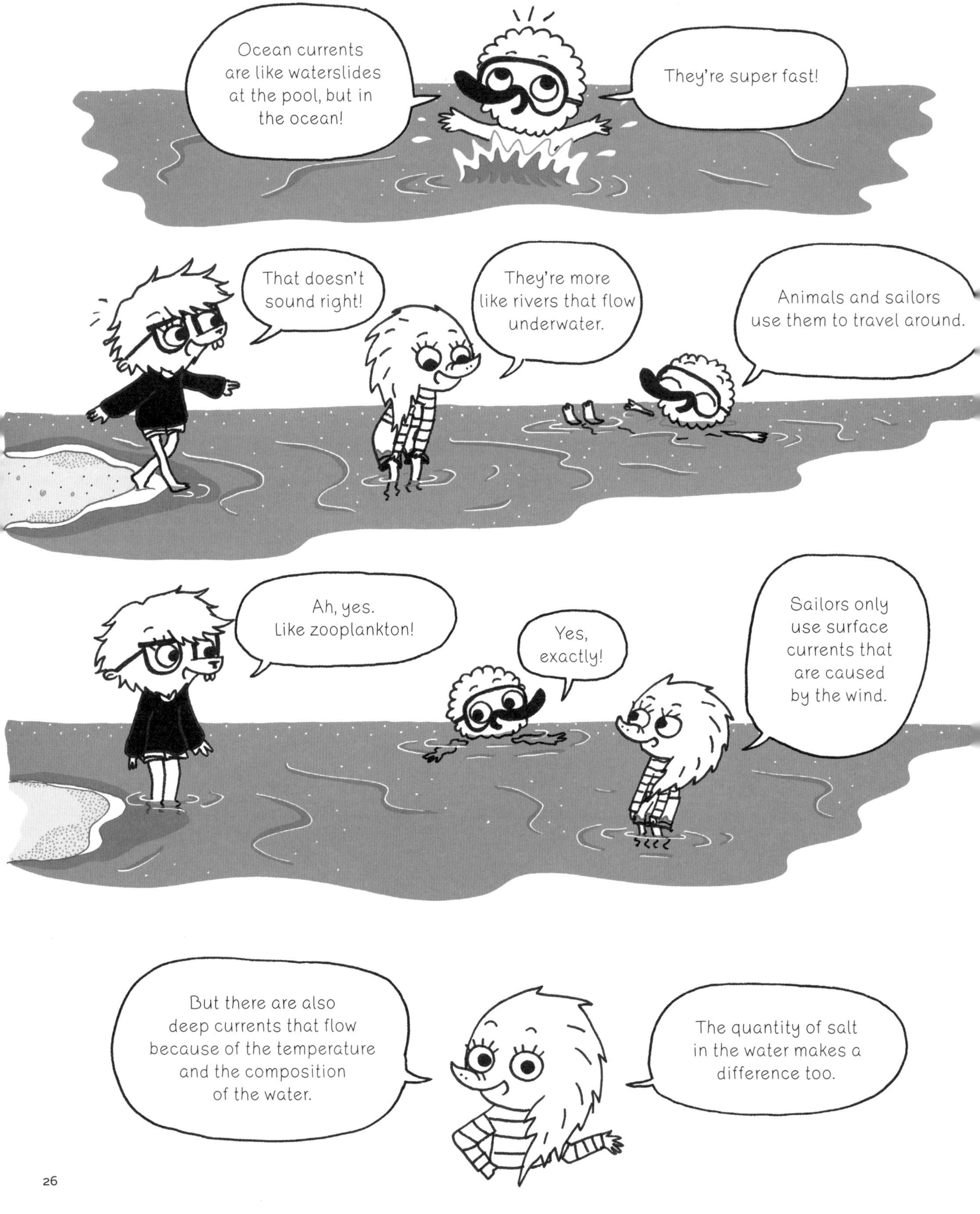
Ocean currents are like waterslides at the pool, but in the ocean!
They're super fast!
That doesn't sound right!
They're more like rivers that flow underwater.
Animals and sailors use them to travel around.
Ah, yes. Like zooplankton!
Yes, exactly!
Sailors only use surface currents that are caused by the wind.
But there are also deep currents that flow because of the temperature and the composition of the water.
The quantity of salt in the water makes a difference too.

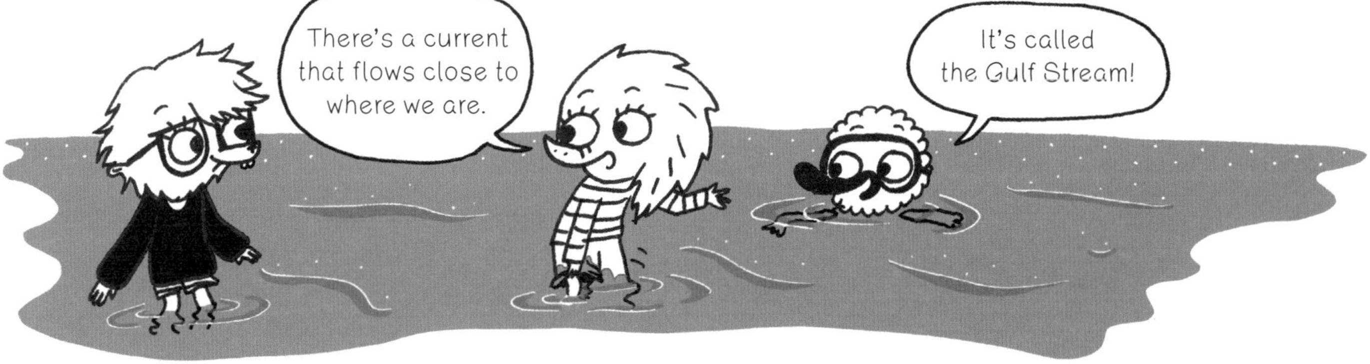
There's a current that flows close to where we are.
It's called the Gulf Stream!

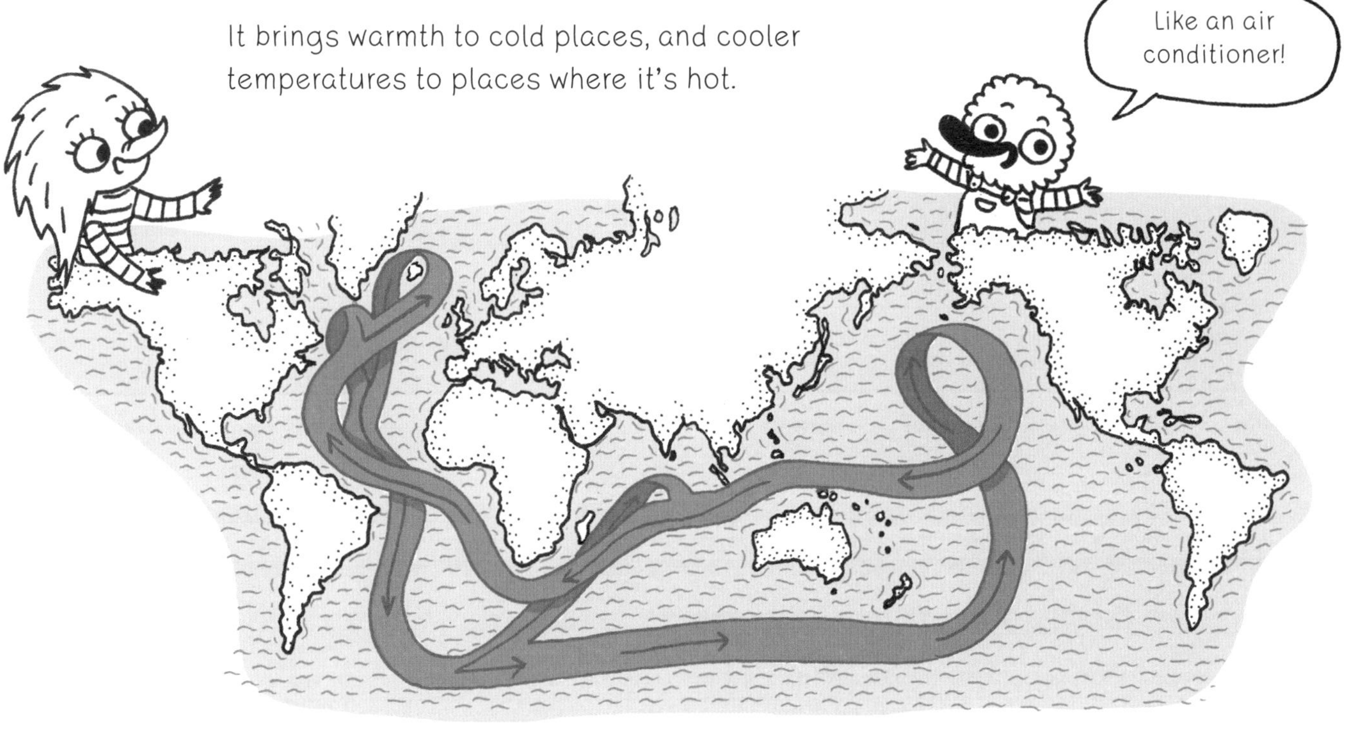
It brings warmth to cold places, and cooler temperatures to places where it's hot.
Like an air conditioner!

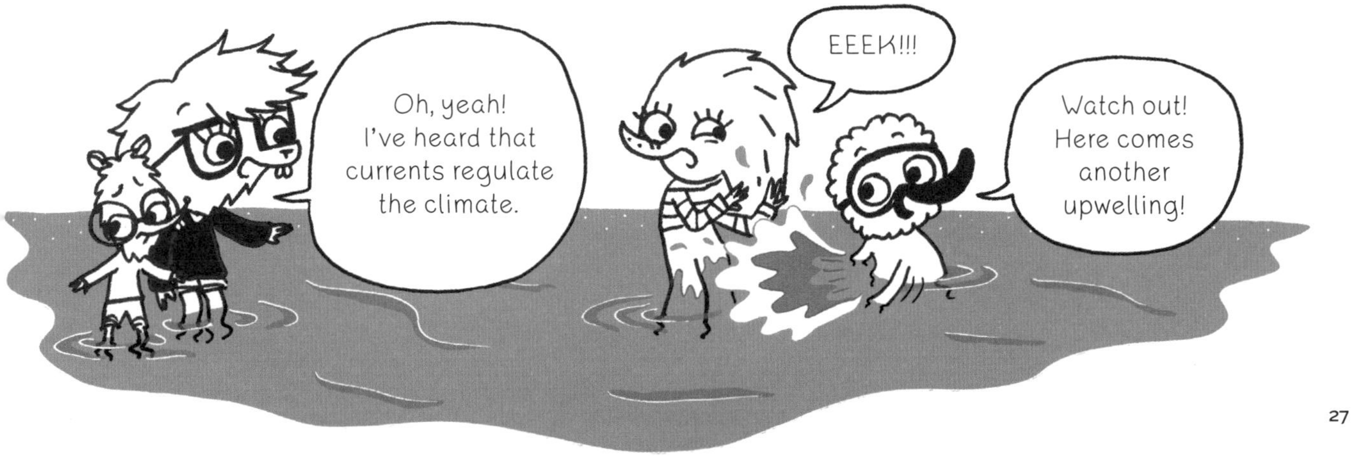
Oh, yeah! I've heard that currents regulate the climate.
EEEK!!!
Watch out! Here comes another upwelling!

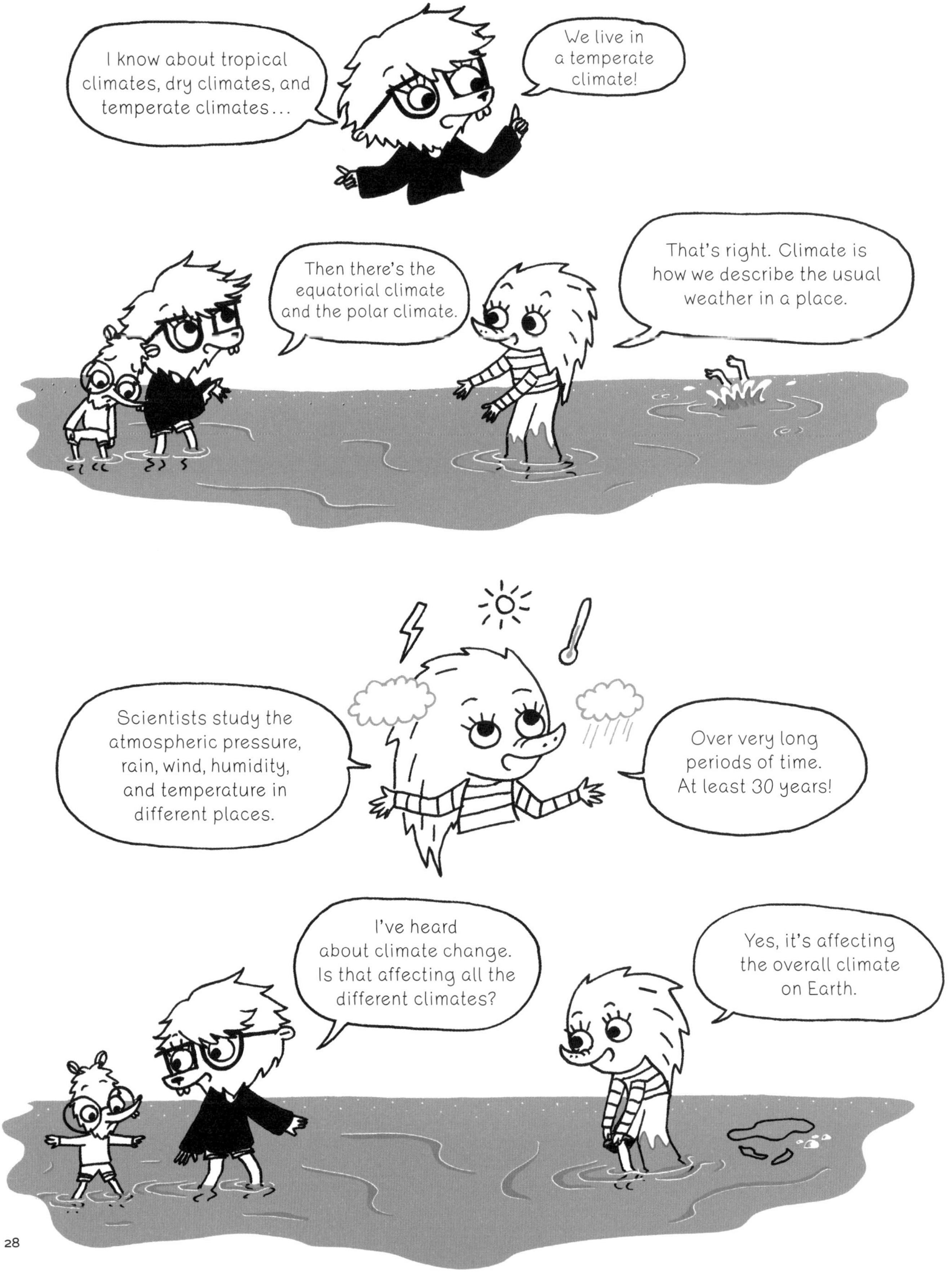

I know about tropical climates, dry climates, and temperate climates…
We live in a temperate climate!
Then there's the equatorial climate and the polar climate.
That's right. Climate is how we describe the usual weather in a place.
Scientists study the atmospheric pressure, rain, wind, humidity, and temperature in different places.
Over very long periods of time. At least 30 years!
I've heard about climate change. Is that affecting all the different climates?
Yes, it's affecting the overall climate on Earth.

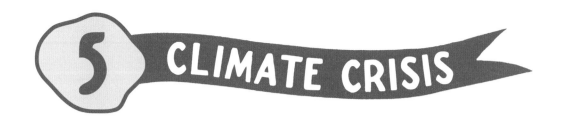

5 CLIMATE CRISIS

Since the very beginning of its history, the Earth's climate has changed regularly.

There's so much ice!
COLD
700 million years ago
HOT
COLD
HOT
200 million years ago
Wow! There's no more ice!
But there are dinosaurs!

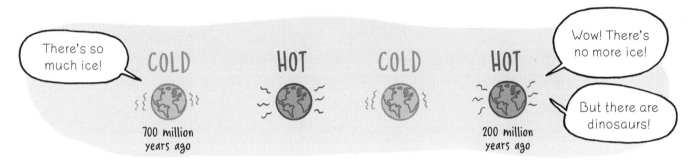

It's a natural phenomenon due to the position of the Earth and the Sun. The heat of the Sun is regulated by greenhouse gases in the Earth's atmosphere. The main greenhouse gases are:

WATER VAPOR
H_2O
METHANE
CH_4
CARBON DIOXIDE
CO_2

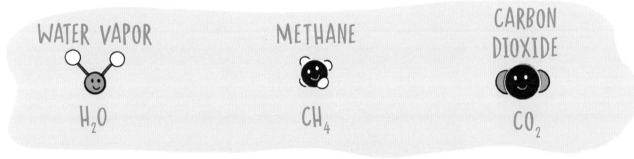

Greenhouse gases are important for the Earth. They trap some of the Sun's heat and keep the Earth at the ideal average temperature of around 59°F (15°C).

0°F (-18°C)
Without them, it would be very cold!
59°F (15°C)
And if there were any more greenhouse gases...
...that would be like a blanket.
It would get very hot!
68°F (20°C)

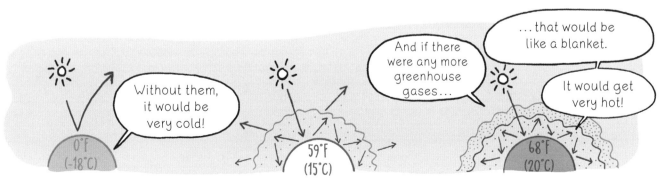

For years, humans have been releasing more and more CO_2 and CH_4, and this has increased the "greenhouse effect."

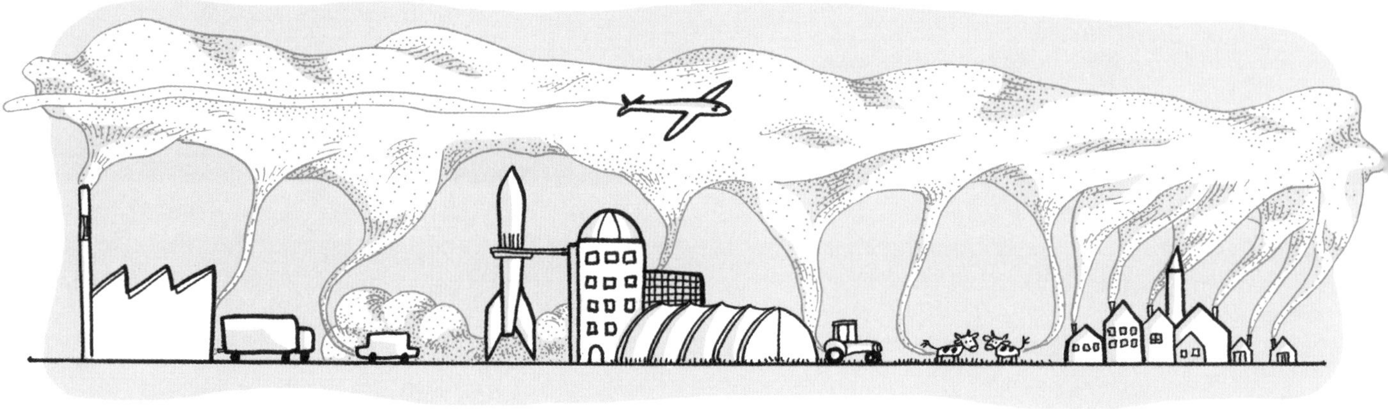

Luckily, the forests (thanks to trees!) and the ocean (thanks to phytoplankton!) can absorb some of these gases and release oxygen (O_2).

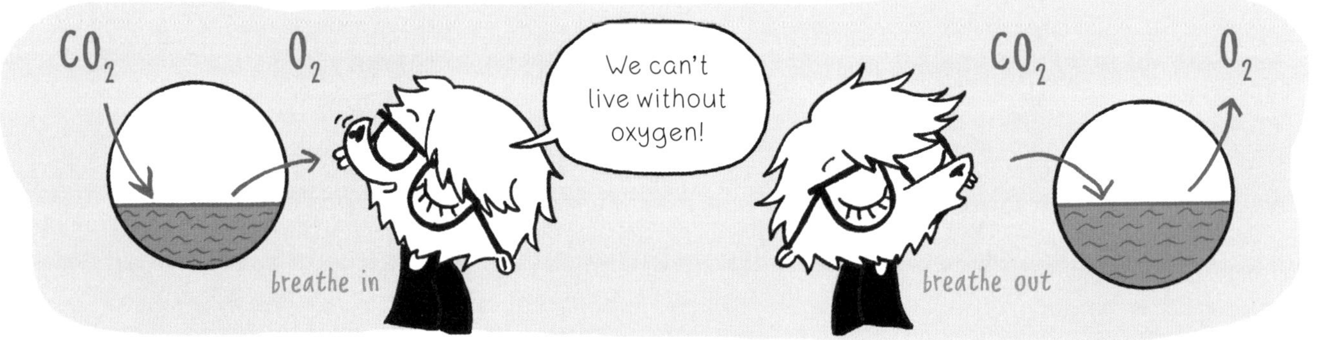
CO_2
O_2
We can't live without oxygen!
breathe in
CO_2
O_2
breathe out

But there's still too much CO_2 and CH_4 in the atmosphere, and temperatures are rising.

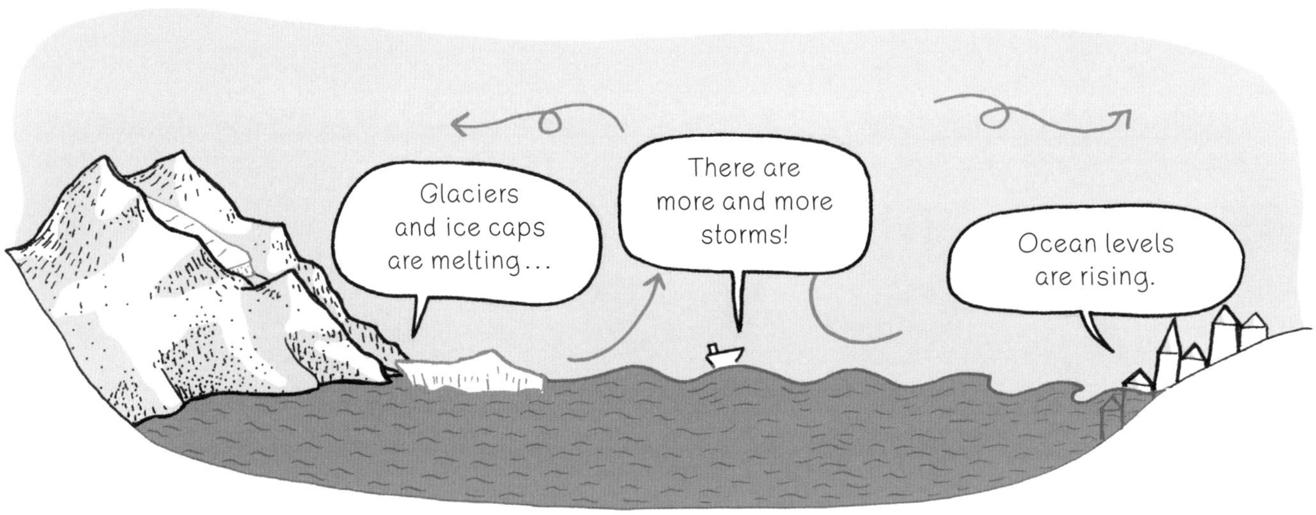
Glaciers and ice caps are melting...
There are more and more storms!
Ocean levels are rising.

Today, there's so much CO_2 in the ocean, the water is getting more acidic. One day, it could start releasing CO_2 instead of oxygen!

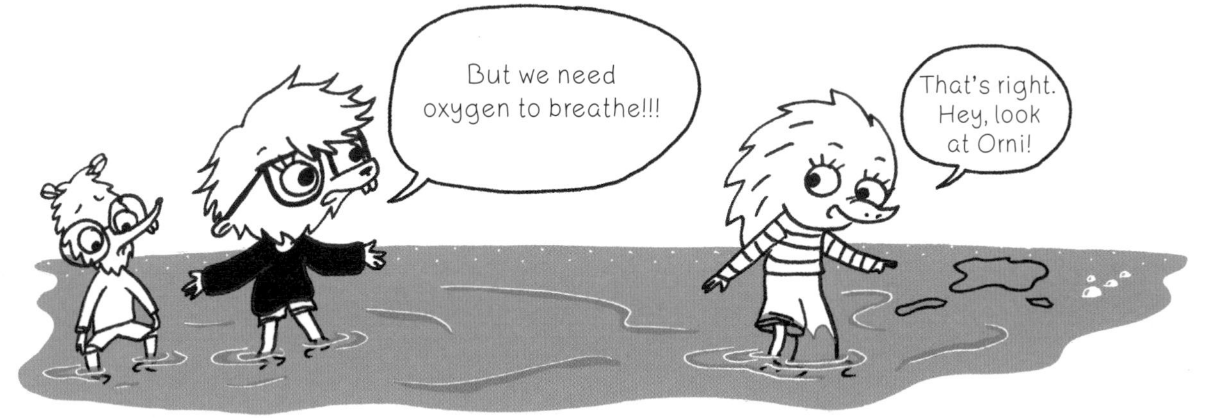
But we need oxygen to breathe!!!
That's right. Hey, look at Orni!

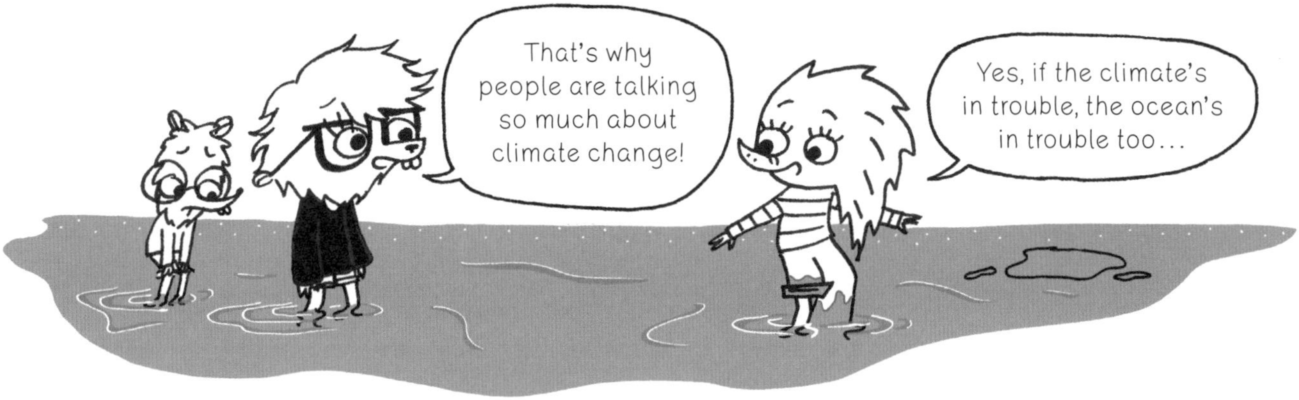
That's why people are talking so much about climate change!
Yes, if the climate's in trouble, the ocean's in trouble too...

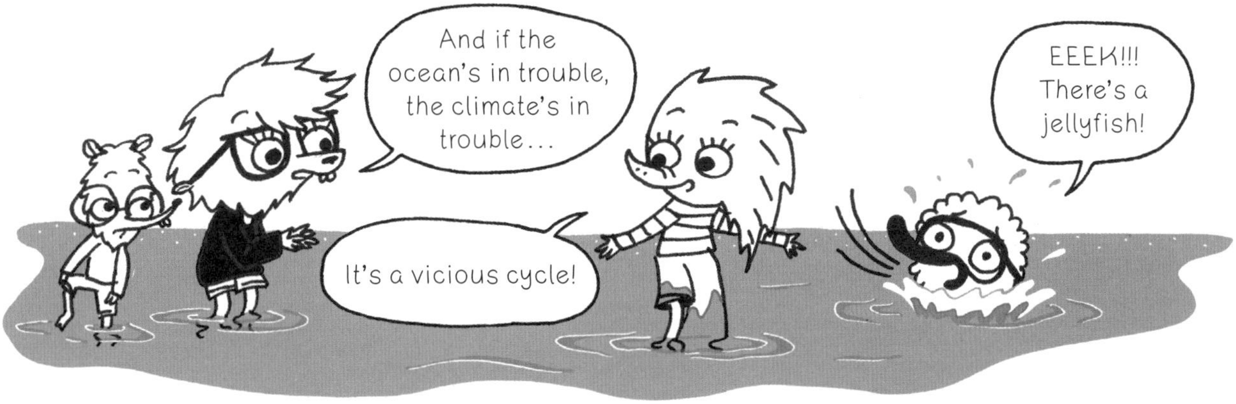
And if the ocean's in trouble, the climate's in trouble...
It's a vicious cycle!
EEEK!!! There's a jellyfish!

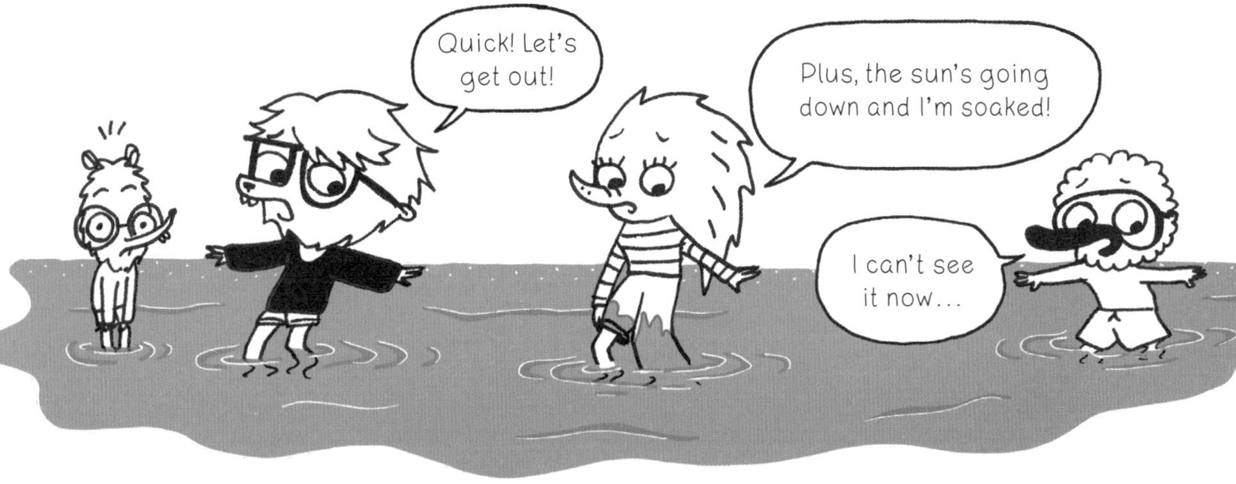
Quick! Let's get out!
Plus, the sun's going down and I'm soaked!
I can't see it now...

JELLYFISH

Some jellyfish are almost invisible.
You have to be careful because their tentacles can sting.

Some jellyfish stings can even be deadly.

Jellyfish are made up of around 98% water!

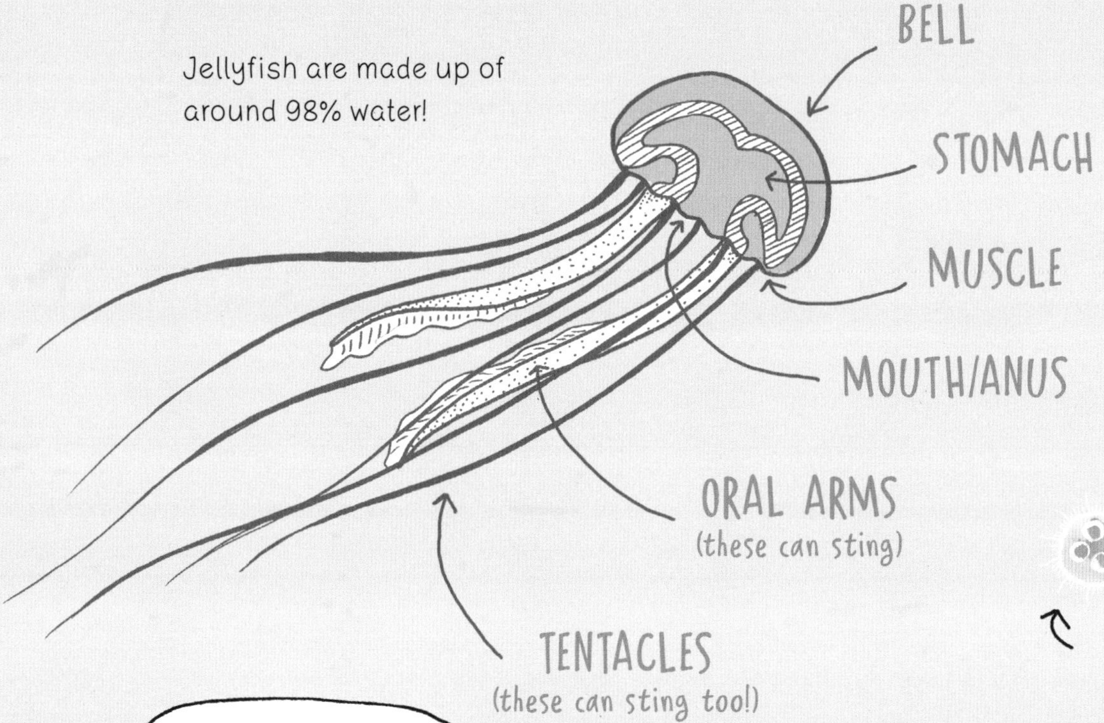

BELL
STOMACH
MUSCLE
MOUTH/ANUS
ORAL ARMS
(these can sting)
TENTACLES
(these can sting too!)

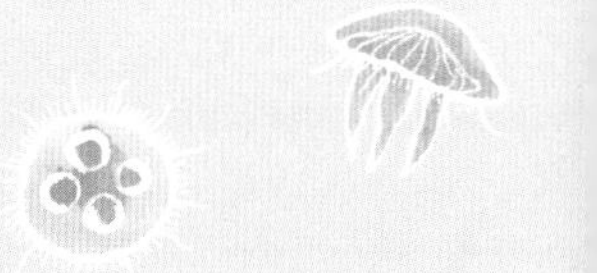

1. MOON JELLYFISH

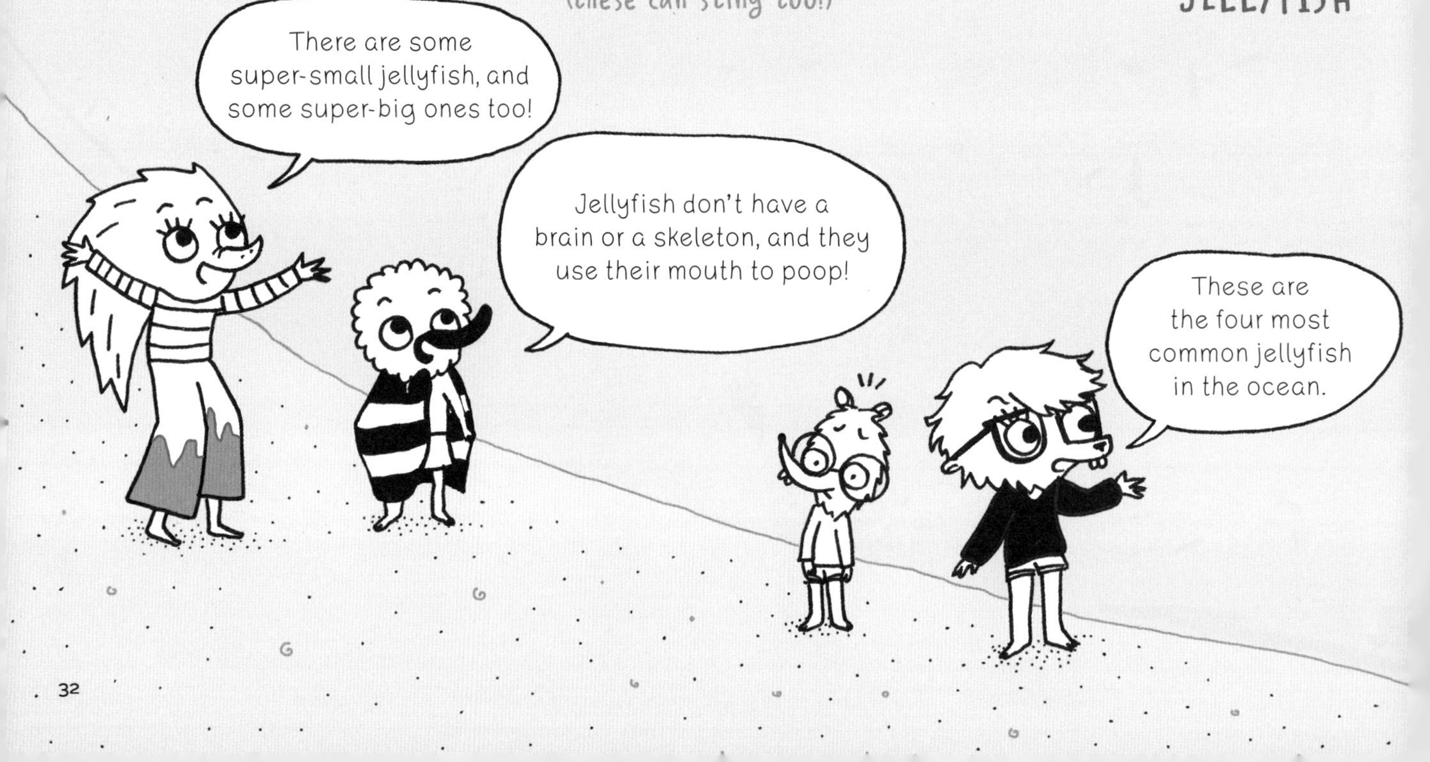

There are some super-small jellyfish, and some super-big ones too!
Jellyfish don't have a brain or a skeleton, and they use their mouth to poop!
These are the four most common jellyfish in the ocean.

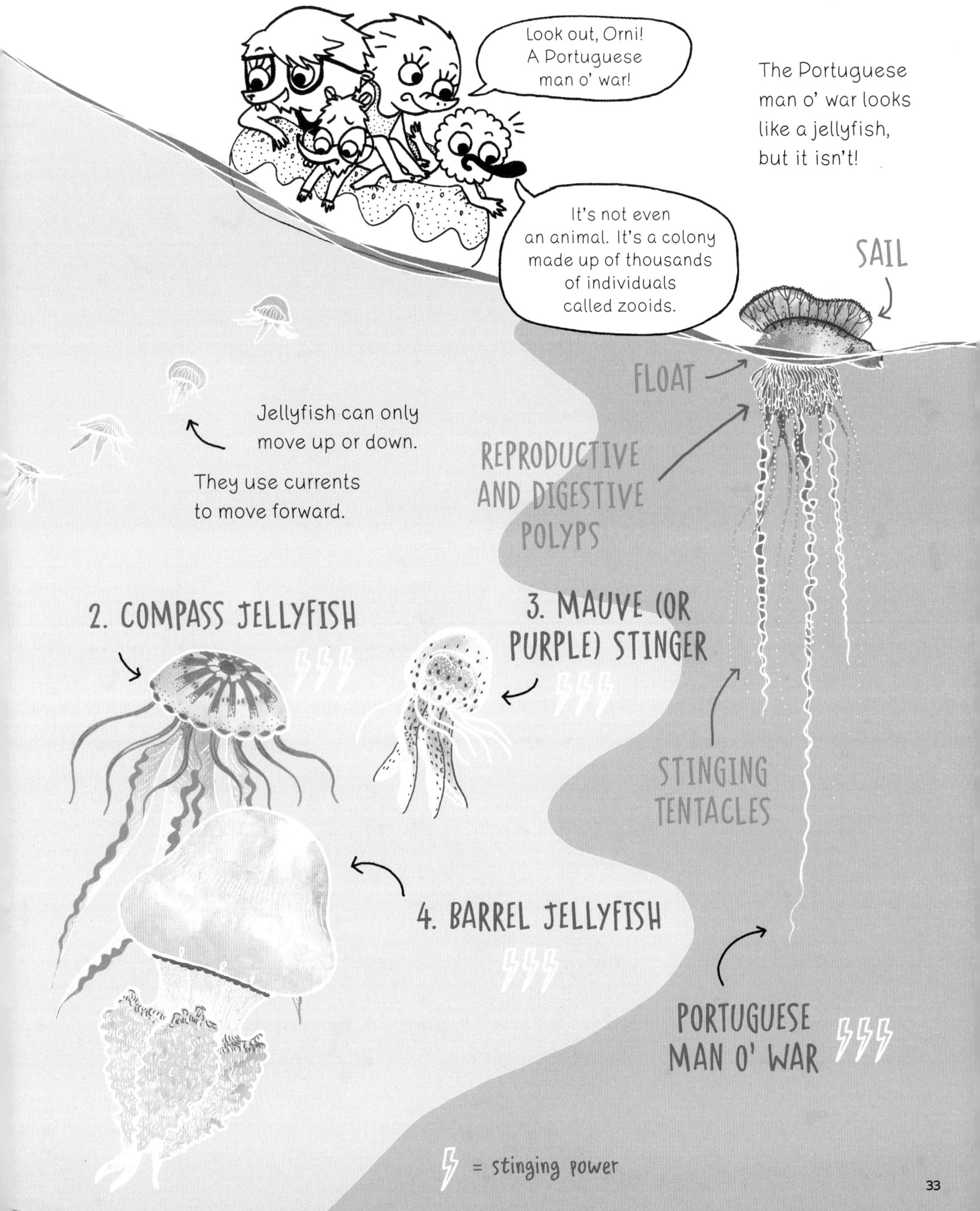

Look out, Orni! A Portuguese man o' war!
The Portuguese man o' war looks like a jellyfish, but it isn't!
It's not even an animal. It's a colony made up of thousands of individuals called zooids.
SAIL
FLOAT
Jellyfish can only move up or down.
They use currents to move forward.
REPRODUCTIVE AND DIGESTIVE POLYPS
2. COMPASS JELLYFISH
3. MAUVE (OR PURPLE) STINGER
STINGING TENTACLES
4. BARREL JELLYFISH
PORTUGUESE MAN O' WAR
= stinging power

6 MAKING WAVES

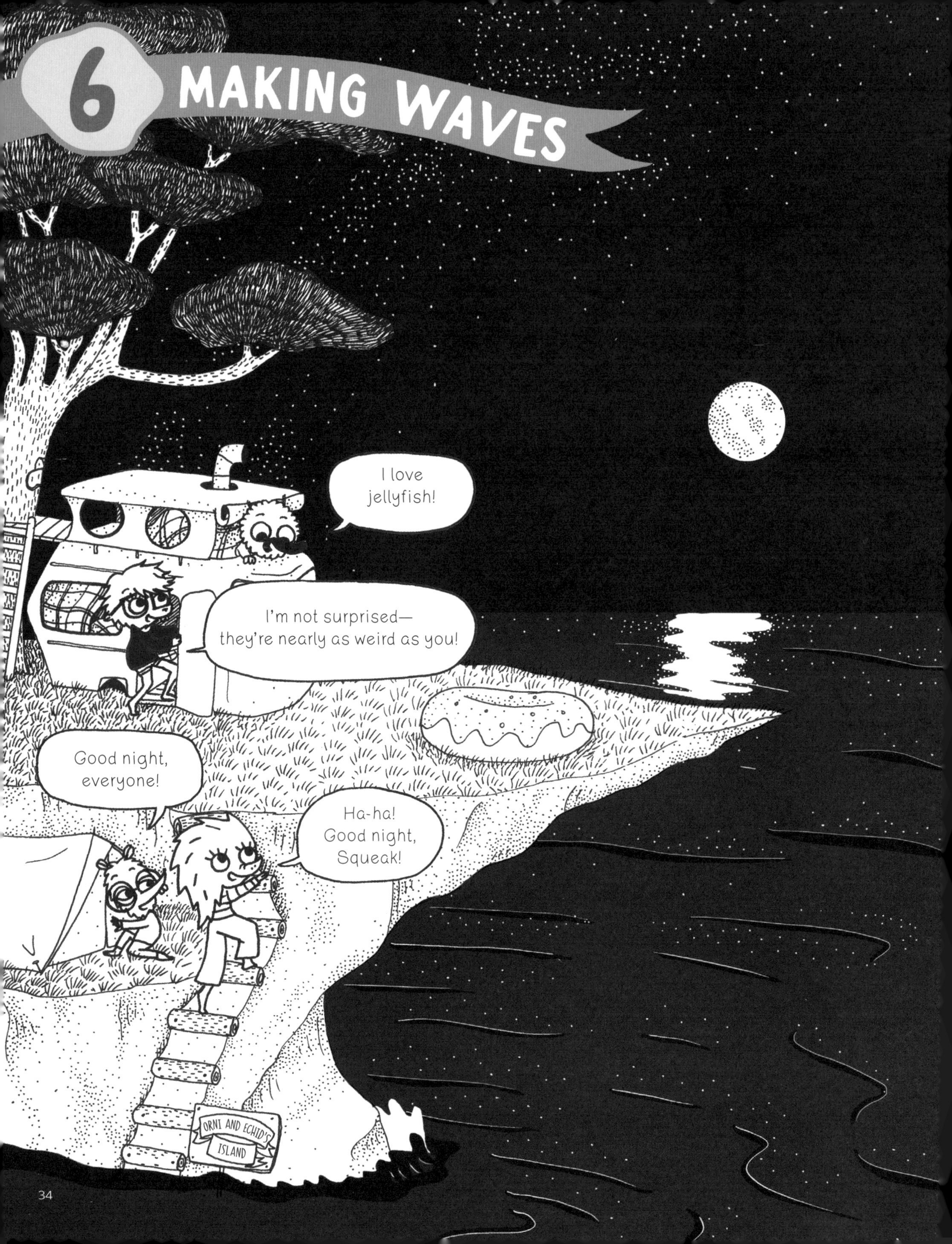
I love jellyfish!
I'm not surprised—they're nearly as weird as you!
Good night, everyone!
Ha-ha! Good night, Squeak!
ORNI AND ECHID'S ISLAND

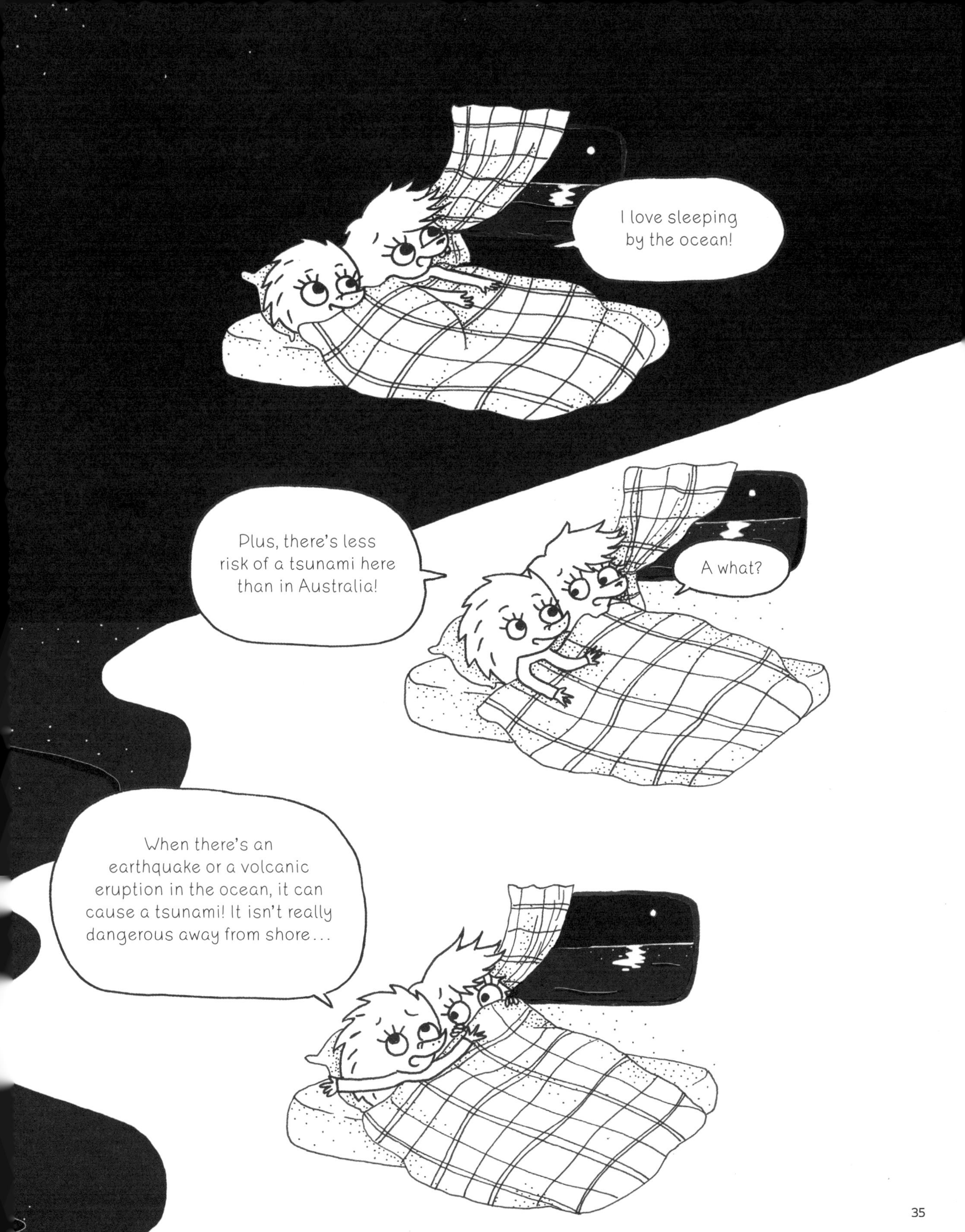
I love sleeping by the ocean!
Plus, there's less risk of a tsunami here than in Australia!
A what?
When there's an earthquake or a volcanic eruption in the ocean, it can cause a tsunami! It isn't really dangerous away from shore...

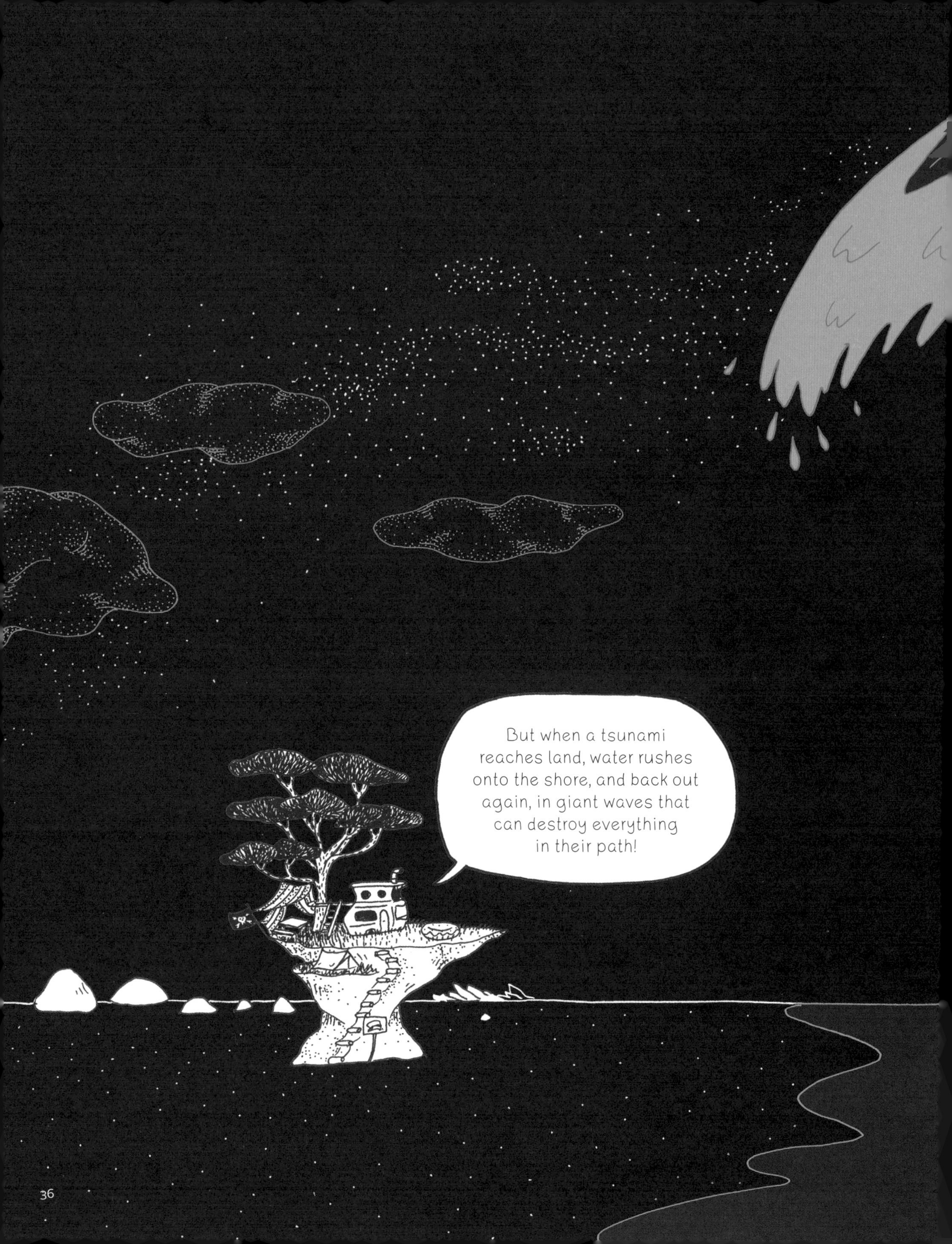
But when a tsunami reaches land, water rushes onto the shore, and back out again, in giant waves that can destroy everything in their path!

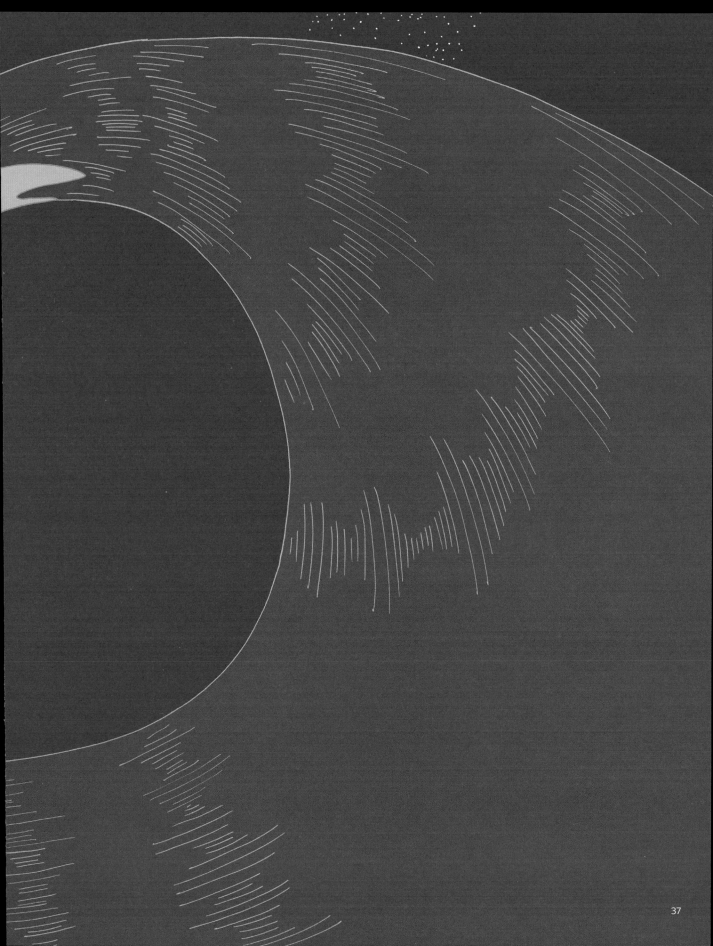

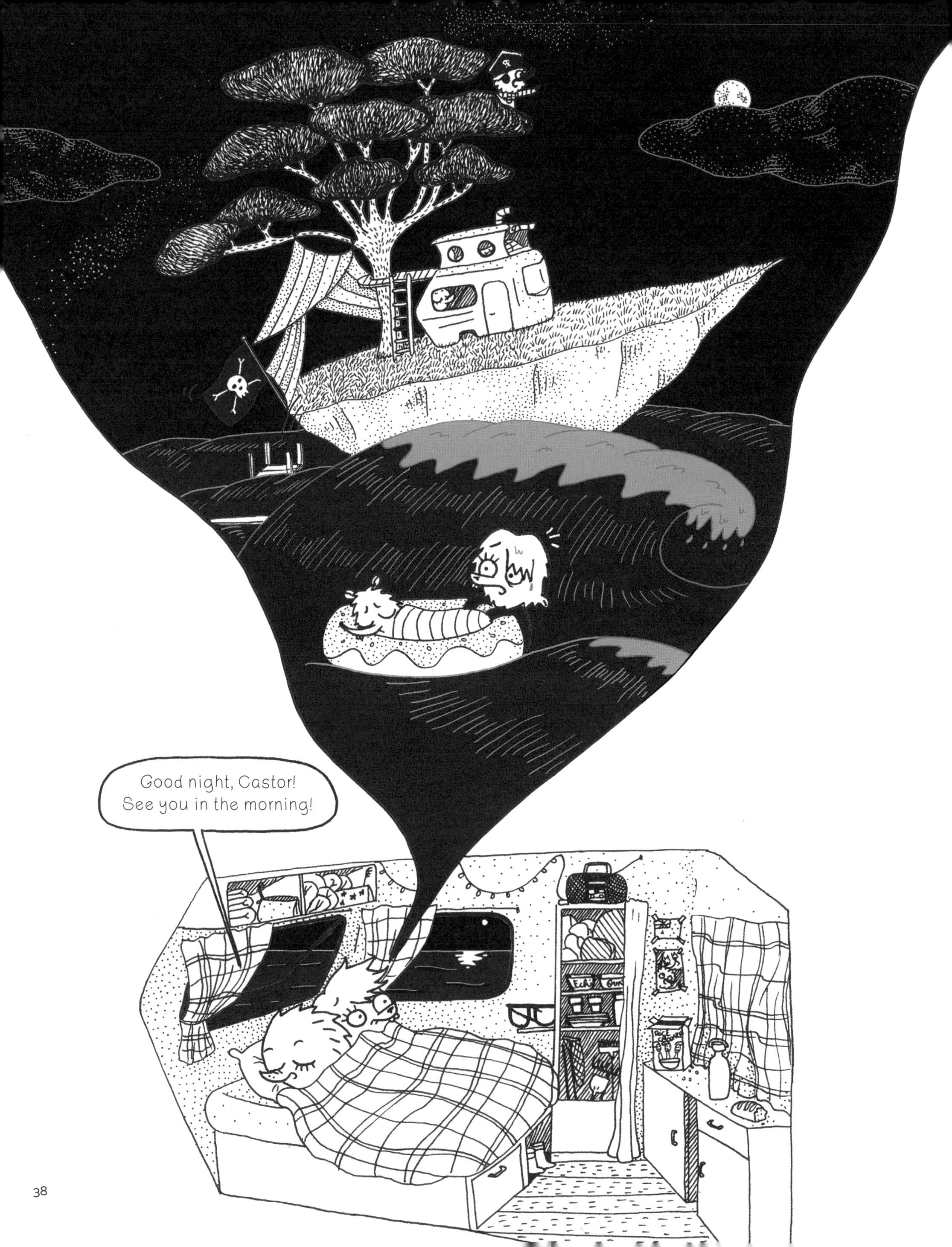
Good night, Castor! See you in the morning!

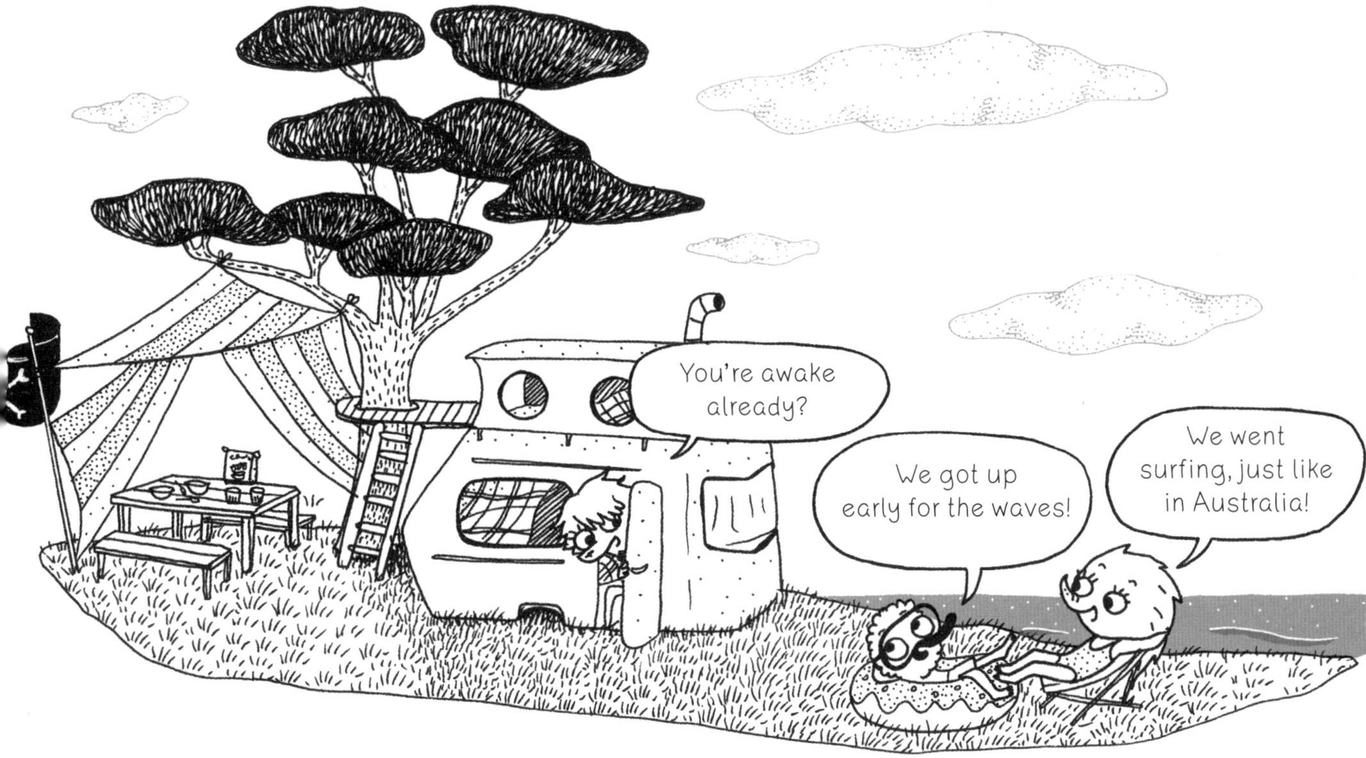
You're awake already?
We got up early for the waves!
We went surfing, just like in Australia!

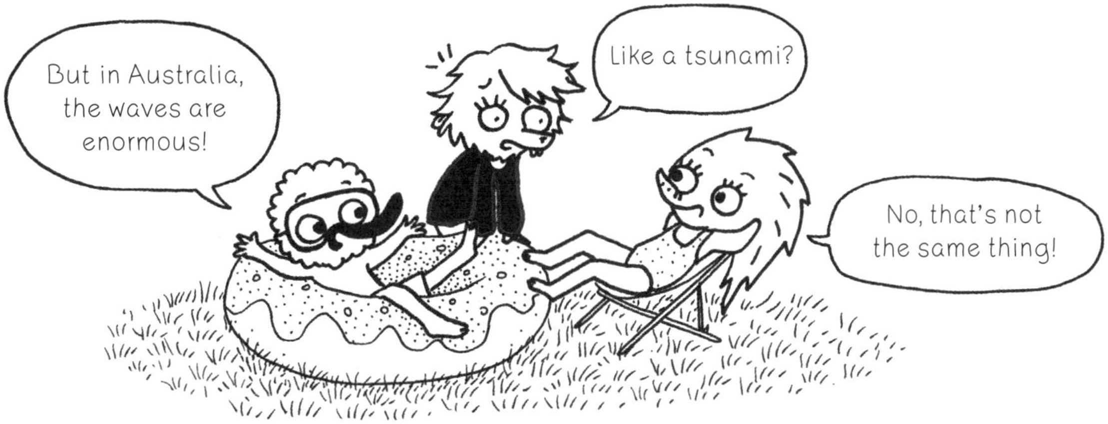
But in Australia, the waves are enormous!
Like a tsunami?
No, that's not the same thing!

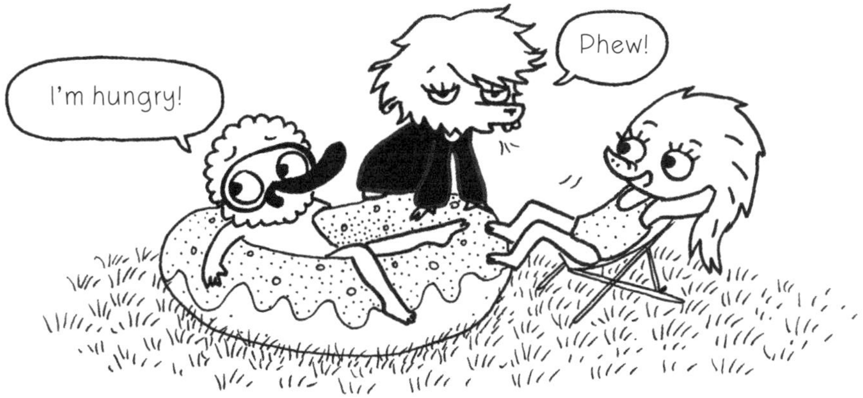
I'm hungry!
Phew!

WAVES, WIND, AND SWELL

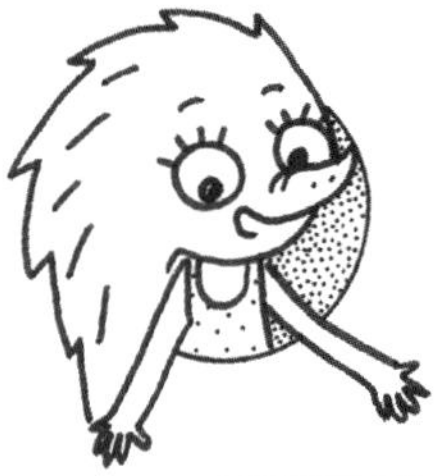

Unlike tsunamis, "regular" waves are created by wind.
A wave can make it look like the water is moving forward,
but it's the energy of the wave that's moving through the water.

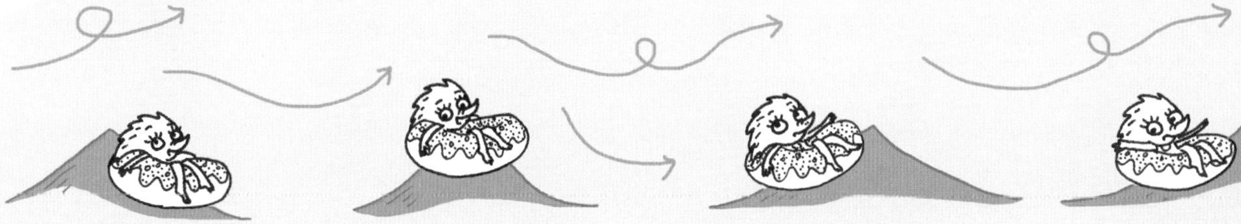

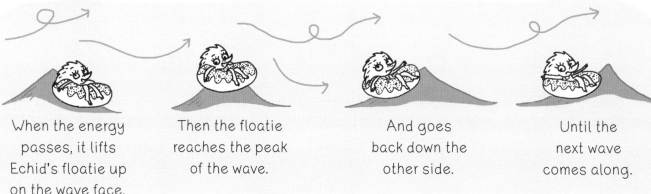

When the energy passes, it lifts Echid's floatie up on the wave face.

Then the floatie reaches the peak of the wave.

And goes back down the other side.

Until the next wave comes along.

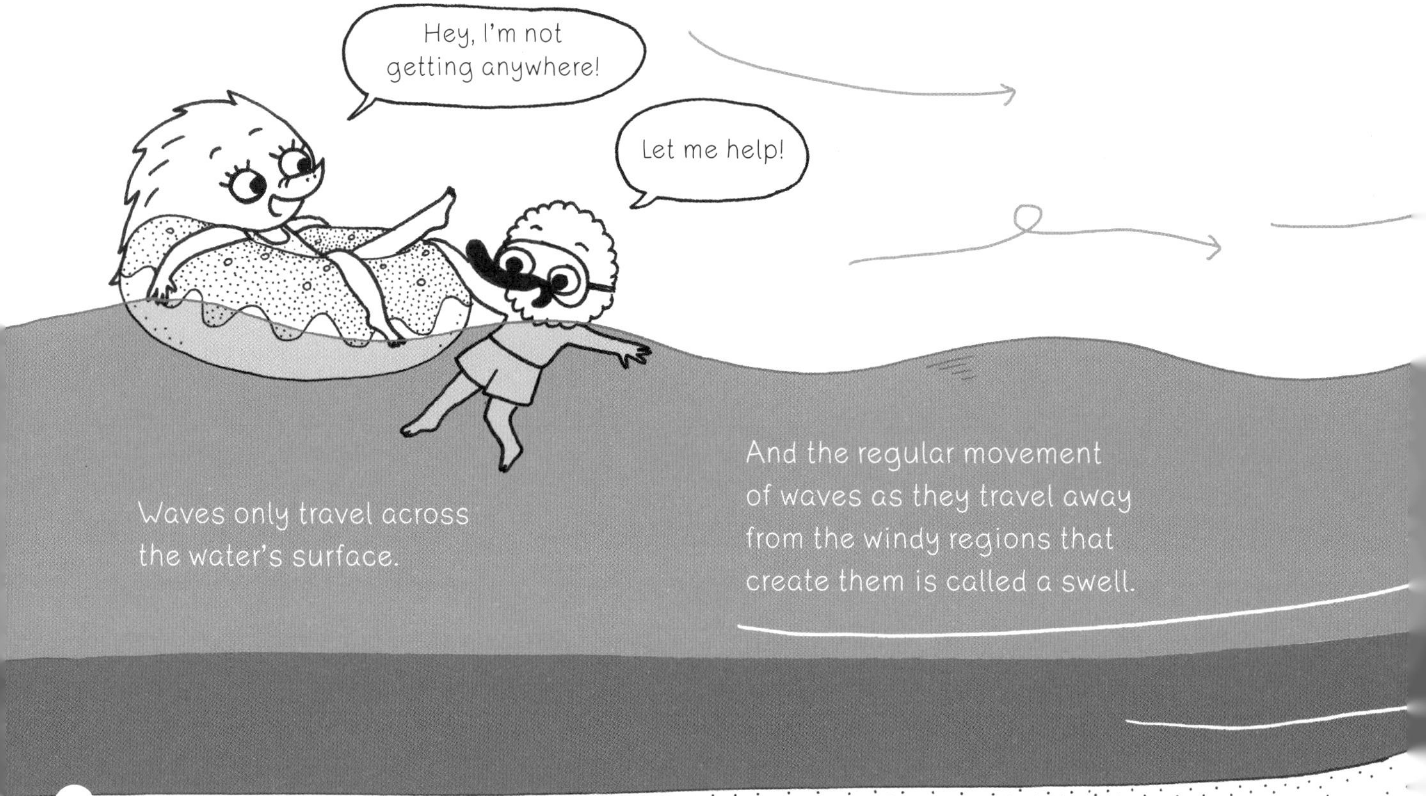
Hey, I'm not getting anywhere!
Let me help!

Waves only travel across the water's surface.

And the regular movement of waves as they travel away from the windy regions that create them is called a swell.

HOW WAVES FORM

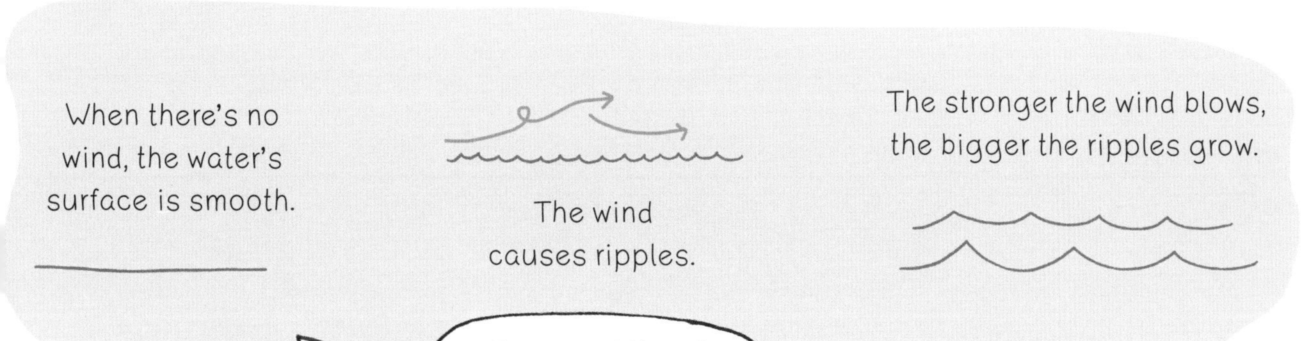
When there's no wind, the water's surface is smooth.
The wind causes ripples.
The stronger the wind blows, the bigger the ripples grow.

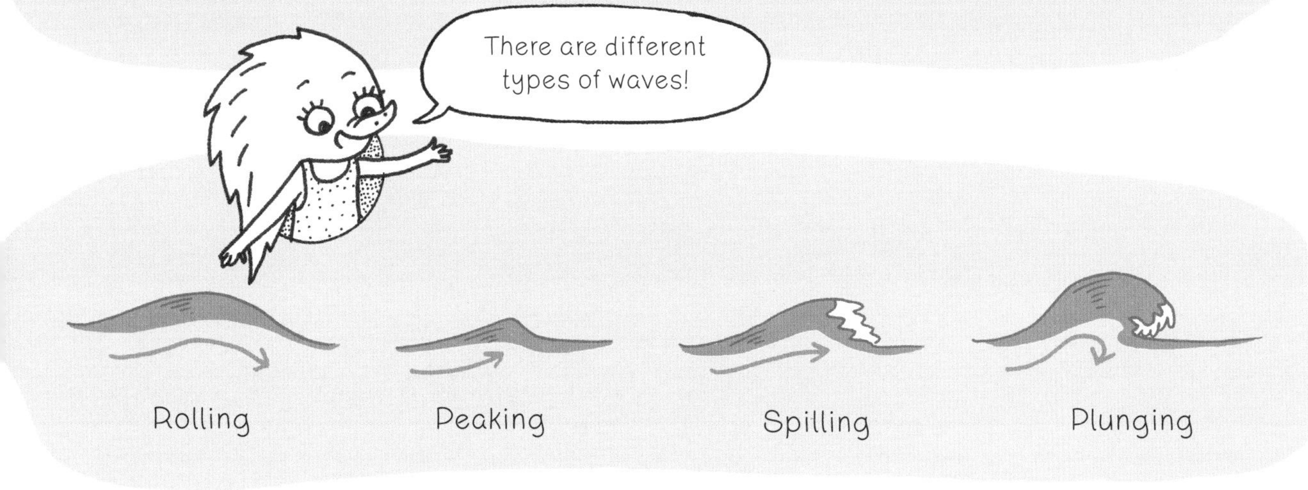
There are different types of waves!
Rolling
Peaking
Spilling
Plunging

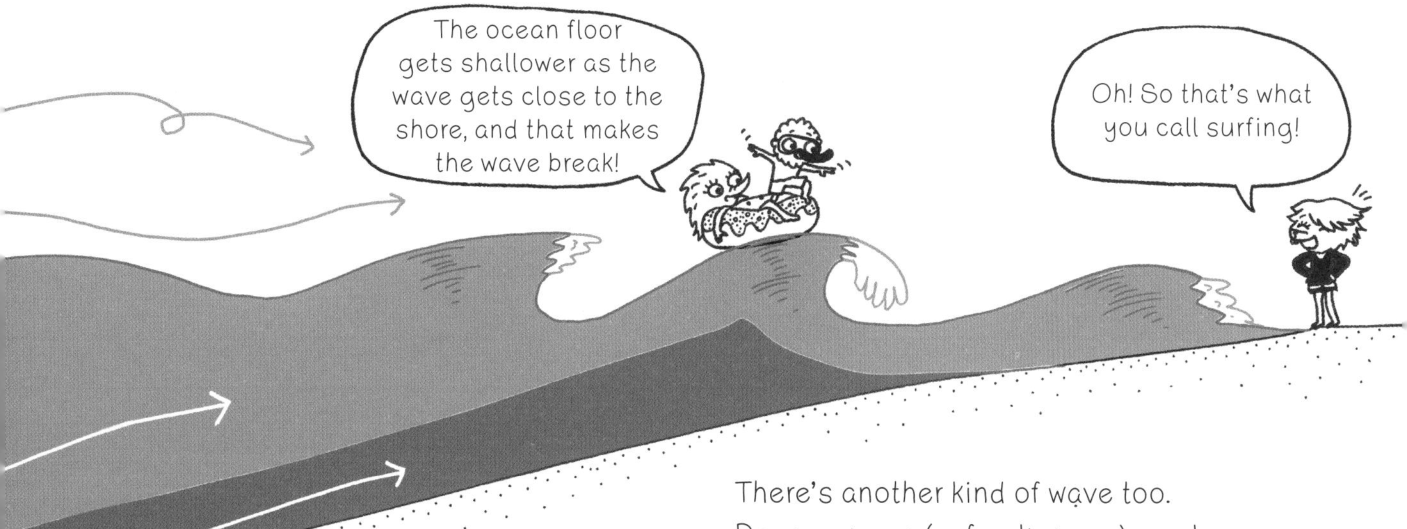
The ocean floor gets shallower as the wave gets close to the shore, and that makes the wave break!
Oh! So that's what you call surfing!

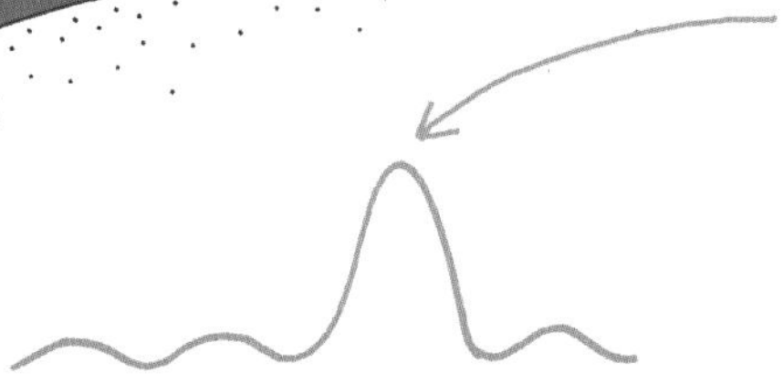

There's another kind of wave too. Rogue waves (or freak waves) can be dangerous because they're much bigger than the ones that come before and after… Rogue waves are rare, and scientists still don't know a lot about them!

7 THE TIDE IS HIGH!

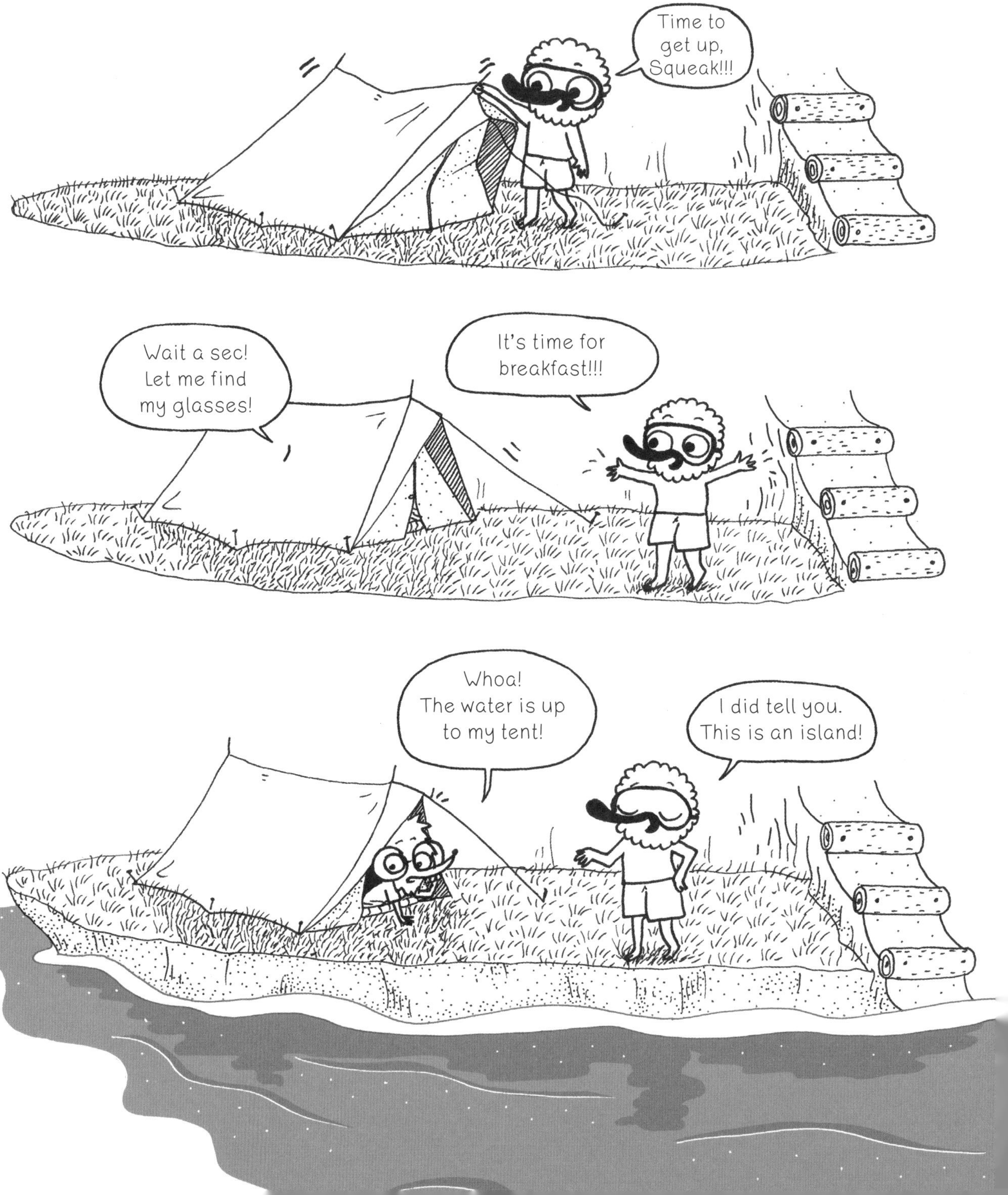

Time to get up, Squeak!!!
Wait a sec! Let me find my glasses!
It's time for breakfast!!!
Whoa! The water is up to my tent!
I did tell you. This is an island!

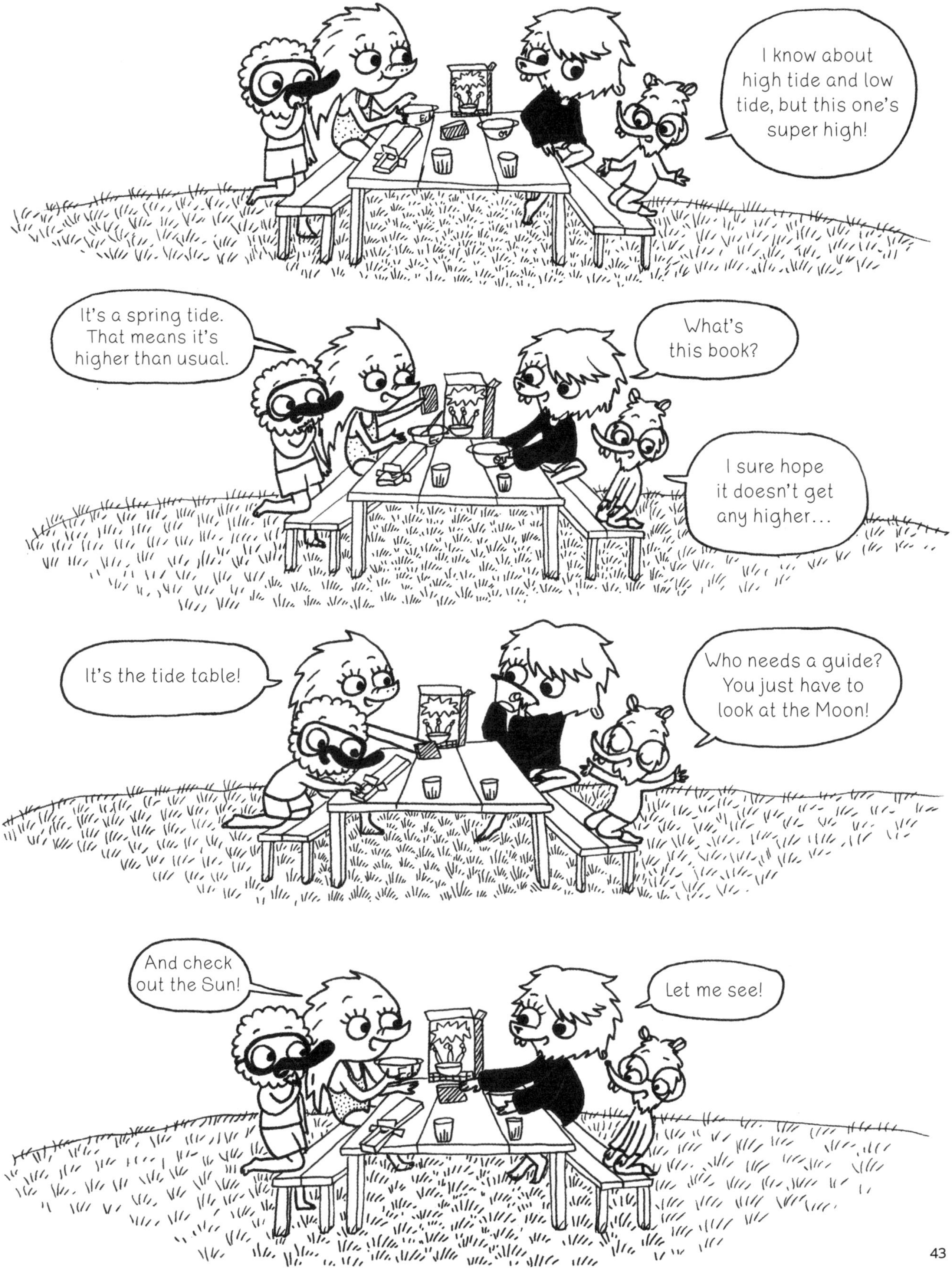
I know about high tide and low tide, but this one's super high!
It's a spring tide. That means it's higher than usual.
What's this book?
I sure hope it doesn't get any higher...
It's the tide table!
Who needs a guide? You just have to look at the Moon!
And check out the Sun!
Let me see!

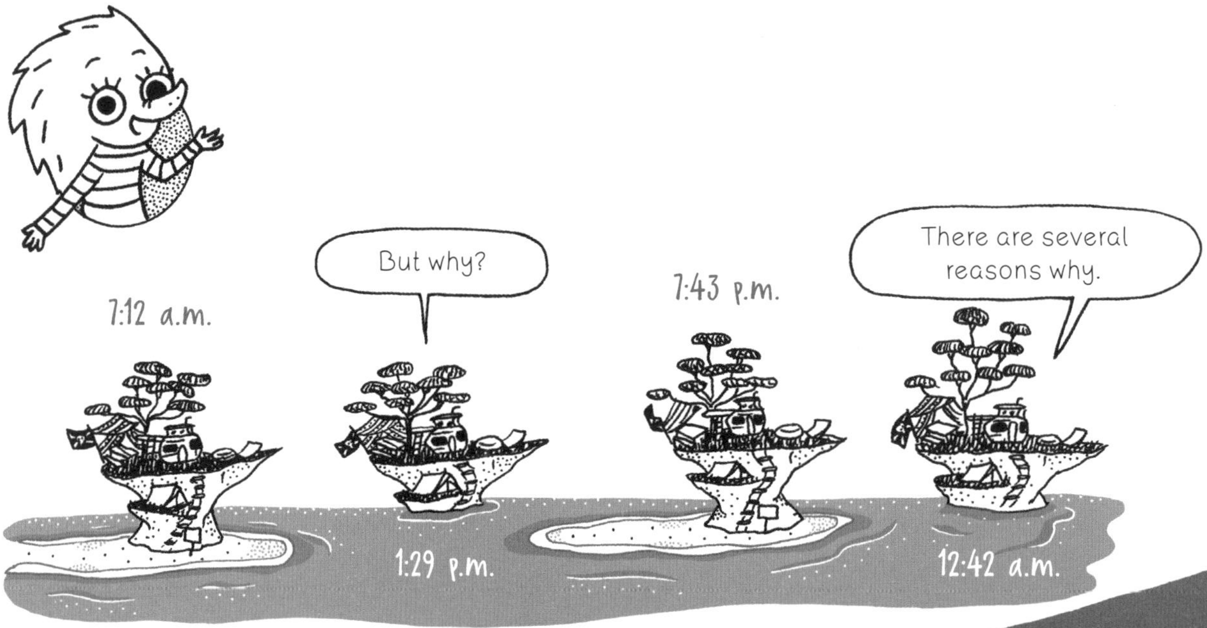
7:12 a.m.
But why?
1:29 p.m.
7:43 p.m.
There are several reasons why.
12:42 a.m.

1. GRAVITATION OF THE MOON

Tides are partly caused by the Moon as its gravitation pulls the water in the oceans on Earth toward it.

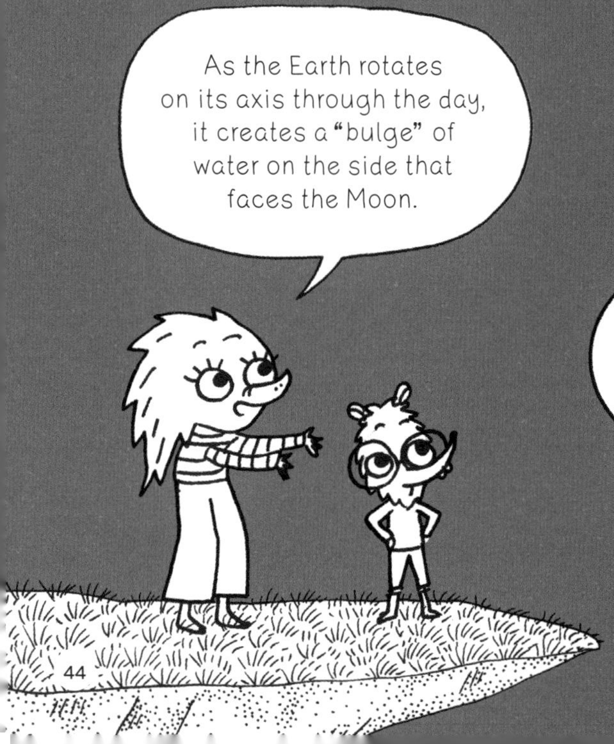
As the Earth rotates on its axis through the day, it creates a "bulge" of water on the side that faces the Moon.

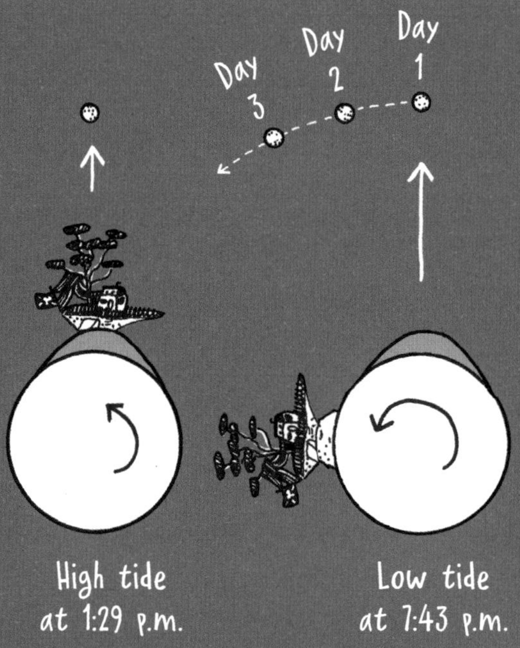
Day 3
Day 2
Day 1
High tide at 1:29 p.m.
Low tide at 7:43 p.m.

It takes the Moon 1 month to rotate around the Earth, so the tide times shift by a few minutes every day.

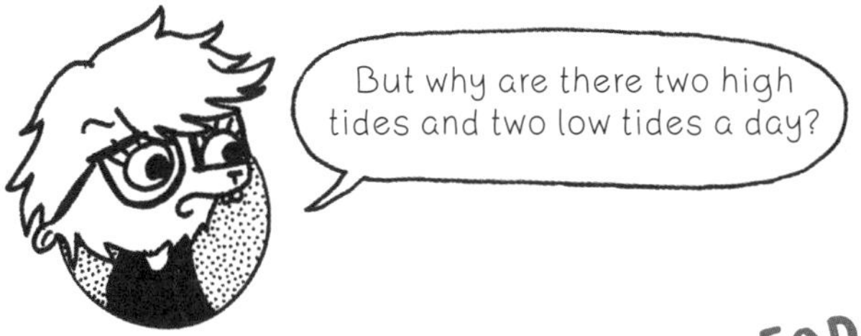
But why are there two high tides and two low tides a day?

2. CENTRIFUGAL FORCE

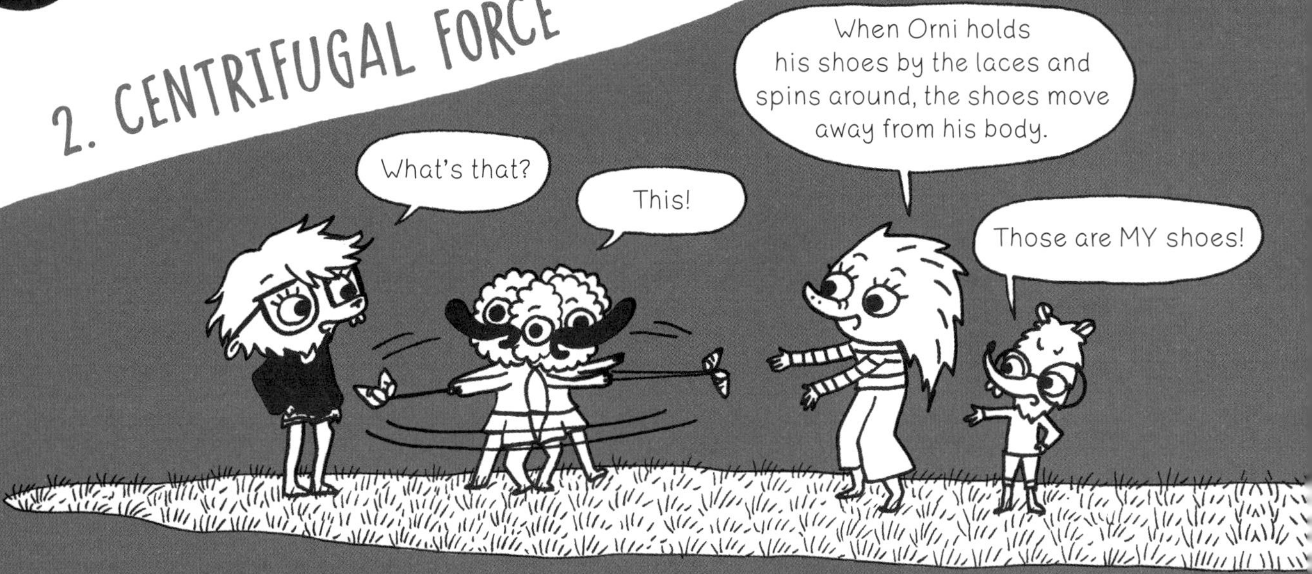
What's that?
This!
When Orni holds his shoes by the laces and spins around, the shoes move away from his body.
Those are MY shoes!

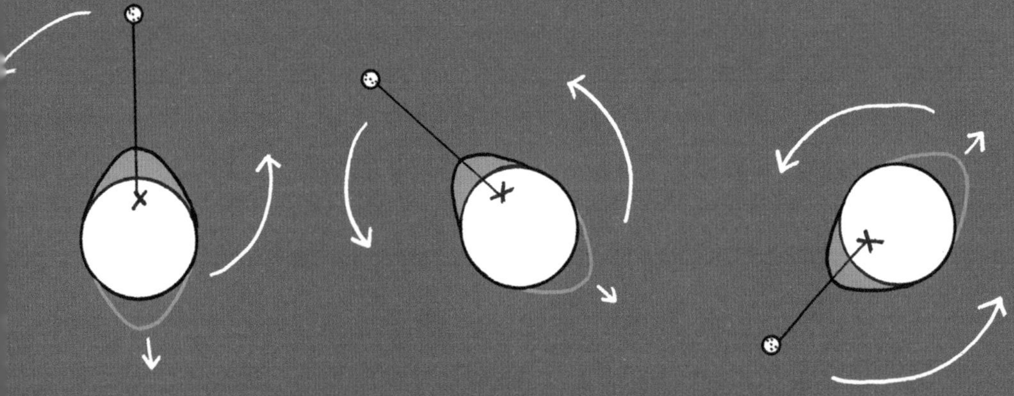

The Earth and the Moon both rotate around a point called the center of gravity.

And the water moves away from the center of gravity, just like the shoes!

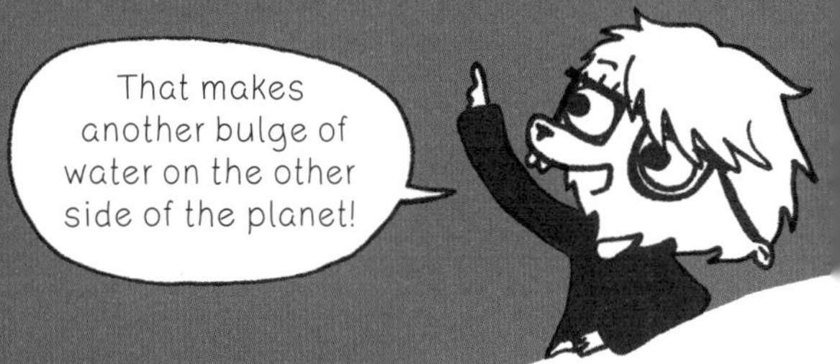
That makes another bulge of water on the other side of the planet!

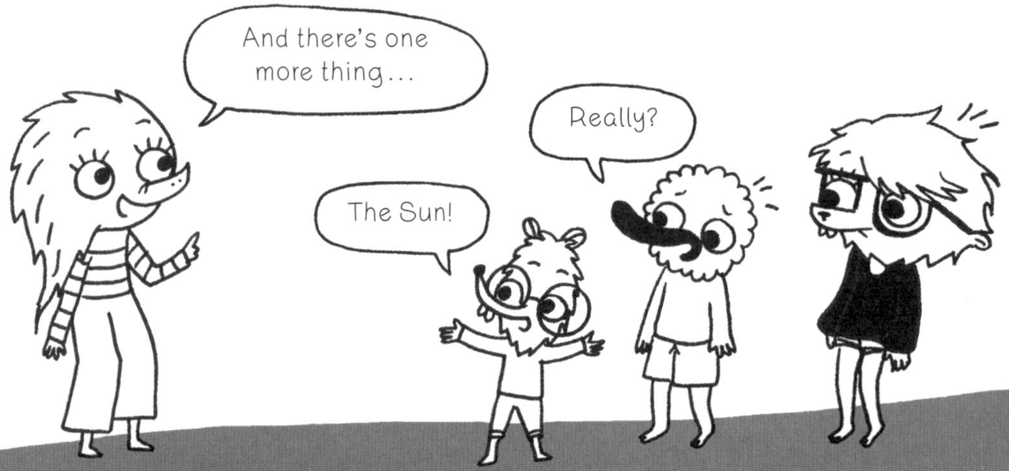
And there's one more thing...
Really?
The Sun!

3. THE SUN

When the Earth, the Moon, and the Sun are in alignment during a new moon or a full moon, the tides are even more impressive!

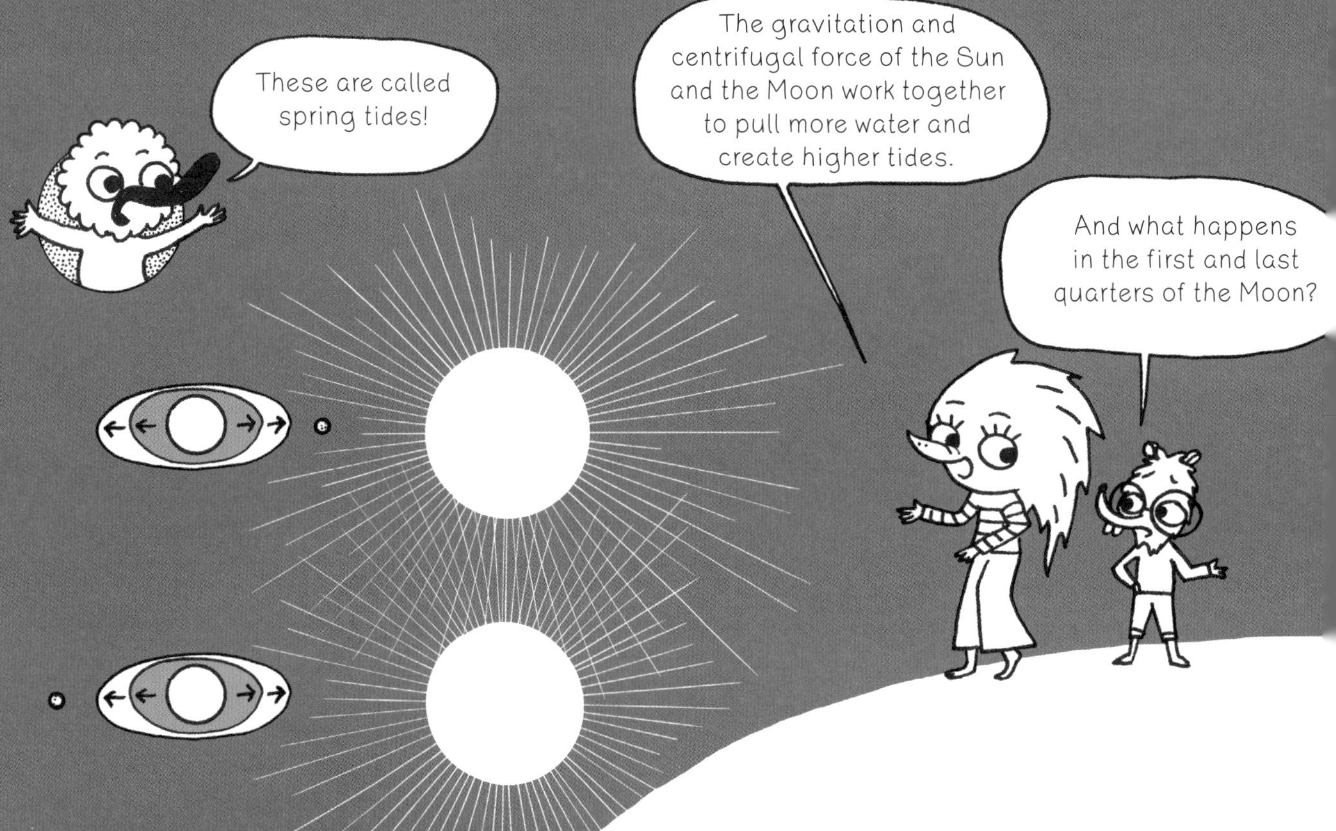
These are called spring tides!
The gravitation and centrifugal force of the Sun and the Moon work together to pull more water and create higher tides.
And what happens in the first and last quarters of the Moon?

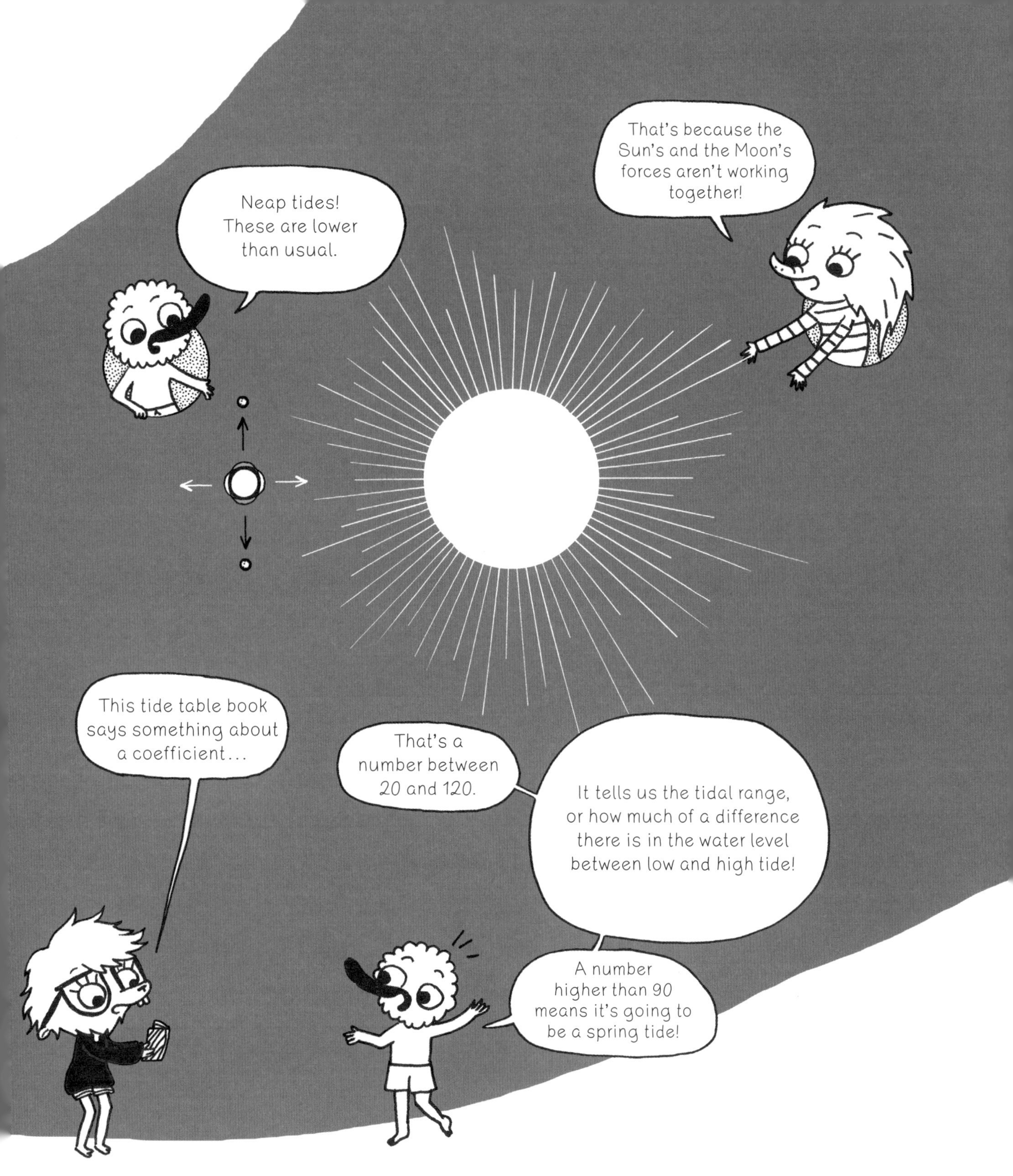

Neap tides! These are lower than usual.
That's because the Sun's and the Moon's forces aren't working together!
This tide table book says something about a coefficient...
That's a number between 20 and 120.
It tells us the tidal range, or how much of a difference there is in the water level between low and high tide!
A number higher than 90 means it's going to be a spring tide!

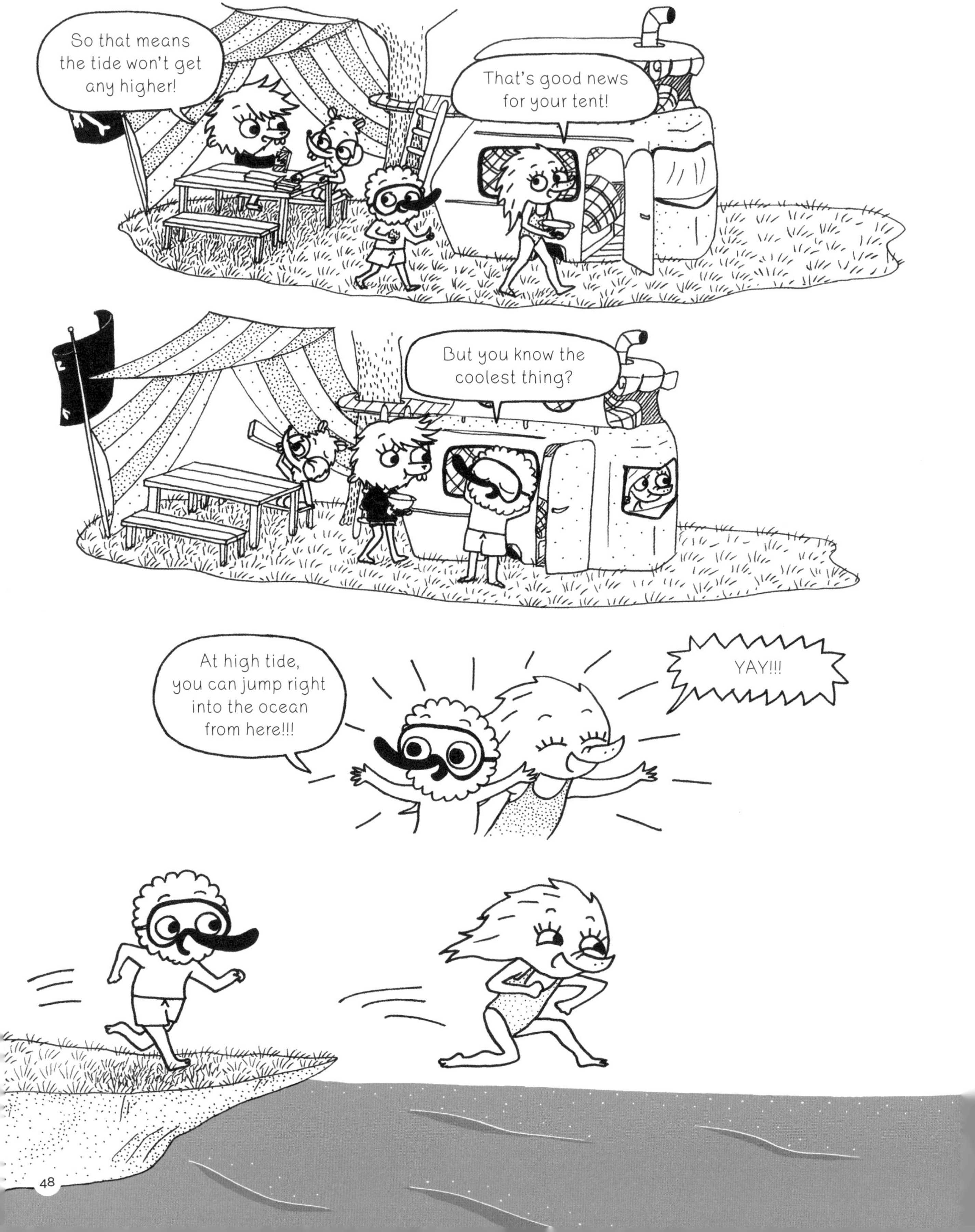
So that means the tide won't get any higher!
That's good news for your tent!
But you know the coolest thing?
At high tide, you can jump right into the ocean from here!!!
YAY!!!

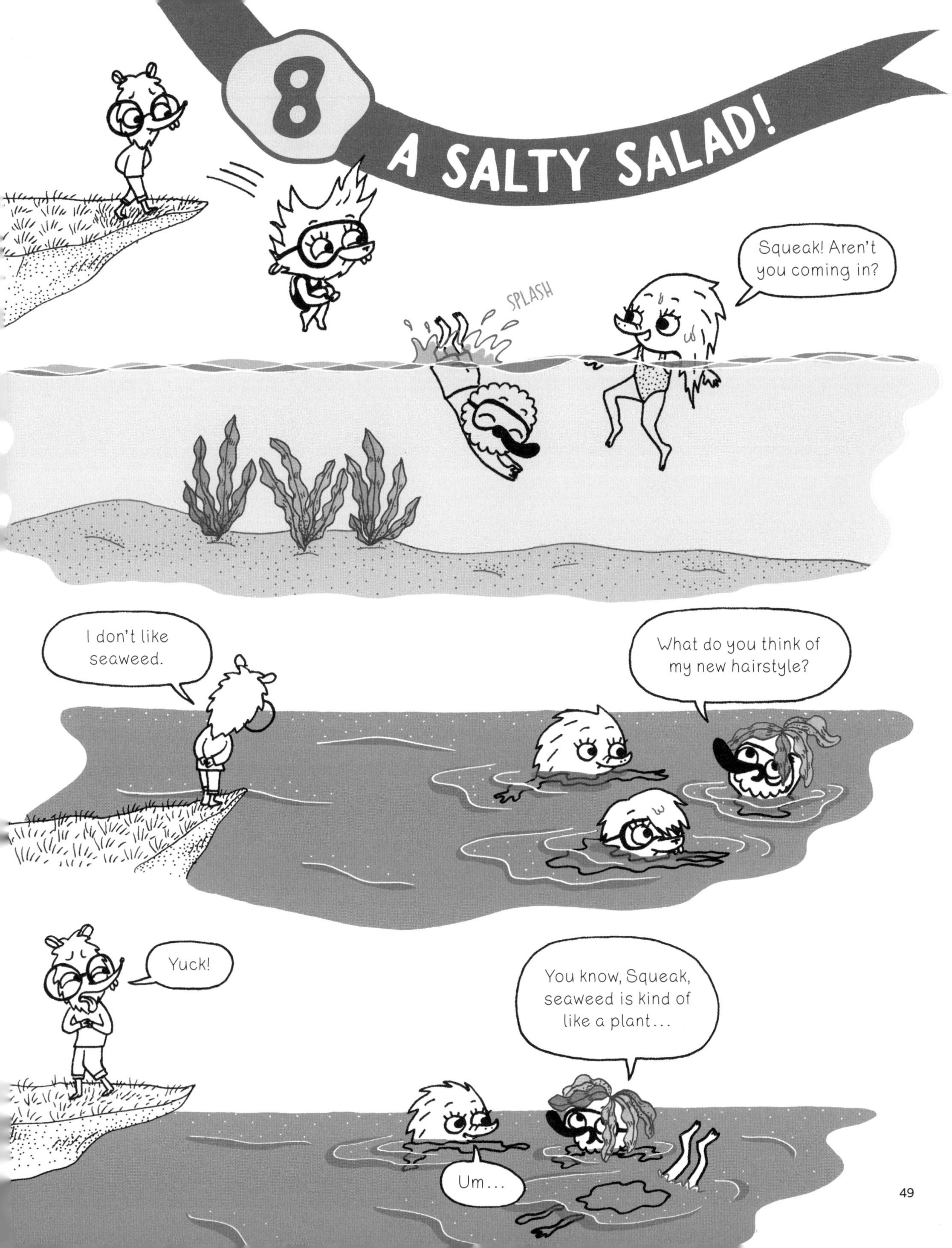
8
A SALTY SALAD!
SPLASH
Squeak! Aren't you coming in?
I don't like seaweed.
What do you think of my new hairstyle?
Yuck!
You know, Squeak, seaweed is kind of like a plant...
Um...

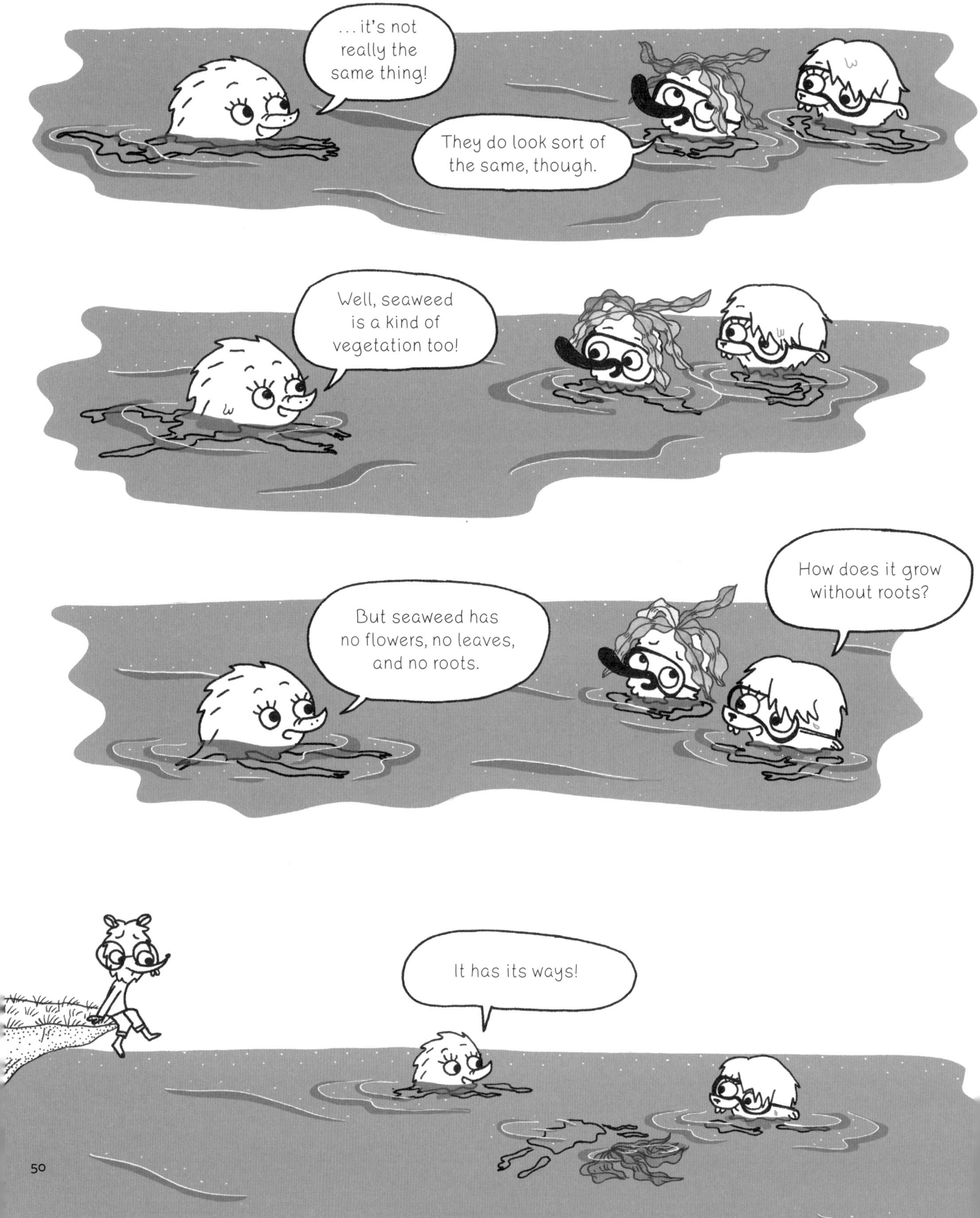
...it's not really the same thing!
They do look sort of the same, though.
Well, seaweed is a kind of vegetation too!
But seaweed has no flowers, no leaves, and no roots.
How does it grow without roots?
It has its ways!

Most types of seaweed are aquatic.
They can live in fresh water or salt water.
There are two main families of seaweed:

SINGLE-CELLED ALGAE

Like the plankton we talked about earlier!

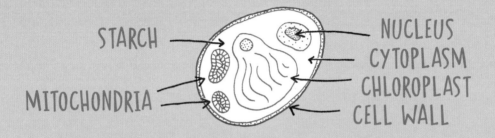

STARCH

NUCLEUS
CYTOPLASM
CHLOROPLAST
CELL WALL

MITOCHONDRIA

MULTICELLULAR ALGAE

This is the most commonly known type of
seaweed. It's the kind you see on the beach,
clinging to rocks, or under the water.

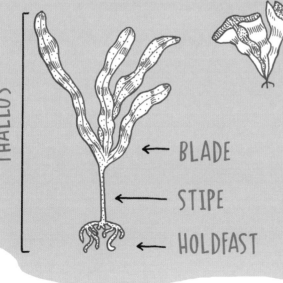

THALLUS

← BLADE

← STIPE

← HOLDFAST

There are lots of
different varieties, but they
all have a rootlike structure
called a holdfast, a stipe,
and one or more blades.

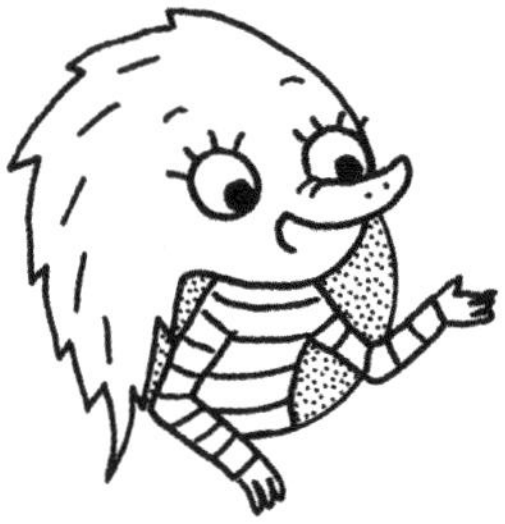

There are three kinds of multicellular algae:
green, brown, and red.

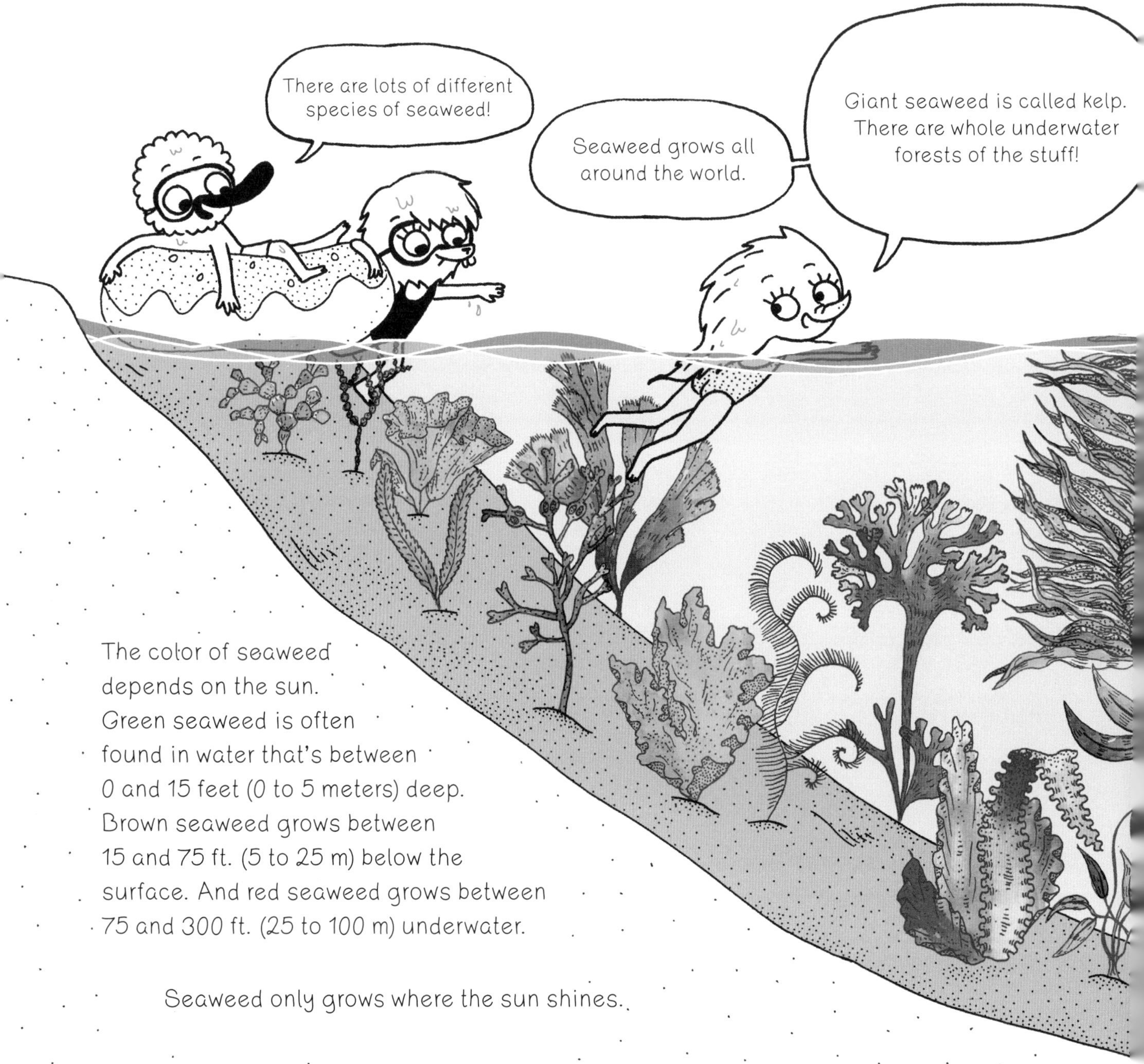

There are lots of different species of seaweed!
Seaweed grows all around the world.
Giant seaweed is called kelp. There are whole underwater forests of the stuff!

The color of seaweed depends on the sun. Green seaweed is often found in water that's between 0 and 15 feet (0 to 5 meters) deep. Brown seaweed grows between 15 and 75 ft. (5 to 25 m) below the surface. And red seaweed grows between 75 and 300 ft. (25 to 100 m) underwater.

Seaweed only grows where the sun shines.

To grow, seaweed needs sunlight for photosynthesis.

Some seaweeds have developed a system of floats to help them get closer to the sunlight.

One of these species is called *FUCUS VESICULOSUS.*

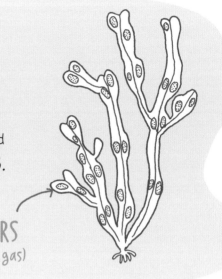

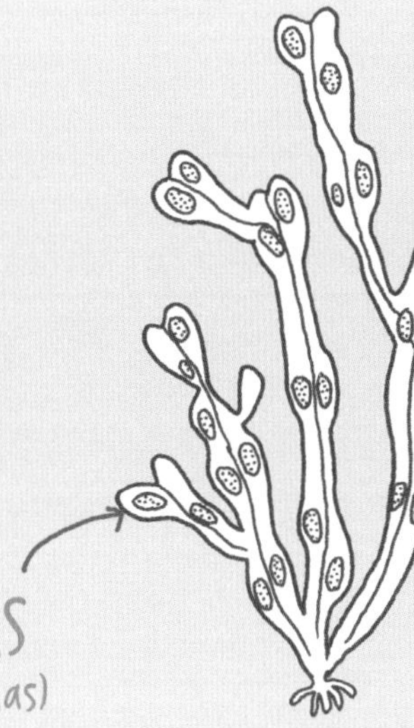
BLADDERS
(filled with gas)

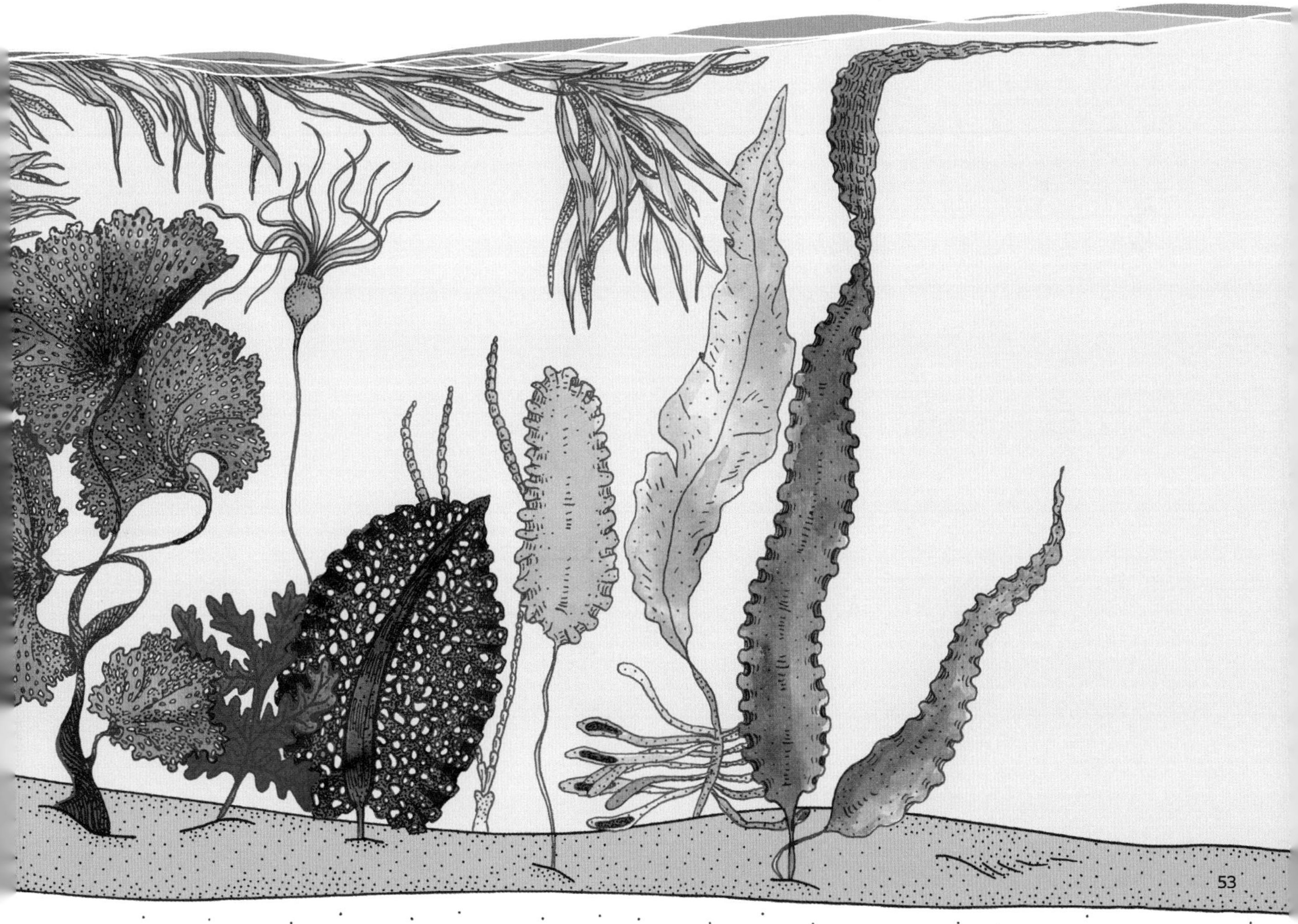

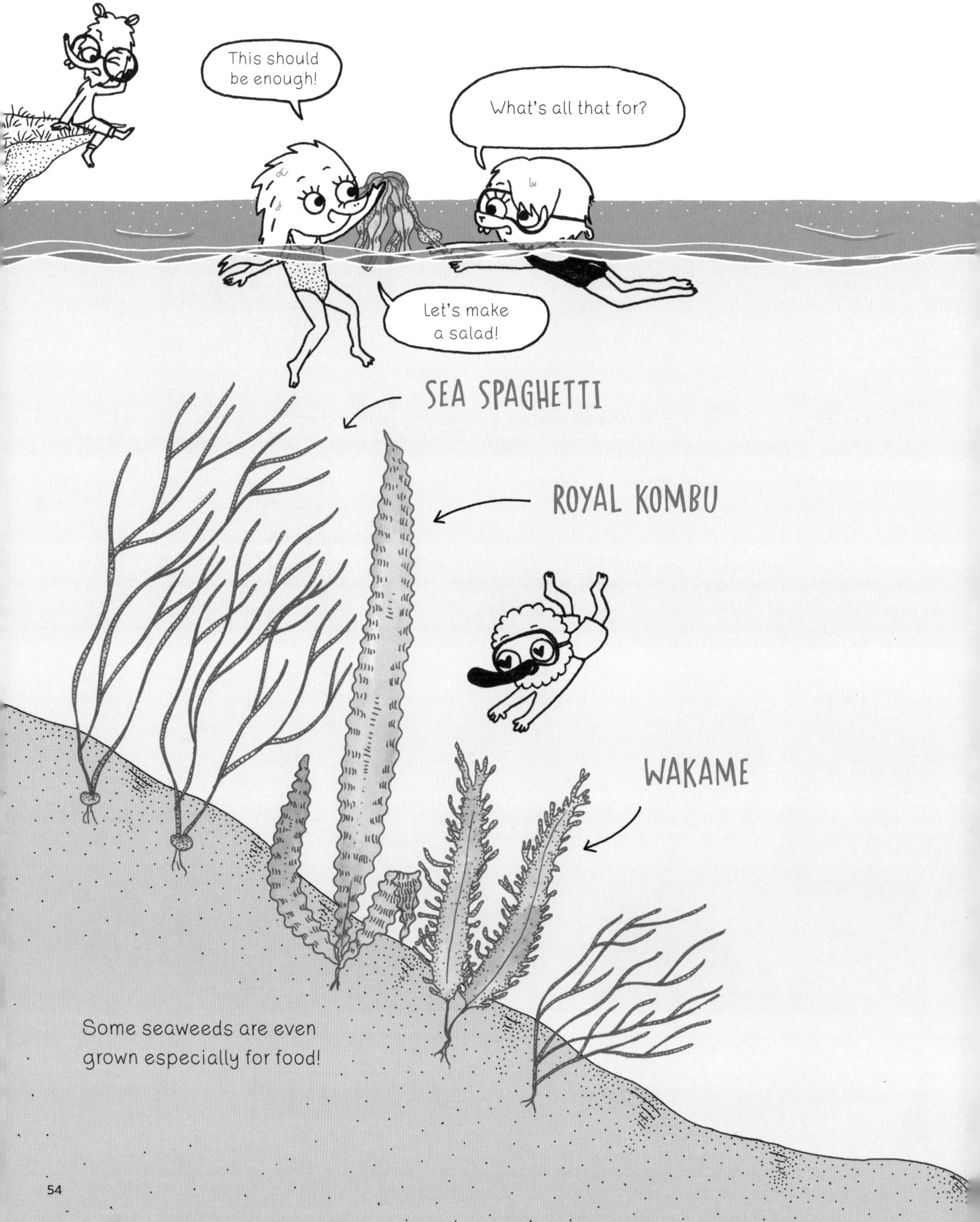
This should be enough!
What's all that for?
Let's make a salad!
SEA SPAGHETTI
ROYAL KOMBU
WAKAME
Some seaweeds are even grown especially for food!

9 ANYONE HUNGRY?

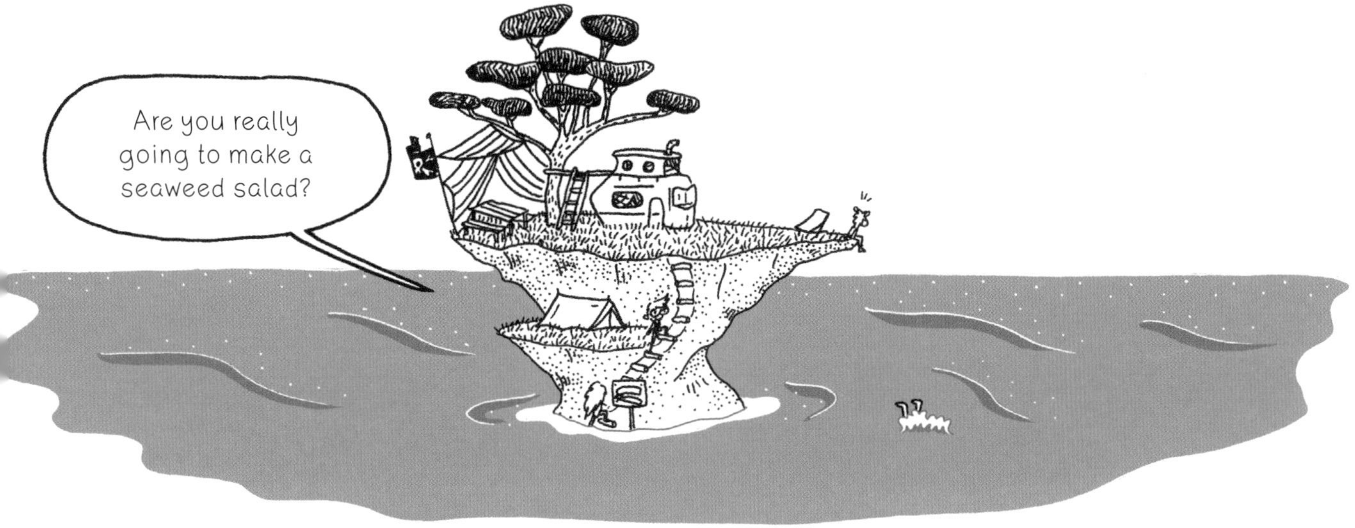
Are you really going to make a seaweed salad?

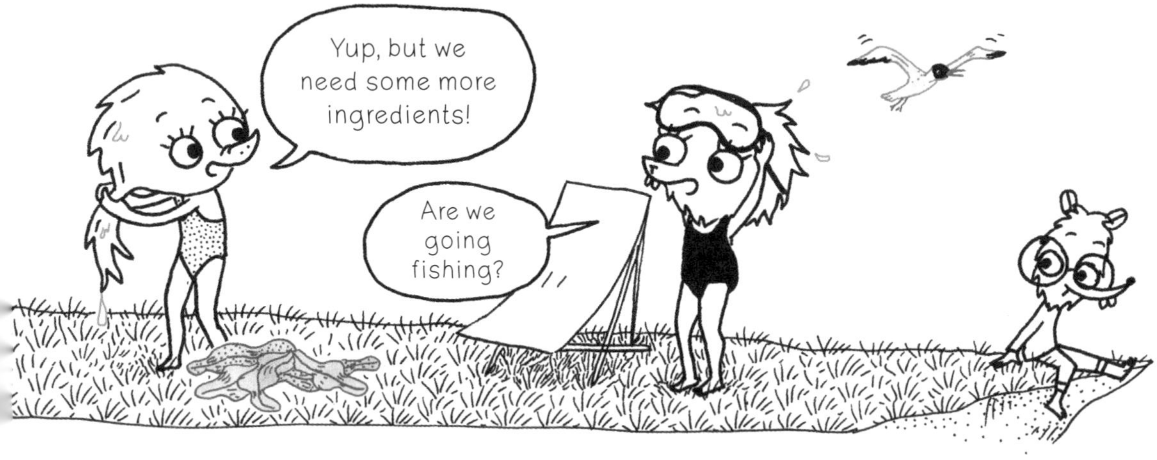
Yup, but we need some more ingredients!
Are we going fishing?

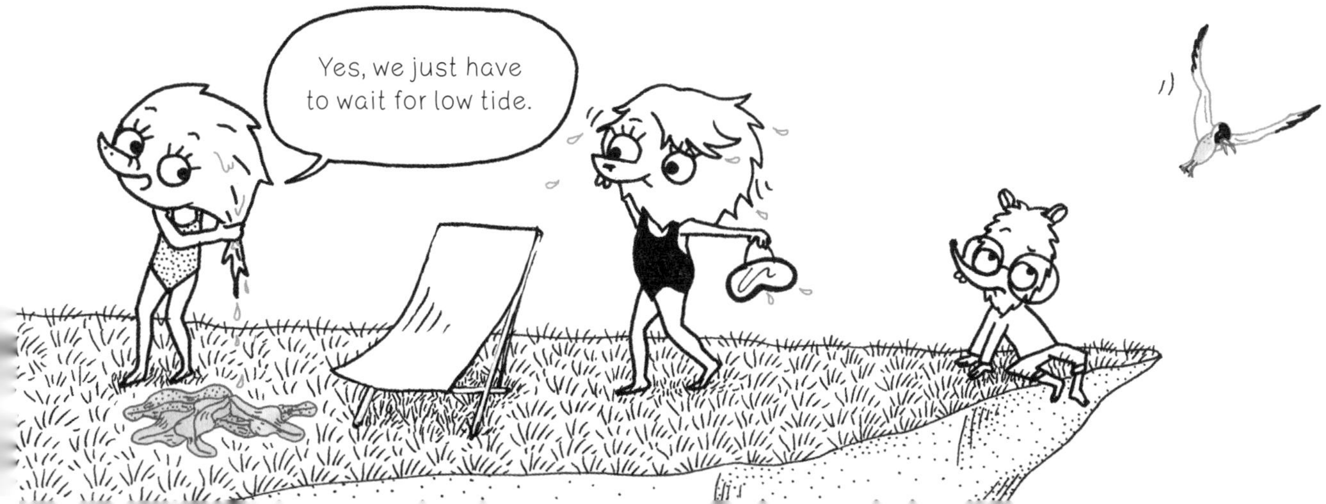
Yes, we just have to wait for low tide.

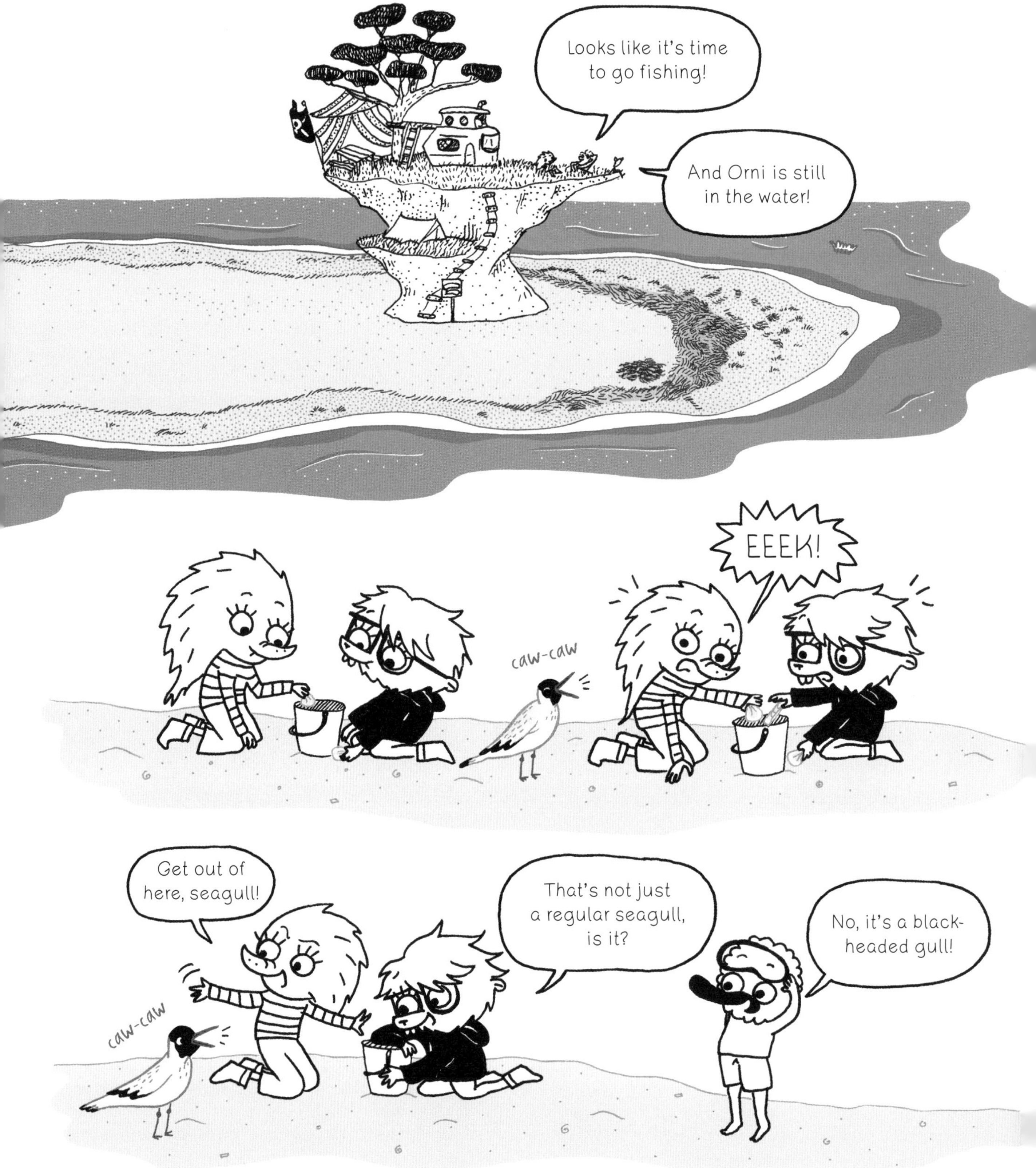

Looks like it's time to go fishing!
And Orni is still in the water!
caw-caw
EEEK!
Get out of here, seagull!
caw-caw
That's not just a regular seagull, is it?
No, it's a black-headed gull!

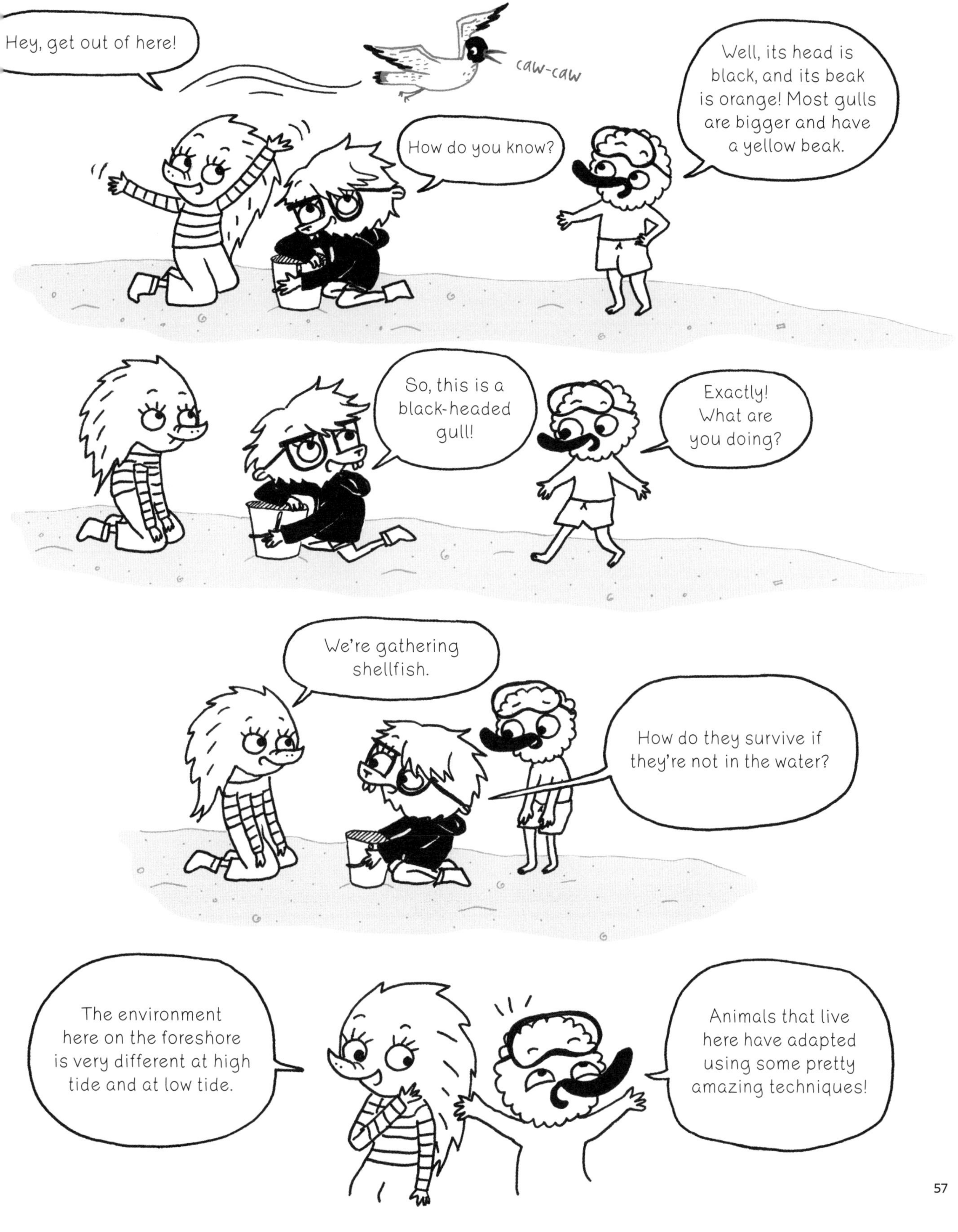
Hey, get out of here!
caw-caw
How do you know?
Well, its head is black, and its beak is orange! Most gulls are bigger and have a yellow beak.
So, this is a black-headed gull!
Exactly! What are you doing?
We're gathering shellfish.
How do they survive if they're not in the water?
The environment here on the foreshore is very different at high tide and at low tide.
Animals that live here have adapted using some pretty amazing techniques!

WHEN THE TIDE GOES OUT

The foreshore, or the intertidal zone, is the part of the beach that's exposed at low tide. Any animal and plant life that develops here must love salt and be okay with being underwater for hours before being exposed to the sun and the wind.

MOLLUSKS...

There are two main families.

Gastropods and bivalves are two different types of mollusk. Their bodies are protected by either one shell or two.

GASTROPODS look a little like snails.

They use their foot to move around!

They drool!

Gastropods make mucus. This is what they use to cling to rocks and keep water inside their shell.

SHELL

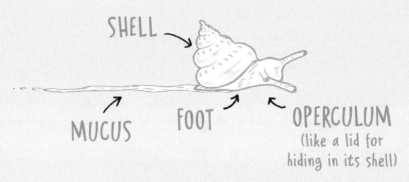

MUCUS   FOOT   OPERCULUM
(like a lid for hiding in its shell)

BIVALVES

Bivalves have two shells that close at low tide...

...so they can keep water inside.

suck in

blow out

They use a siphon to breathe.

...AND CRUSTACEANS

There are lots of very different kinds of crustaceans. The most well known of all is the crab.

Like most crustaceans, crabs have a skeleton on the outside of their body. This is called an **EXOSKELETON.**
It's also known as a shell.

In molting season, crabs cast off their shell and wait for another one to grow. During that time, their soft body is exposed and vulnerable.

Look at its claws!

Shrimp, crawfish, and lobsters are crustaceans too.

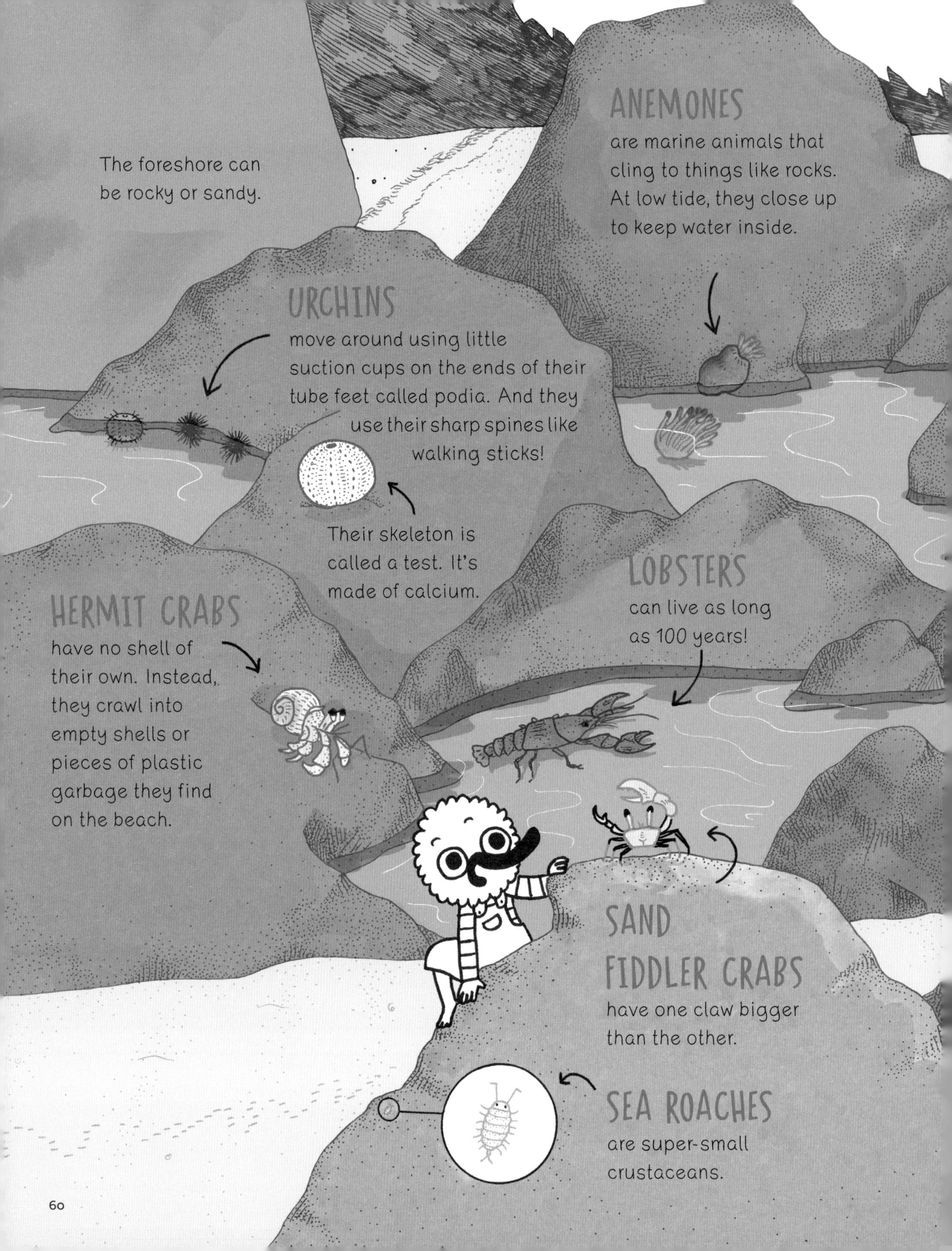

The foreshore can be rocky or sandy.

ANEMONES

are marine animals that cling to things like rocks. At low tide, they close up to keep water inside.

URCHINS

move around using little suction cups on the ends of their tube feet called podia. And they use their sharp spines like walking sticks!

Their skeleton is called a test. It's made of calcium.

HERMIT CRABS

have no shell of their own. Instead, they crawl into empty shells or pieces of plastic garbage they find on the beach.

LOBSTERS

can live as long as 100 years!

SAND FIDDLER CRABS

have one claw bigger than the other.

SEA ROACHES

are super-small crustaceans.

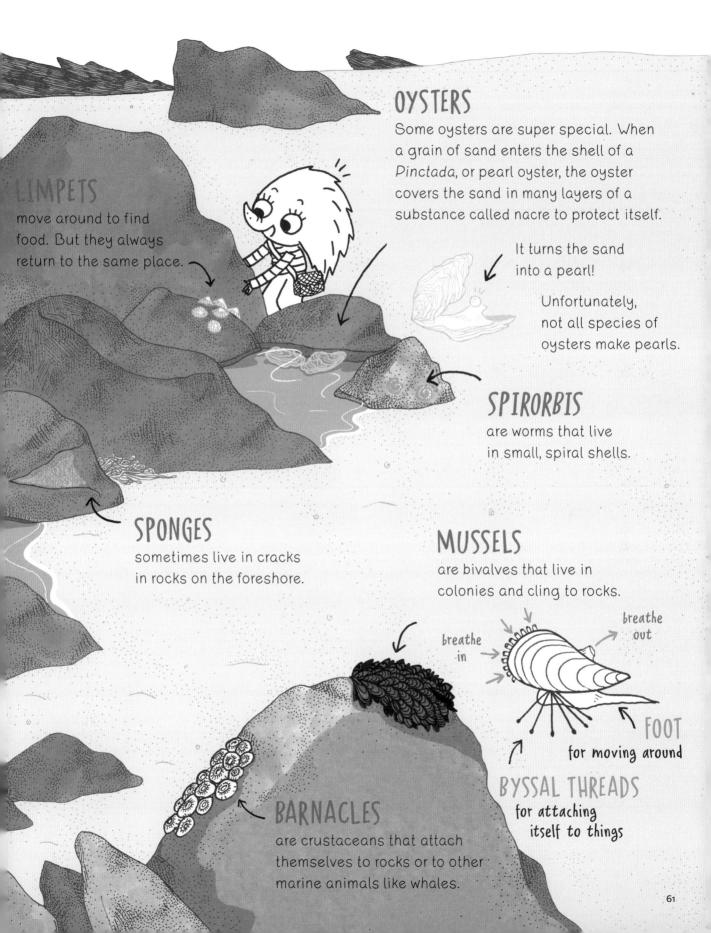

OYSTERS

Some oysters are super special. When a grain of sand enters the shell of a *Pinctada*, or pearl oyster, the oyster covers the sand in many layers of a substance called nacre to protect itself.

It turns the sand into a pearl!

Unfortunately, not all species of oysters make pearls.

LIMPETS

move around to find food. But they always return to the same place.

SPIRORBIS

are worms that live in small, spiral shells.

SPONGES

sometimes live in cracks in rocks on the foreshore.

MUSSELS

are bivalves that live in colonies and cling to rocks.

breathe in

breathe out

FOOT

for moving around

BYSSAL THREADS

for attaching itself to things

BARNACLES

are crustaceans that attach themselves to rocks or to other marine animals like whales.

SAND

is made up of tiny rocks and crushed shells, urchin tests (the name scientists use for urchin shells), and coral.

HERRING GULLS

are the big birds we often call seagulls.

BLACK-HEADED GULLS

are smaller. Their heads turn white in winter.

MEIOFAUNA

is the name for a group of tiny organisms, all smaller than 0.04 inche (1 millimeter). They live in the sand—both close to shore and deep in the ocean.

PERIWINKLES

leave trails in the sand.

IN THE SAND

Some animals hide in the sand at low tide.

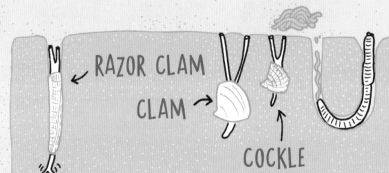

← RAZOR CLAM

CLAM →

COCKLE

LUGWORMS

are worms that dig themselves into the sand and leave little sand spirals behind.

SAND HOPPERS

are crustaceans

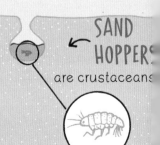

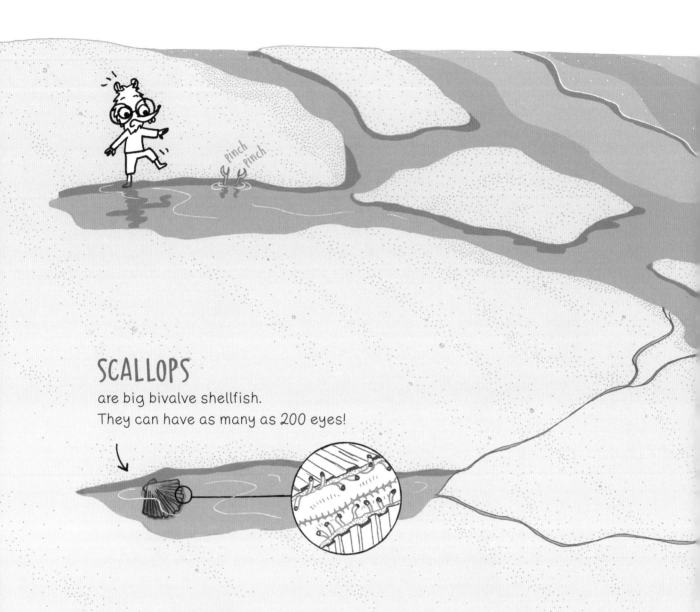

SCALLOPS

are big bivalve shellfish.
They can have as many as 200 eyes!

SHRIMP

have claws on their front legs like
crabs do, but they're much smaller.

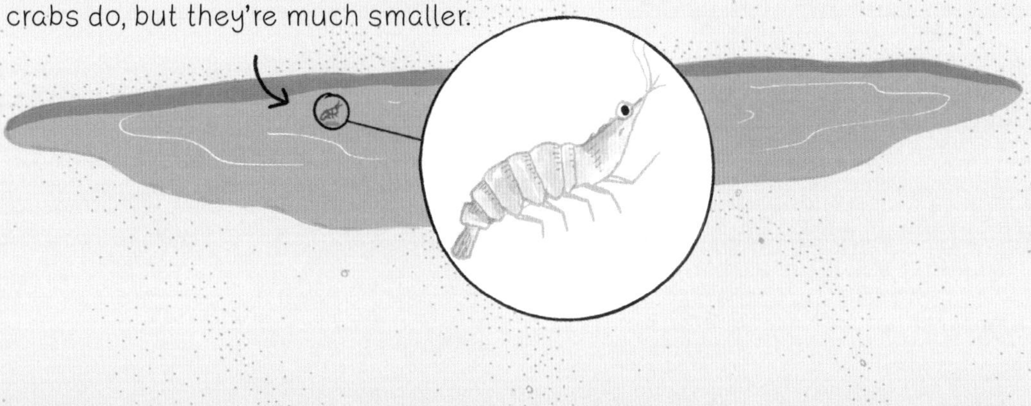

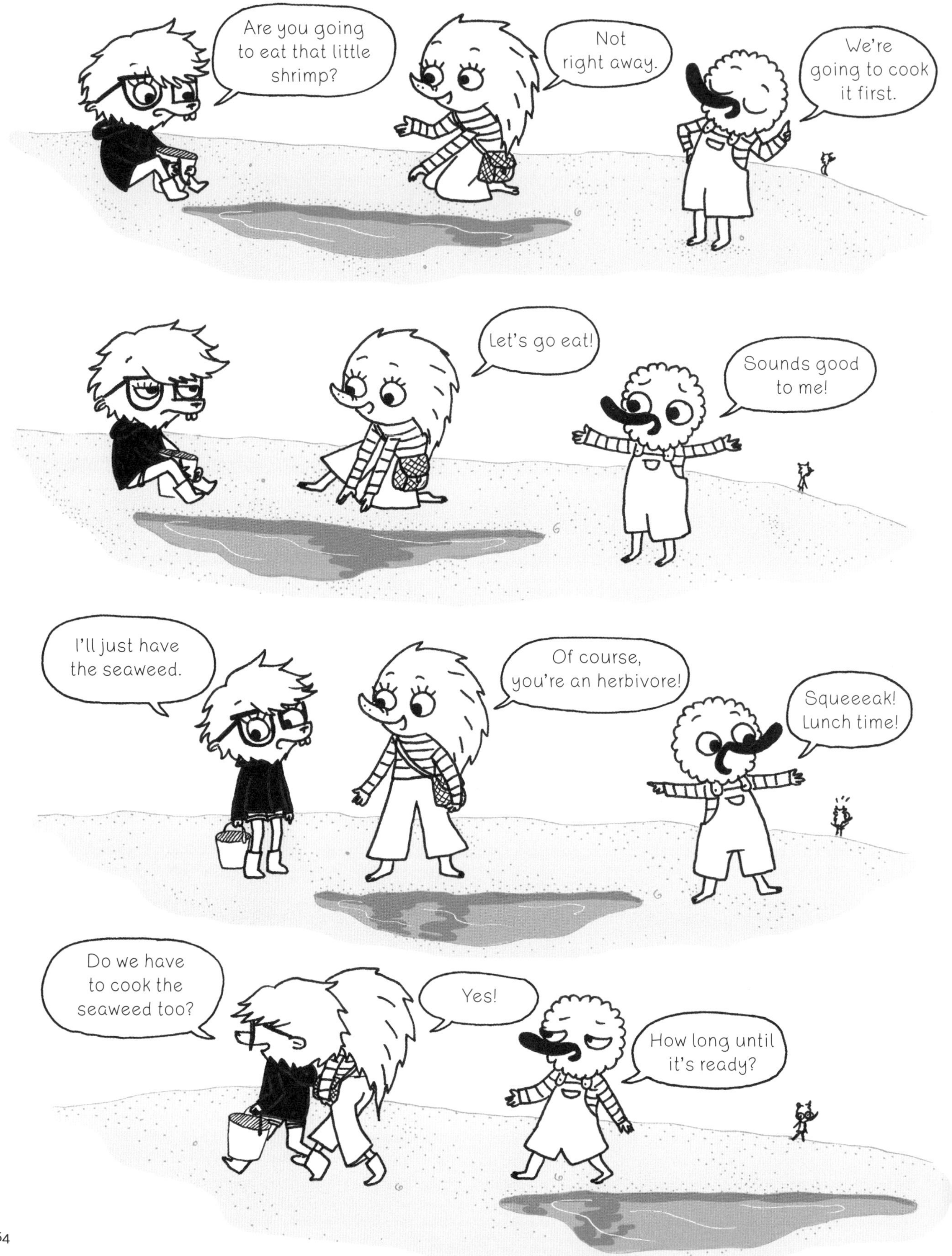
Are you going to eat that little shrimp?
Not right away.
We're going to cook it first.
Let's go eat!
Sounds good to me!
I'll just have the seaweed.
Of course, you're an herbivore!
Squeeeak! Lunch time!
Do we have to cook the seaweed too?
Yes!
How long until it's ready?

10 JAWS!

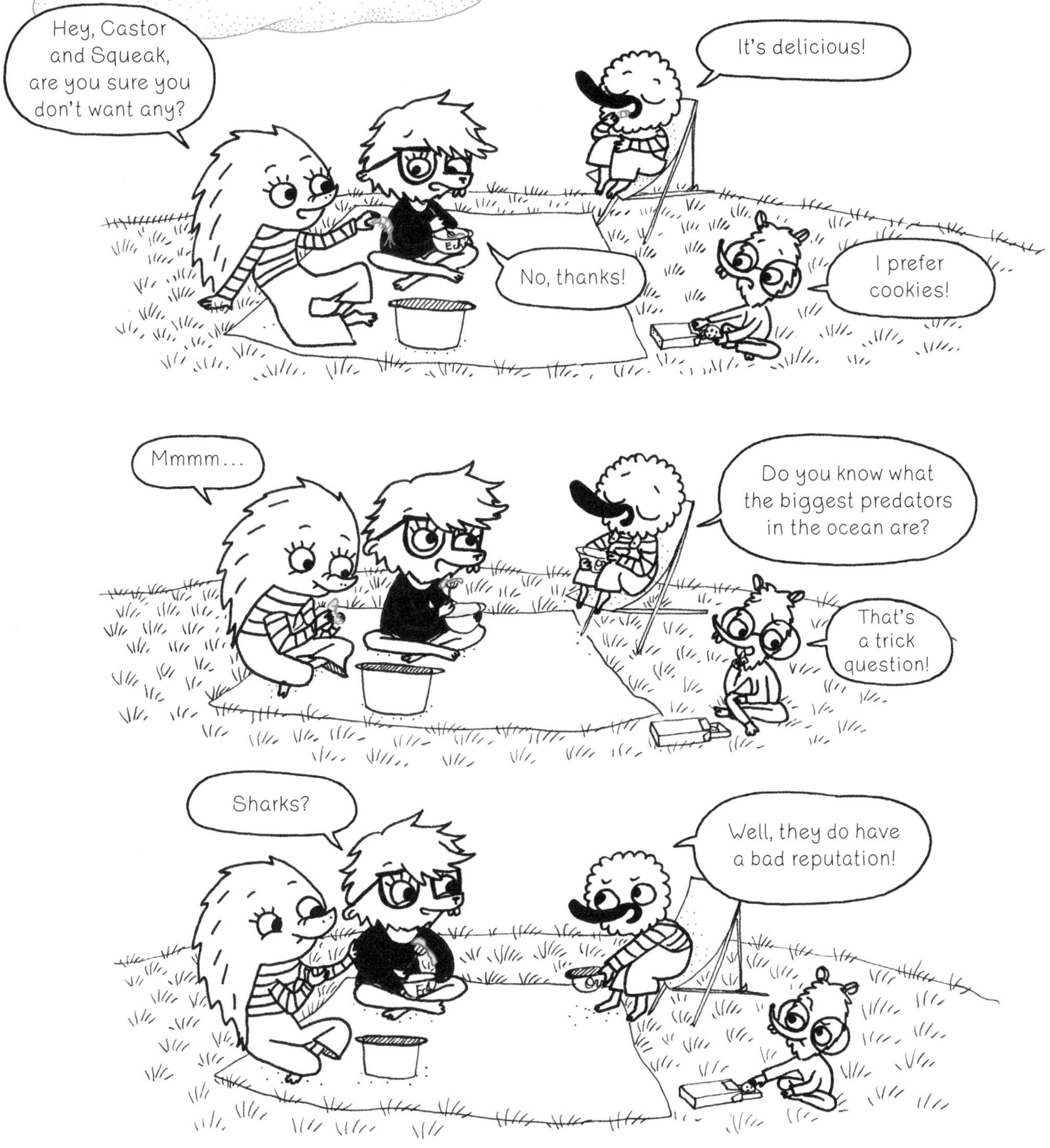
Hey, Castor and Squeak, are you sure you don't want any?
It's delicious!
No, thanks!
I prefer cookies!
Mmmm...
Do you know what the biggest predators in the ocean are?
That's a trick question!
Sharks?
Well, they do have a bad reputation!

SHARKS

are cartilaginous fish. There are more than 500 species of sharks. Only around 10 of those are dangerous to humans.

GREAT WHITE SHARK

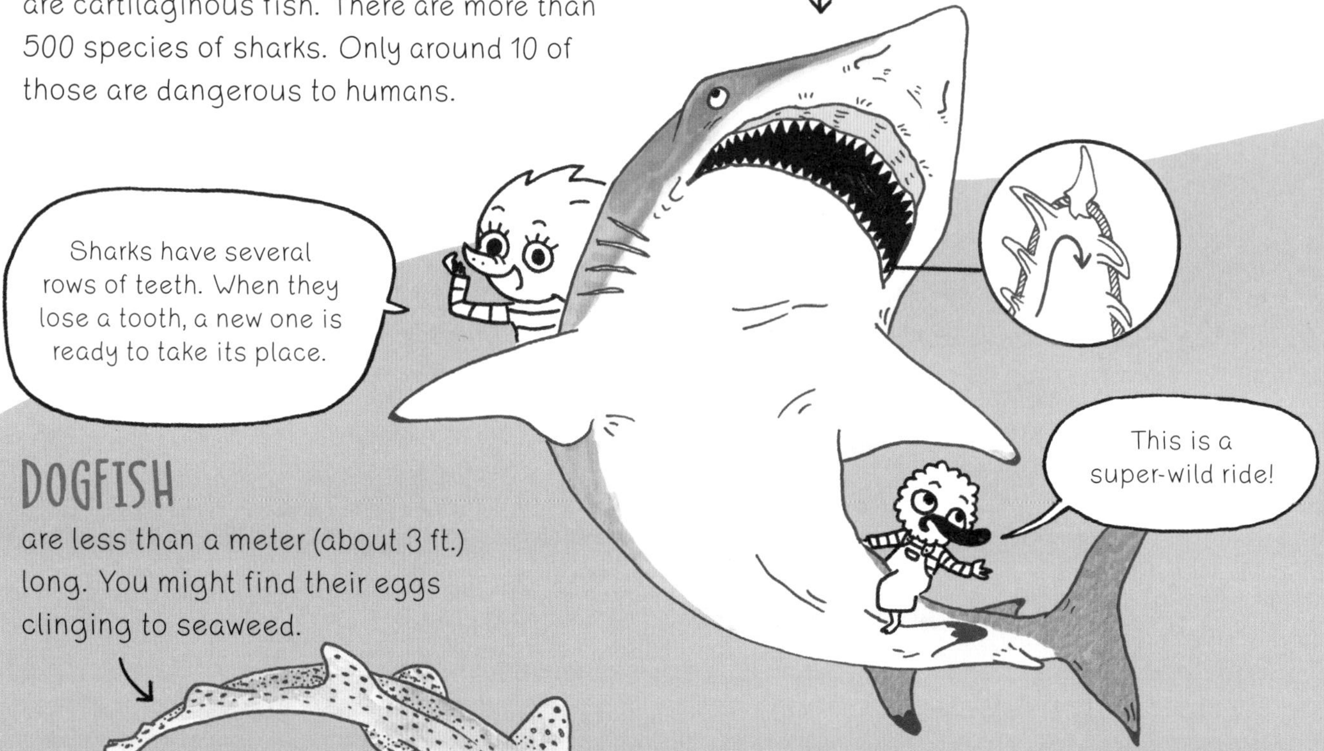
Sharks have several rows of teeth. When they lose a tooth, a new one is ready to take its place.
This is a super-wild ride!

DOGFISH

are less than a meter (about 3 ft.) long. You might find their eggs clinging to seaweed.

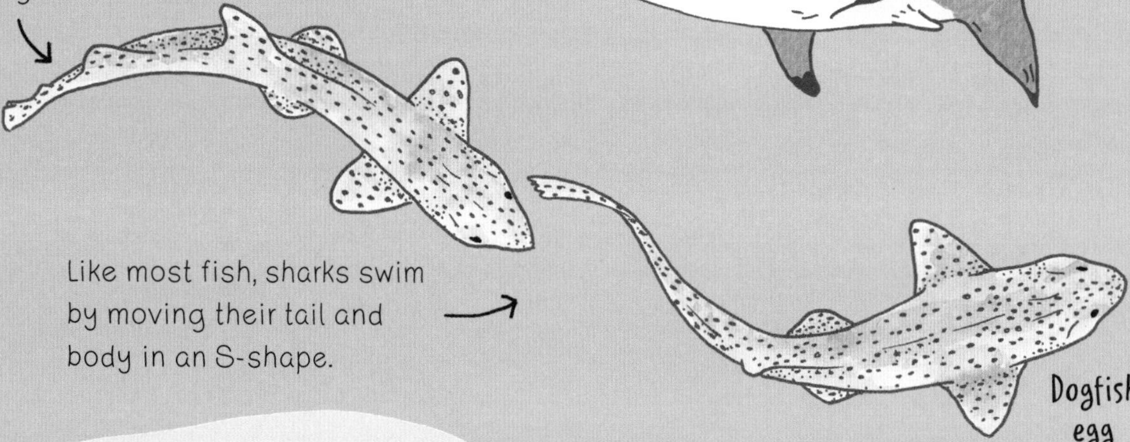

Like most fish, sharks swim by moving their tail and body in an S-shape.

Dogfish egg

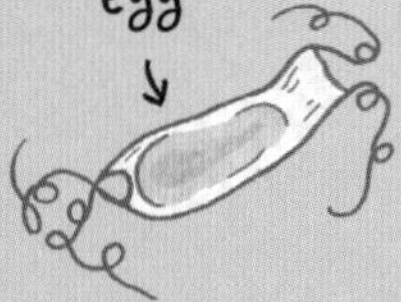

SPOTTED EAGLE RAY

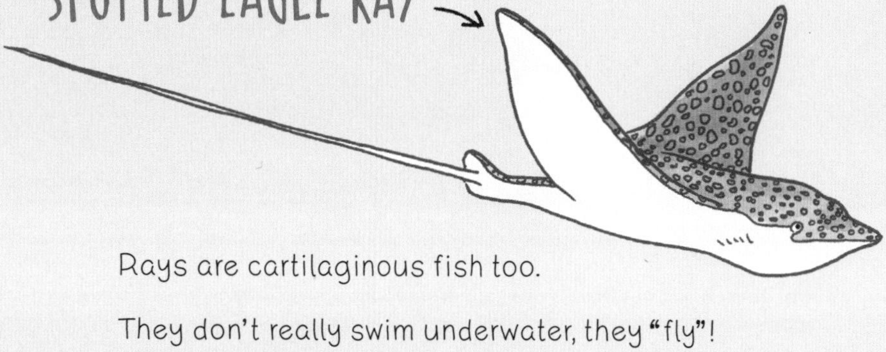

Rays are cartilaginous fish too.

They don't really swim underwater, they "fly"!

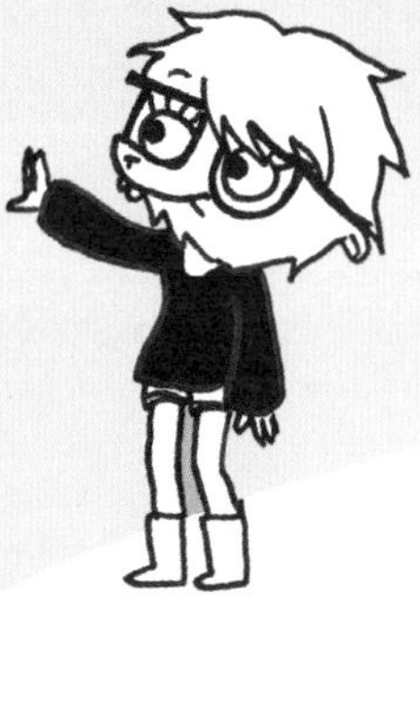

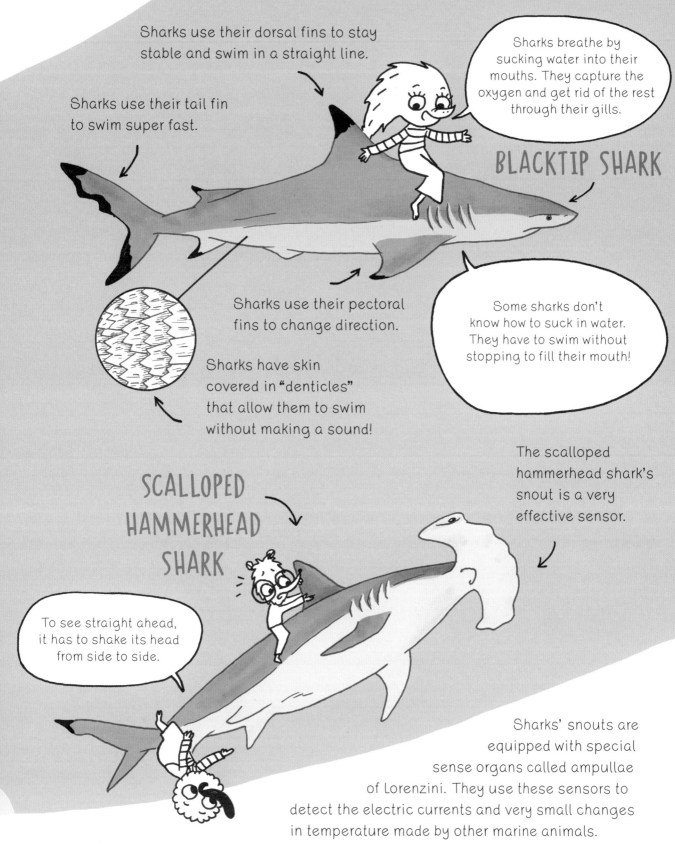

Sharks use their dorsal fins to stay stable and swim in a straight line.

Sharks breathe by sucking water into their mouths. They capture the oxygen and get rid of the rest through their gills.

Sharks use their tail fin to swim super fast.

BLACKTIP SHARK

Sharks use their pectoral fins to change direction.

Some sharks don't know how to suck in water. They have to swim without stopping to fill their mouth!

Sharks have skin covered in "denticles" that allow them to swim without making a sound!

The scalloped hammerhead shark's snout is a very effective sensor.

SCALLOPED HAMMERHEAD SHARK

To see straight ahead, it has to shake its head from side to side.

Sharks' snouts are equipped with special sense organs called ampullae of Lorenzini. They use these sensors to detect the electric currents and very small changes in temperature made by other marine animals.

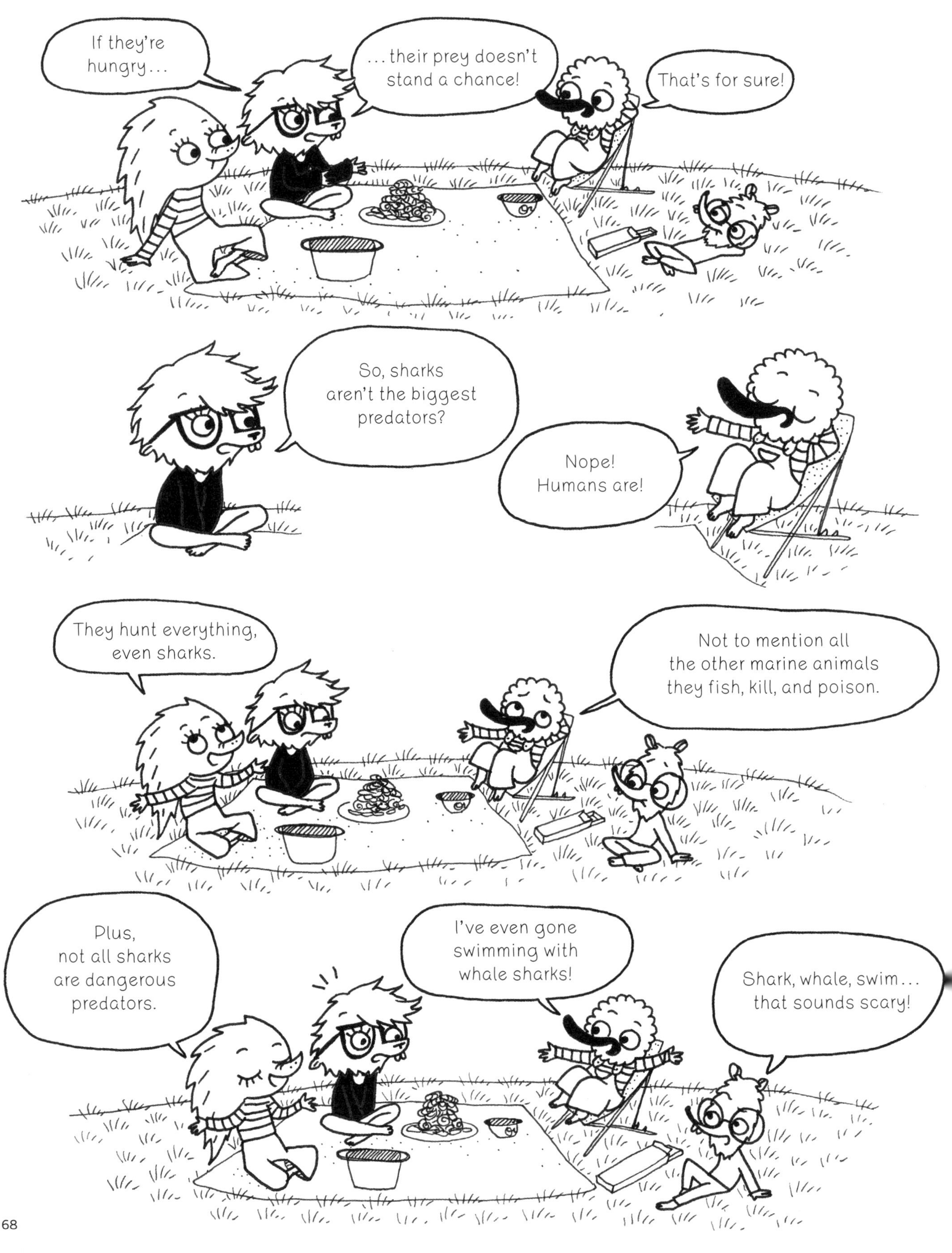
If they're hungry . . .
. . . their prey doesn't stand a chance!
That's for sure!
So, sharks aren't the biggest predators?
Nope! Humans are!
They hunt everything, even sharks.
Not to mention all the other marine animals they fish, kill, and poison.
Plus, not all sharks are dangerous predators.
I've even gone swimming with whale sharks!
Shark, whale, swim . . . that sounds scary!

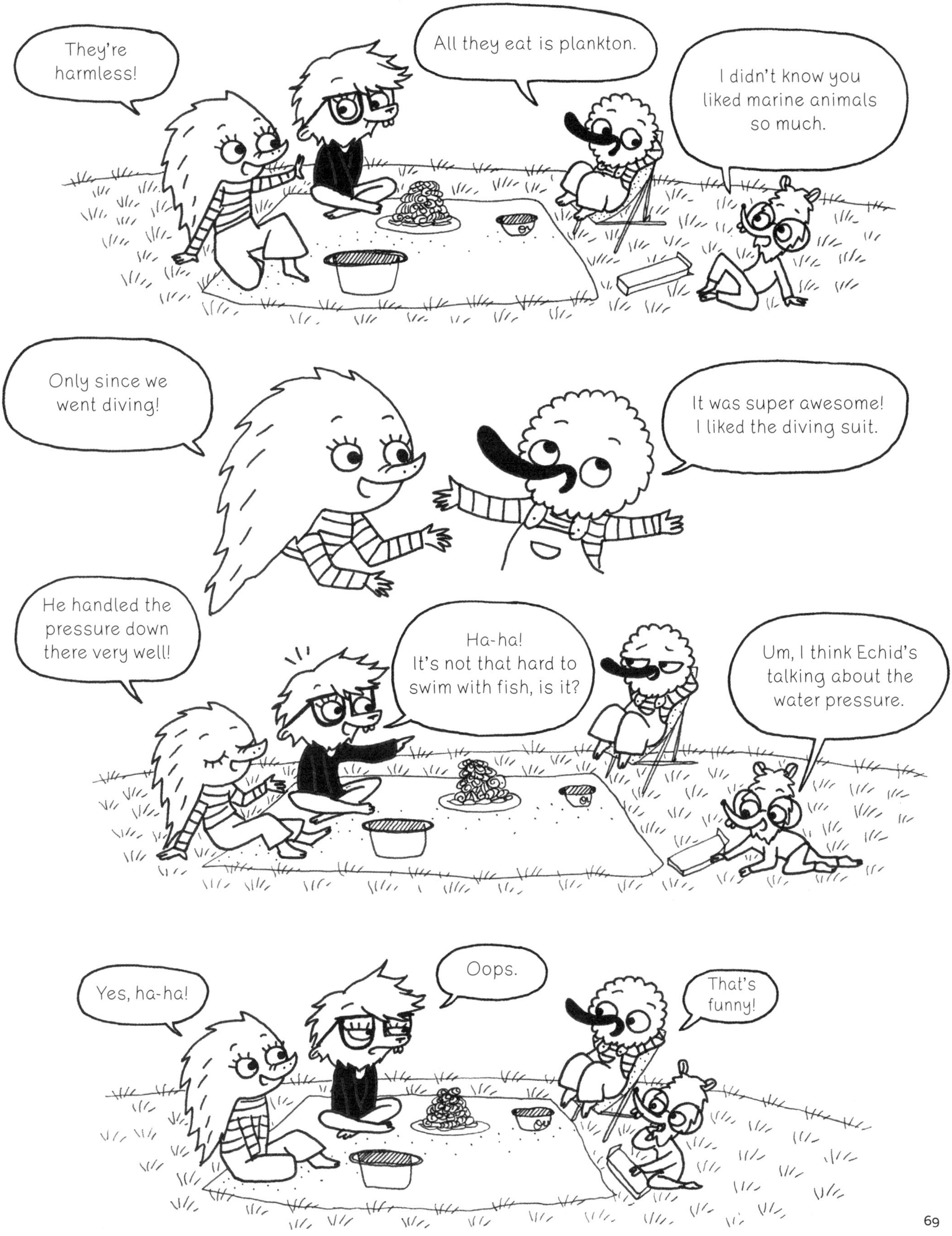
They're harmless!
All they eat is plankton.
I didn't know you liked marine animals so much.
Only since we went diving!
It was super awesome! I liked the diving suit.
He handled the pressure down there very well!
Ha-ha! It's not that hard to swim with fish, is it?
Um, I think Echid's talking about the water pressure.
Yes, ha-ha!
Oops.
That's funny!

The layer of air surrounding the Earth is called the atmosphere. It's made up of about 78% nitrogen, 21% oxygen, and small amounts of rare gases.

The air puts pressure on everything on Earth.
This is called ATMOSPHERIC PRESSURE.

Water has a pressure too.

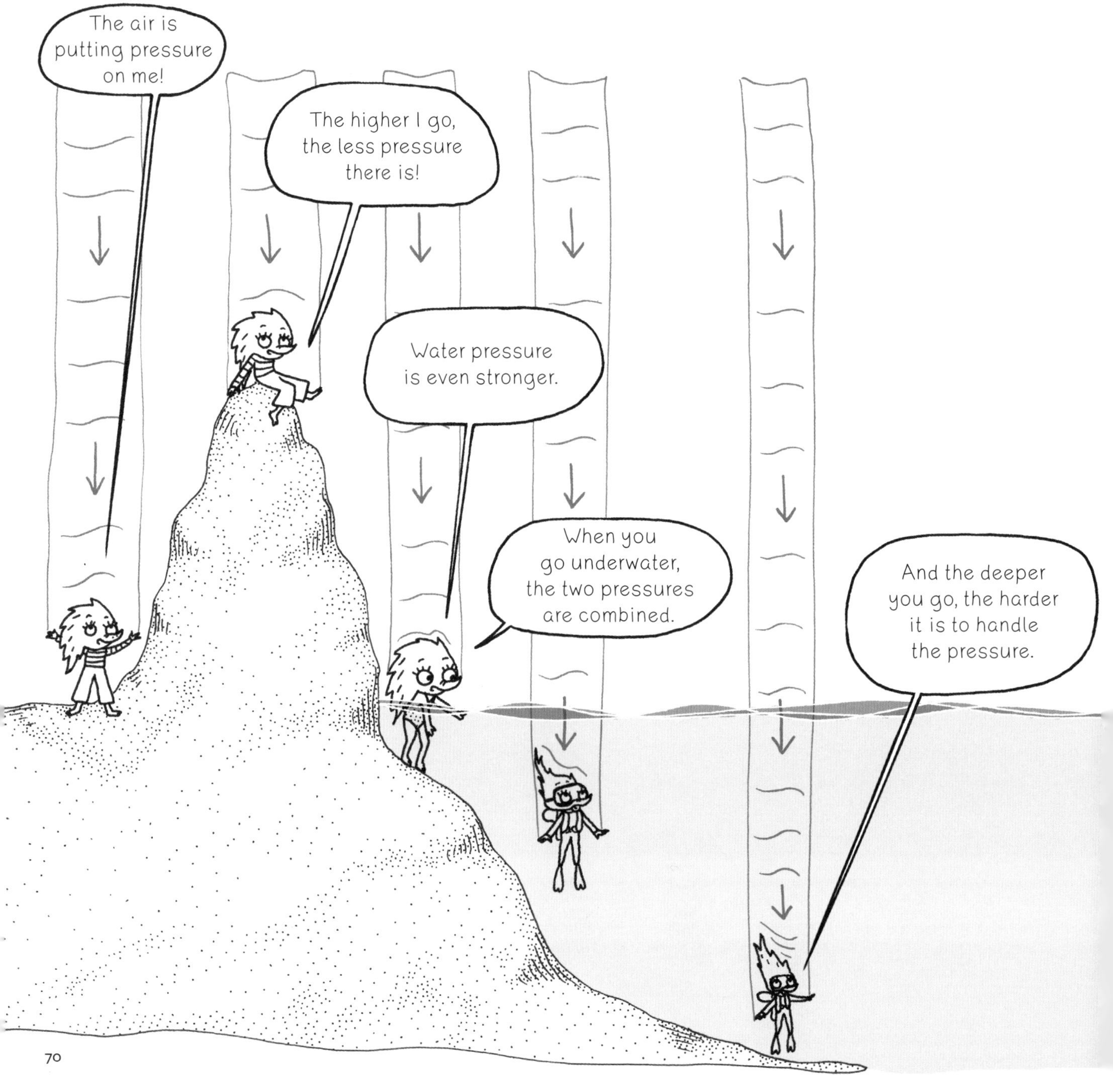

The air is putting pressure on me!
The higher I go, the less pressure there is!
Water pressure is even stronger.
When you go underwater, the two pressures are combined.
And the deeper you go, the harder it is to handle the pressure.

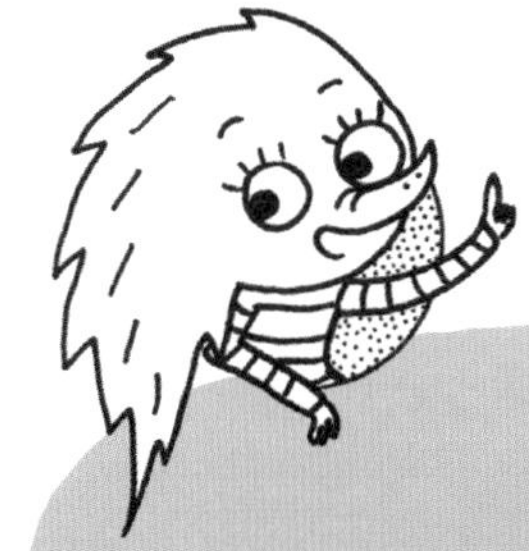

When you go diving, it's important not to go alone, and to use the right equipment.

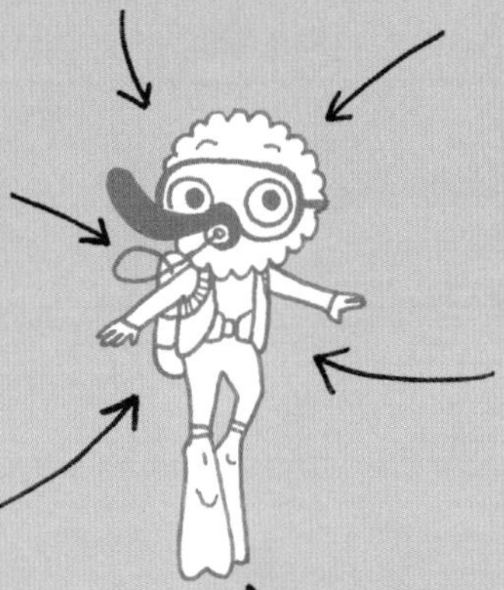

DIVING SUIT
Protects from the cold

MASK
Lets divers keep their eyes open underwater

VEST
Inflatable to help divers float, balance, and come back to the surface

TANKS
Filled with compressed air, so divers can breathe underwater

BELT
Weighted to help divers sink more easily

FINS
Make it easier to swim, so divers use less oxygen and can stay underwater for longer

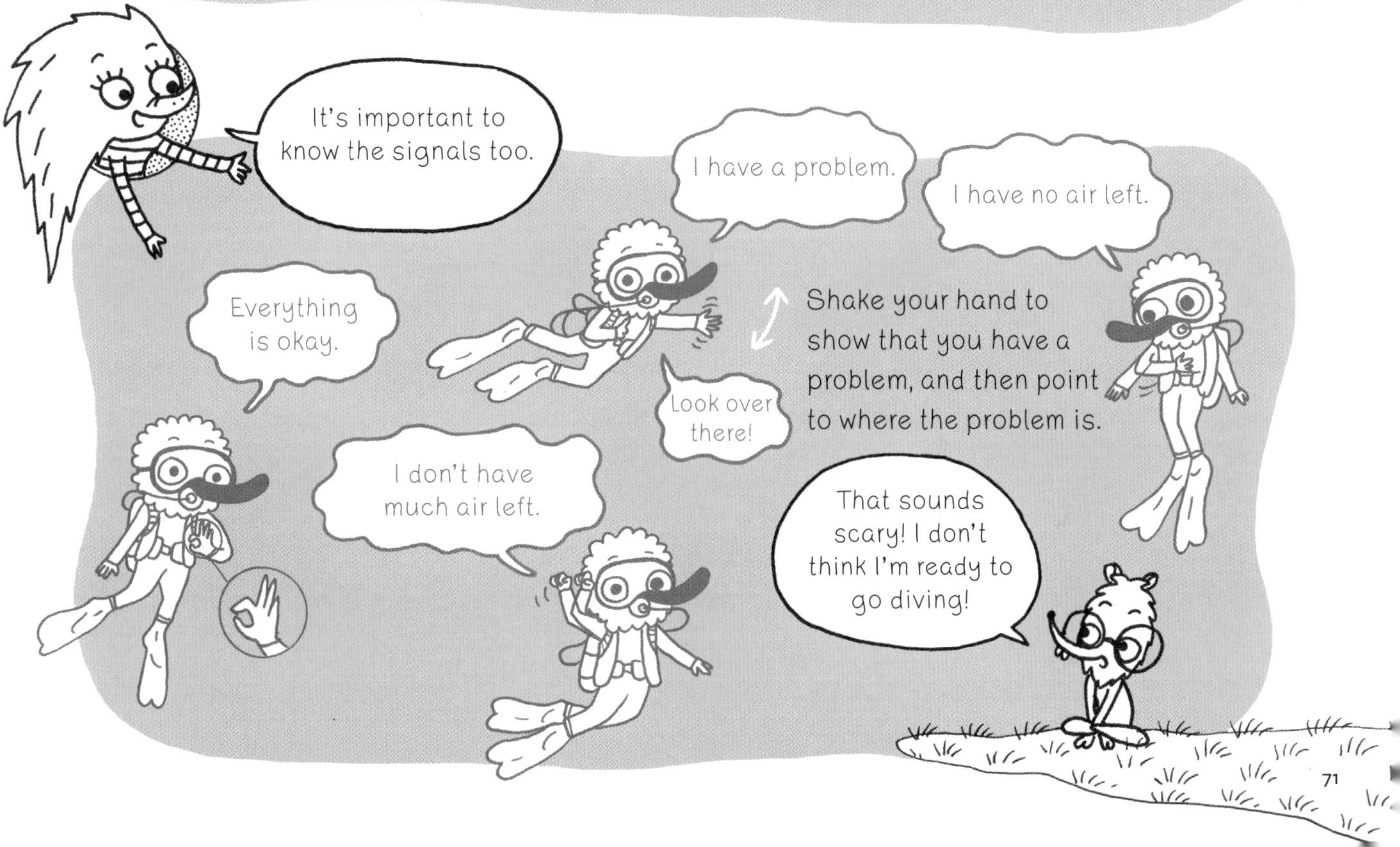
It's important to know the signals too.
I have a problem.
I have no air left.
Everything is okay.
Shake your hand to show that you have a problem, and then point to where the problem is.
Look over there!
I don't have much air left.
That sounds scary! I don't think I'm ready to go diving!

11 SUPER CORAL!

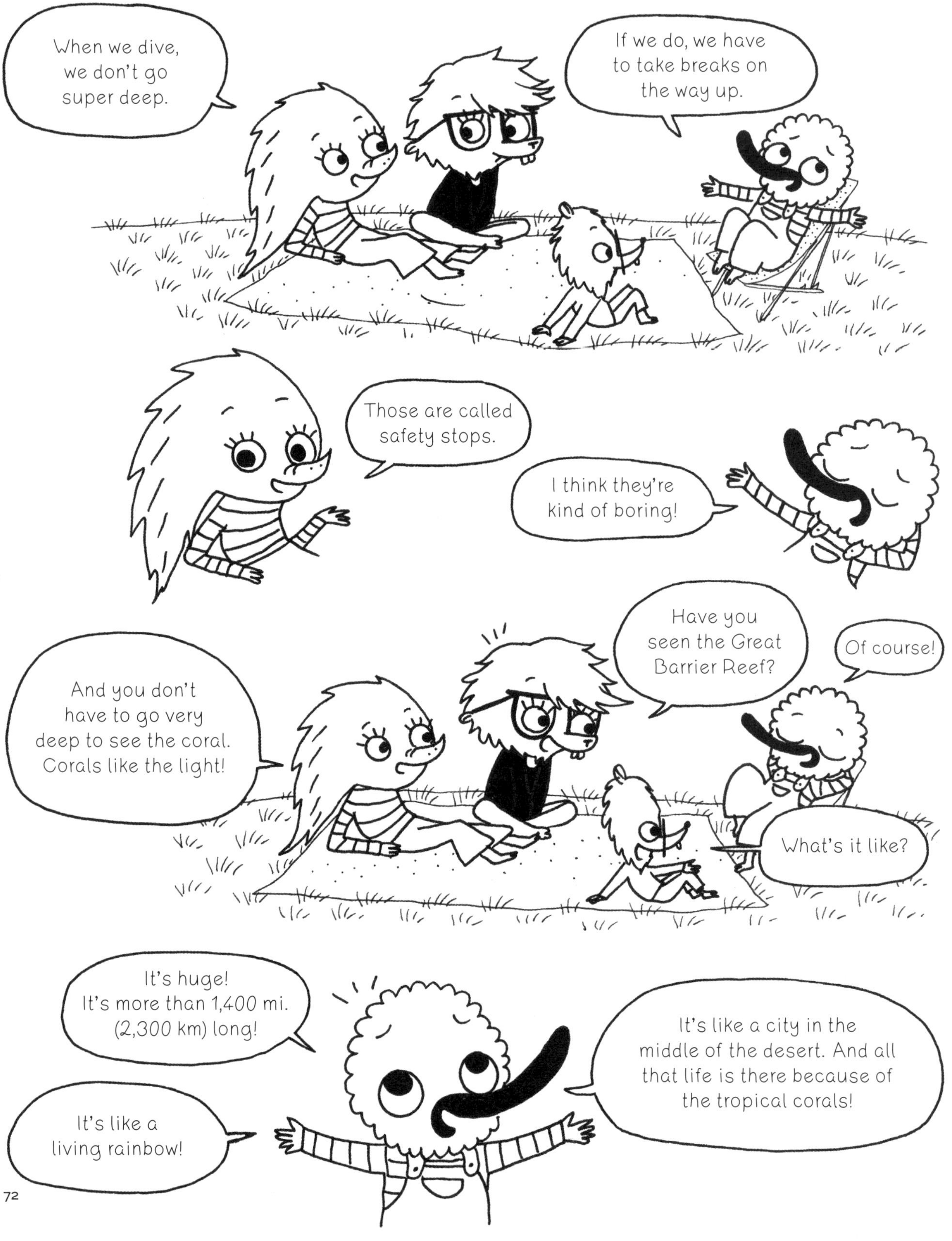
When we dive, we don't go super deep.
If we do, we have to take breaks on the way up.
Those are called safety stops.
I think they're kind of boring!
And you don't have to go very deep to see the coral. Corals like the light!
Have you seen the Great Barrier Reef?
Of course!
What's it like?
It's huge! It's more than 1,400 mi. (2,300 km) long!
It's like a living rainbow!
It's like a city in the middle of the desert. And all that life is there because of the tropical corals!

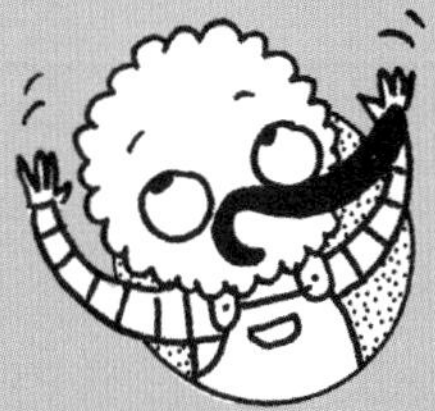

TROPICAL CORALS

have calcium skeletons that house lots of tiny organisms called polyps. They live in colonies in symbiosis with a kind of algae called zooxanthellae.

There are lots of different species of coral: soft, flat, red, blue, and more!

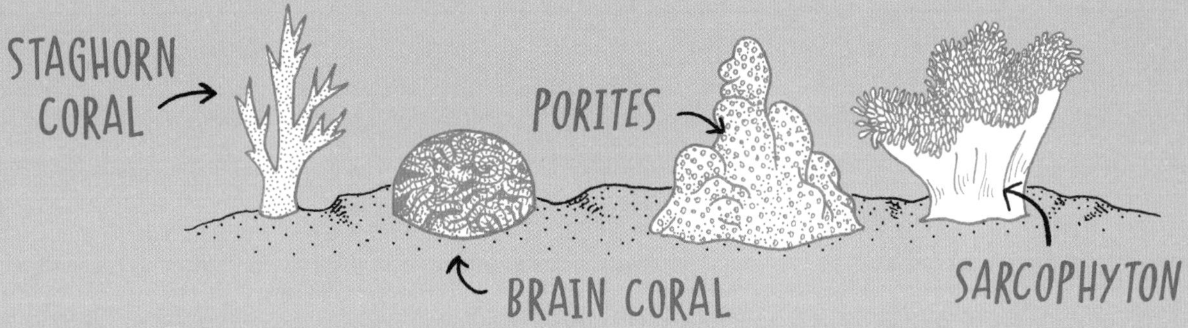
STAGHORN CORAL
PORITES
BRAIN CORAL
SARCOPHYTON

What you see here are the calcium skeletons.
After dark, the polyps wake up and start hunting for zooplankton!

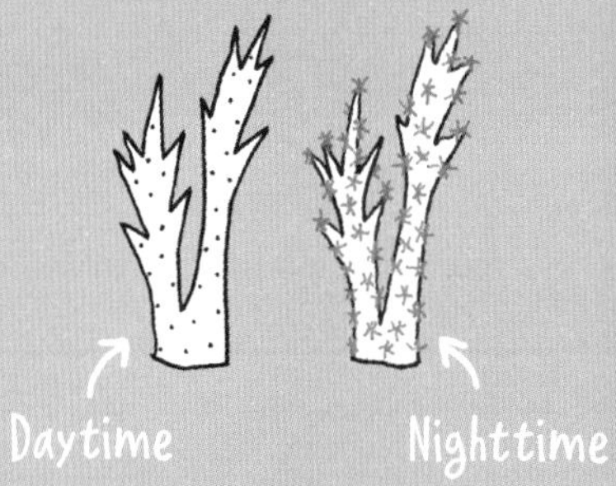
Daytime
Nighttime

CORAL POLYPS

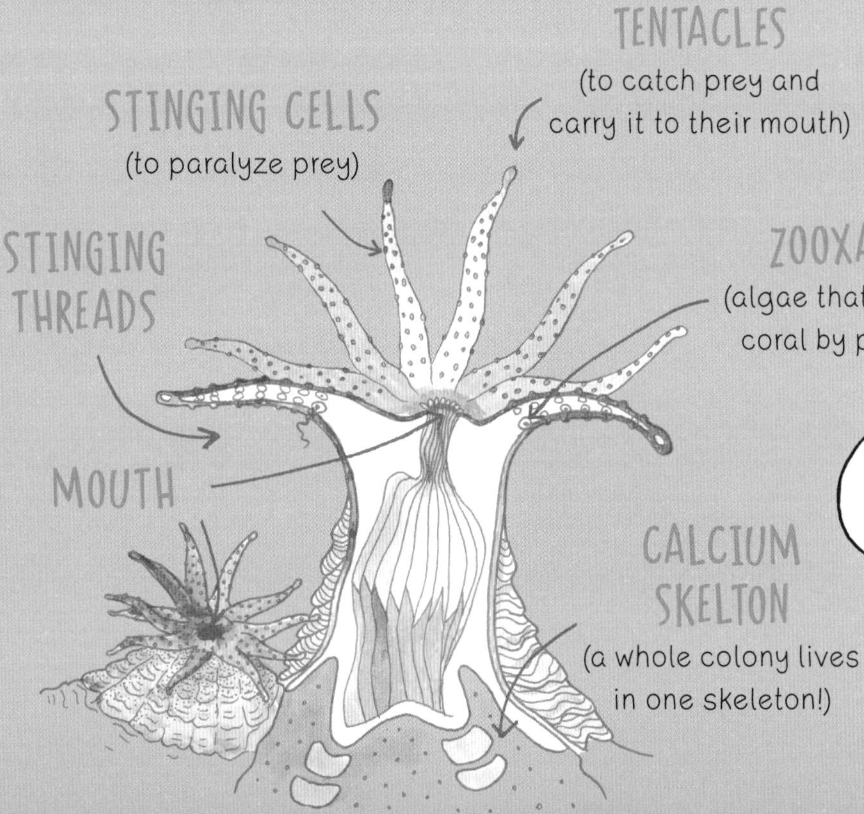
TENTACLES
(to catch prey and carry it to their mouth)
STINGING CELLS
(to paralyze prey)
STINGING THREADS
ZOOXANTHELLAE
(algae that gives energy to coral by photosynthesis)
MOUTH
CALCIUM SKELTON
(a whole colony lives in one skeleton!)

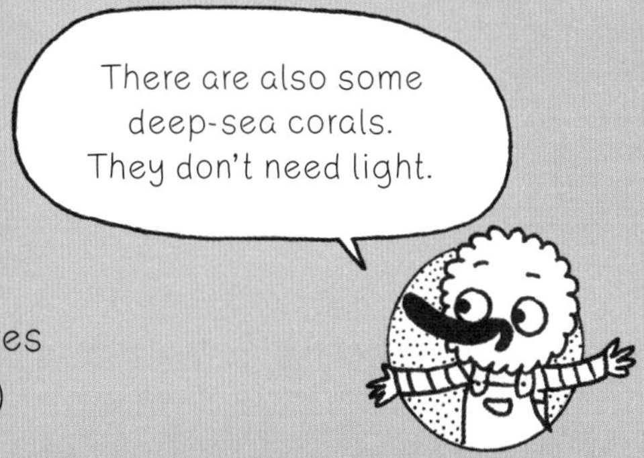
There are also some deep-sea corals. They don't need light.

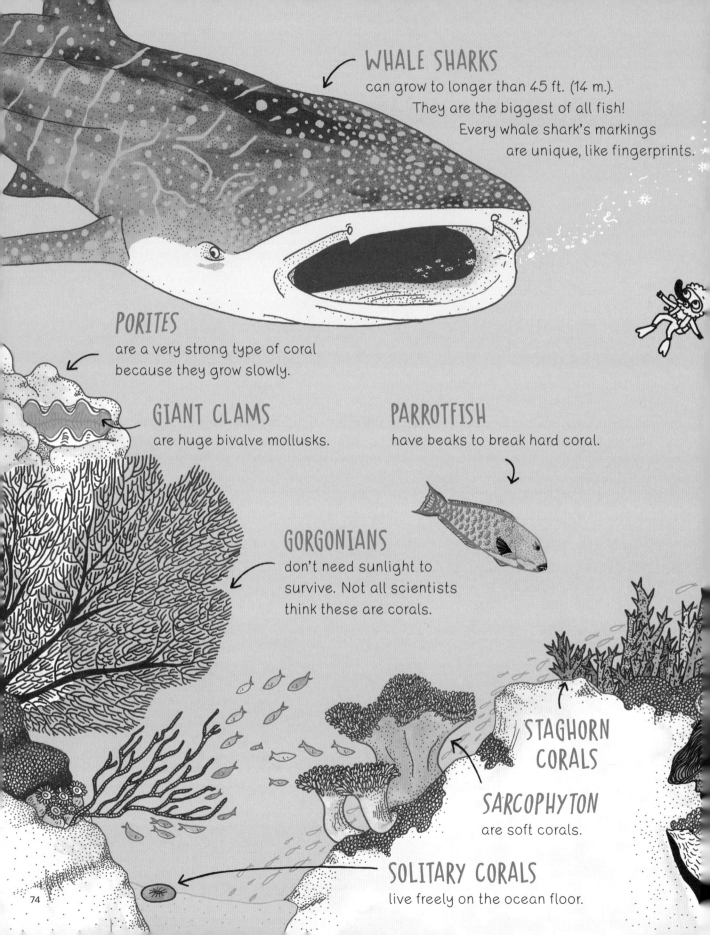

WHALE SHARKS

can grow to longer than 45 ft. (14 m.).
They are the biggest of all fish!
Every whale shark's markings
are unique, like fingerprints.

PORITES

are a very strong type of coral
because they grow slowly.

GIANT CLAMS

are huge bivalve mollusks.

PARROTFISH

have beaks to break hard coral.

GORGONIANS

don't need sunlight to
survive. Not all scientists
think these are corals.

STAGHORN CORALS

SARCOPHYTON

are soft corals.

SOLITARY CORALS

live freely on the ocean floor.

Coral reefs and atolls make up less than 1% of the World Ocean, but they are home to a big part of all marine life.

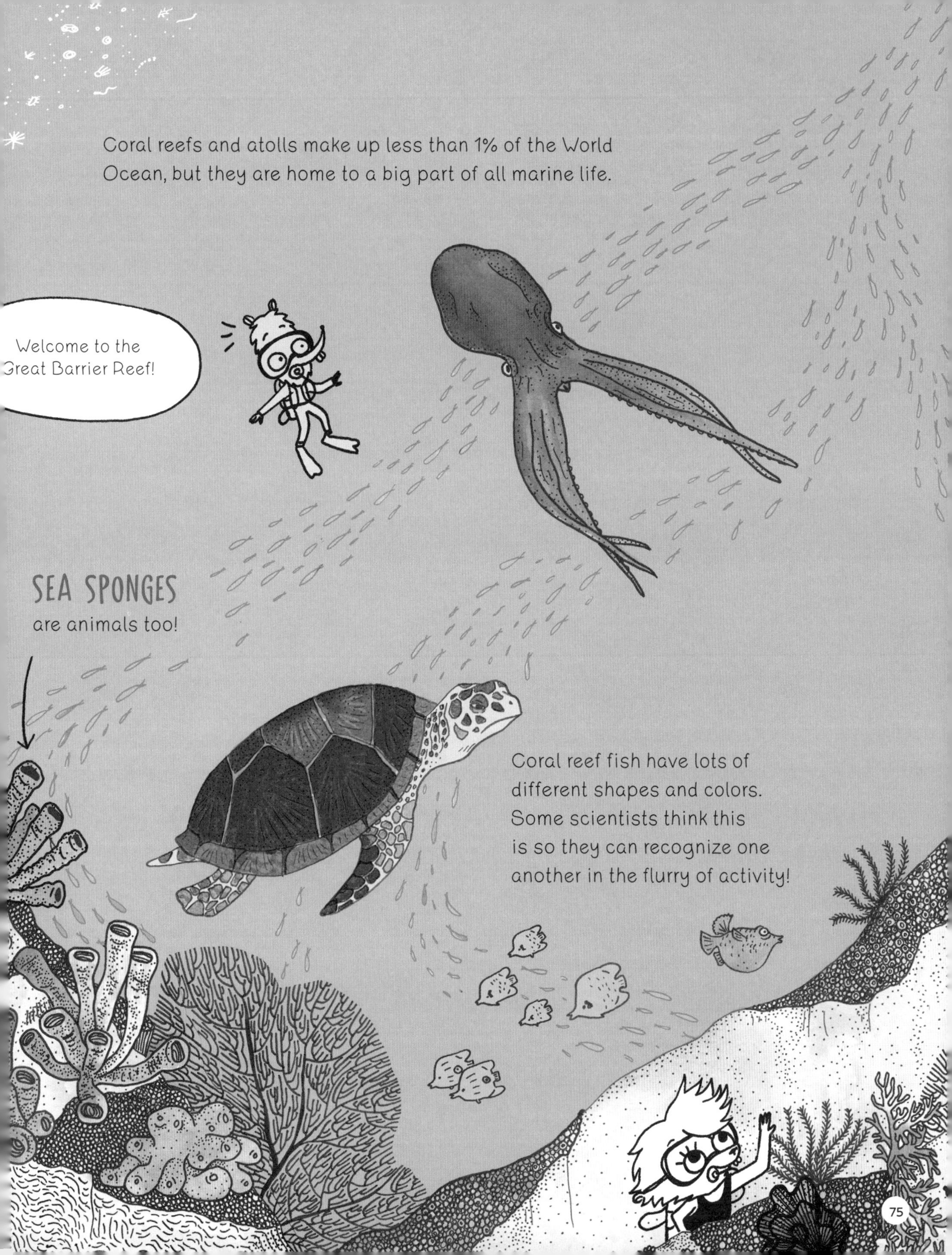
Welcome to the
Great Barrier Reef!

SEA SPONGES

are animals too!

Coral reef fish have lots of different shapes and colors. Some scientists think this is so they can recognize one another in the flurry of activity!

SEA ANEMONES

are animals with stinging tentacles. Clown fish are born immune to the sting, so they can take shelter among the anemones. But they need to rub up against the tentacles every day to build up their protective mucous layer and can't stray too far.

MANTA RAYS

are super impressive with their big mouths!

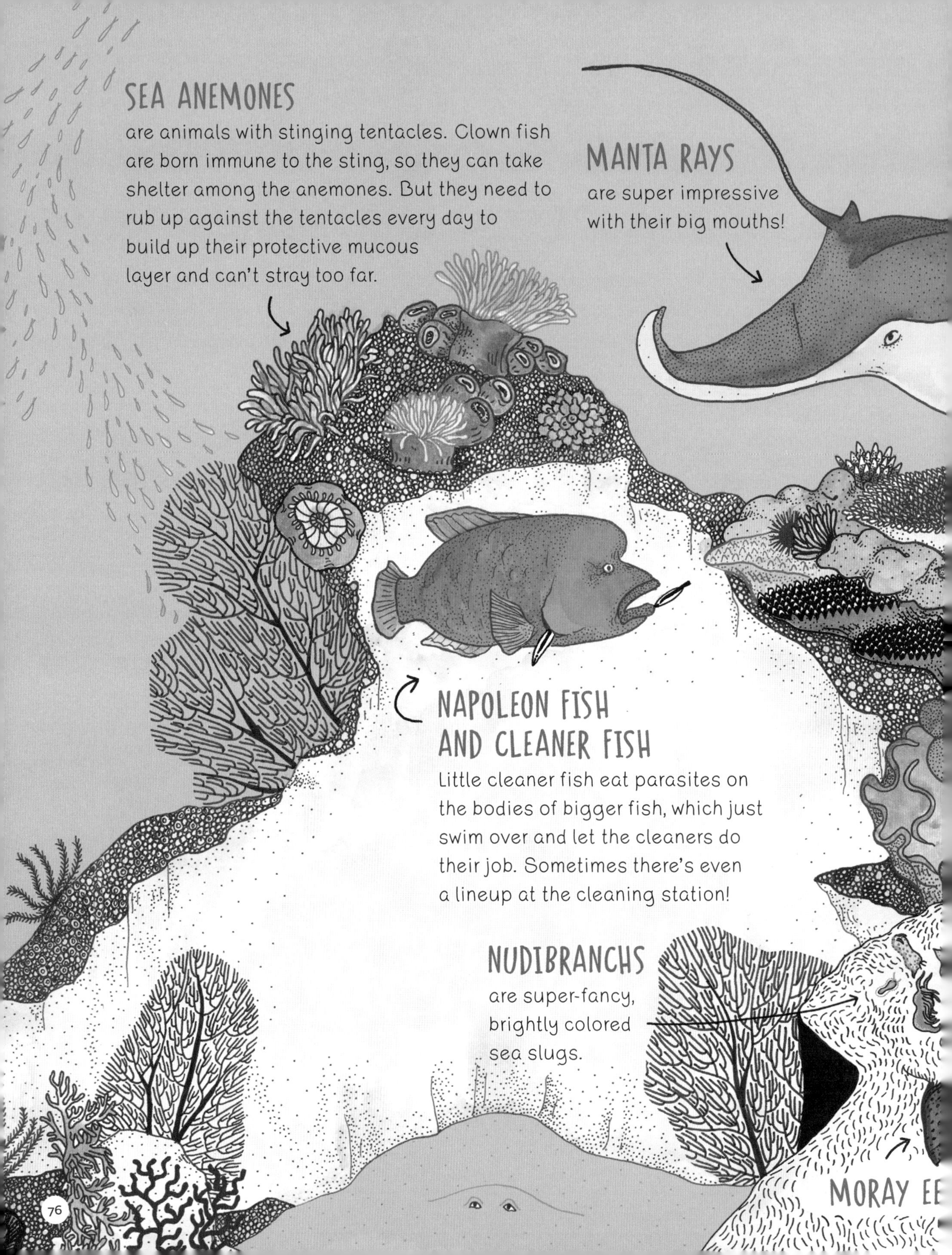

NAPOLEON FISH AND CLEANER FISH

Little cleaner fish eat parasites on the bodies of bigger fish, which just swim over and let the cleaners do their job. Sometimes there's even a lineup at the cleaning station!

NUDIBRANCHS

are super-fancy, brightly colored sea slugs.

MORAY EE

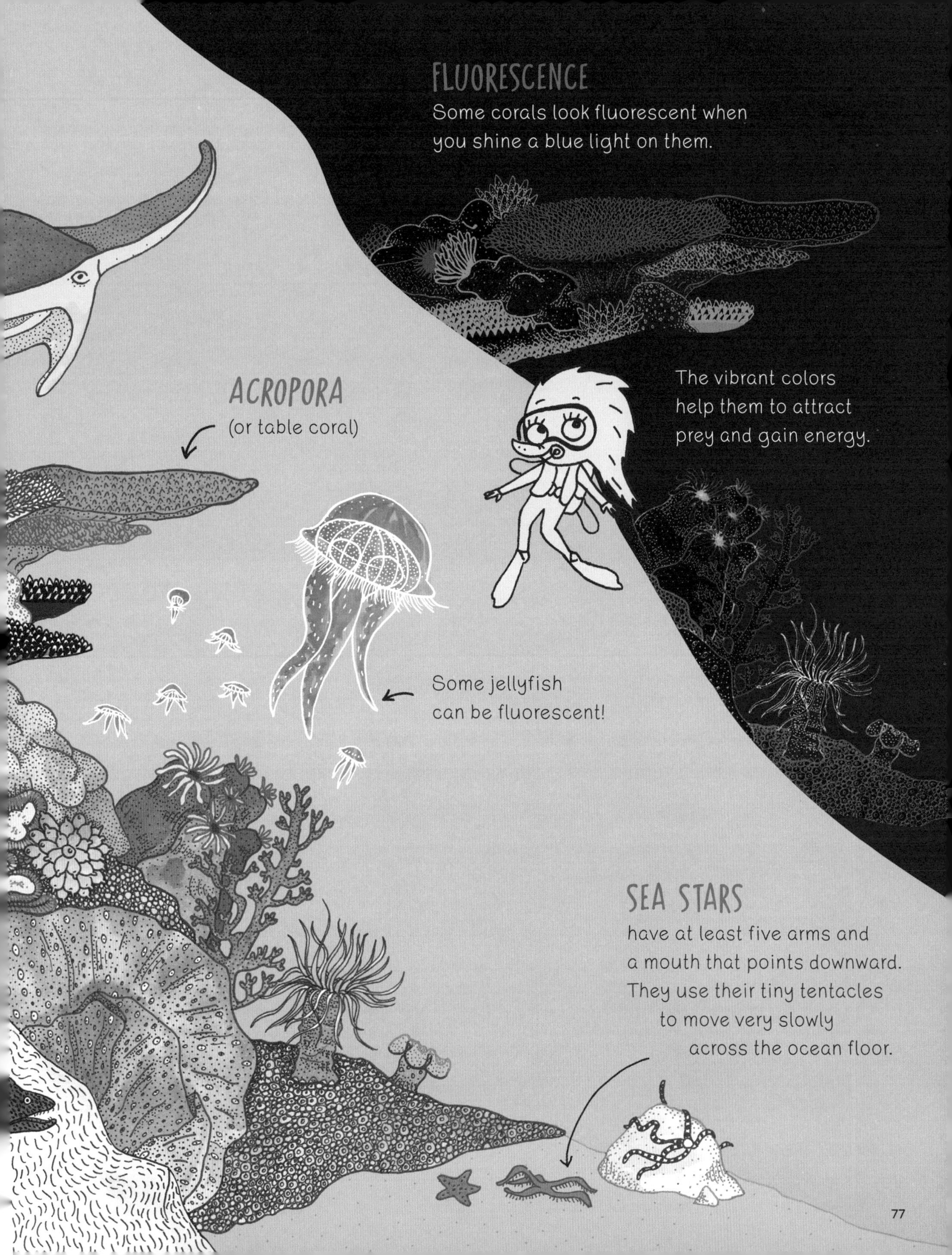

FLUORESCENCE

Some corals look fluorescent when you shine a blue light on them.

The vibrant colors help them to attract prey and gain energy.

ACROPORA

(or table coral)

Some jellyfish can be fluorescent!

SEA STARS

have at least five arms and a mouth that points downward. They use their tiny tentacles to move very slowly across the ocean floor.

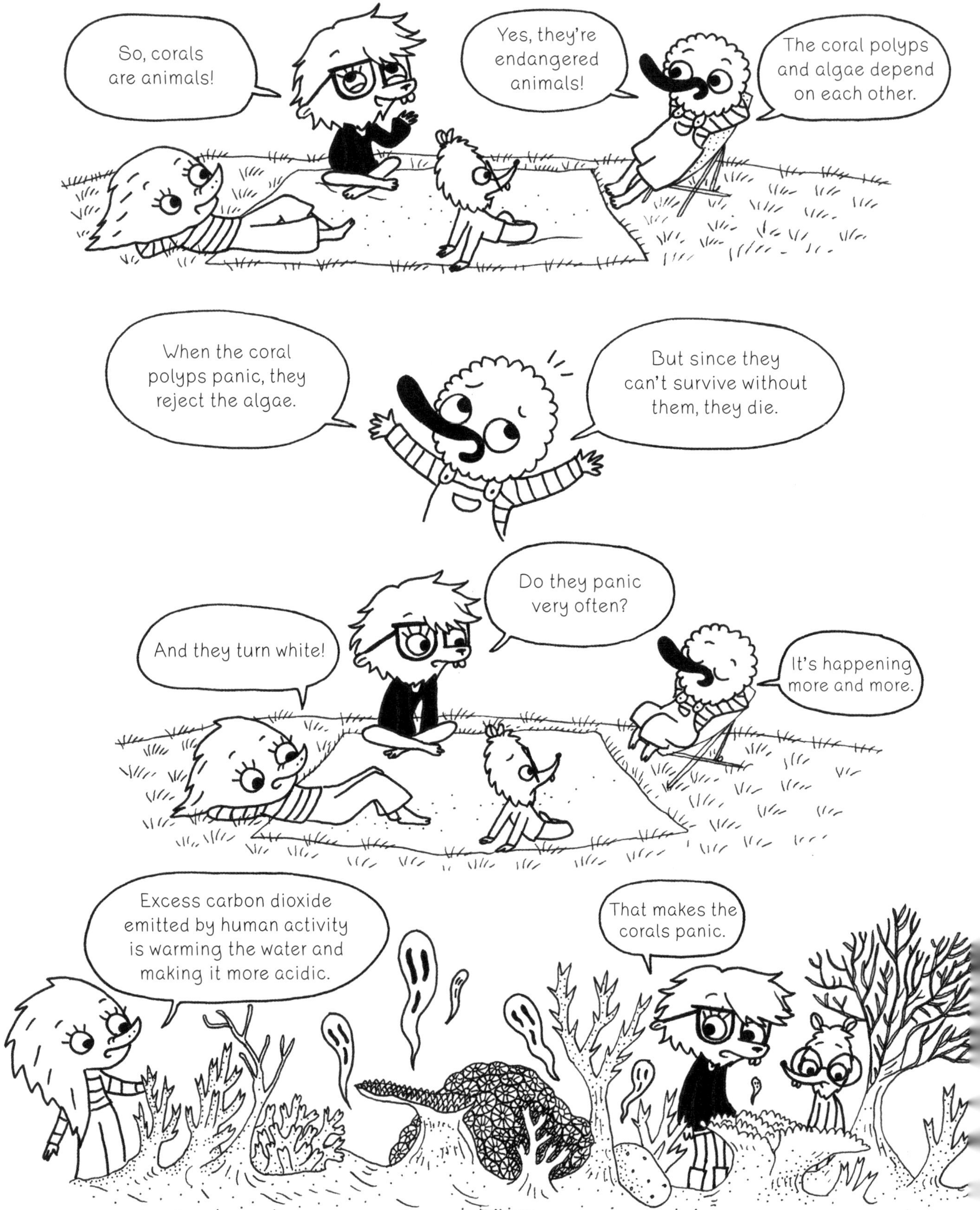
So, corals are animals!
Yes, they're endangered animals!
The coral polyps and algae depend on each other.
When the coral polyps panic, they reject the algae.
But since they can't survive without them, they die.
And they turn white!
Do they panic very often?
It's happening more and more.
Excess carbon dioxide emitted by human activity is warming the water and making it more acidic.
That makes the corals panic.

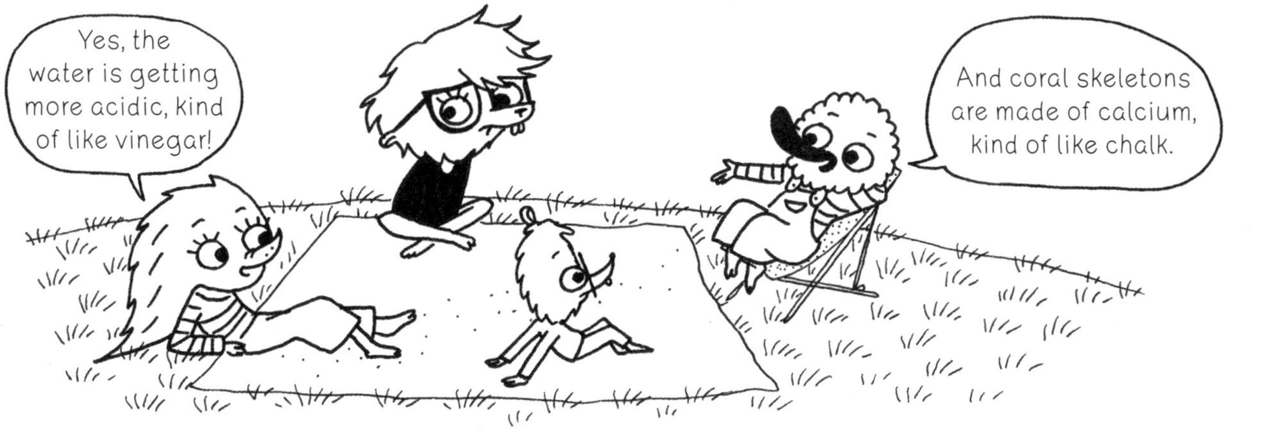
Yes, the water is getting more acidic, kind of like vinegar!
And coral skeletons are made of calcium, kind of like chalk.

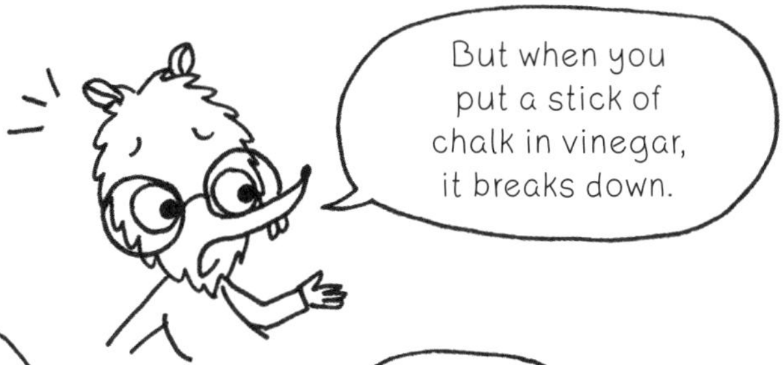
But when you put a stick of chalk in vinegar, it breaks down.

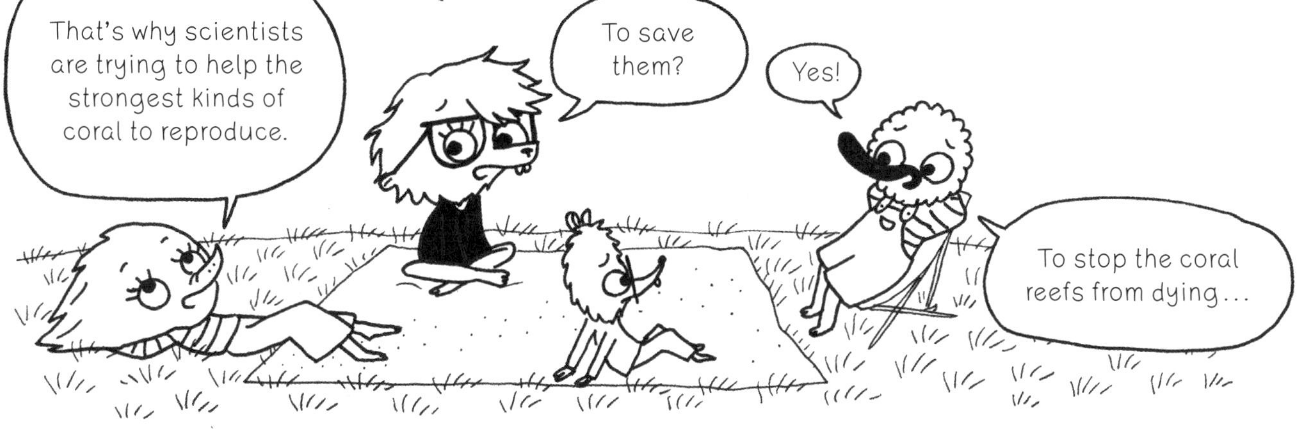
That's why scientists are trying to help the strongest kinds of coral to reproduce.
To save them?
Yes!
To stop the coral reefs from dying . . .

. . . and turning into ghost towns.

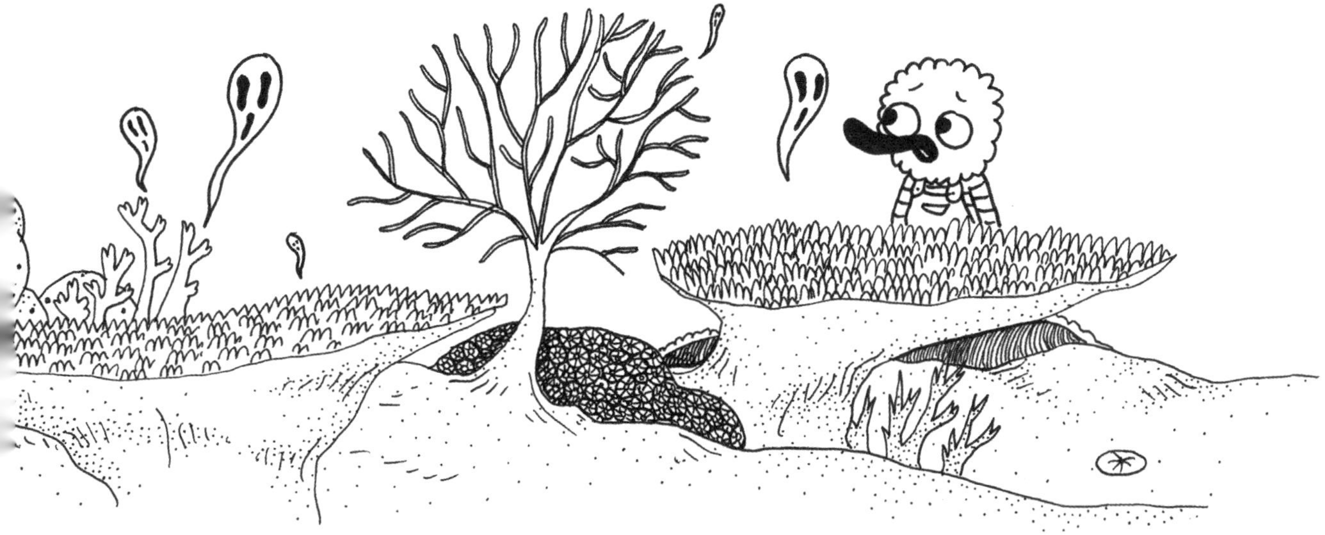

12 EXPERTS IN CAMOUFLAGE

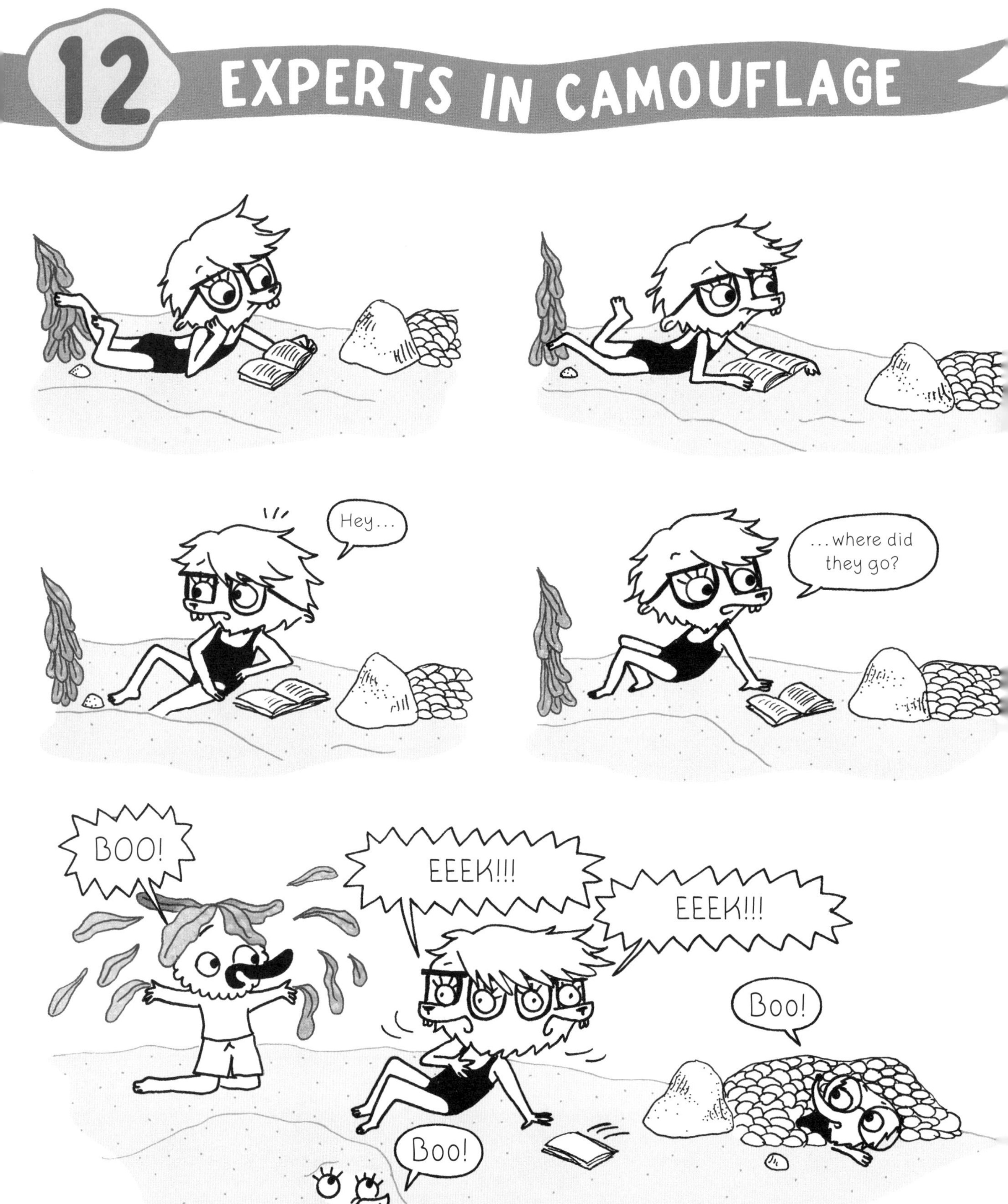

Hey...
...where did they go?
BOO!
EEEK!!!
EEEK!!!
Boo!
Boo!

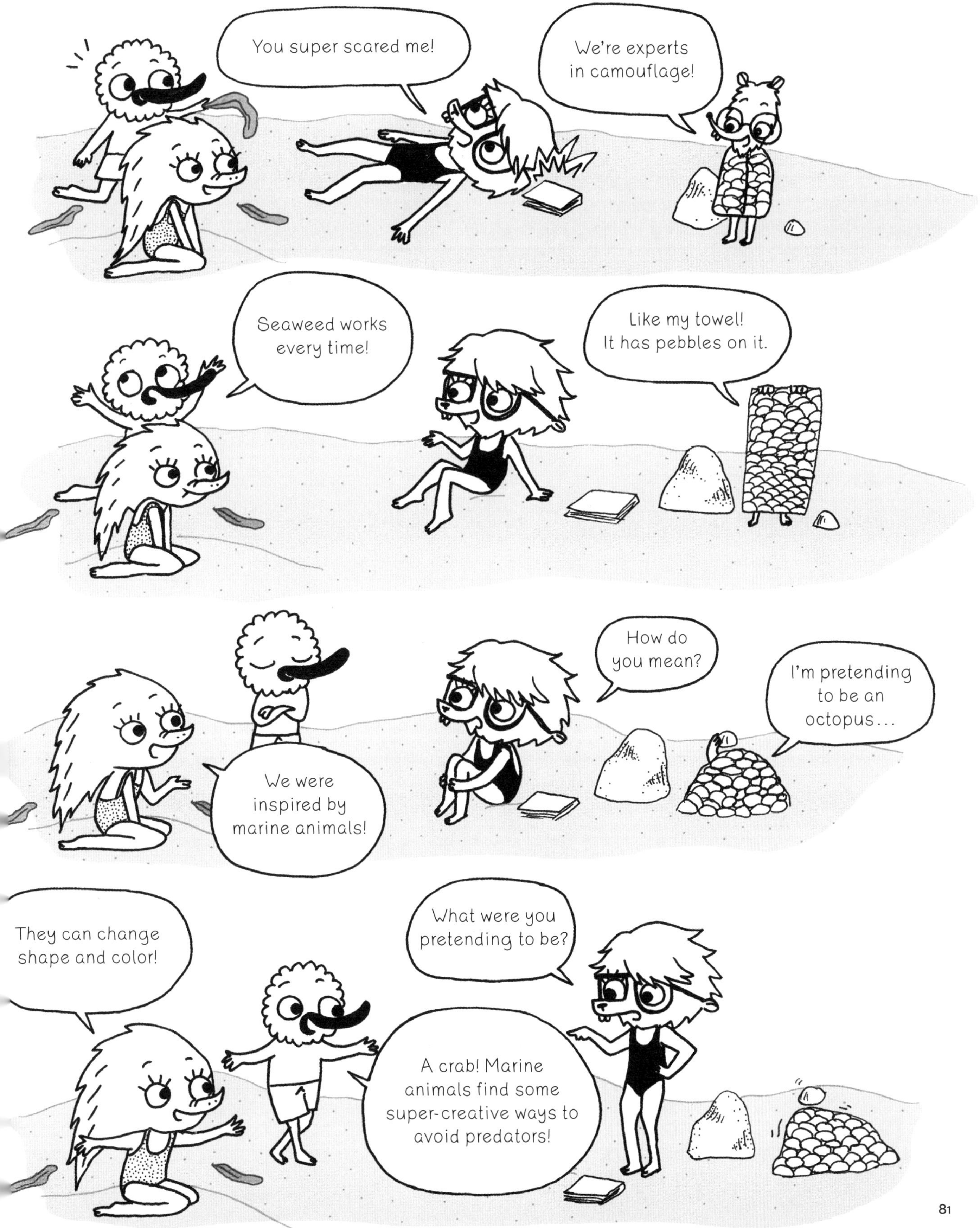
You super scared me!
We're experts in camouflage!
Seaweed works every time!
Like my towel! It has pebbles on it.
We were inspired by marine animals!
How do you mean?
I'm pretending to be an octopus...
They can change shape and color!
What were you pretending to be?
A crab! Marine animals find some super-creative ways to avoid predators!

Everything in the ocean is either a predator
or prey. Together, predators and prey form

THE FOOD CHAIN.

PHYTOPLANKTON
is right at the start
of the food chain.

ZOOPLANKTON
basically feeds on phytoplankton.
And it gets eaten by...

Even super predators are part of
the chain. Like all living beings,
when they die their bodies decompose
and nourish smaller organisms.

Every link in the chain
is important for the
balance of marine life.

When humans catch too
many fish in the ocean, it
messes up that balance.

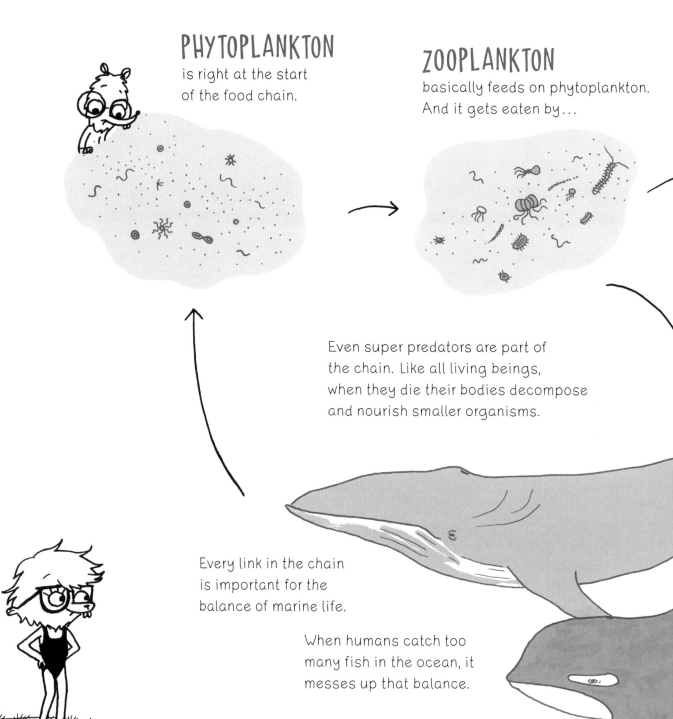

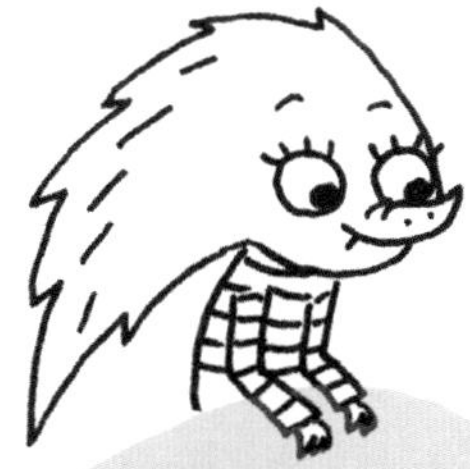

JELLYFISH, SMALL FISH, CUTTLEFISH...

and they get eaten by...

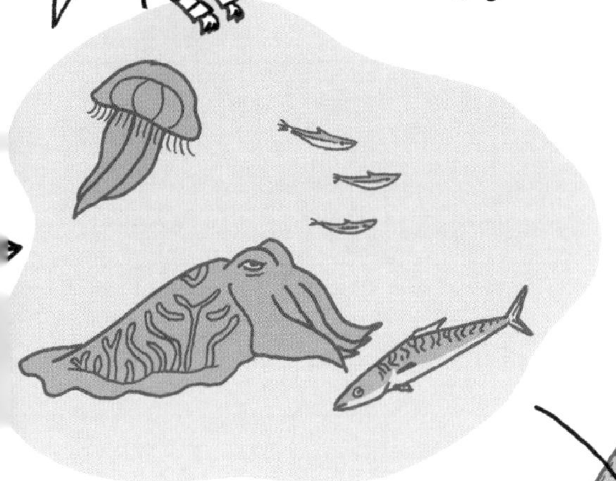

BIG FISH, SEALS, TURTLES, DOLPHINS, AND MARINE MAMMALS...

and they get eaten by...

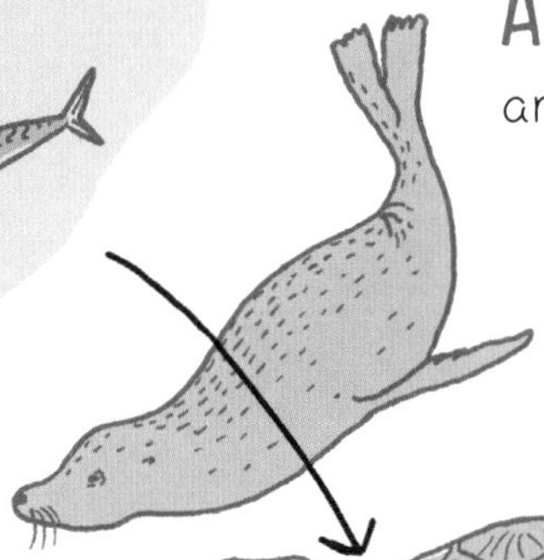

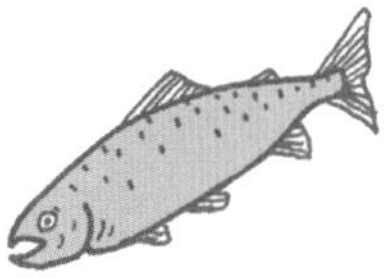

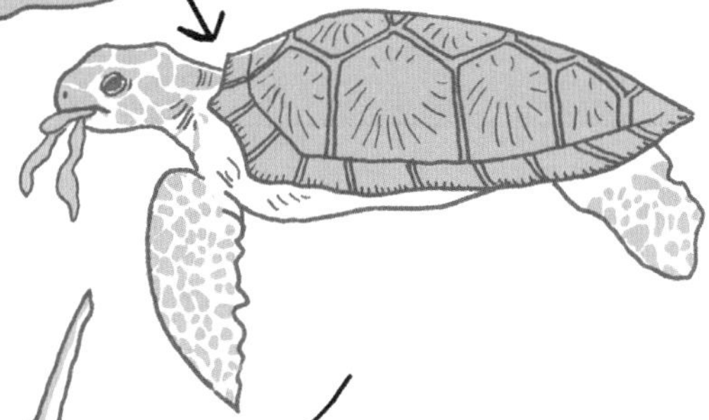

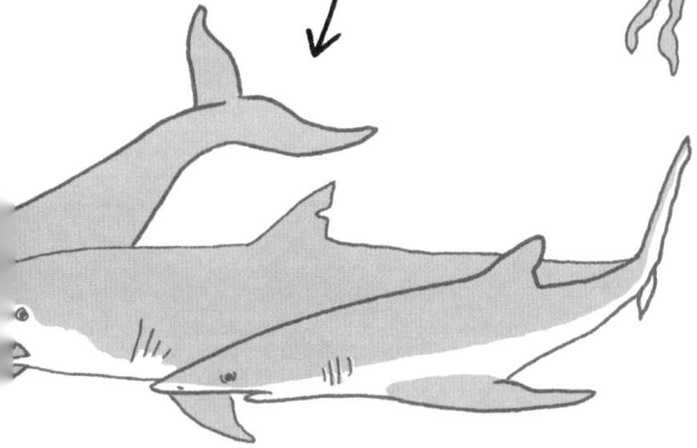

SUPER PREDATORS

like orcas and sharks.

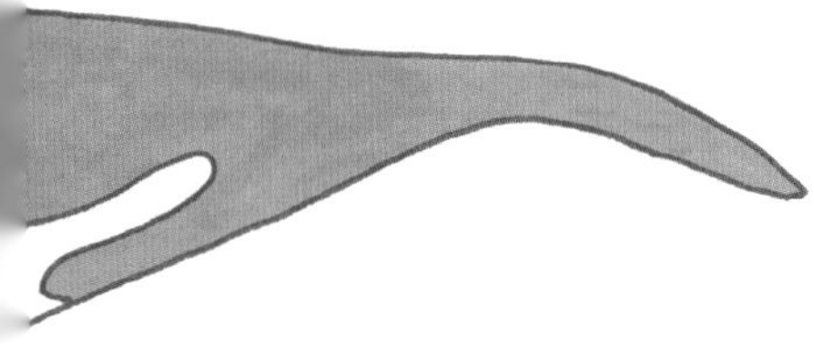

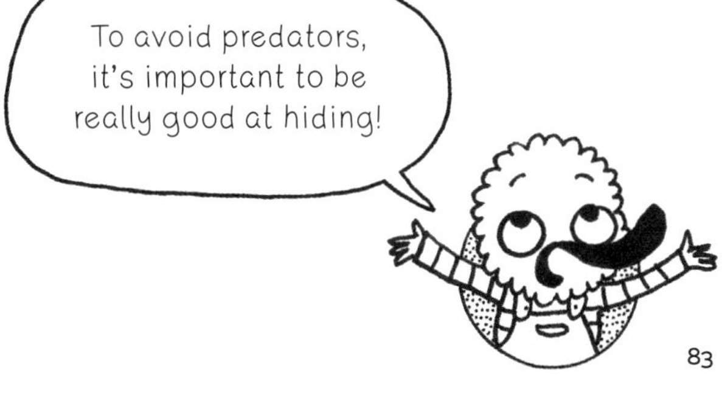
To avoid predators, it's important to be really good at hiding!

CAMOUFLAGE AND CONFUSION*

Lots of marine animals are experts in camouflage. They can be super hard to see.

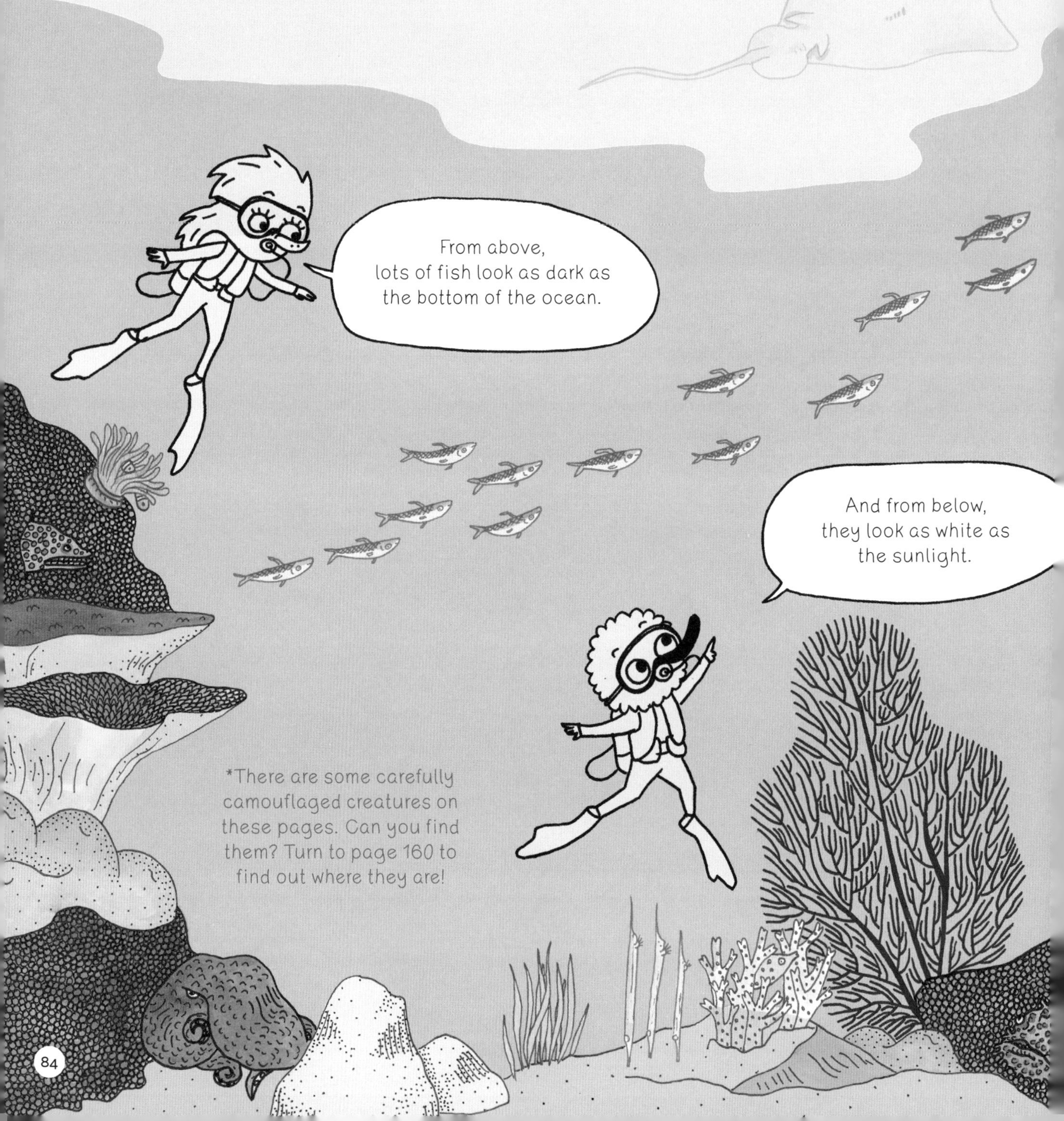
From above, lots of fish look as dark as the bottom of the ocean.
And from below, they look as white as the sunlight.

*There are some carefully camouflaged creatures on these pages. Can you find them? Turn to page 160 to find out where they are!

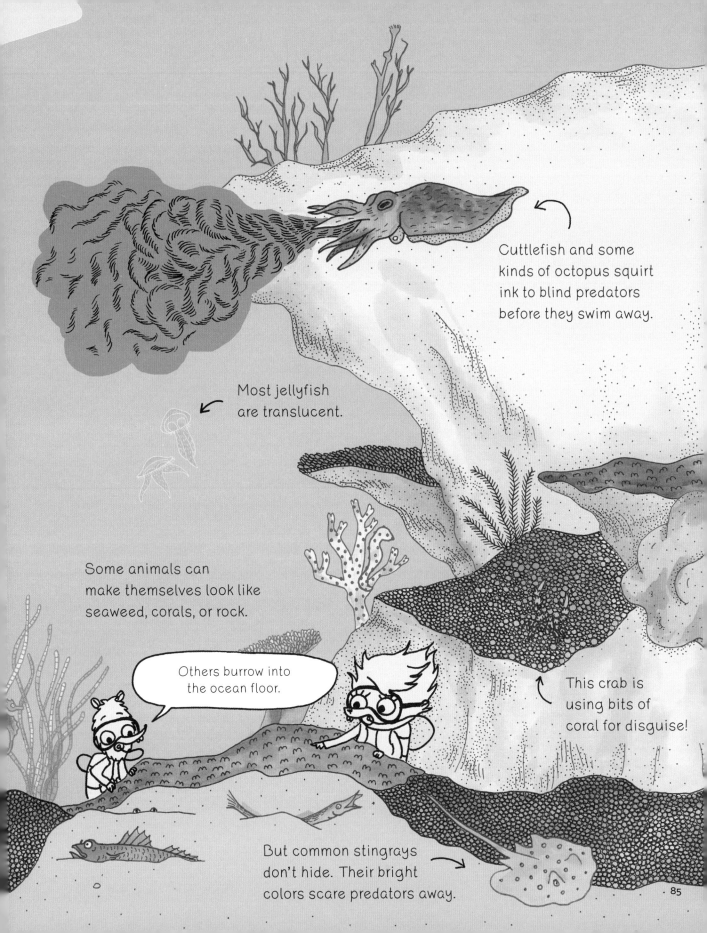

Cuttlefish and some kinds of octopus squirt ink to blind predators before they swim away.

Most jellyfish are translucent.

Some animals can make themselves look like seaweed, corals, or rock.

Others burrow into the ocean floor.

This crab is using bits of coral for disguise!

But common stingrays don't hide. Their bright colors scare predators away.

OCTOPUSES

Octopuses can change their texture using special "papillae" on their skin!

Their skin is smooth when the papillae are closed. And when the papillae open up, their skin is as rough as rock!

They can also change color, thanks to cells called chromatophores that fill with pigment.

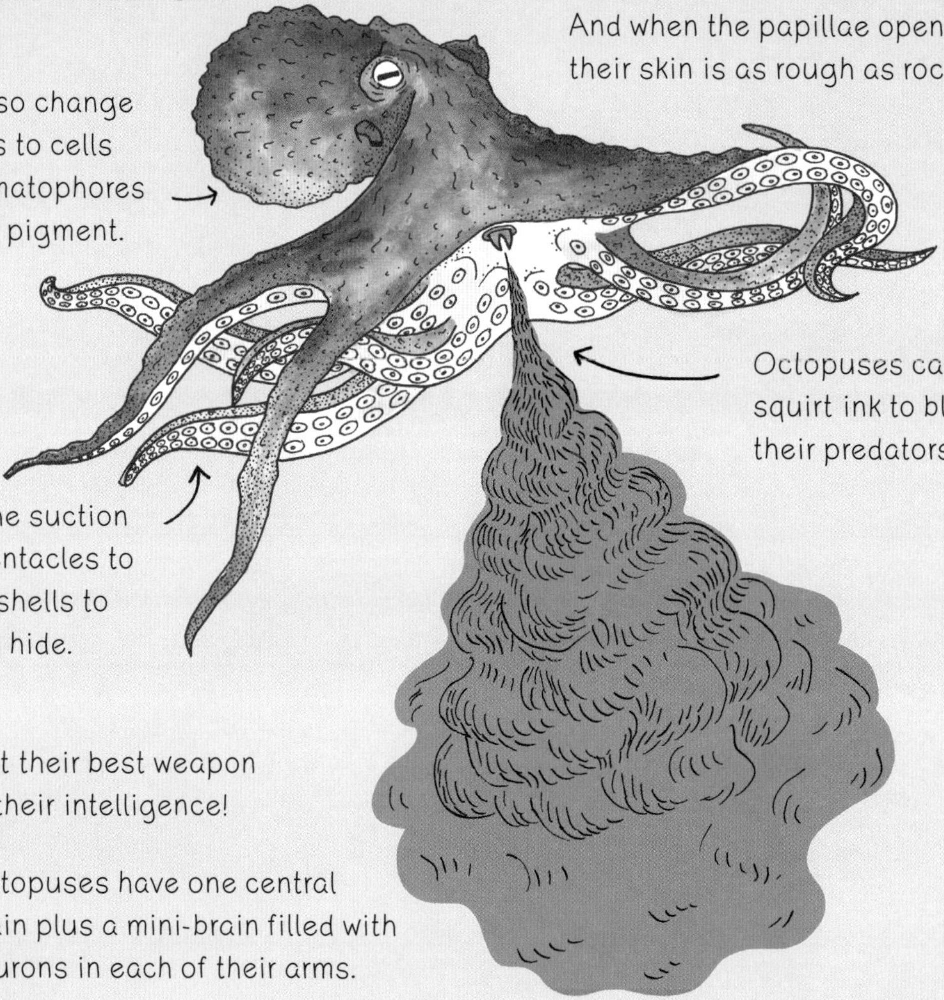

Oclopuses can squirt ink to blind their predators.

They can use the suction cups on their tentacles to stick pieces of shells to themselves and hide.

But their best weapon is their intelligence!

Octopuses have one central brain plus a mini-brain filled with neurons in each of their arms.

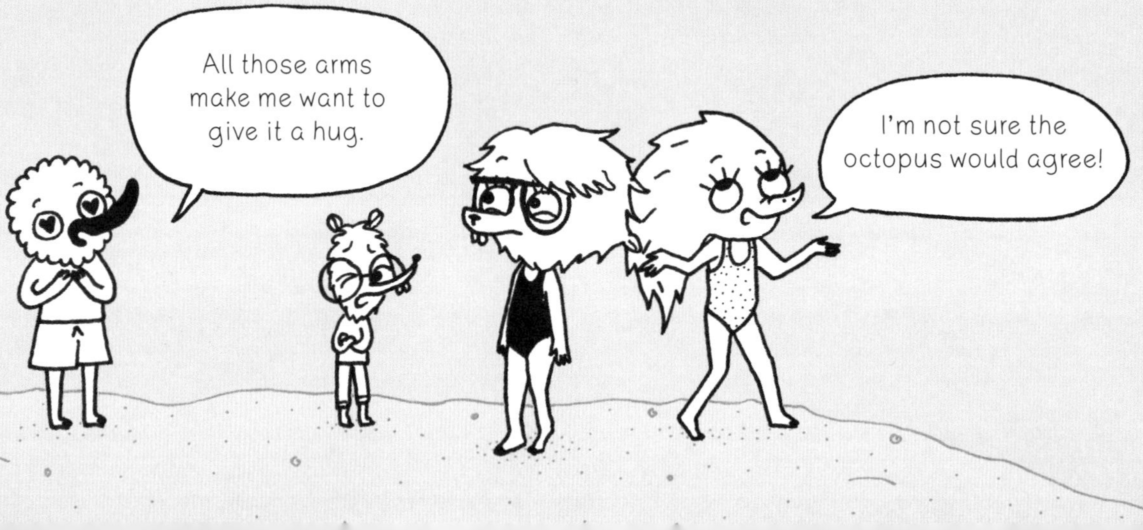
All those arms make me want to give it a hug.
I'm not sure the octopus would agree!

13 ALL ABOUT BUOYANCY

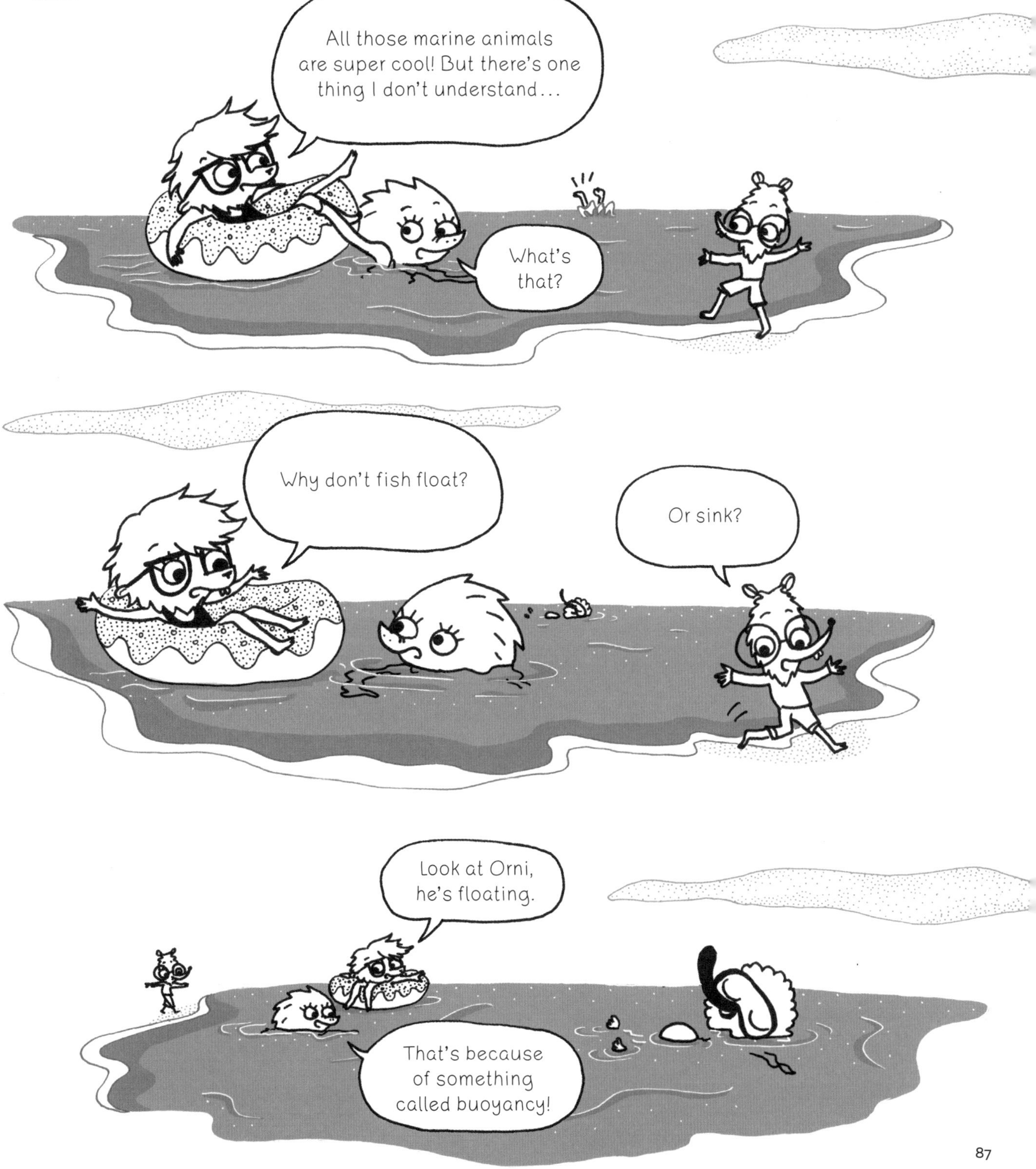

BUOYANCY

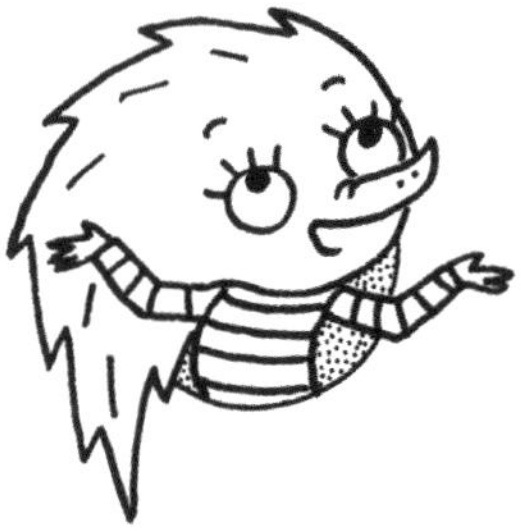

Buoyancy is a force that "lifts" any object put into a liquid.

For an object to stay at the surface, the object must weigh less than the volume of the liquid it displaces.

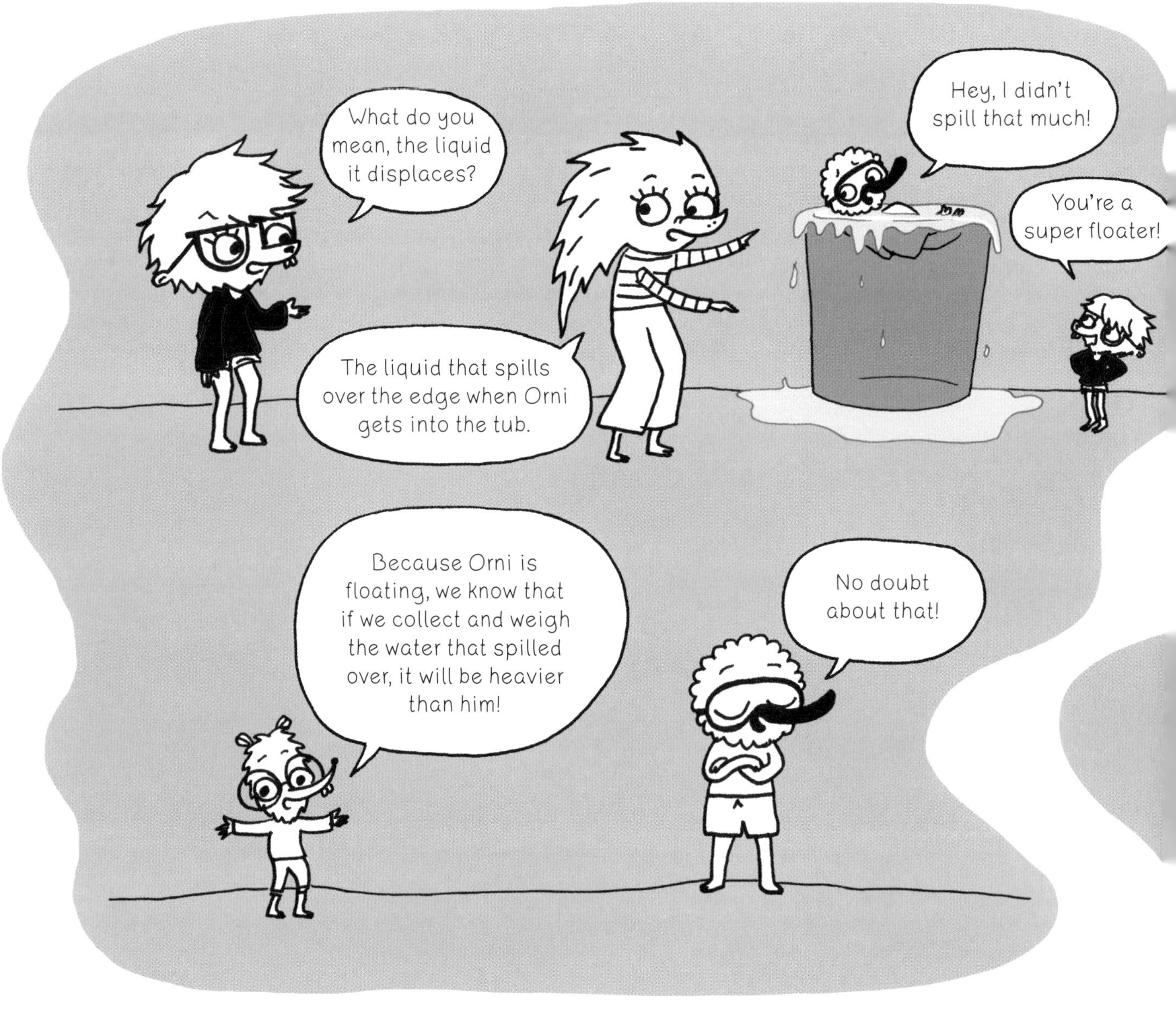

What do you mean, the liquid it displaces?
The liquid that spills over the edge when Orni gets into the tub.
Hey, I didn't spill that much!
You're a super floater!
Because Orni is floating, we know that if we collect and weigh the water that spilled over, it will be heavier than him!
No doubt about that!

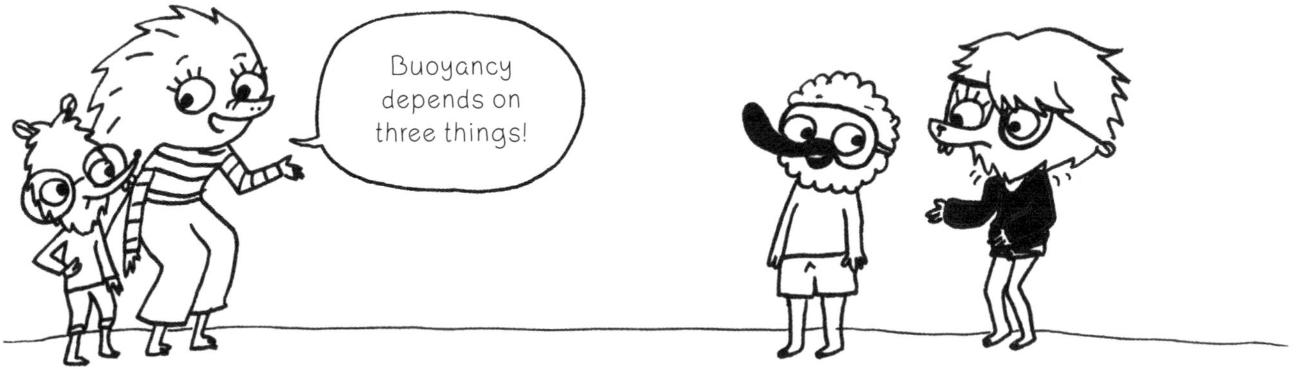
Buoyancy depends on three things!

1. THE WEIGHT OF THE OBJECT

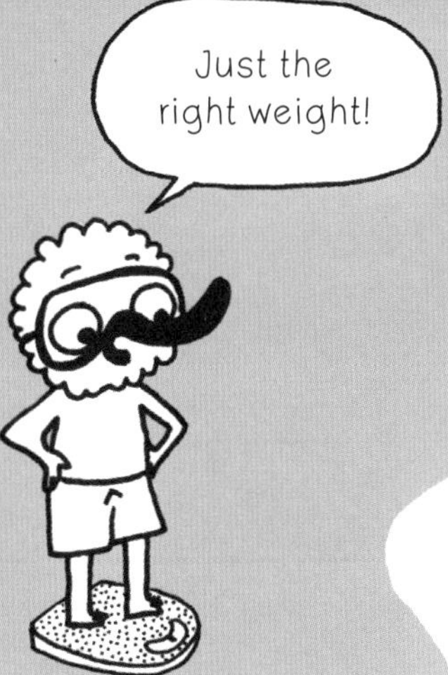
Just the right weight!

2. THE VOLUME OF THE OBJECT

The more water displaced by an object, the greater the buoyant force.

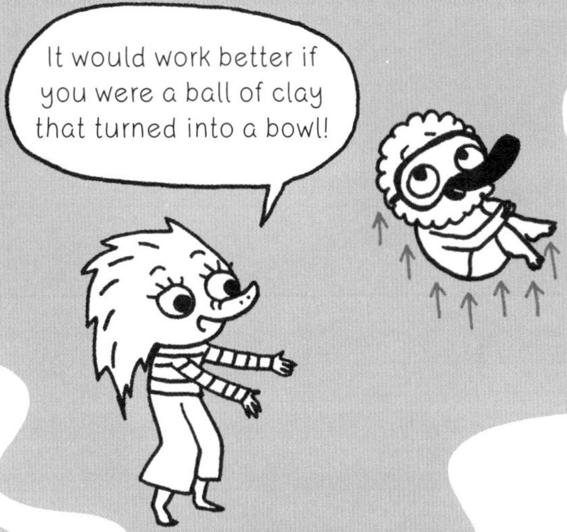
It would work better if you were a ball of clay that turned into a bowl!

3. THE WEIGHT OF THE LIQUID

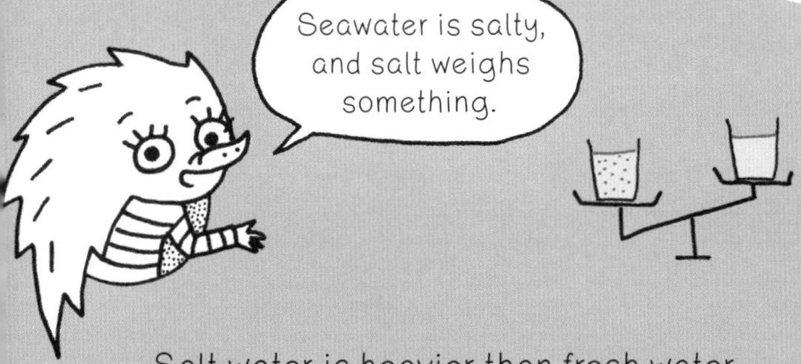
Seawater is salty, and salt weighs something.

Salt water is heavier than fresh water. That's why we float more easily in the ocean.

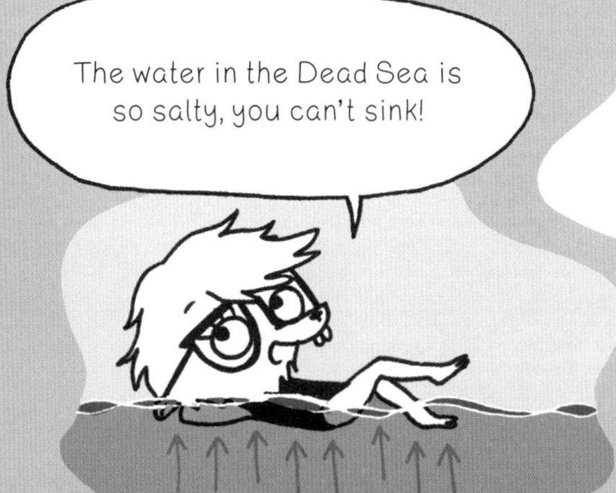
The water in the Dead Sea is so salty, you can't sink!

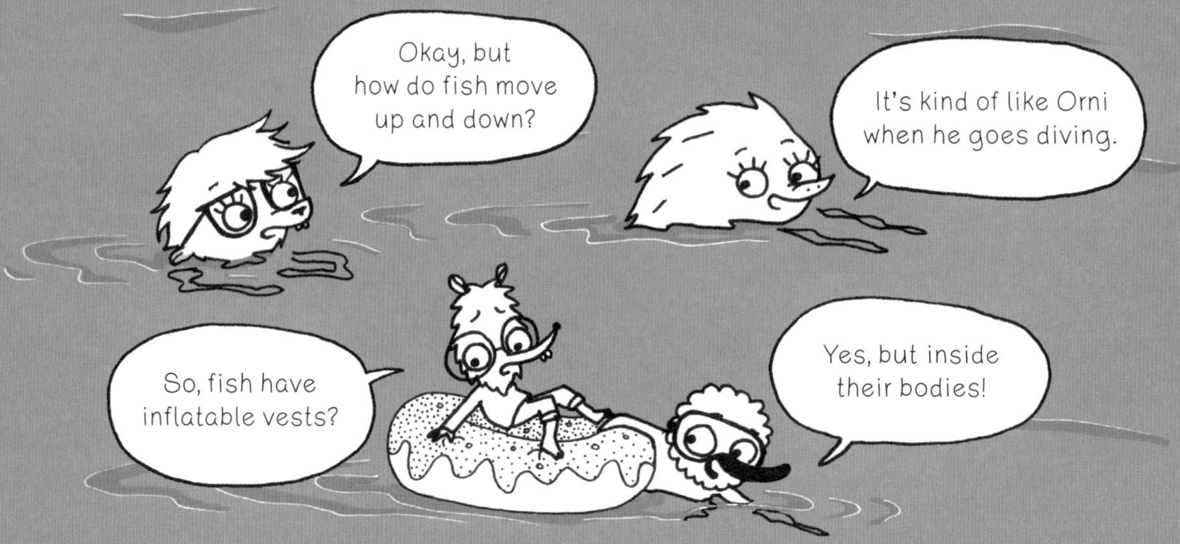
Okay, but how do fish move up and down?
It's kind of like Orni when he goes diving.
So, fish have inflatable vests?
Yes, but inside their bodies!

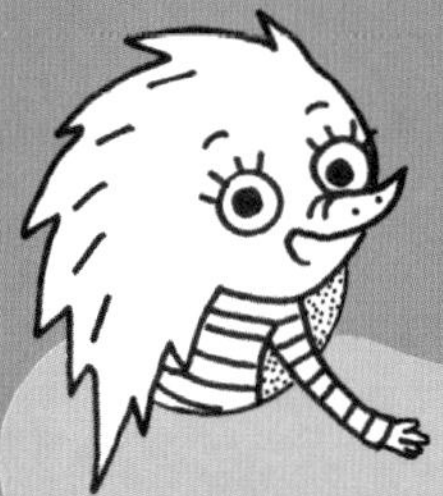

Fish have a SWIM BLADDER.

It's like a balloon that they can make bigger and smaller.

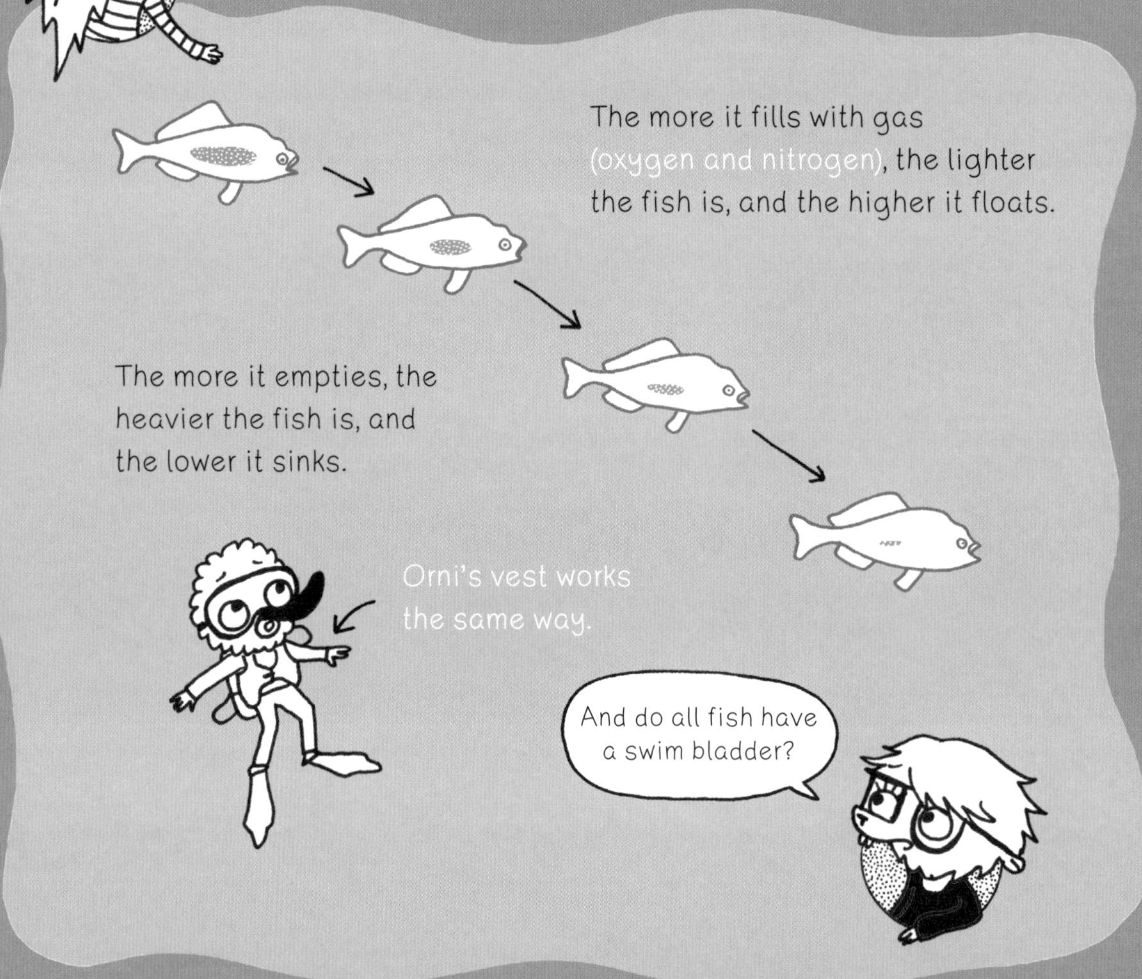
The more it fills with gas (oxygen and nitrogen), the lighter the fish is, and the higher it floats.
The more it empties, the heavier the fish is, and the lower it sinks.
Orni's vest works the same way.
And do all fish have a swim bladder?

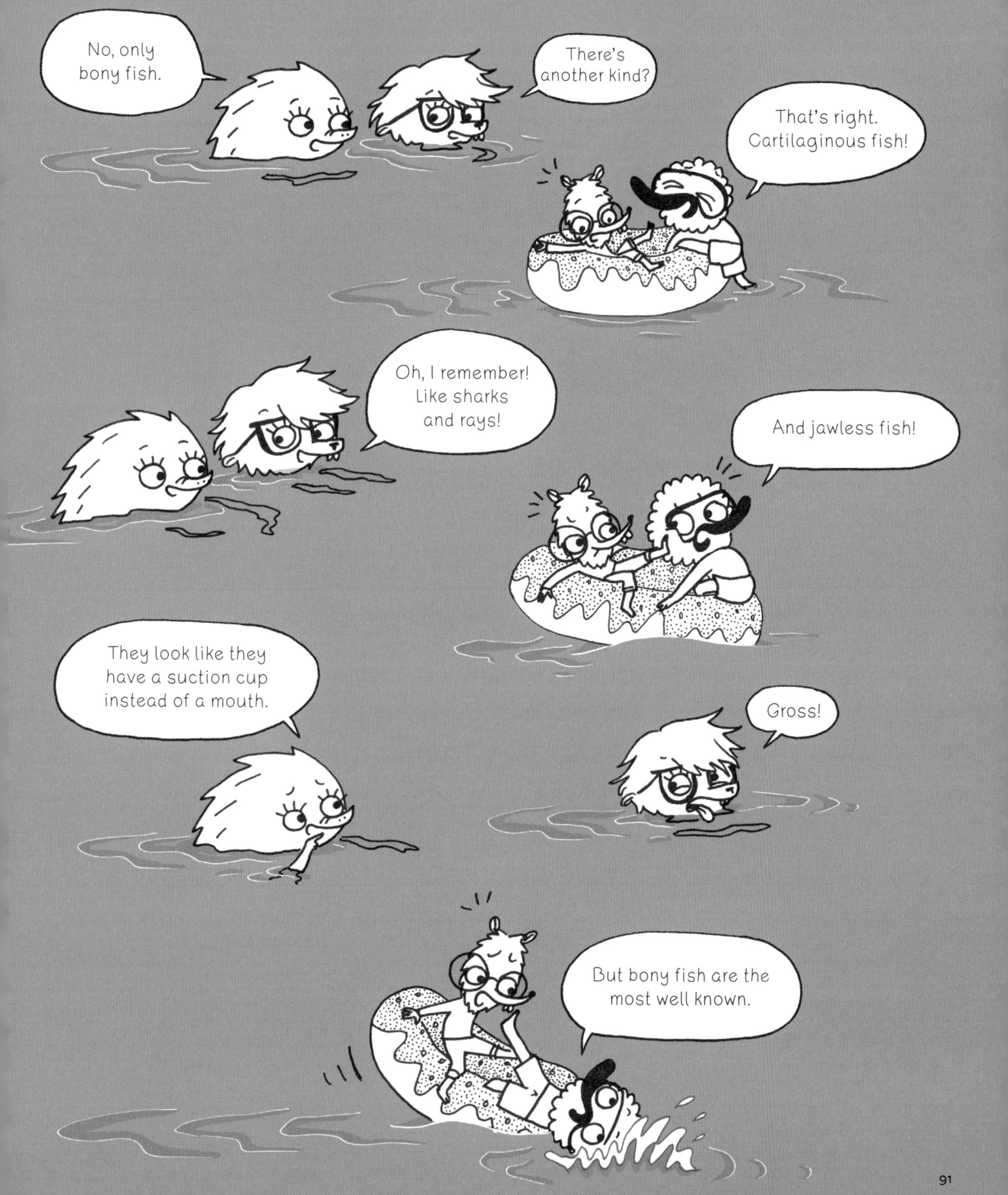
No, only bony fish.
There's another kind?
That's right. Cartilaginous fish!
Oh, I remember! Like sharks and rays!
And jawless fish!
They look like they have a suction cup instead of a mouth.
Gross!
But bony fish are the most well known.

BONY SALTWATER FISH

There are lots of different species of bony fish that live in salt water. You'll see different fish in different oceans, depending on the depth and temperature of the water, and even which predators are around. Some are super small, and some are very big. Some are super brightly colored, and some are not so colorful.

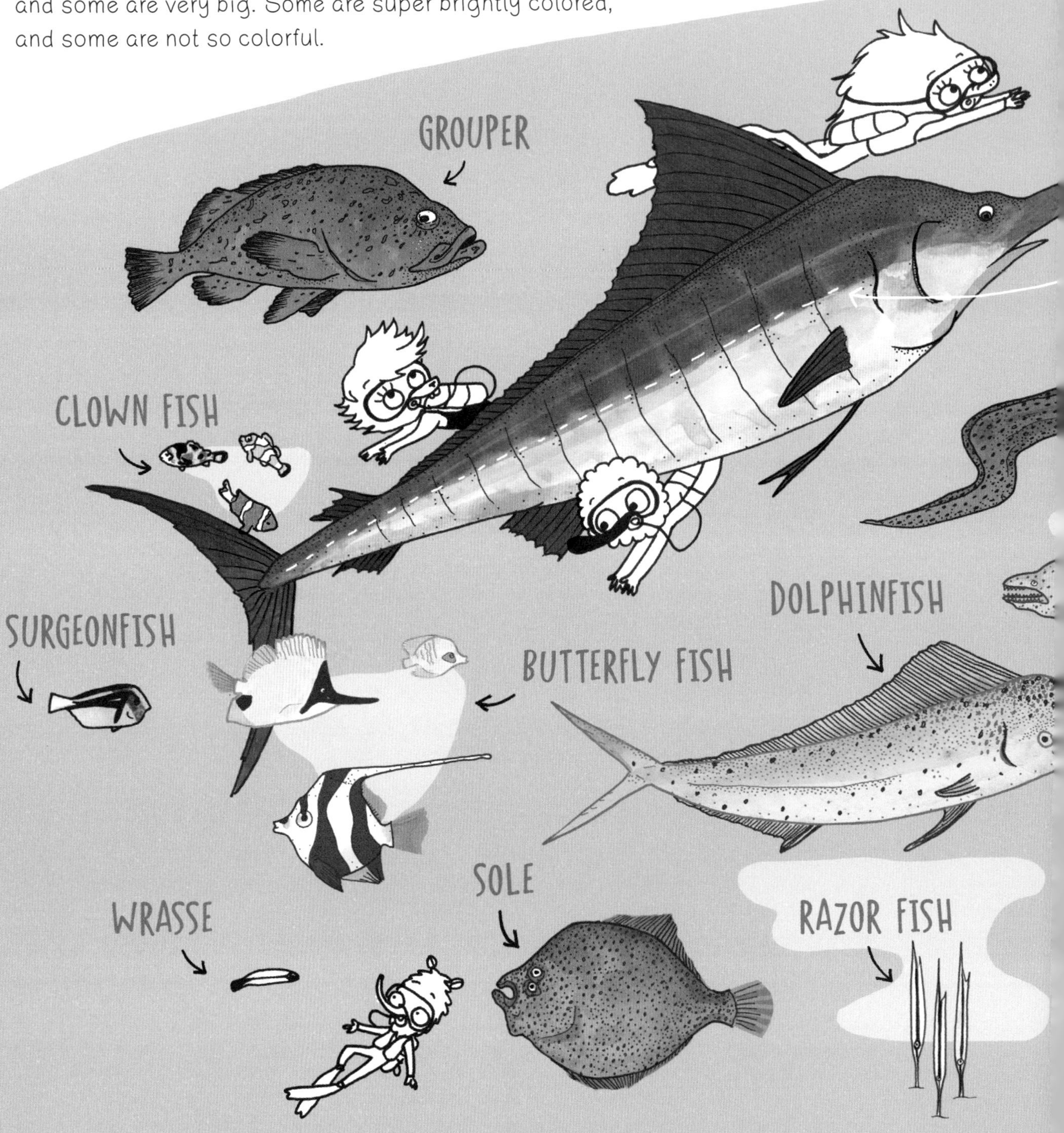

GROUPER
CLOWN FISH
SURGEONFISH
BUTTERFLY FISH
DOLPHINFISH
SOLE
WRASSE
RAZOR FISH

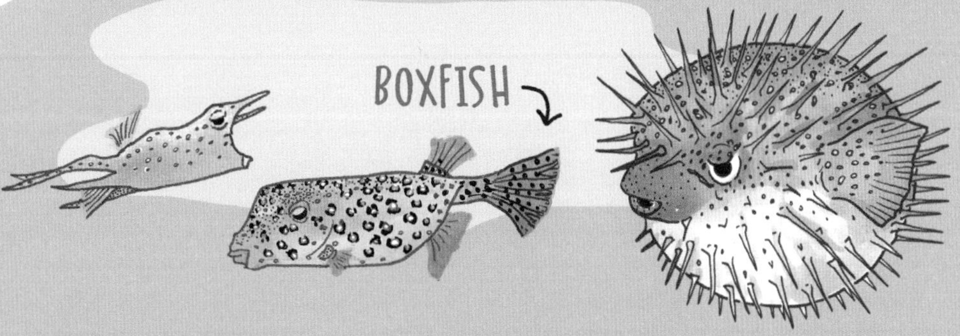

BOXFISH

SWORDFISH

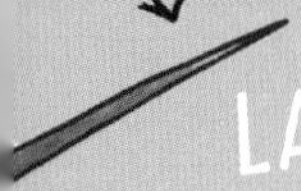

LATERAL LINE

All fish have a lateral line on their body that helps them to feel vibrations from far away.

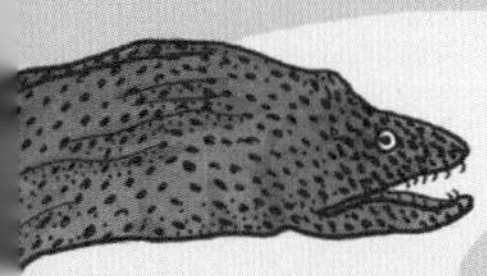

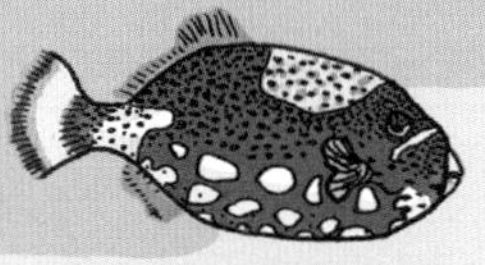

TRIGGERFISH

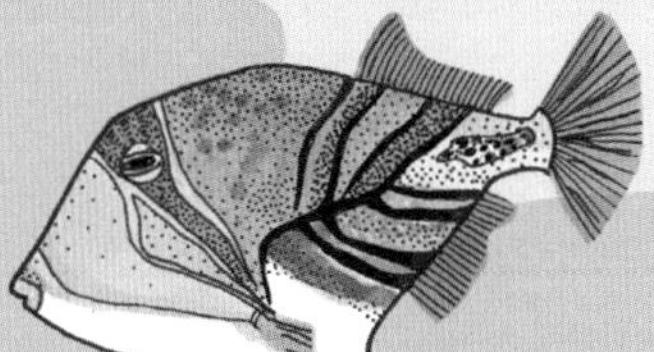

MORAY EEL

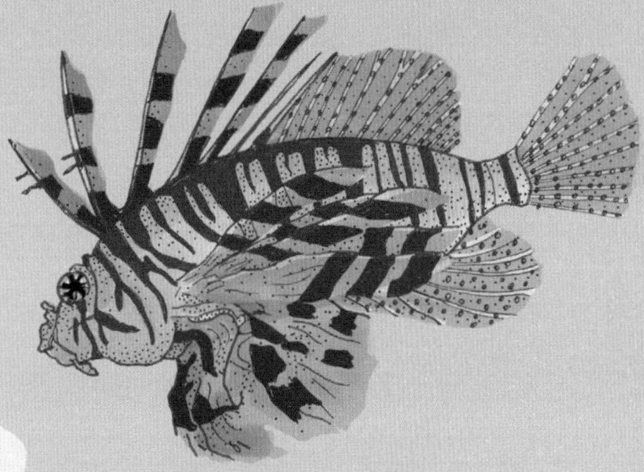

RED LIONFISH

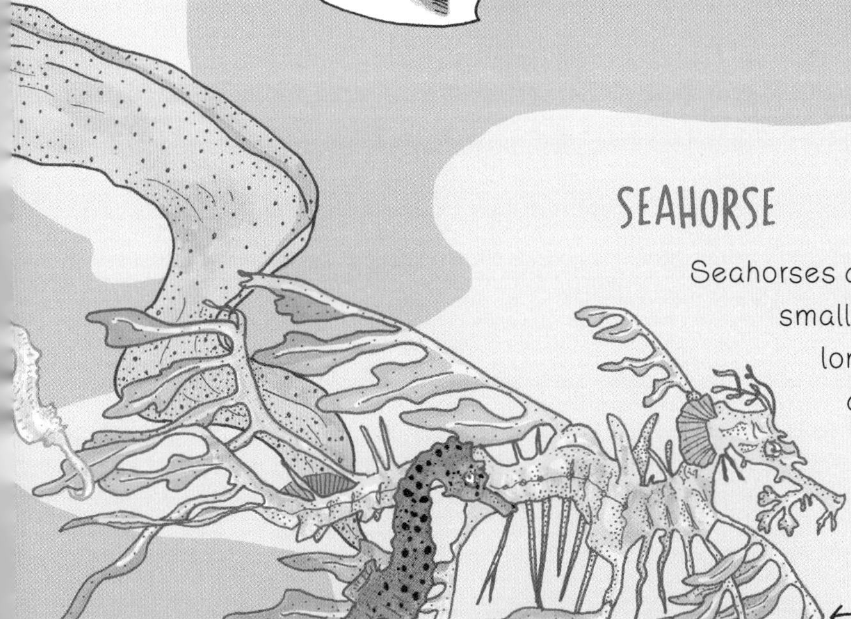

SEAHORSE

Seahorses are fish too! Some are super small, about 1 inch (2 centimeters) long, and others are longer, about 12 in. (30 cm).

Some species are really good at camouflage.

The leafy sea dragon looks like seaweed!

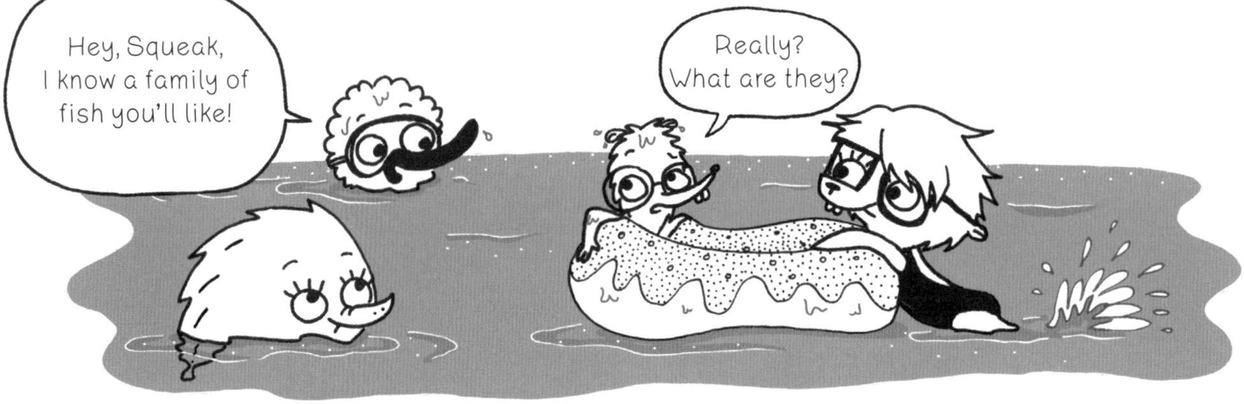
Hey, Squeak, I know a family of fish you'll like!
Really? What are they?

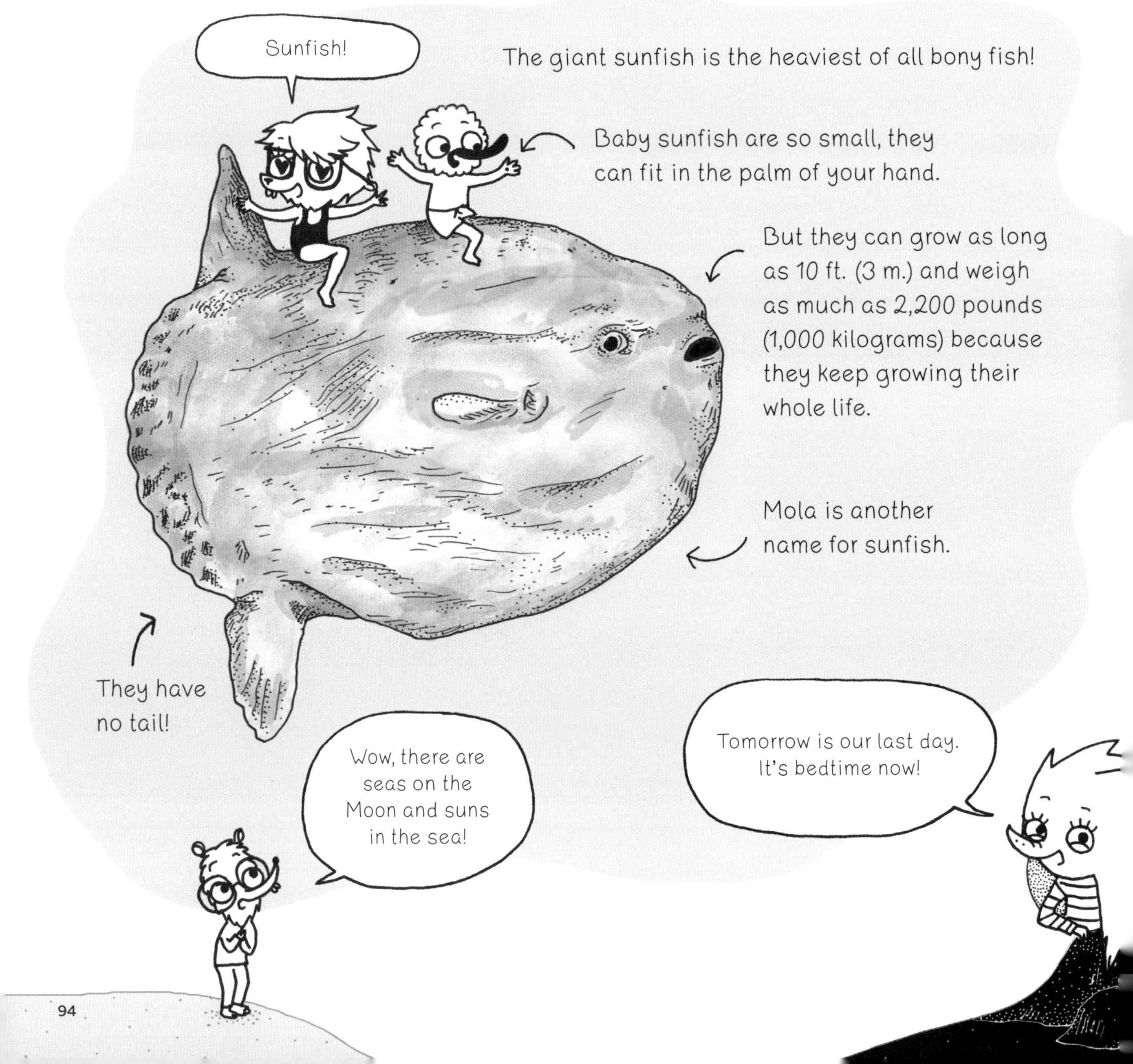
Sunfish!
The giant sunfish is the heaviest of all bony fish!
Baby sunfish are so small, they can fit in the palm of your hand.
But they can grow as long as 10 ft. (3 m.) and weigh as much as 2,200 pounds (1,000 kilograms) because they keep growing their whole life.
Mola is another name for sunfish.
They have no tail!
Wow, there are seas on the Moon and suns in the sea!
Tomorrow is our last day. It's bedtime now!

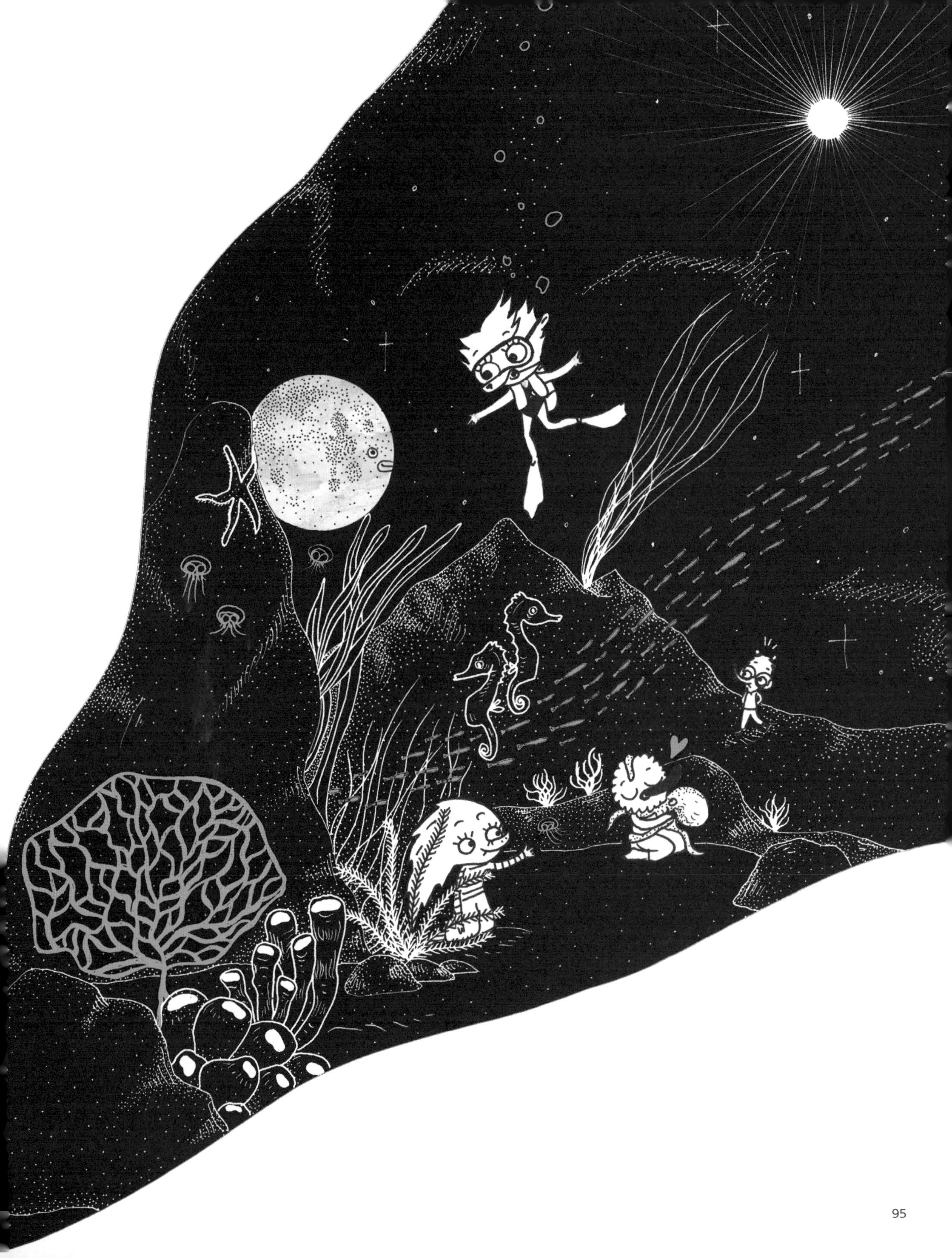

14 SWIMMING SCHOOL

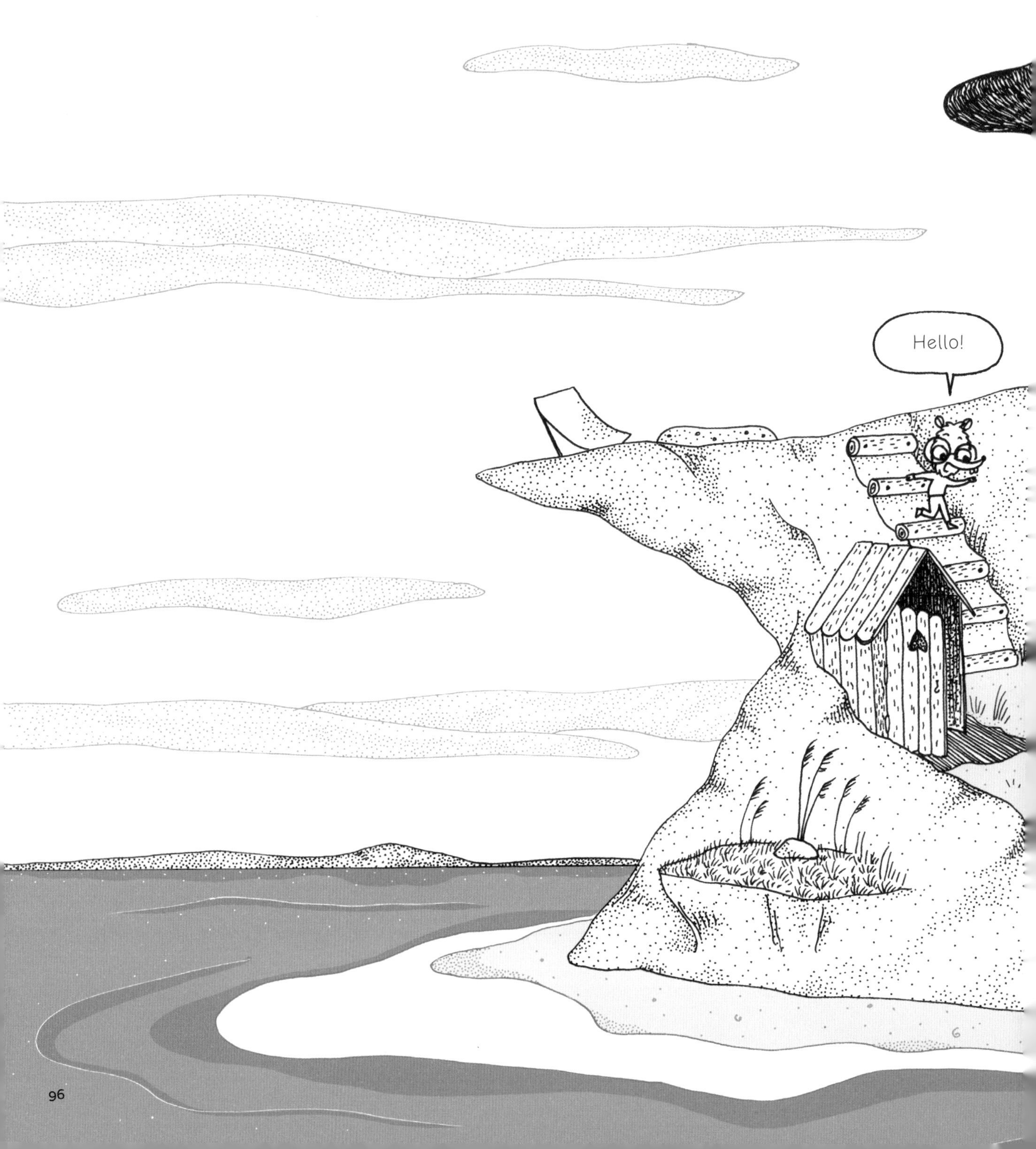
Hello!

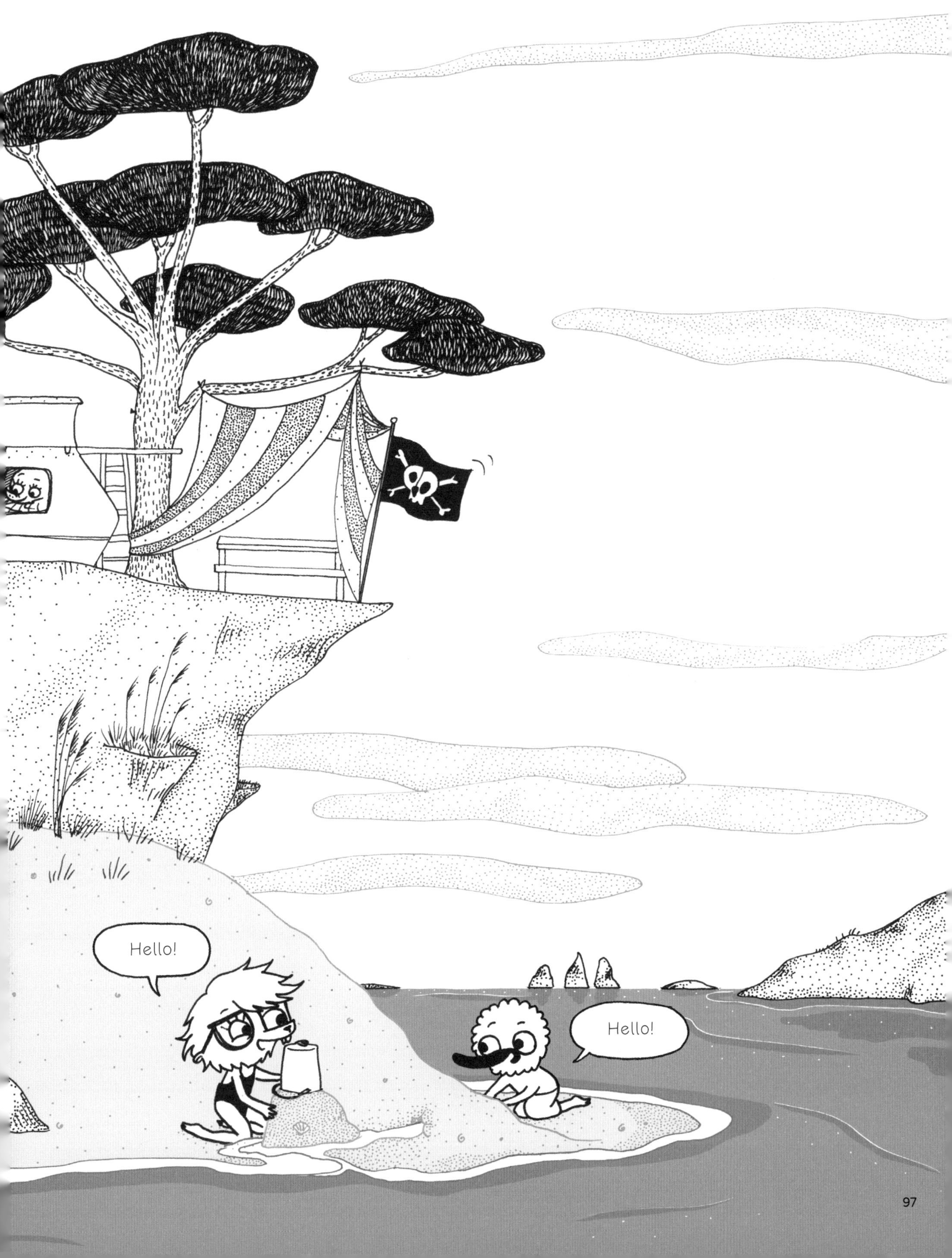
Hello!
Hello!

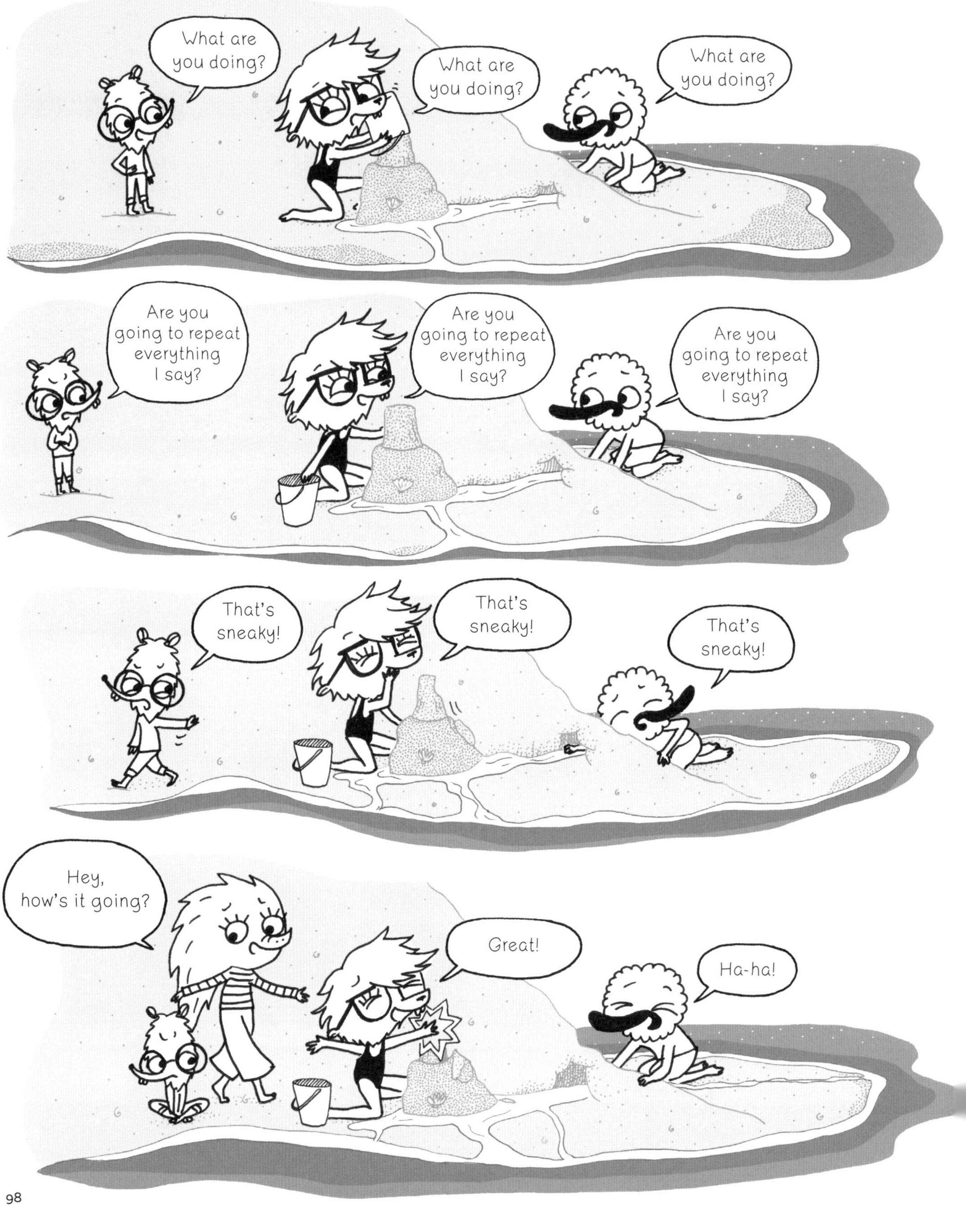
What are you doing?
What are you doing?
What are you doing?
Are you going to repeat everything I say?
Are you going to repeat everything I say?
Are you going to repeat everything I say?
That's sneaky!
That's sneaky!
That's sneaky!
Hey, how's it going?
Great!
Ha-ha!

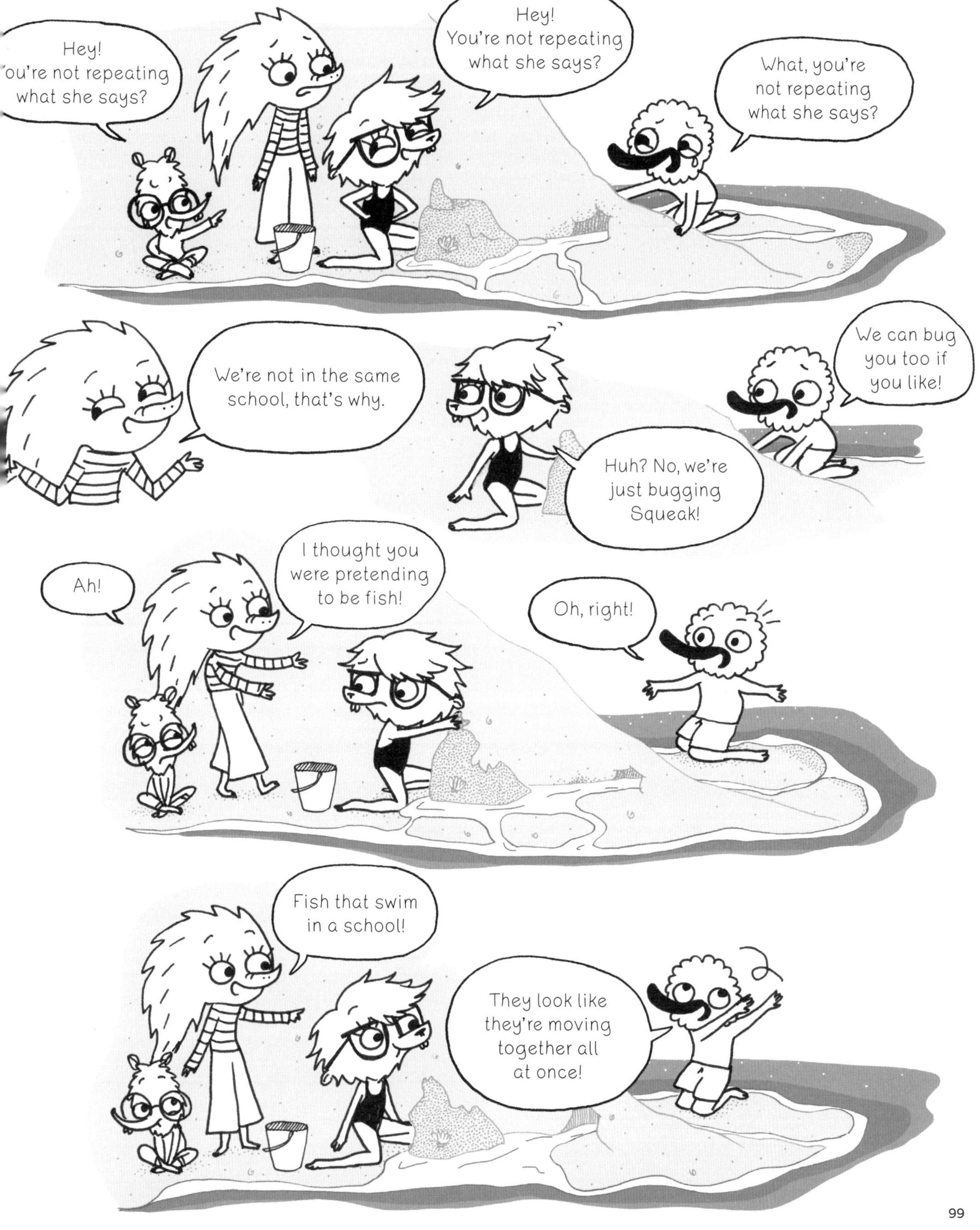

Hey! ou're not repeating what she says?
Hey! You're not repeating what she says?
What, you're not repeating what she says?
We're not in the same school, that's why.
Huh? No, we're just bugging Squeak!
We can bug you too if you like!
Ah!
I thought you were pretending to be fish!
Oh, right!
Fish that swim in a school!
They look like they're moving together all at once!

SWIMMING IN SCHOOLS

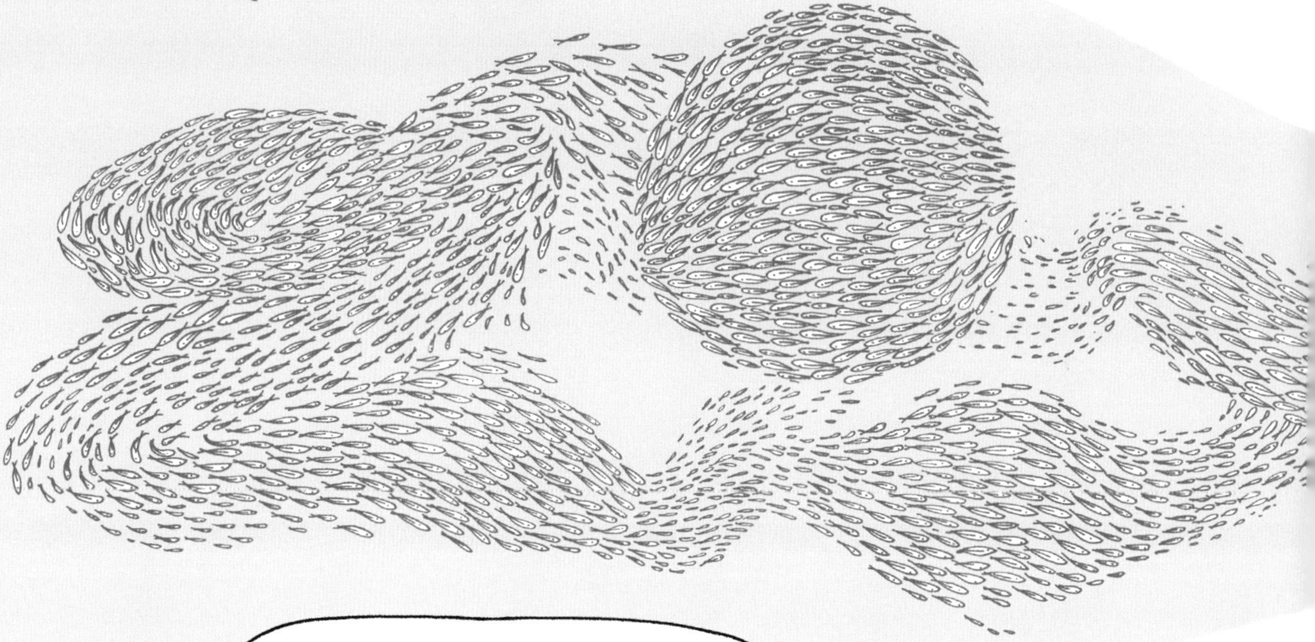

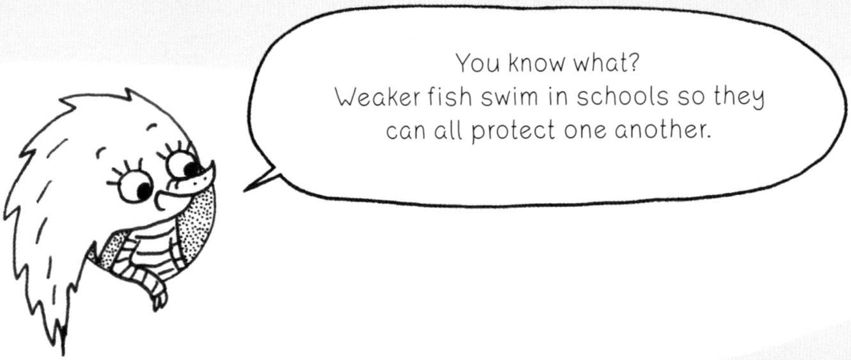
You know what? Weaker fish swim in schools so they can all protect one another.

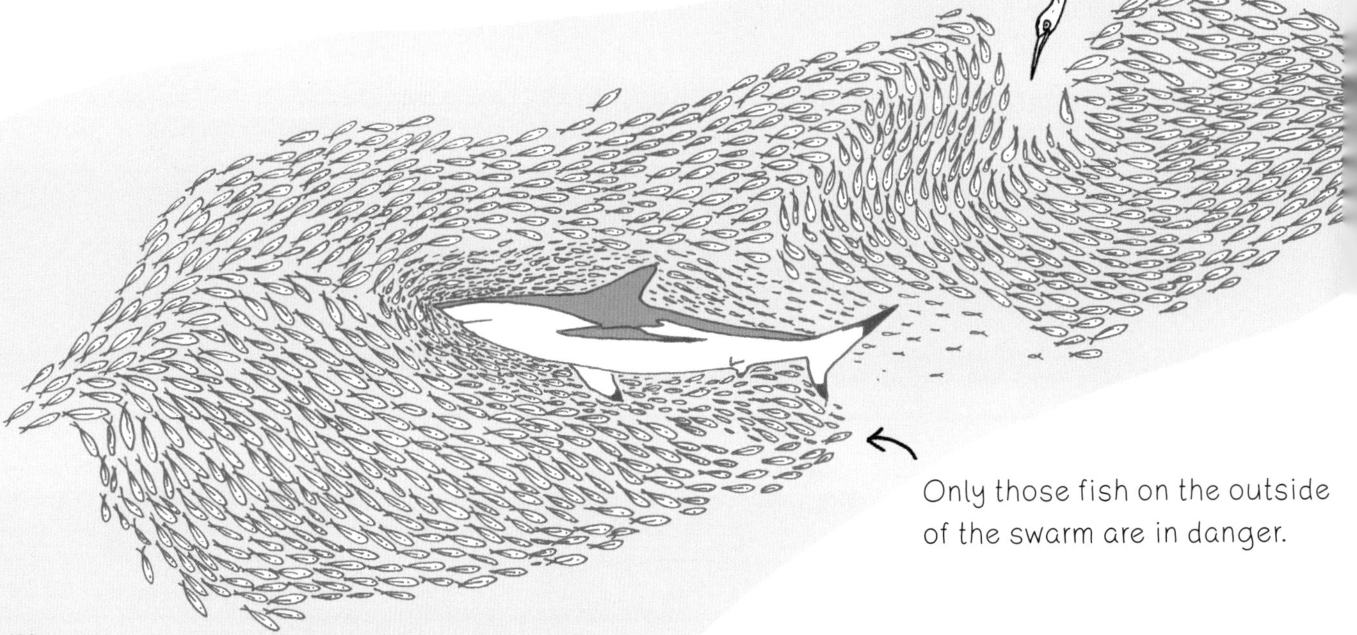
Only those fish on the outside of the swarm are in danger.

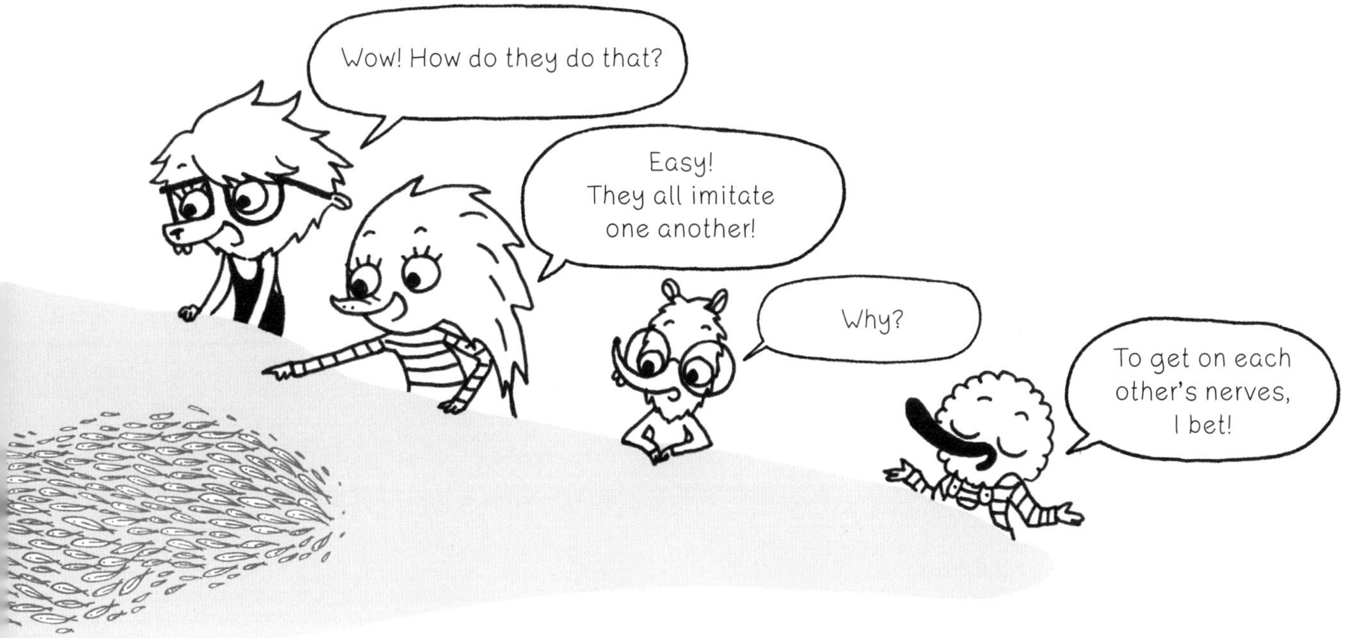
Wow! How do they do that?
Easy! They all imitate one another!
Why?
To get on each other's nerves, I bet!

Predators like sharks, dolphins, and gulls have to split the school up to have any chance of eating the fish.

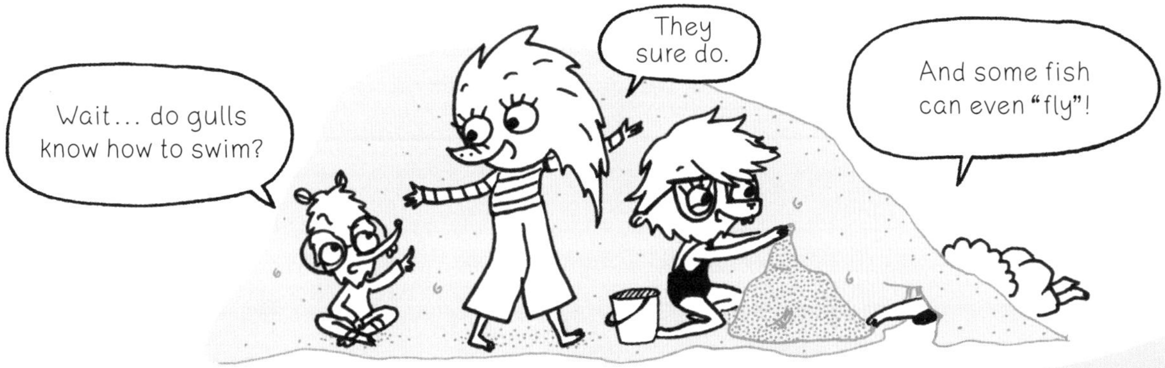
Wait… do gulls know how to swim?
They sure do.
And some fish can even "fly"!

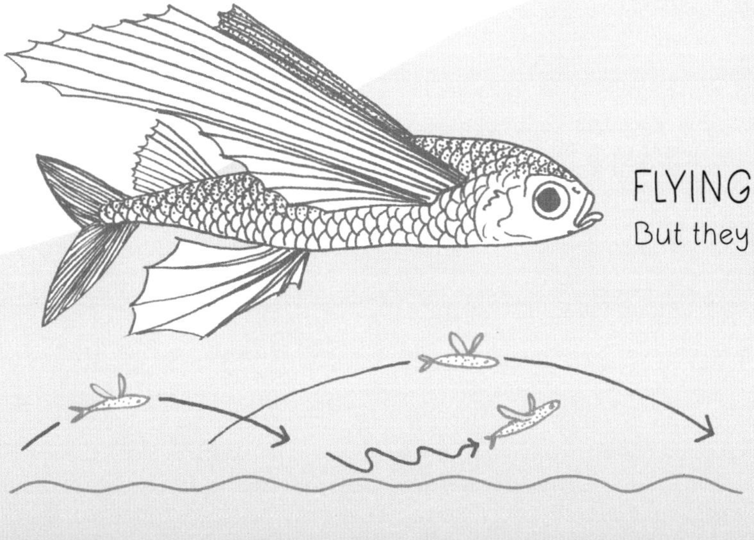

FLYING FISH don't really fly.
But they can jump and glide as far as 60 ft. (20 m).

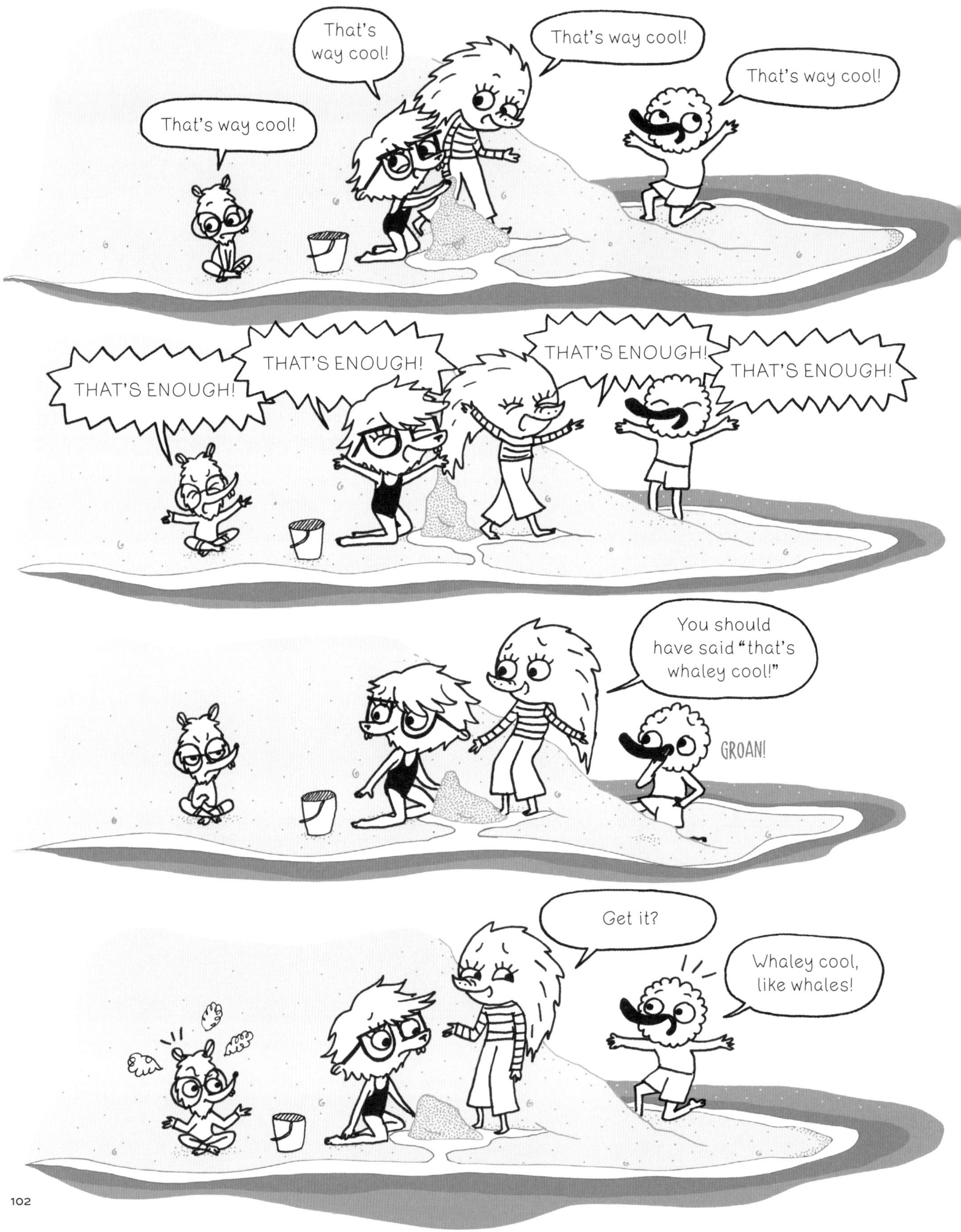
That's way cool!
That's way cool!
That's way cool!
That's way cool!
THAT'S ENOUGH!
THAT'S ENOUGH!
THAT'S ENOUGH!
THAT'S ENOUGH!
You should have said "that's whaley cool!"
GROAN!
Get it?
Whaley cool, like whales!

15 WHALES ARE COOL

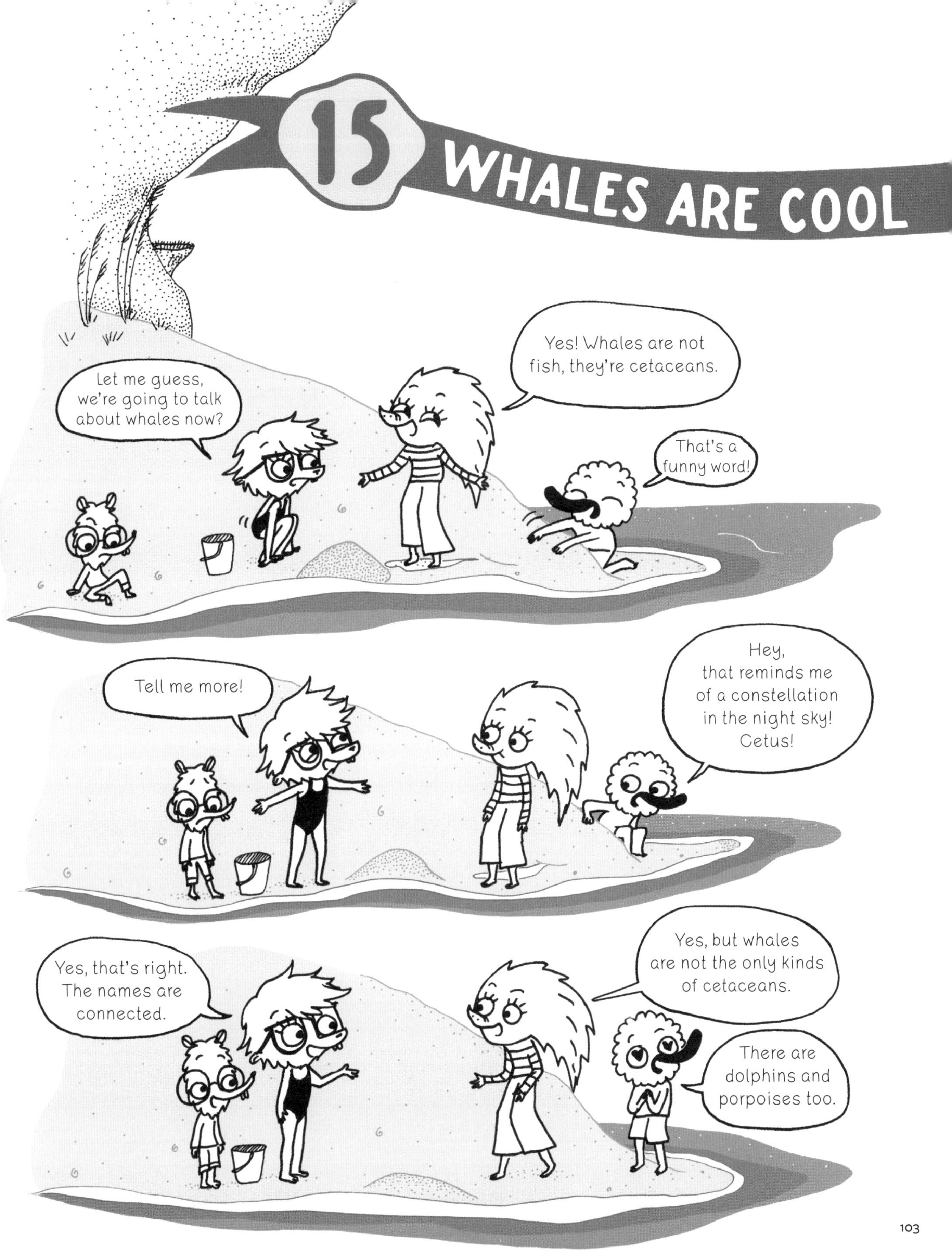
Let me guess, we're going to talk about whales now?
Yes! Whales are not fish, they're cetaceans.
That's a funny word!
Tell me more!
Hey, that reminds me of a constellation in the night sky! Cetus!
Yes, that's right. The names are connected.
Yes, but whales are not the only kinds of cetaceans.
There are dolphins and porpoises too.

CETACEANS

Cetaceans can travel hundreds of miles a day.

There are two main families. Those with teeth, like dolphins, are called Odontoceti. And those with baleen instead of teeth, like most whales, are called Mysticeti!

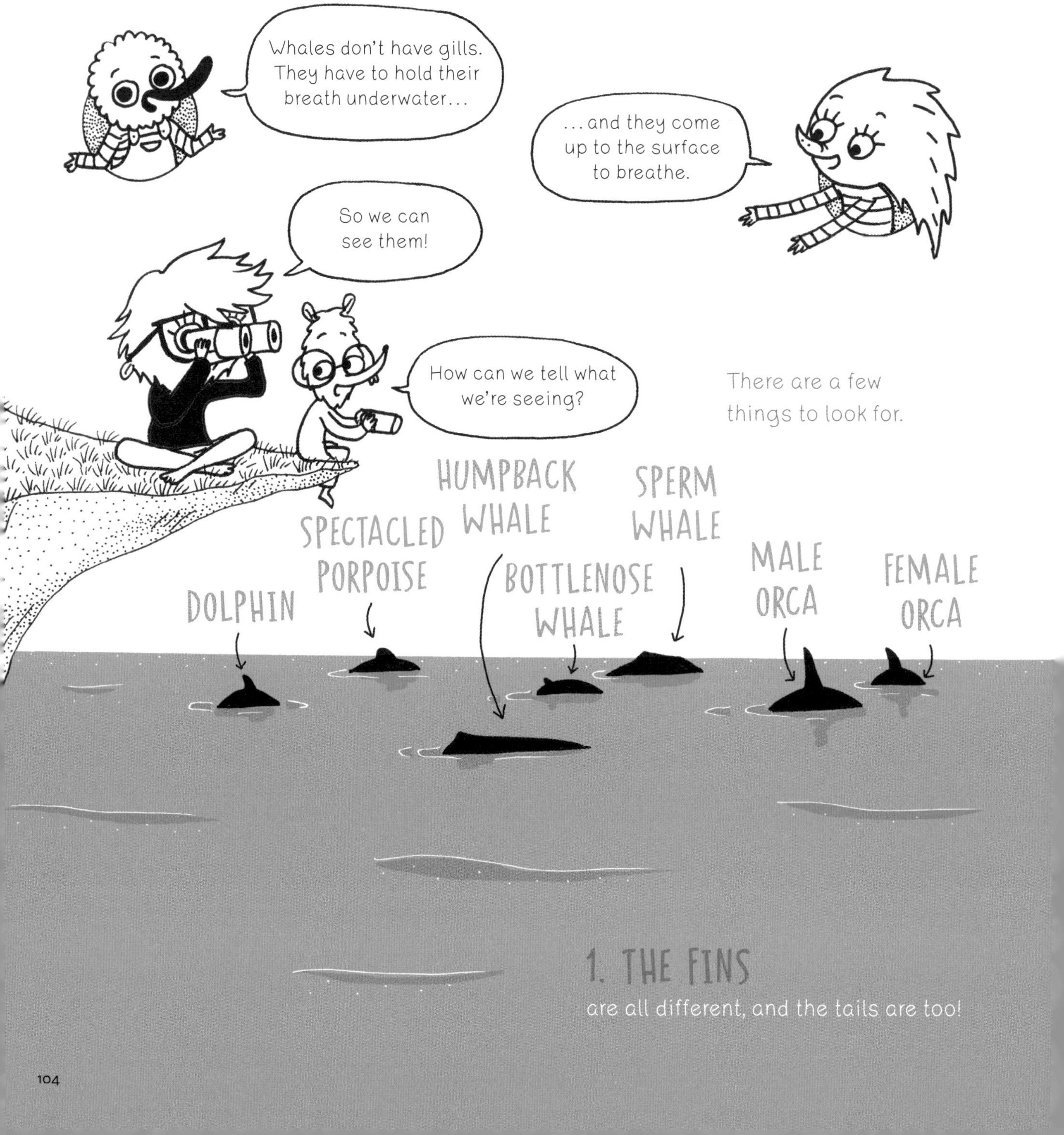
Whales don't have gills. They have to hold their breath underwater...
...and they come up to the surface to breathe.
So we can see them!
How can we tell what we're seeing?
There are a few things to look for.
DOLPHIN
SPECTACLED PORPOISE
HUMPBACK WHALE
BOTTLENOSE WHALE
SPERM WHALE
MALE ORCA
FEMALE ORCA

1. THE FINS

are all different, and the tails are too!

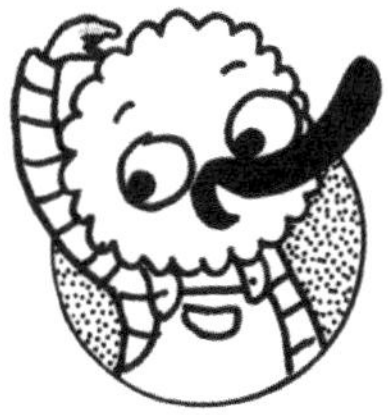

2. THE SPOUTS

Cetaceans breathe through nostrils on their heads that are called blowholes.

Baleen cetaceans have two blowholes, and toothed cetaceans only have one!

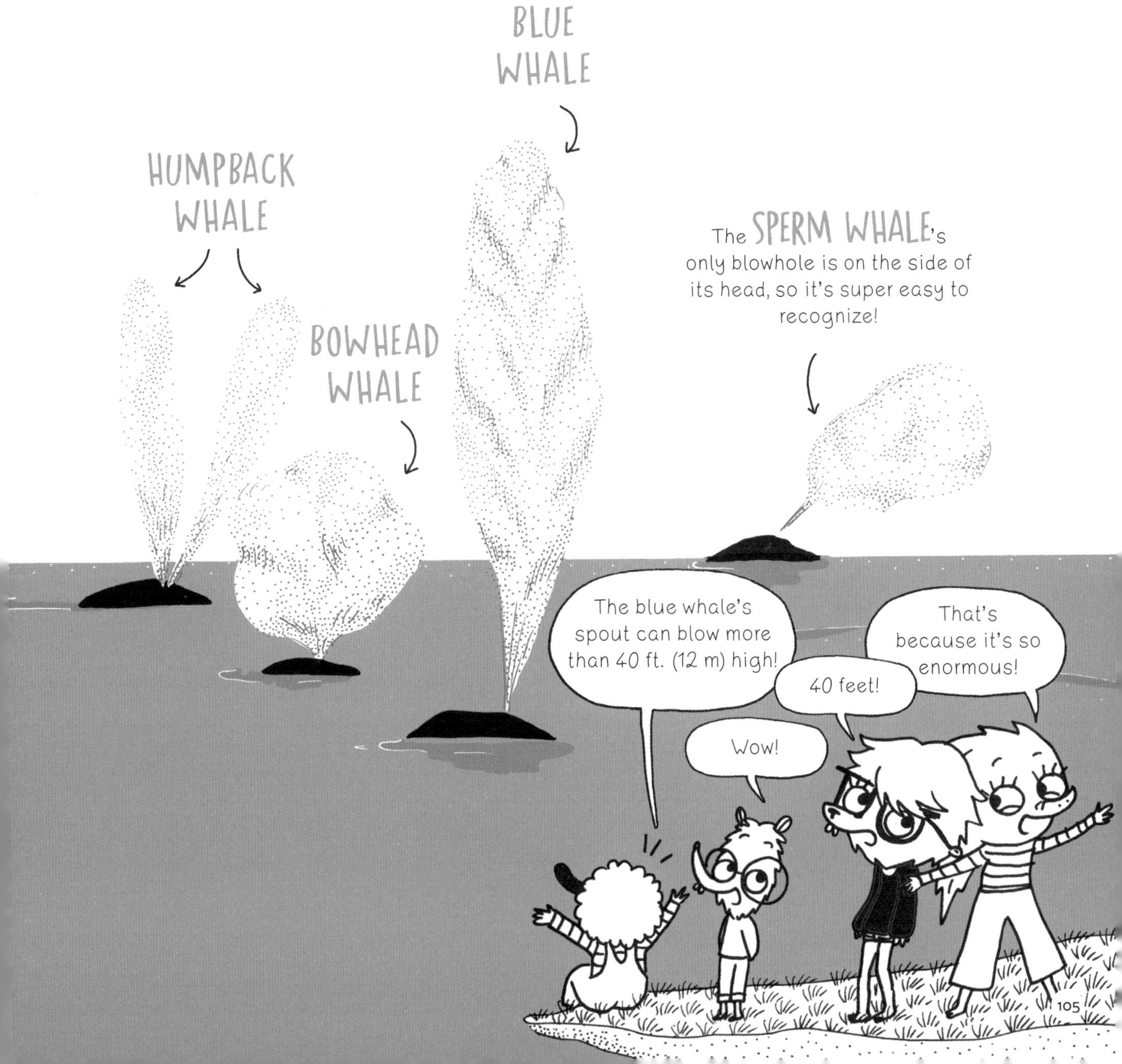

HUMPBACK WHALE
BOWHEAD WHALE
BLUE WHALE
The SPERM WHALE's only blowhole is on the side of its head, so it's super easy to recognize!
The blue whale's spout can blow more than 40 ft. (12 m) high!
Wow!
40 feet!
That's because it's so enormous!

THE BLUE WHALE

Like all cetaceans, the blue whale is a mammal. There are lots of baleen cetaceans, but the blue whale is the most well known of them all.

Blue whales can grow to more than 100 ft. (30 m) long and weigh as much as 330,000 lbs. (150,000 kg)!

Their young weigh more than 4,000 lbs. (2,000 kg) at birth!

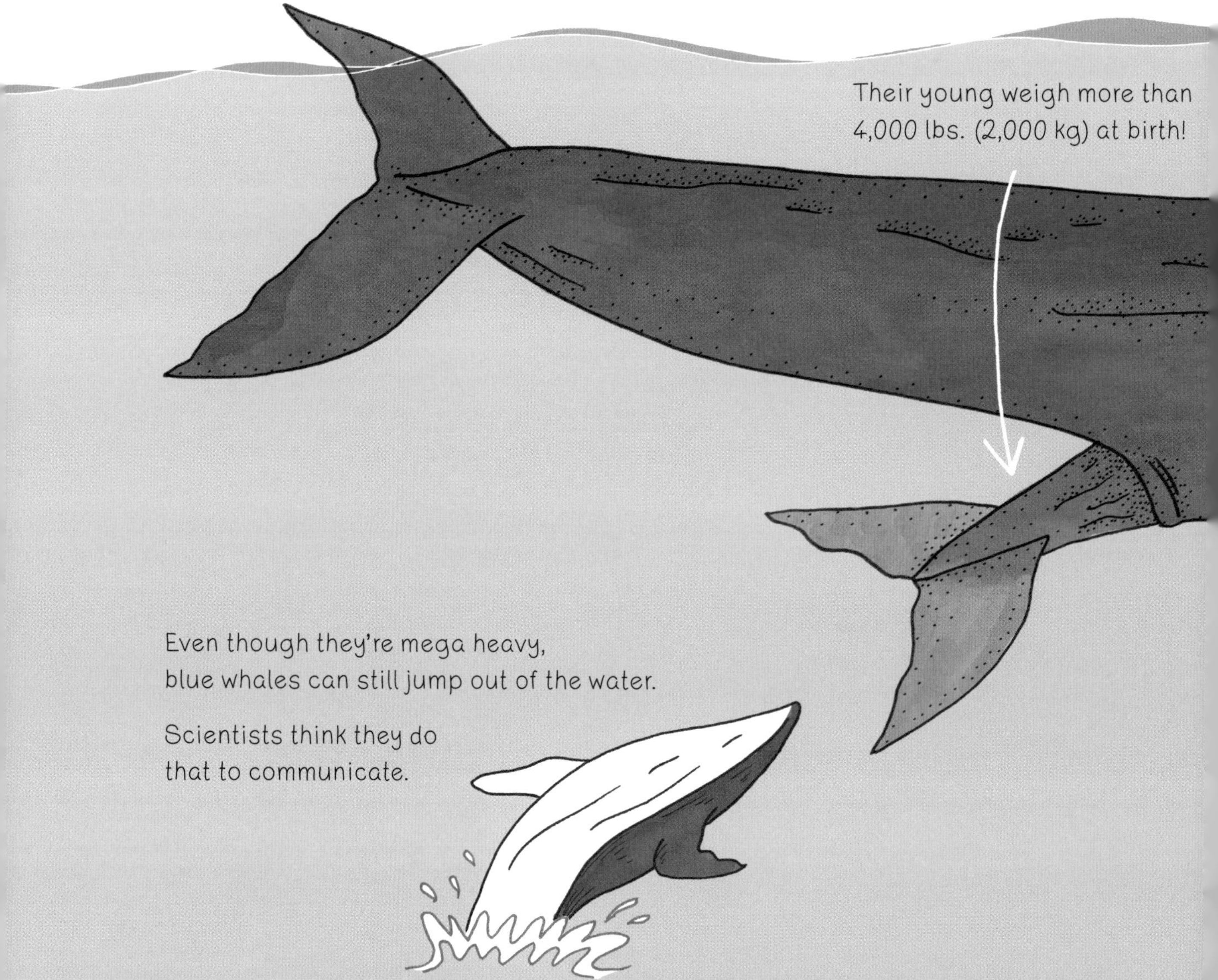

Even though they're mega heavy, blue whales can still jump out of the water.

Scientists think they do that to communicate.

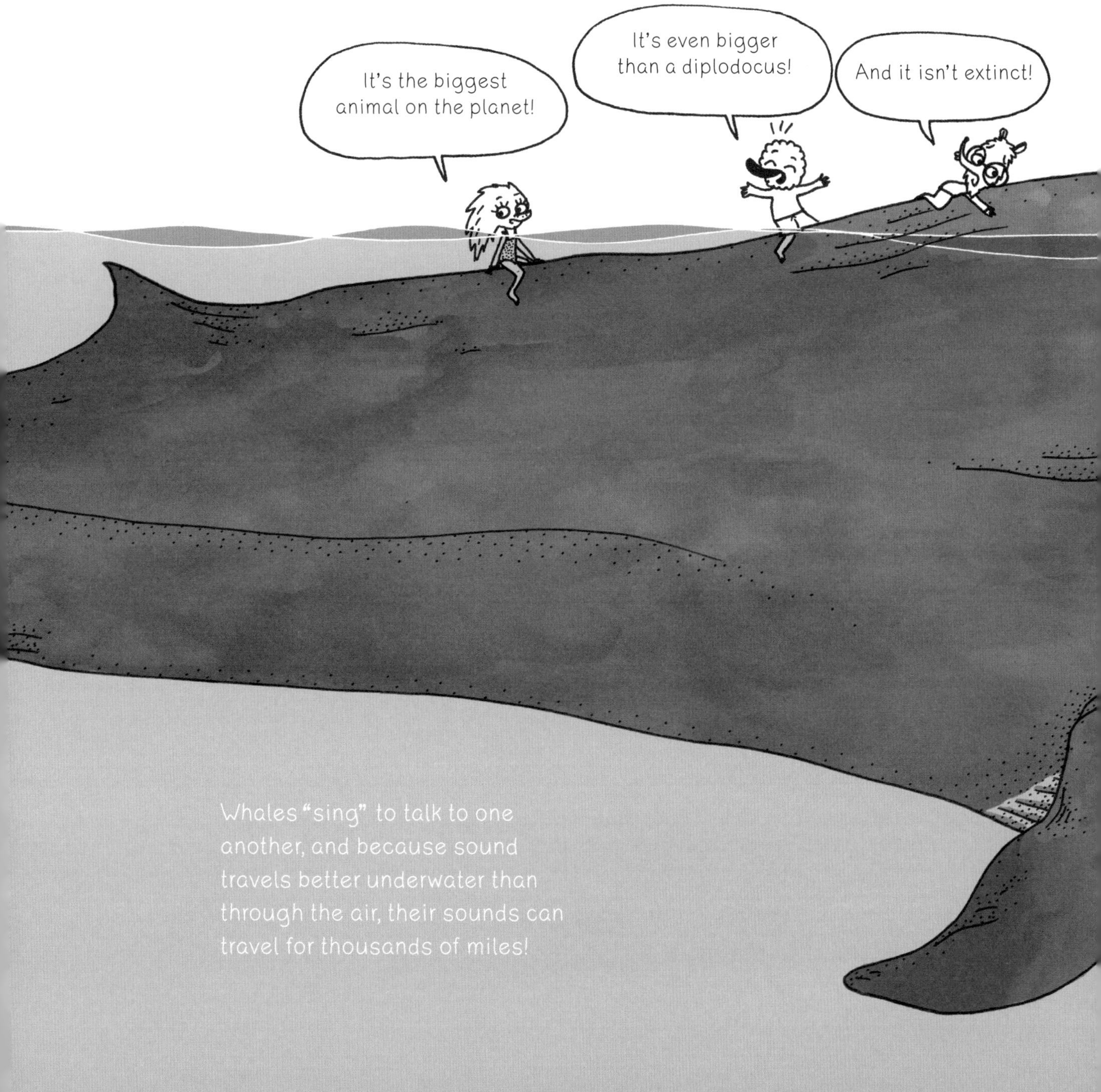
It's the biggest animal on the planet!
It's even bigger than a diplodocus!
And it isn't extinct!
Whales "sing" to talk to one another, and because sound travels better underwater than through the air, their sounds can travel for thousands of miles!

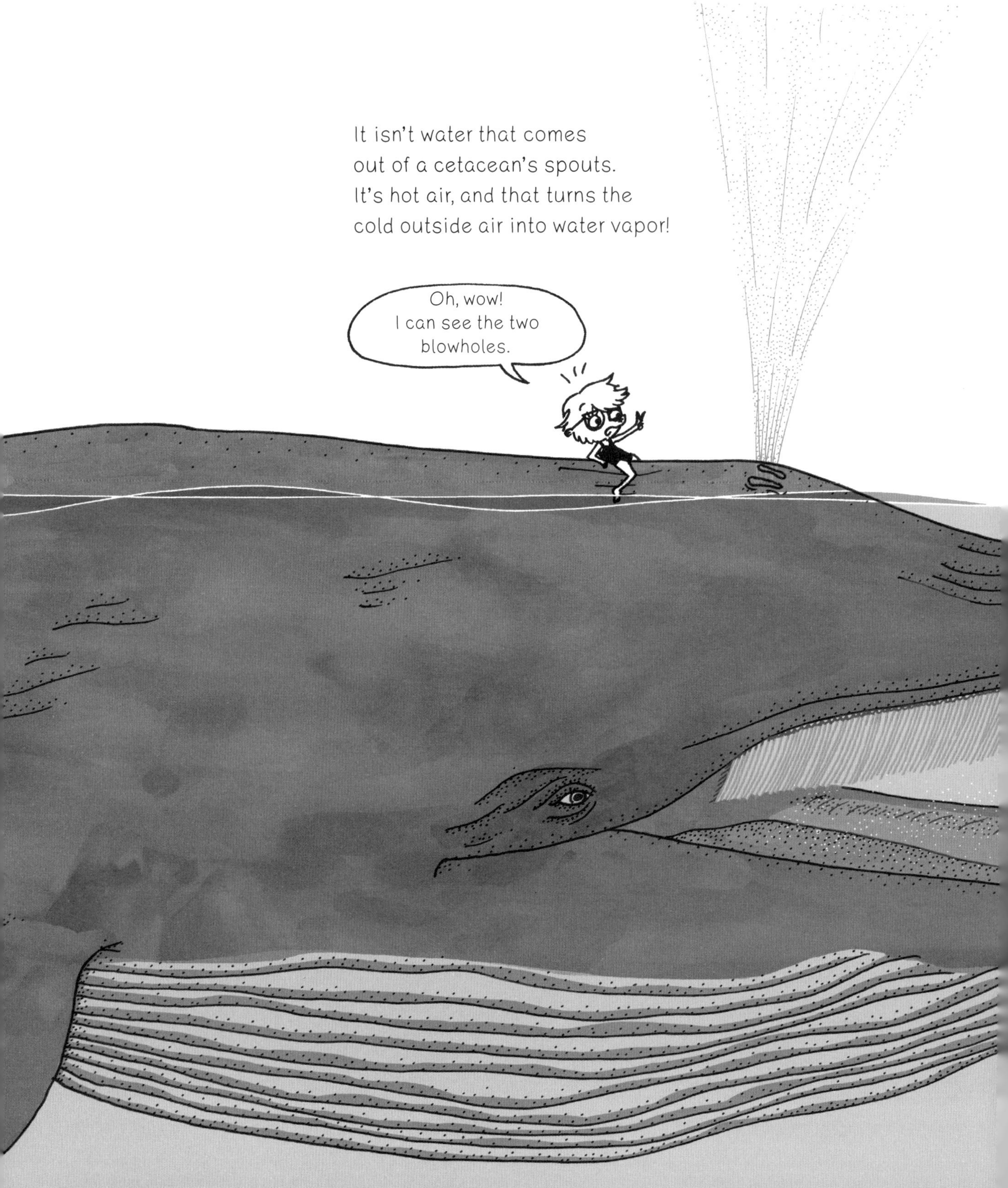
It isn't water that comes out of a cetacean's spouts. It's hot air, and that turns the cold outside air into water vapor!
Oh, wow! I can see the two blowholes.

What's baleen?

BALEEN

is made up of lots of strips of keratin (the stuff that fingernails are made of)! These strips are like the bristles of a brush. They keep food in the whale's mouth and let water filter out.

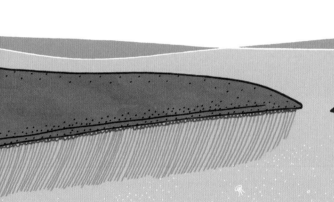

Plankton can come in, but it can't get out.

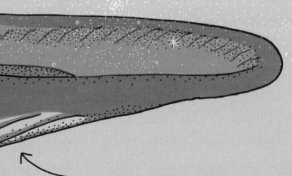

They may be massive, but whales feed on plankton. Their favorite food is krill, a tiny crustacean.

The folds under a blue whale's mouth expand!

It can drink nearly 16,000 gallons (60,000 liters) of water in one gulp!

TOOTHED CETACEANS

There are lots more species of cetaceans with teeth than with baleen. Some of these creatures are fearsome predators, with sharp teeth and a fatty organ on their head called a melon. The sperm whale has an enormous melon!

DOLPHINS

There are many species in the dolphin family, including orcas and pilot whales. There are even pink river dolphins that live in fresh water!

BOTTLENOSE DOLPHIN

COMMON DOLPHIN

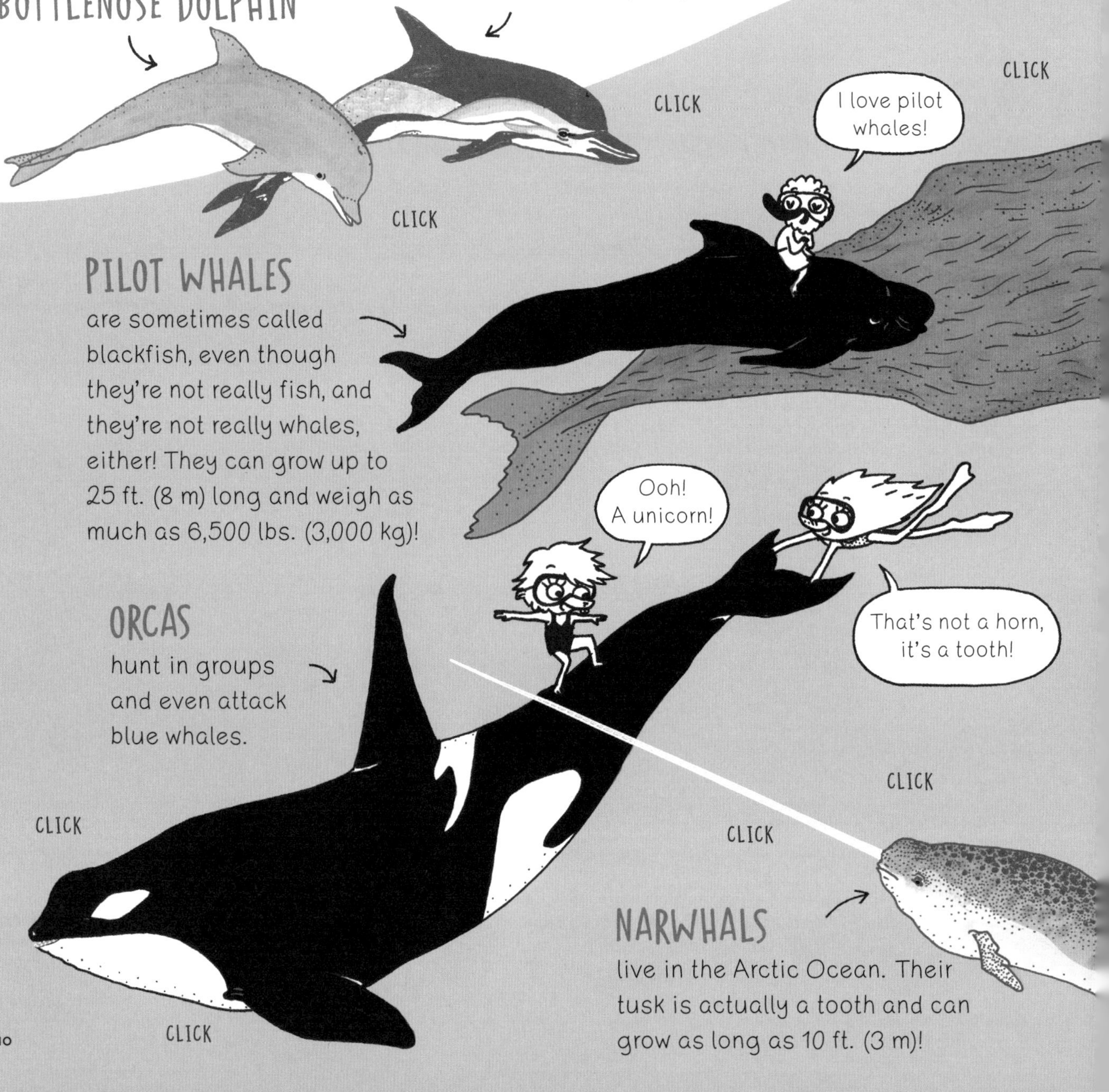
CLICK
CLICK
CLICK
I love pilot whales!
Ooh! A unicorn!
That's not a horn, it's a tooth!
CLICK
CLICK
CLICK
CLICK

PILOT WHALES

are sometimes called blackfish, even though they're not really fish, and they're not really whales, either! They can grow up to 25 ft. (8 m) long and weigh as much as 6,500 lbs. (3,000 kg)!

ORCAS

hunt in groups and even attack blue whales.

NARWHALS

live in the Arctic Ocean. Their tusk is actually a tooth and can grow as long as 10 ft. (3 m)!

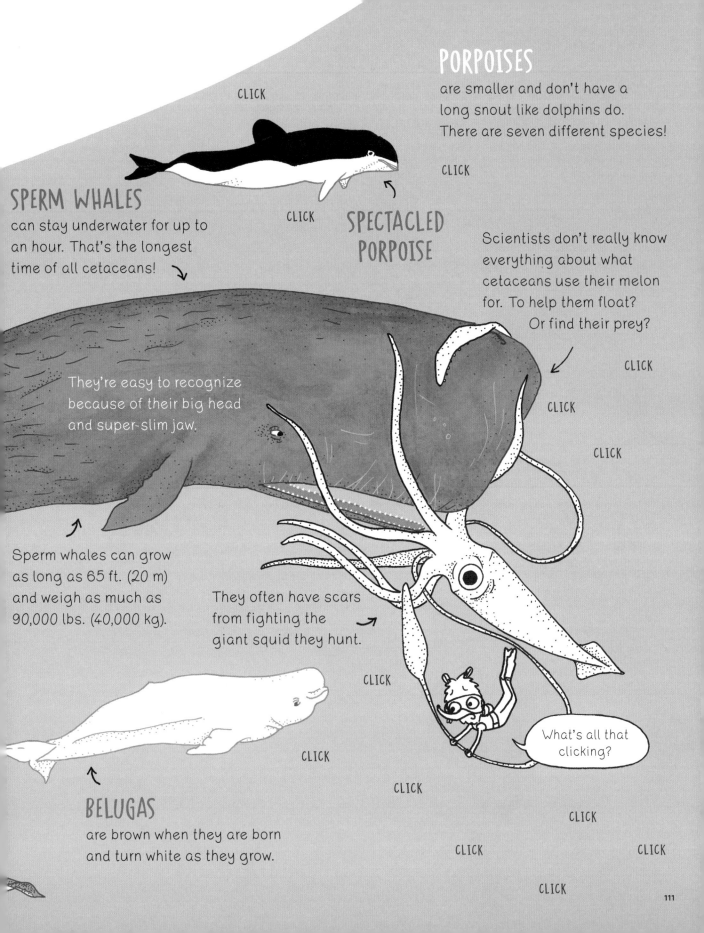

CLICK

PORPOISES

are smaller and don't have a
long snout like dolphins do.
There are seven different species!

CLICK

SPERM WHALES

can stay underwater for up to
an hour. That's the longest
time of all cetaceans!

CLICK

SPECTACLED
PORPOISE

Scientists don't really know
everything about what
cetaceans use their melon
for. To help them float?
Or find their prey?

CLICK

CLICK

CLICK

They're easy to recognize
because of their big head
and super-slim jaw.

Sperm whales can grow
as long as 65 ft. (20 m)
and weigh as much as
90,000 lbs. (40,000 kg).

They often have scars
from fighting the
giant squid they hunt.

CLICK

CLICK

What's all that
clicking?

CLICK

CLICK

CLICK

BELUGAS

are brown when they are born
and turn white as they grow.

CLICK

CLICK

CLICK

111

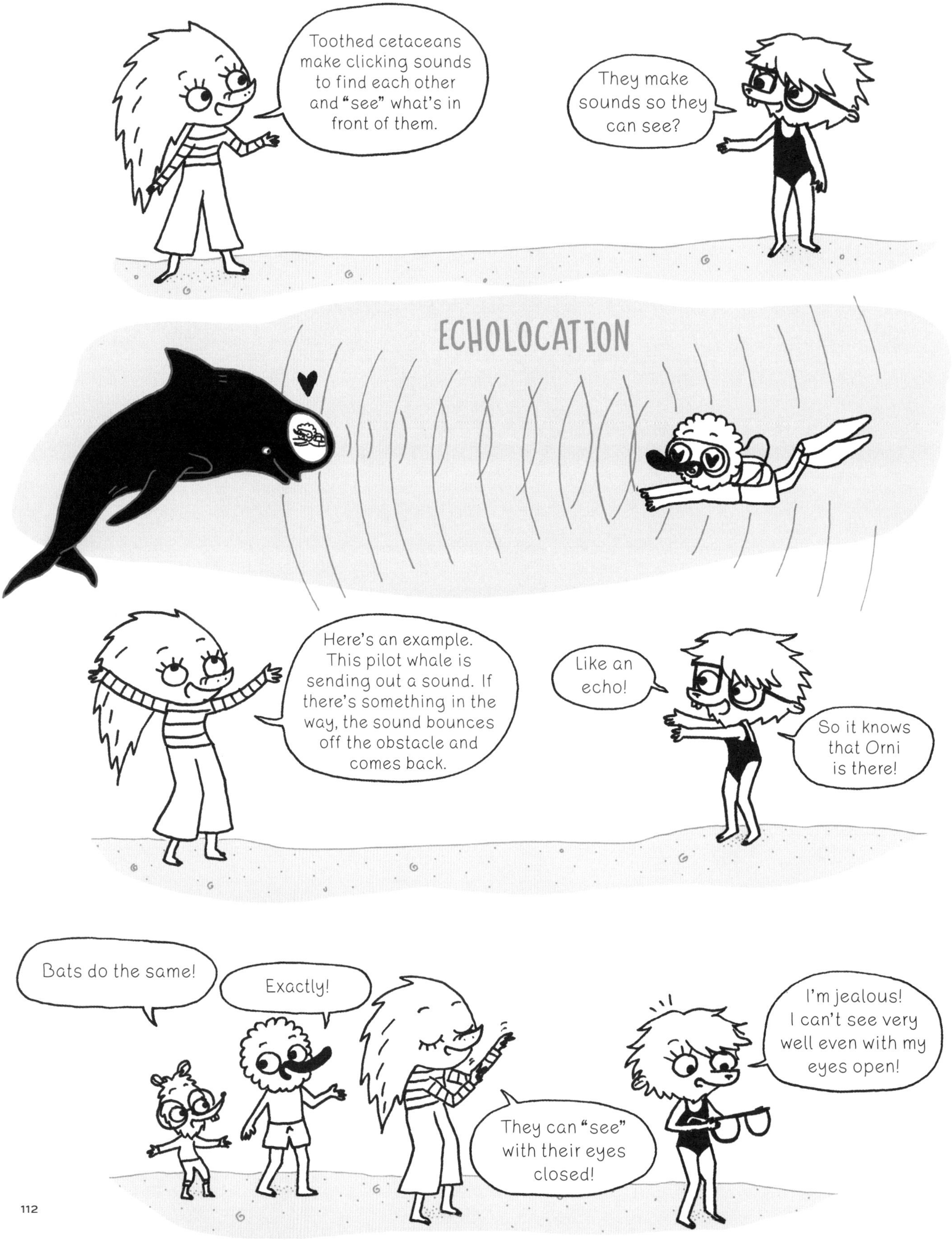
Toothed cetaceans make clicking sounds to find each other and "see" what's in front of them.
They make sounds so they can see?
ECHOLOCATION
Here's an example. This pilot whale is sending out a sound. If there's something in the way, the sound bounces off the obstacle and comes back.
Like an echo!
So it knows that Orni is there!
Bats do the same!
Exactly!
They can "see" with their eyes closed!
I'm jealous! I can't see very well even with my eyes open!

16 SIRENIANS AND PINNIPEDS

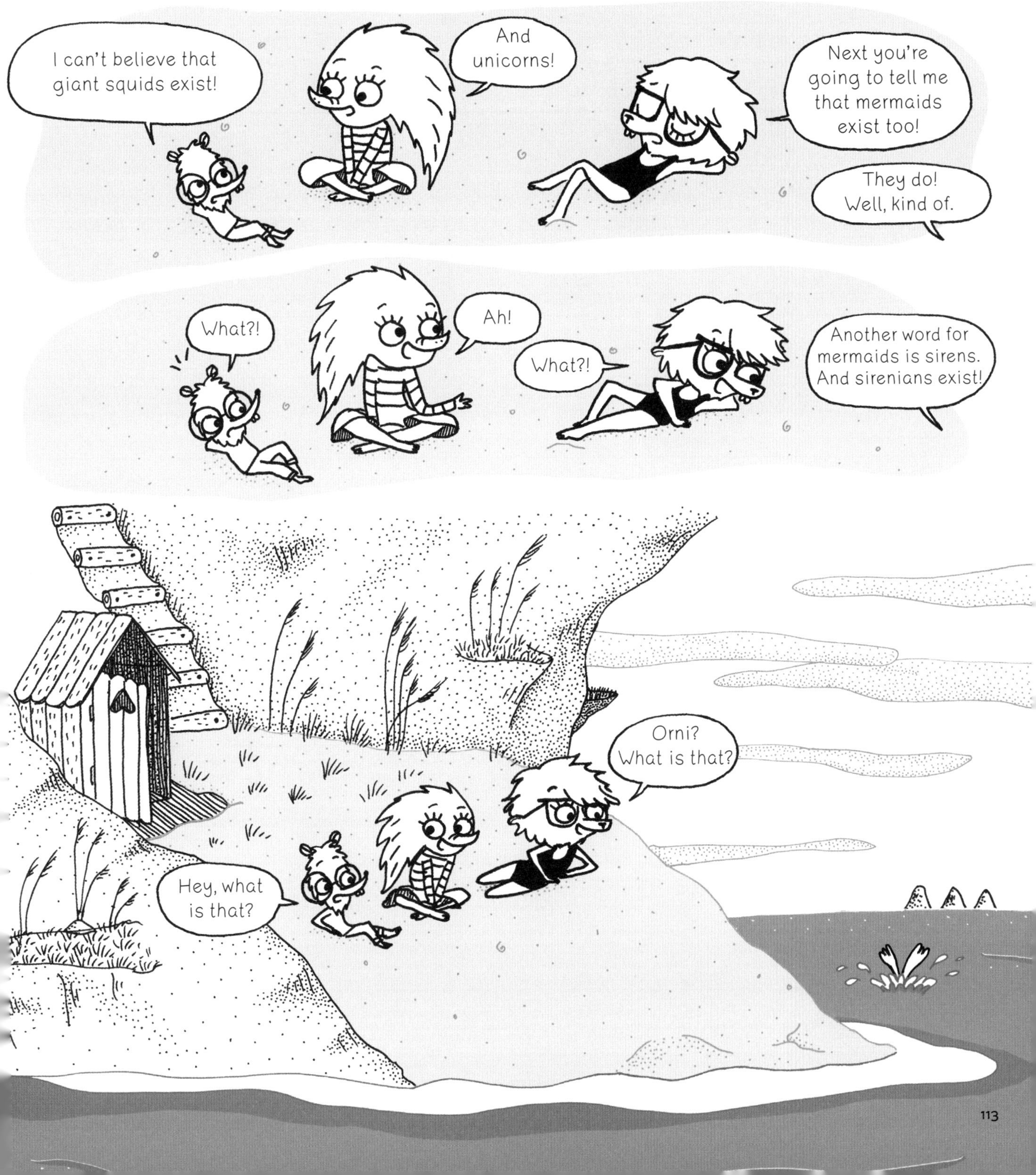
I can't believe that giant squids exist!
And unicorns!
Next you're going to tell me that mermaids exist too!
They do! Well, kind of.
What?!
Ah!
What?!
Another word for mermaids is sirens. And sirenians exist!
Orni? What is that?
Hey, what is that?

SIRENIANS

are peaceful mammals. They are mainly herbivores, and they live close to shore because they can't stay underwater for very long. There are four different species of sirenians. They're not the same as pinnipeds, which look similar but are a different family.

DUGONG

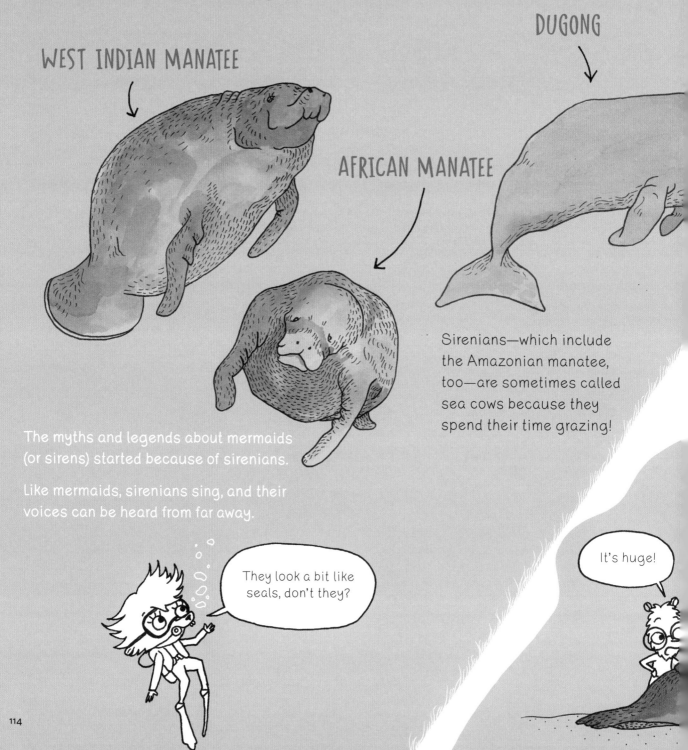

WEST INDIAN MANATEE

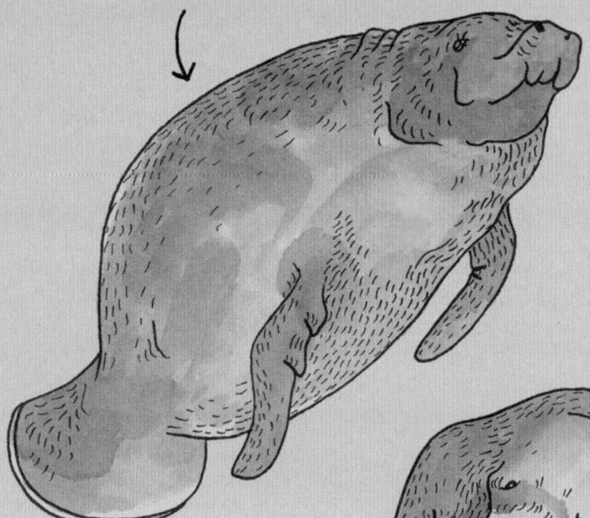

AFRICAN MANATEE

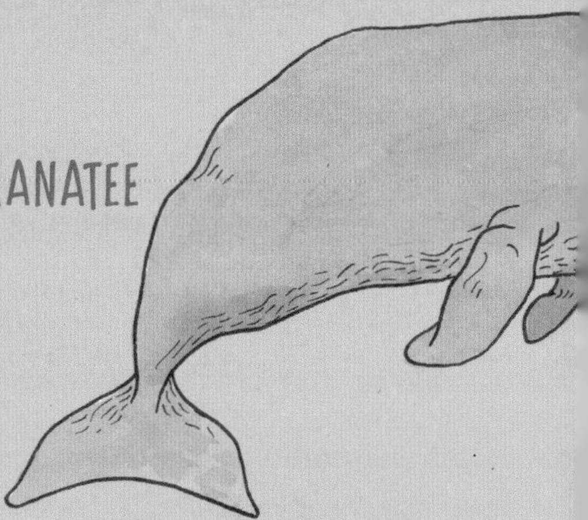

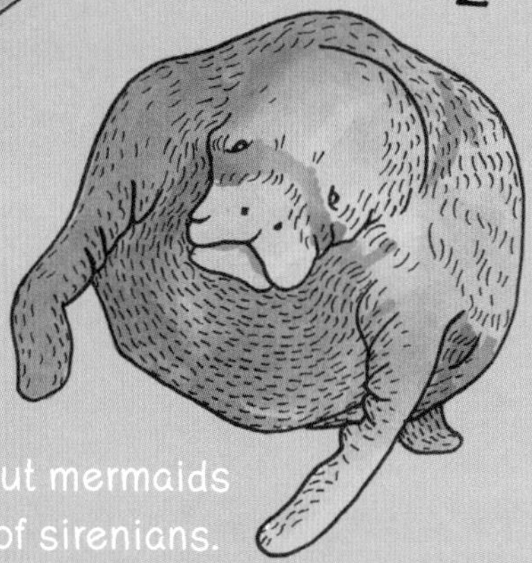

Sirenians—which include the Amazonian manatee, too—are sometimes called sea cows because they spend their time grazing!

The myths and legends about mermaids (or sirens) started because of sirenians.

Like mermaids, sirenians sing, and their voices can be heard from far away.

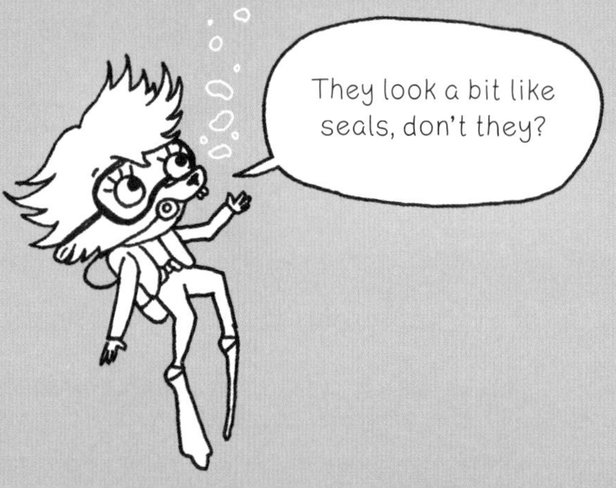
They look a bit like seals, don't they?

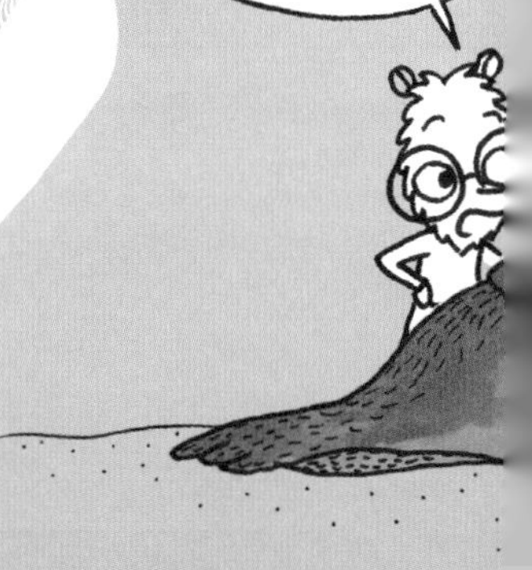
It's huge!

PINNIPEDS

are carnivorous mammals.

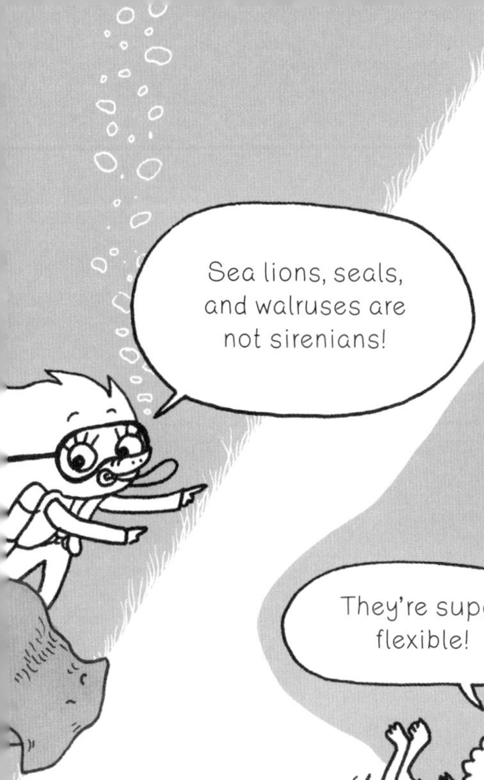

Sea lions, seals, and walruses are not sirenians!

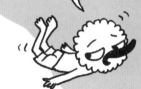

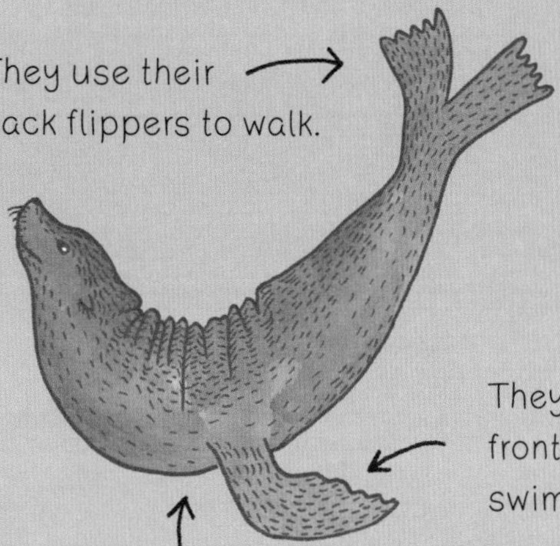

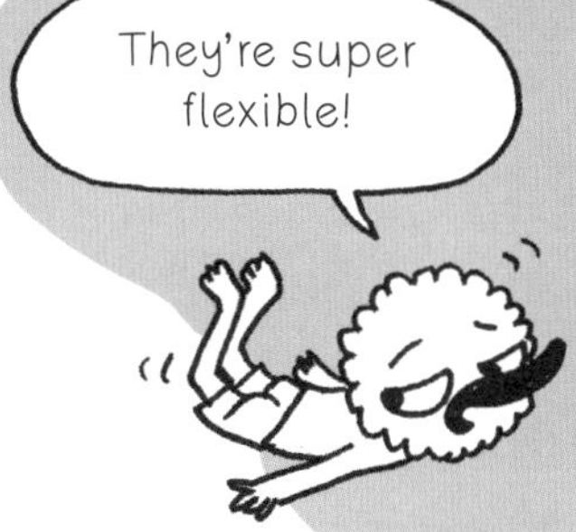

SEA LIONS

They have ears!

They use their back flippers to walk.

They're super flexible!

They use their big front flippers to swim extremely fast!

CALIFORNIA SEA LION

STELLER'S SEA LION

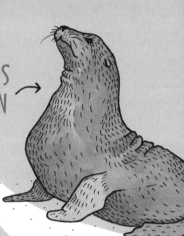

SEALS

There are different species of seals.

They have holes instead of ears.

It's hard for them to sit up when they're out of the water.

Their back flippers make them super-good swimmers.

A baby seal is called a seal pup!

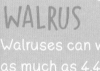

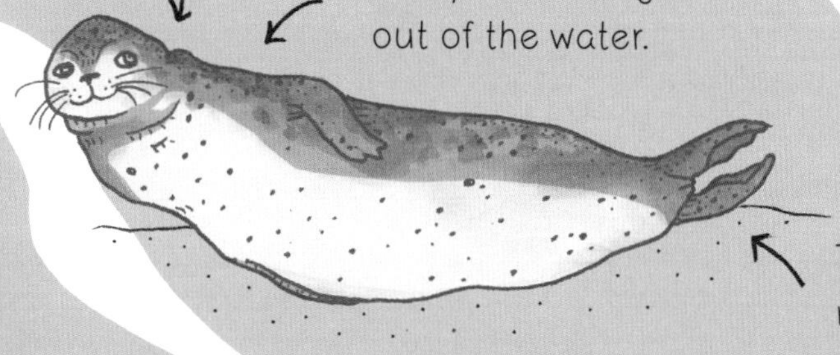

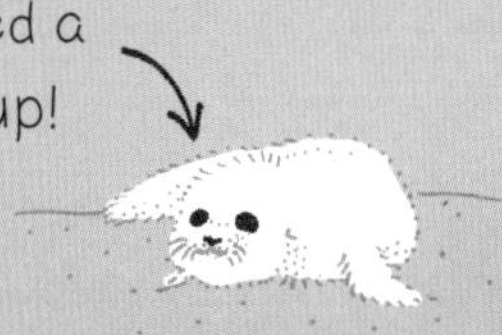

WALRUS

Walruses can weigh as much as 4,400 lbs. (2,000 kg)!

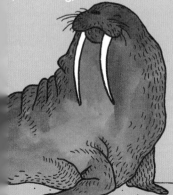

There's only one species in the walrus family.

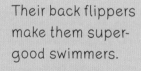

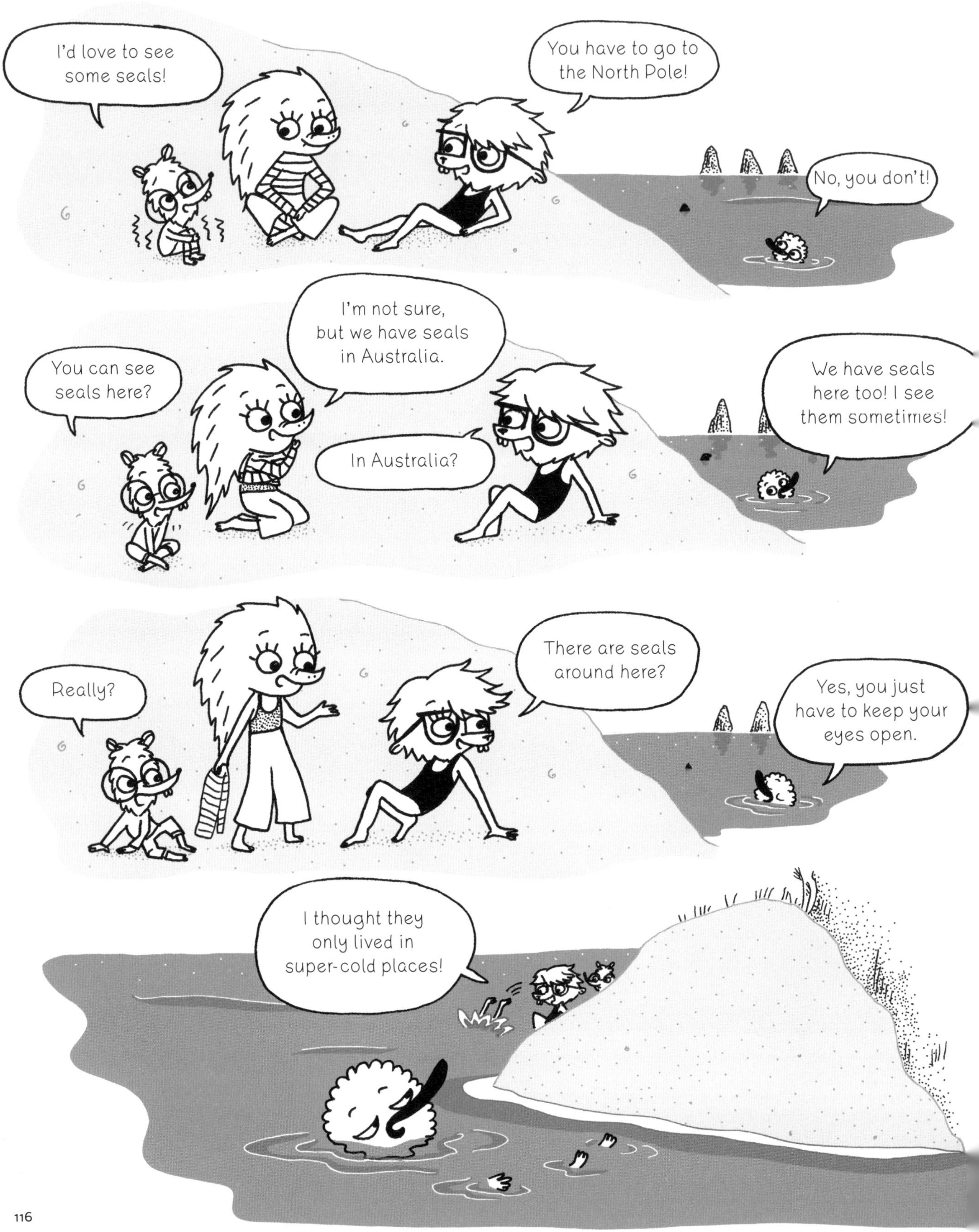
I'd love to see some seals!
You have to go to the North Pole!
No, you don't!
You can see seals here?
I'm not sure, but we have seals in Australia.
In Australia?
We have seals here too! I see them sometimes!
Really?
There are seals around here?
Yes, you just have to keep your eyes open.
I thought they only lived in super-cold places!

17 IT'S FREEZING!

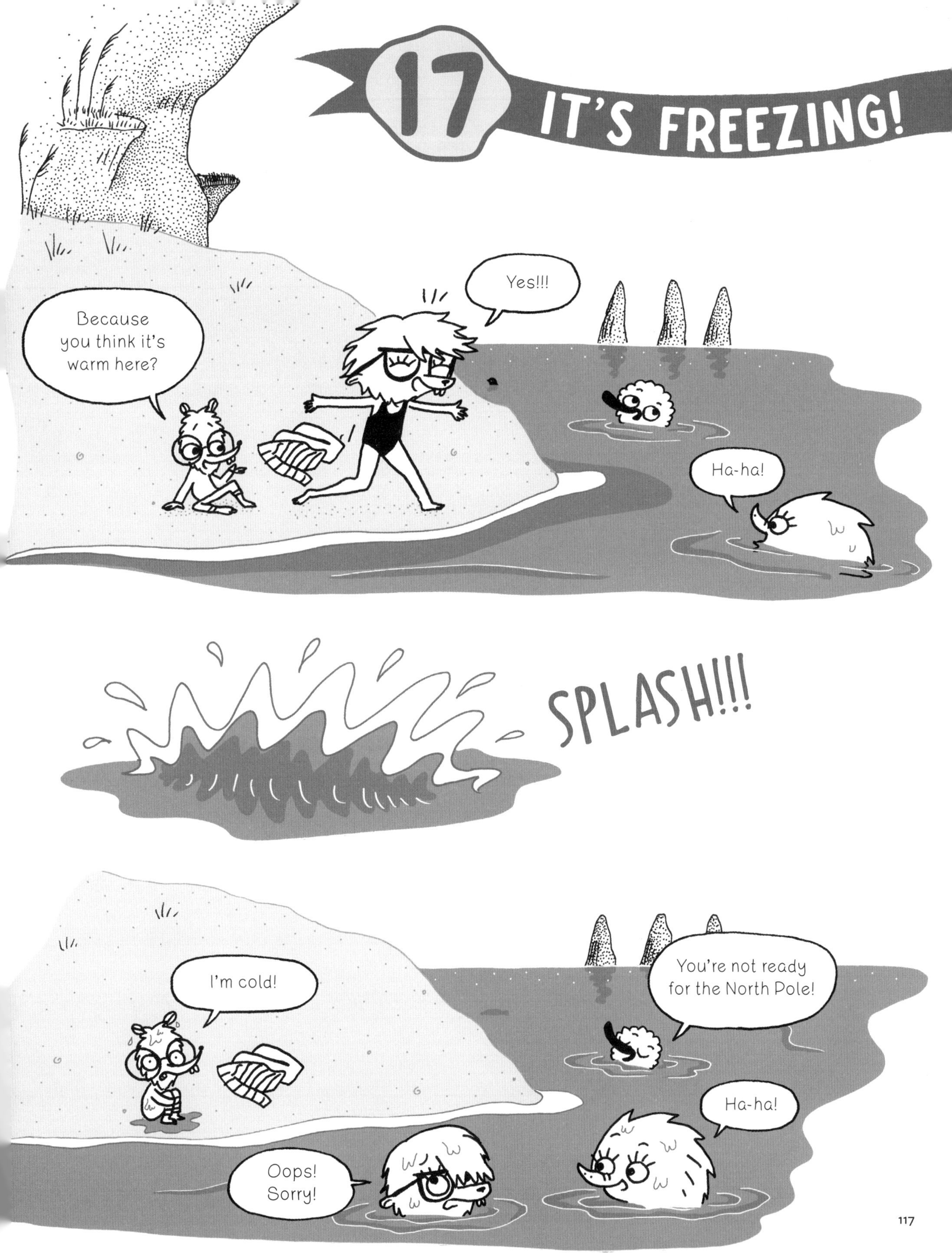

Because you think it's warm here?
Yes!!!
Ha-ha!
SPLASH!!!
I'm cold!
You're not ready for the North Pole!
Ha-ha!
Oops! Sorry!

THE ARCTIC OCEAN AND THE SOUTHERN OCEAN

are the oceans around the North Pole and the South Pole. The water there is very cold!

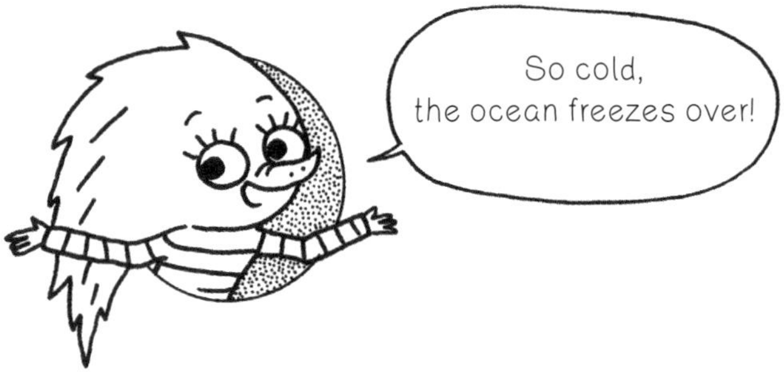
So cold,
the ocean freezes over!

This is called SEA ICE. That's ice that floats. There are two kinds of sea ice.

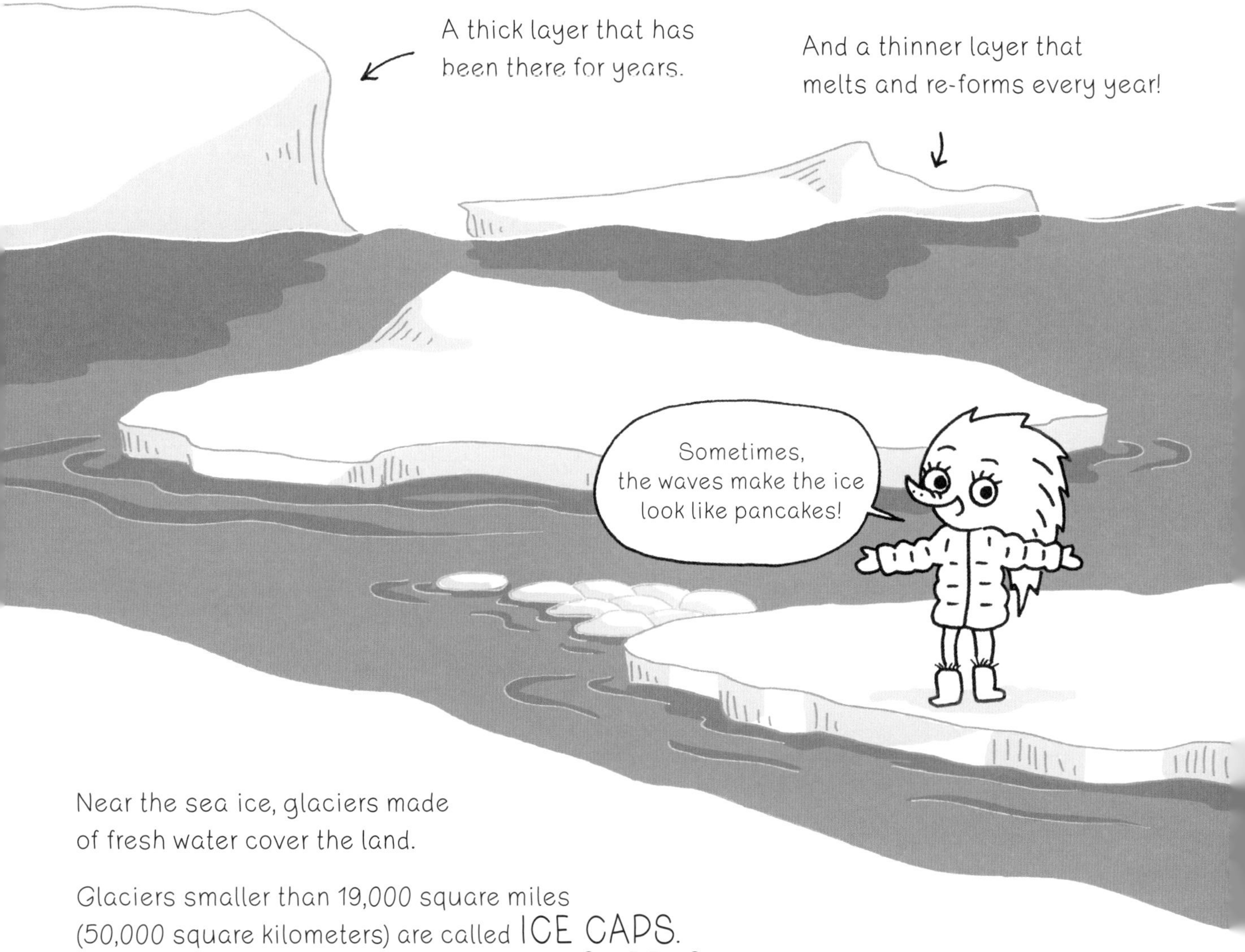
A thick layer that has been there for years.
And a thinner layer that melts and re-forms every year!
Sometimes, the waves make the ice look like pancakes!

Near the sea ice, glaciers made of fresh water cover the land.

Glaciers smaller than 19,000 square miles (50,000 square kilometers) are called ICE CAPS. Glaciers smaller than that are called ICE SHEETS.

Sometimes, big chunks of ice can break off from glaciers. These are called icebergs. They are made up of fresh water and can have different shapes.

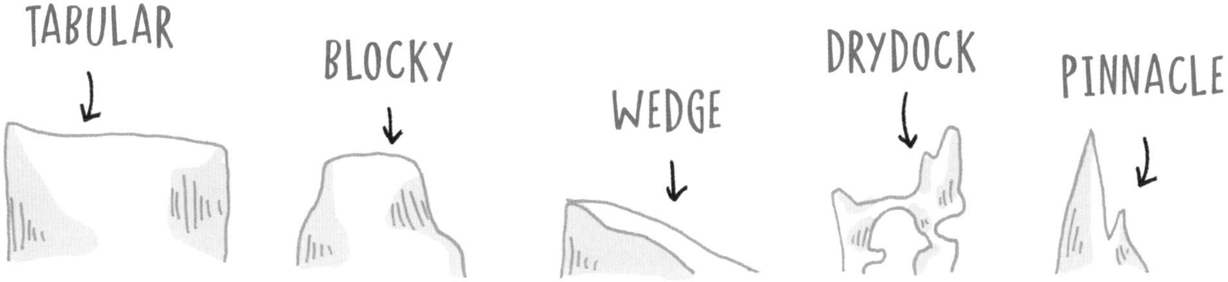
TABULAR
BLOCKY
WEDGE
DRYDOCK
PINNACLE

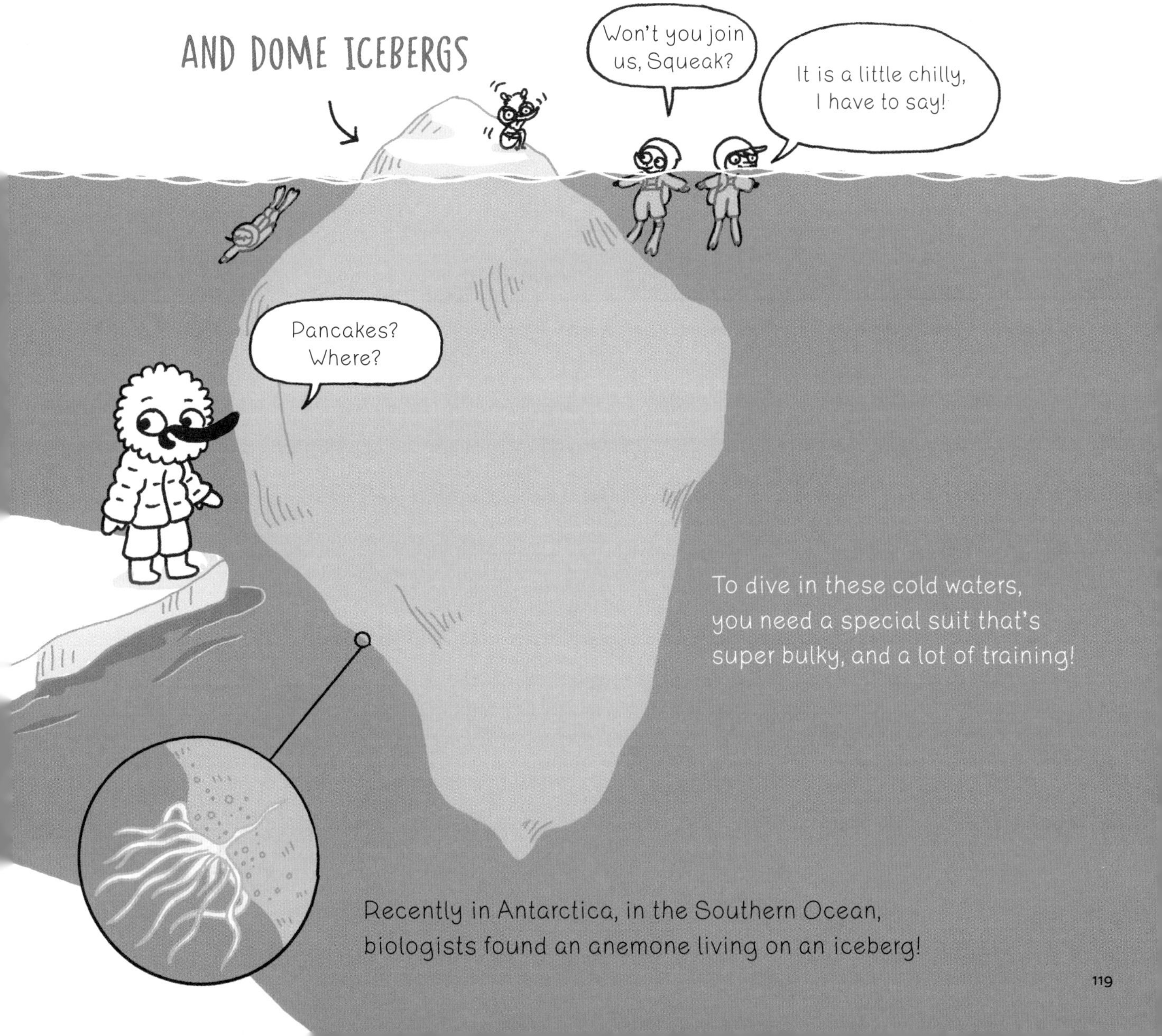
AND DOME ICEBERGS
Won't you join us, Squeak?
It is a little chilly, I have to say!
Pancakes? Where?

To dive in these cold waters, you need a special suit that's super bulky, and a lot of training!

Recently in Antarctica, in the Southern Ocean, biologists found an anemone living on an iceberg!

THE ARCTIC OCEAN

The Arctic Ocean is the smallest of all the oceans.
It's also the shallowest. It's extremely cold, but lots of animals live there!

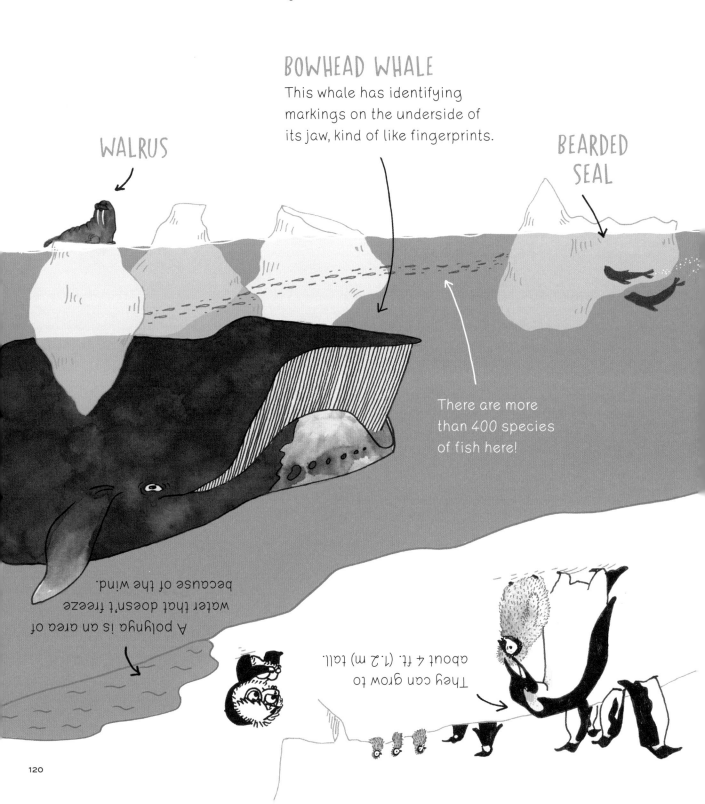

WALRUS

BOWHEAD WHALE

This whale has identifying
markings on the underside of
its jaw, kind of like fingerprints.

BEARDED SEAL

There are more
than 400 species
of fish here!

A polynya is an area of
water that doesn't freeze
because of the wind.

They can grow to
about 4 ft. (1.2 m) tall.

THE POLAR BEAR

is the symbol of the North Pole! The word "arctic" comes from "arktos," the Greek word for bear.

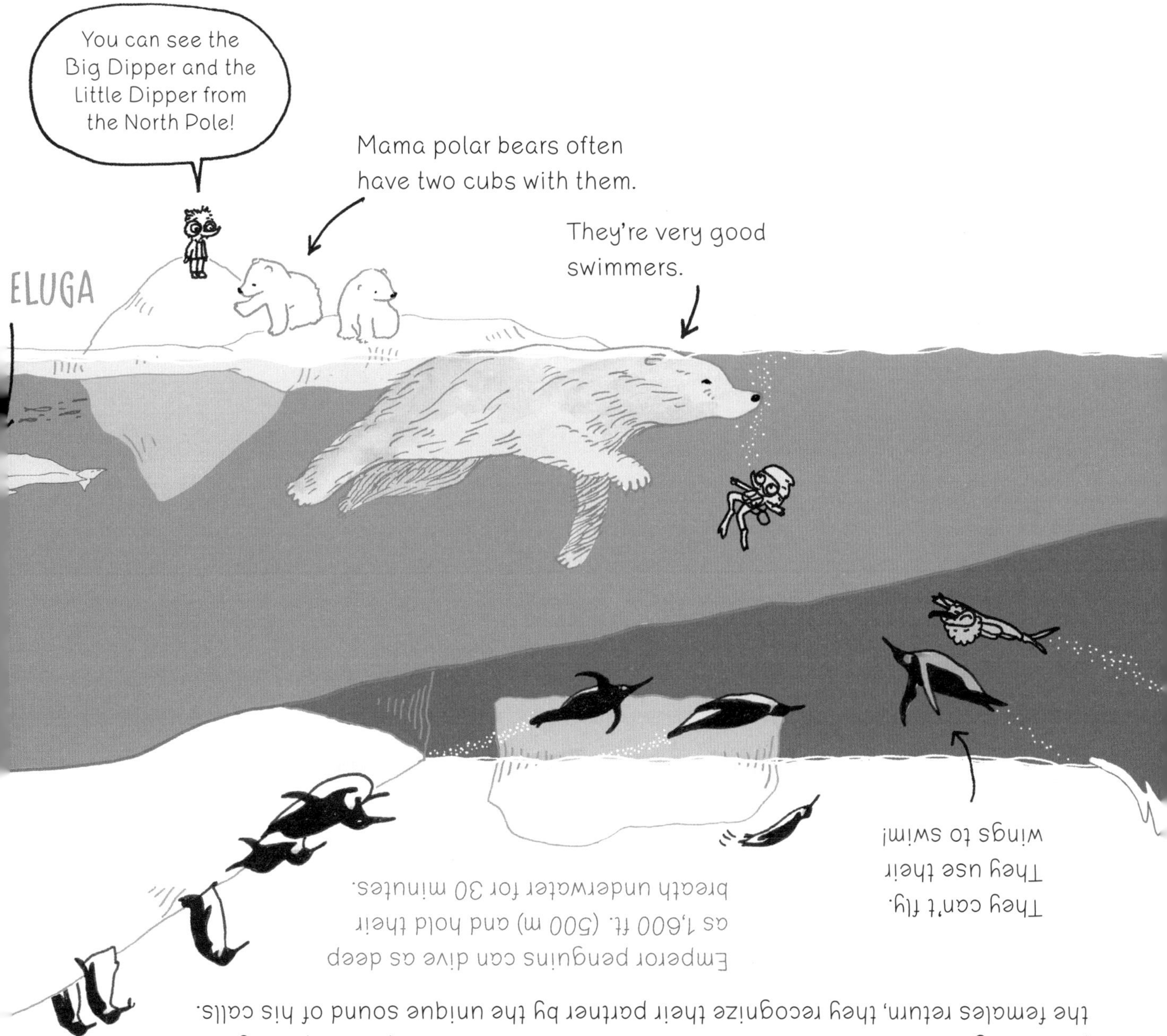
You can see the Big Dipper and the Little Dipper from the North Pole!
Mama polar bears often have two cubs with them.
They're very good swimmers.
ELUGA
They can't fly. They use their wings to swim!
Emperor penguins can dive as deep as 1,600 ft. (500 m) and hold their breath underwater for 30 minutes.

THE SOUTHERN OCEAN

EMPEROR PENGUINS

live in colonies. Every year, the females lay an egg and the males incubate it while their partners go off in search of food, sometimes as far as 200 mi. (300 km) away. When the females return, they recognize their partner by the unique sound of his calls.

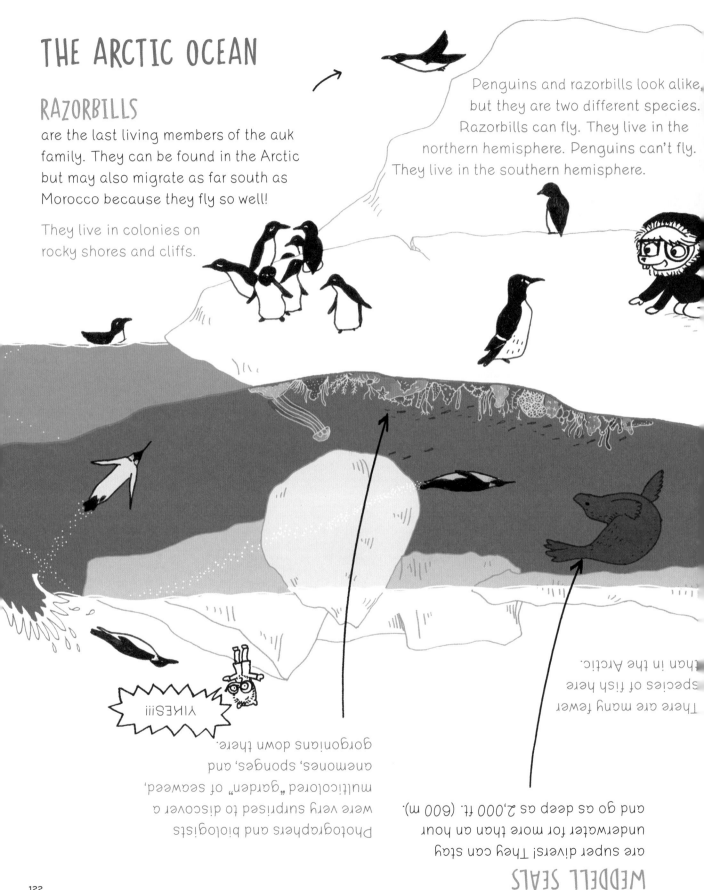

THE ARCTIC OCEAN

RAZORBILLS

are the last living members of the auk family. They can be found in the Arctic but may also migrate as far south as Morocco because they fly so well!

They live in colonies on rocky shores and cliffs.

Penguins and razorbills look alike, but they are two different species. Razorbills can fly. They live in the northern hemisphere. Penguins can't fly. They live in the southern hemisphere.

There are many fewer species of fish here than in the Arctic.

YIKES!!!

Photographers and biologists were very surprised to discover a multicolored "garden" of seaweed, anemones, sponges, and gorgonians down there.

WEDDELL SEALS

are super divers! They can stay underwater for more than an hour and go as deep as 2,000 ft. (600 m).

THE SOUTHERN OCEAN

The Southern Ocean is on the completely opposite side of the planet! It's the coldest of all the oceans, but lots of animals still live there or feed there.

Species in the Antarctic are isolated from the other oceans because of a current that flows around the continent.

They only exist here.

ADÉLIE PENGUINS

spend most of their lives fishing underwater.

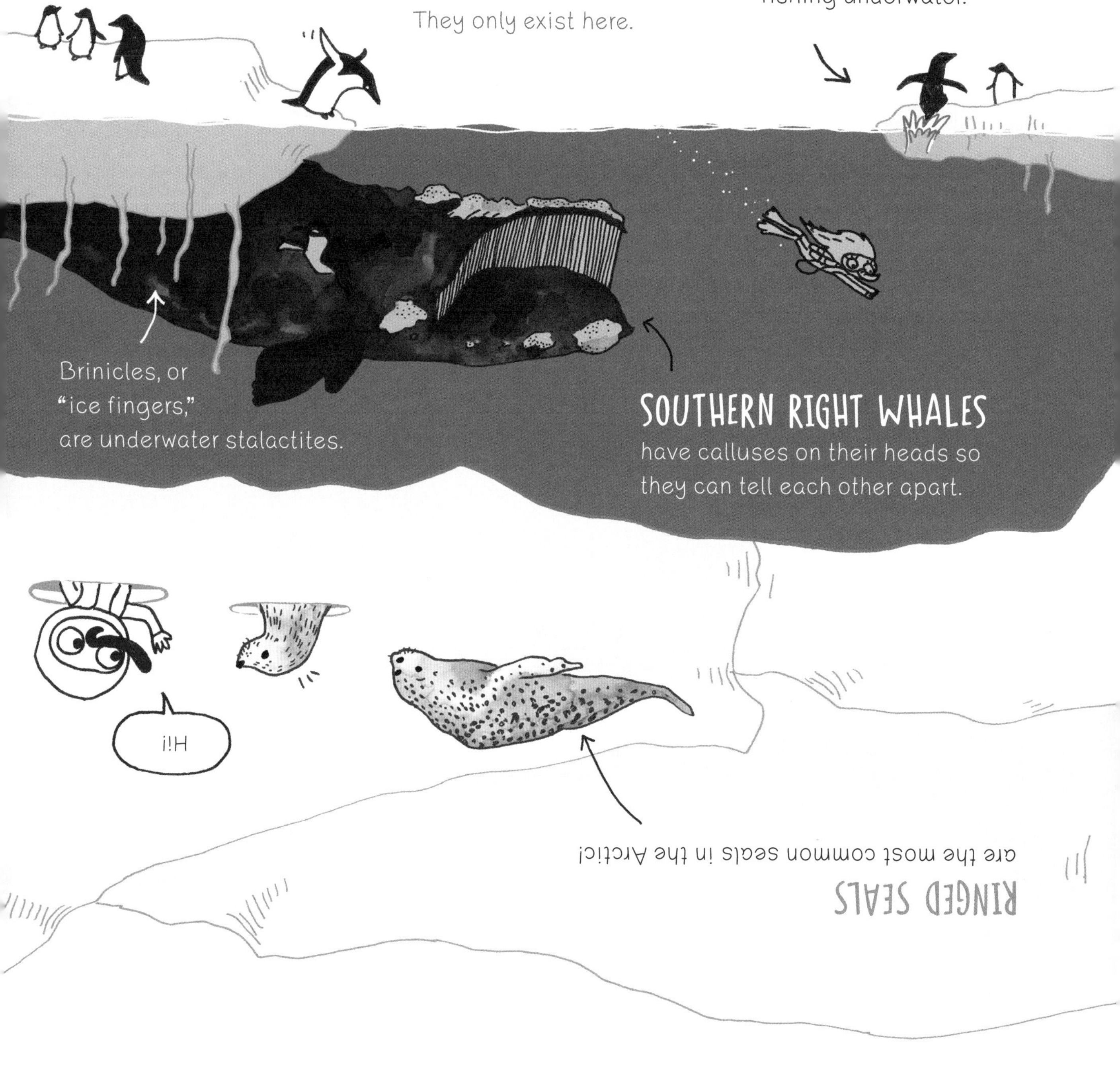
Hi!

Brinicles, or "ice fingers," are underwater stalactites.

SOUTHERN RIGHT WHALES

have calluses on their heads so they can tell each other apart.

RINGED SEALS

are the most common seals in the Arctic!

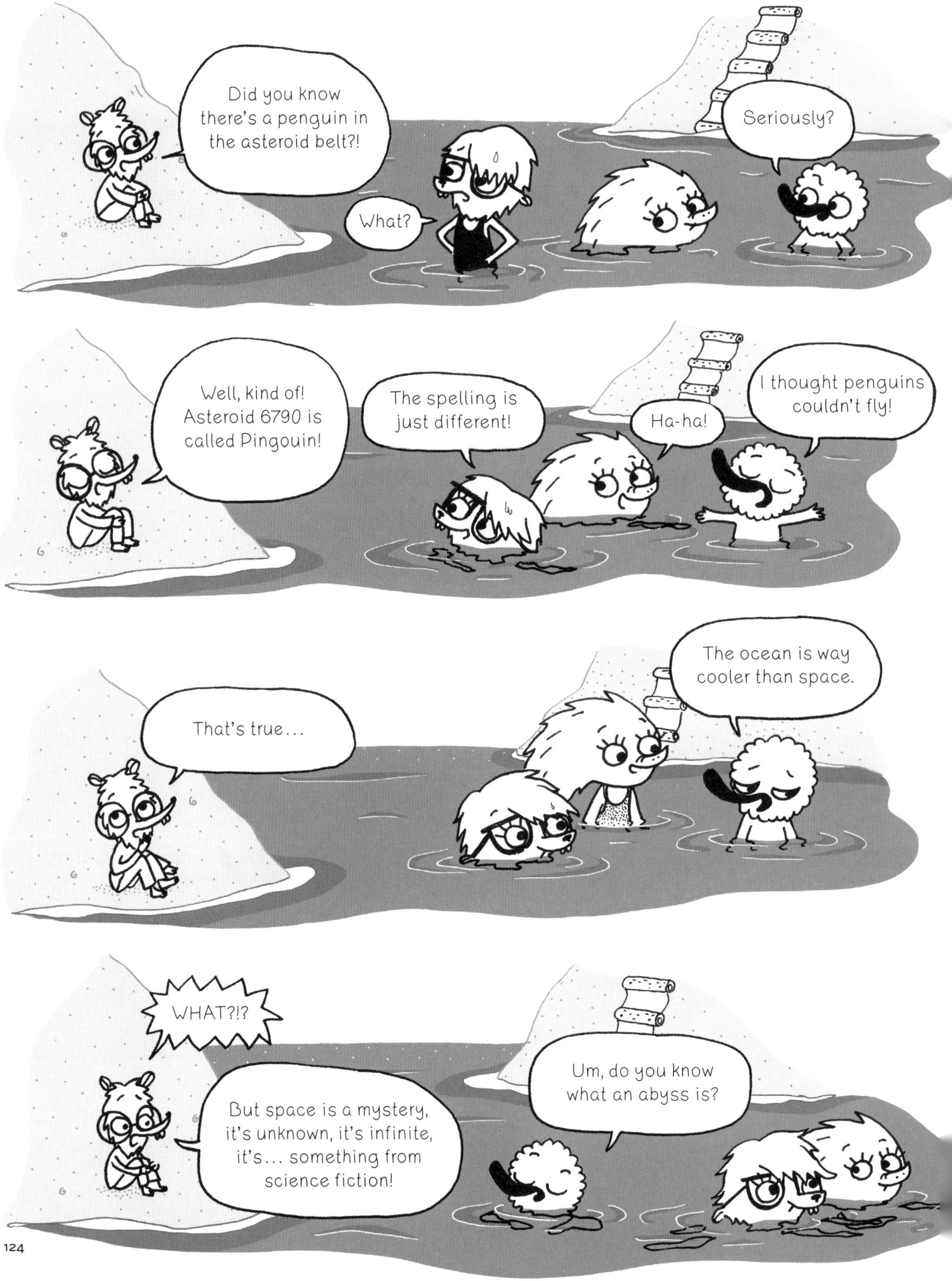
Did you know there's a penguin in the asteroid belt?!
What?
Seriously?
Well, kind of! Asteroid 6790 is called Pingouin!
The spelling is just different!
Ha-ha!
I thought penguins couldn't fly!
That's true...
The ocean is way cooler than space.
WHAT?!?
But space is a mystery, it's unknown, it's infinite, it's... something from science fiction!
Um, do you know what an abyss is?

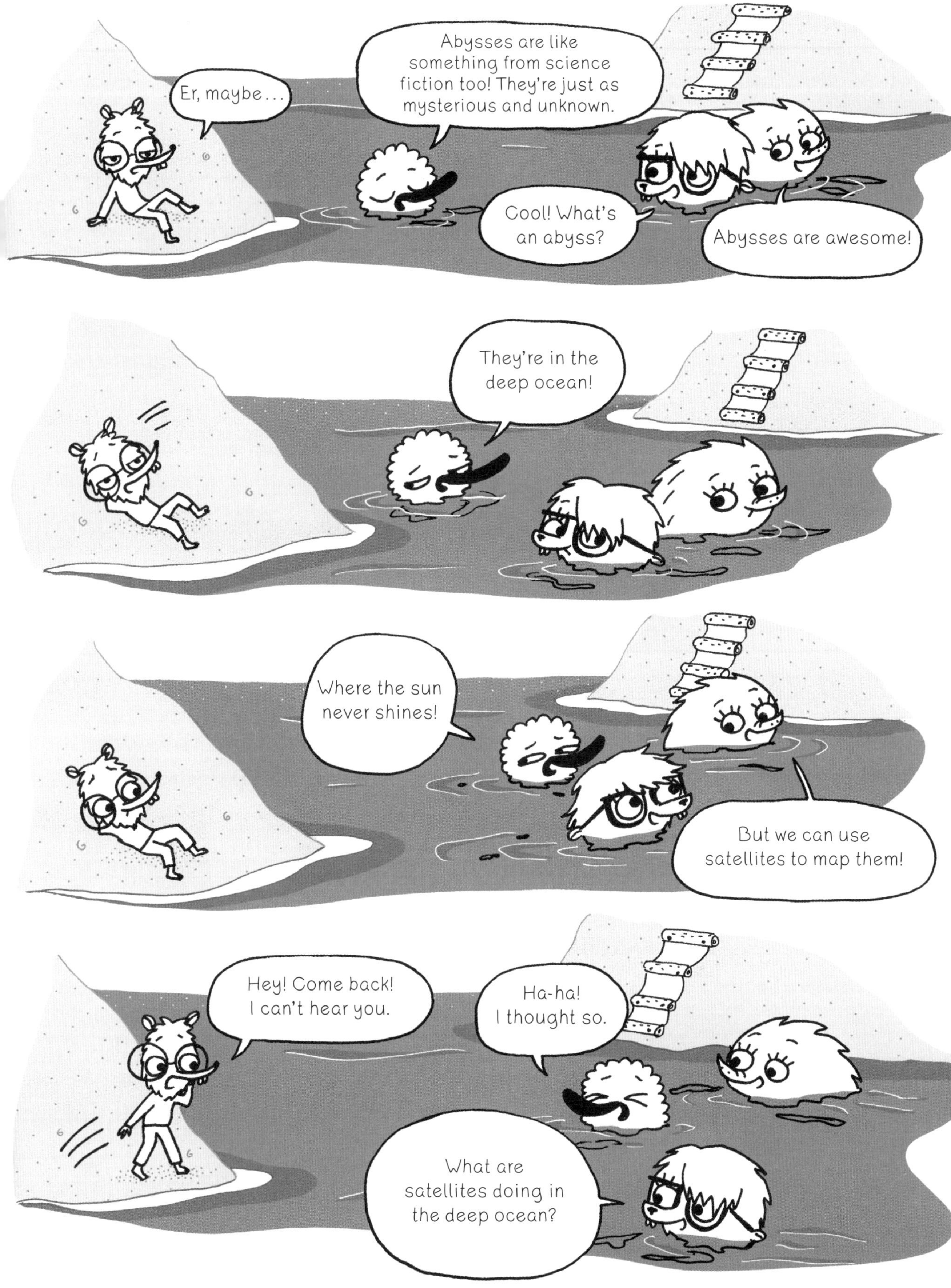

Er, maybe...
Abysses are like something from science fiction too! They're just as mysterious and unknown.
Cool! What's an abyss?
Abysses are awesome!
They're in the deep ocean!
Where the sun never shines!
But we can use satellites to map them!
Hey! Come back! I can't hear you.
Ha-ha! I thought so.
What are satellites doing in the deep ocean?

18 TO THE BOTTOM OF THE OCEAN!

Oceanographers have used satellites in space to make a map of the ocean floor. Now we know that there are mountains, volcanoes, and trenches under the ocean!

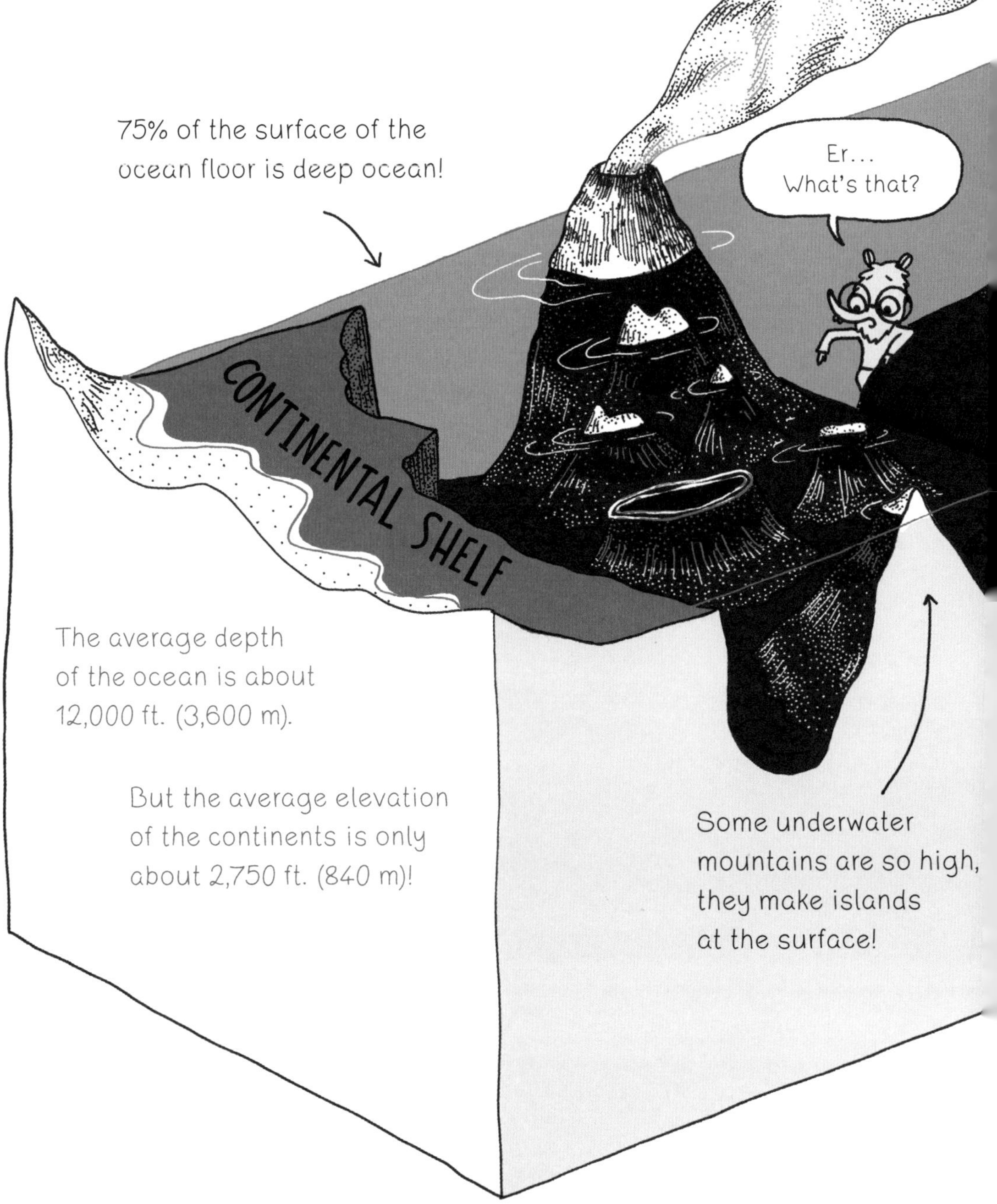

75% of the surface of the ocean floor is deep ocean!
Er... What's that?
CONTINENTAL SHELF
The average depth of the ocean is about 12,000 ft. (3,600 m).
But the average elevation of the continents is only about 2,750 ft. (840 m)!
Some underwater mountains are so high, they make islands at the surface!

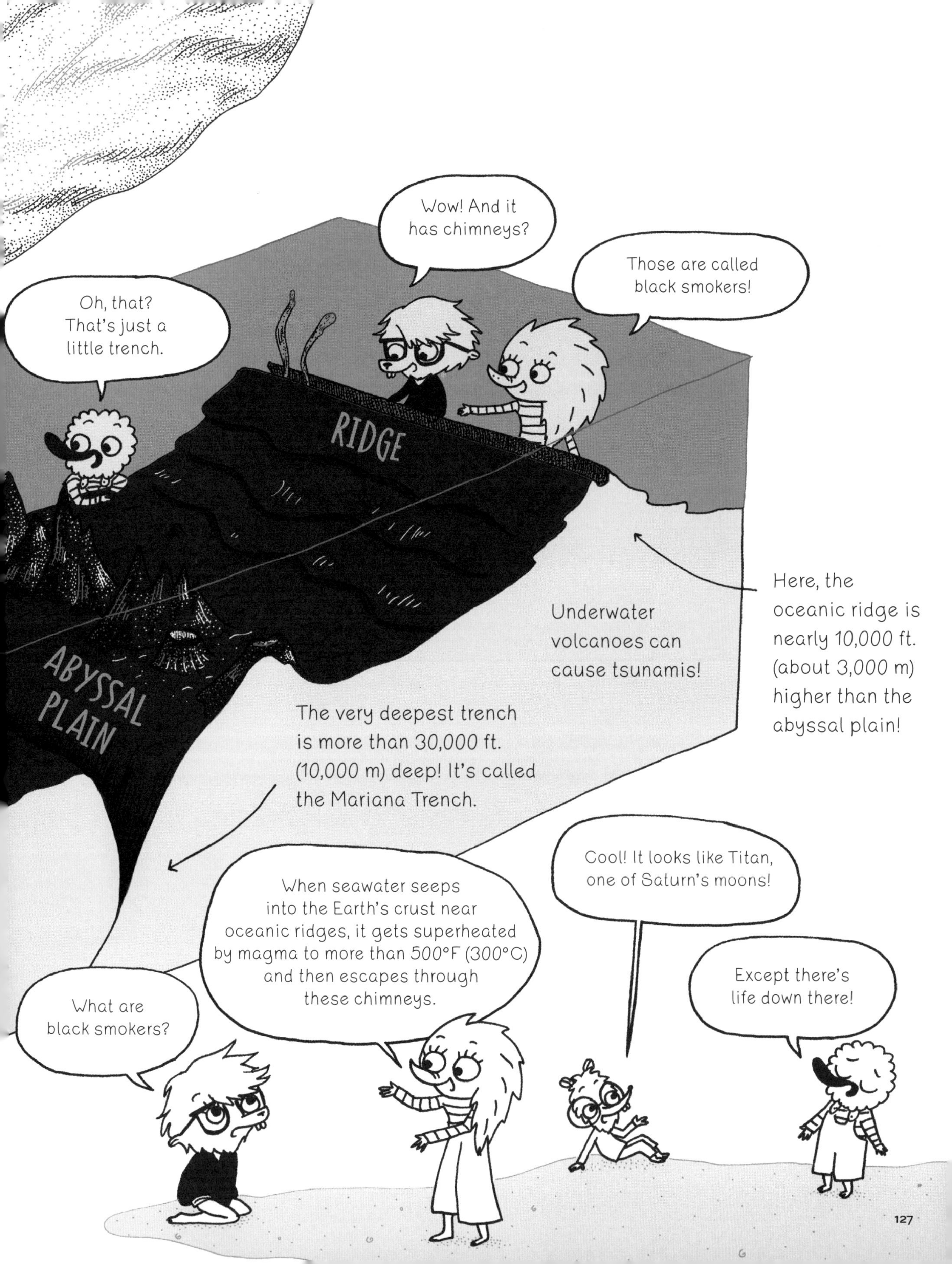
Oh, that? That's just a little trench.
Wow! And it has chimneys?
Those are called black smokers!
RIDGE
ABYSSAL PLAIN
Underwater volcanoes can cause tsunamis!
Here, the oceanic ridge is nearly 10,000 ft. (about 3,000 m) higher than the abyssal plain!
The very deepest trench is more than 30,000 ft. (10,000 m) deep! It's called the Mariana Trench.
What are black smokers?
When seawater seeps into the Earth's crust near oceanic ridges, it gets superheated by magma to more than 500°F (300°C) and then escapes through these chimneys.
Cool! It looks like Titan, one of Saturn's moons!
Except there's life down there!

In 1977, three American oceanographers in the submersible *Alvin* made an incredible discovery.

BLACK SMOKERS are hydrothermal vents.

They are chimneys formed by a build-up of metal sulfides. Some of the metals they contain are very valuable.

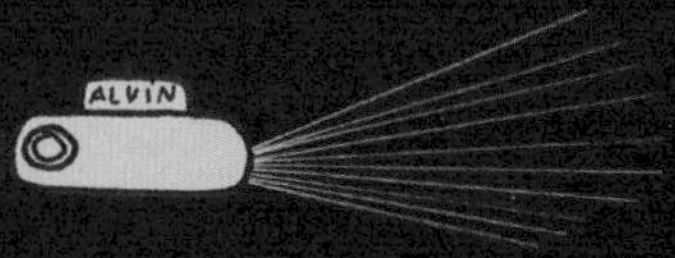
ALVIN

The crew of the *Alvin* discovered the black smokers at about 8,000 ft. (2,500 m) beneath the surface.

The scientists were surprised to see an oasis of life near the chimneys...

... even though the temperature at the very top was nearly 750°F (400°C)!

The highest of them is called Poseidon. It's almost 200 ft. (60 m) high!

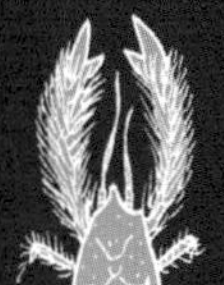

YETI CRABS

were discovered in 2005. They're completely white and are probably blind.

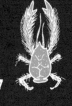

There's life down here, but it's kind of weird!

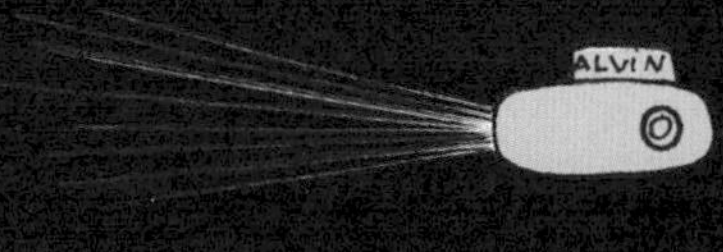
ALVIN

Life near black smokers is very different from what we know. It doesn't depend on sunlight. Instead, it depends on the chemical energy released by the chimneys.

GIANT TUBE WORMS

are worms in big tubes that live in colonies. Some can be about 6 ft. (2 m) long!

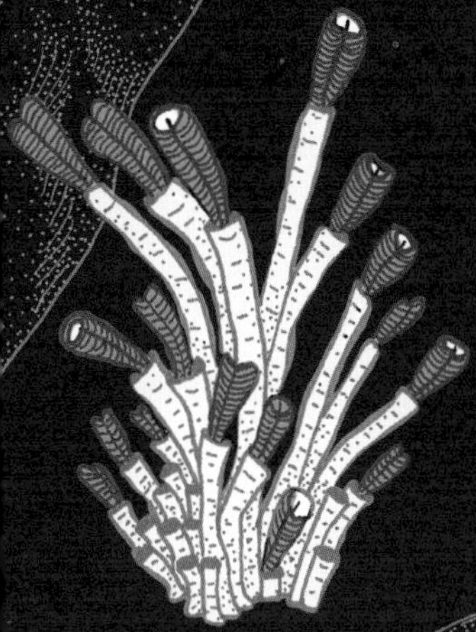

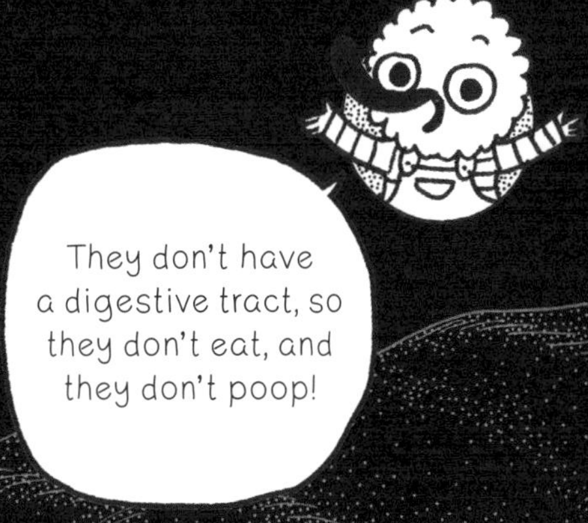
They don't have a digestive tract, so they don't eat, and they don't poop!

TWOLINE EELPOUTS

feed on small organisms that live in the mud on the ocean floor.

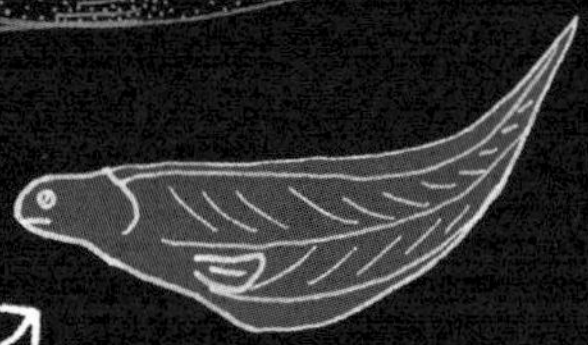

POMPEII WORMS

get their name from the hot environment they live in. Pompeii was a city in Italy that was destroyed when Mount Vesuvius—a volcano—erupted!

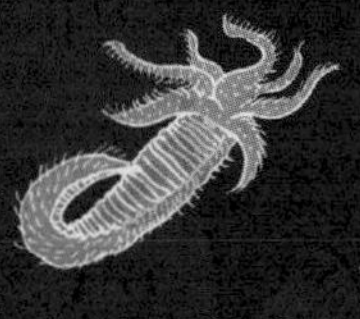

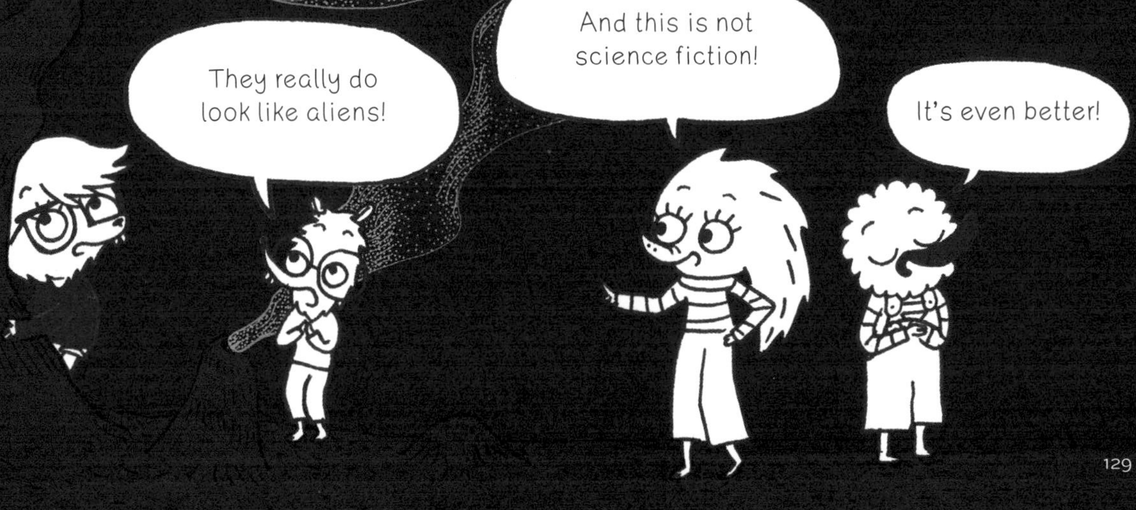
They really do look like aliens!
And this is not science fiction!
It's even better!

UNDERWATER EXPLORATION

Because of the colossal water pressure at these depths and the total darkness, it's a big challenge to explore the ocean abysses.

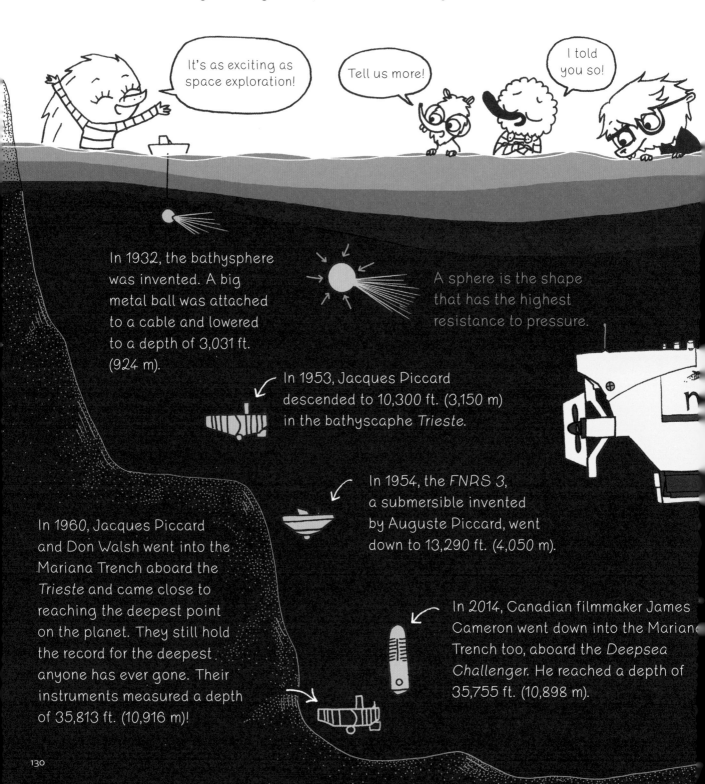

It's as exciting as space exploration!

Tell us more!

I told you so!

In 1932, the bathysphere was invented. A big metal ball was attached to a cable and lowered to a depth of 3,031 ft. (924 m).

A sphere is the shape that has the highest resistance to pressure.

In 1953, Jacques Piccard descended to 10,300 ft. (3,150 m) in the bathyscaphe *Trieste*.

In 1954, the *FNRS 3*, a submersible invented by Auguste Piccard, went down to 13,290 ft. (4,050 m).

In 1960, Jacques Piccard and Don Walsh went into the Mariana Trench aboard the *Trieste* and came close to reaching the deepest point on the planet. They still hold the record for the deepest anyone has ever gone. Their instruments measured a depth of 35,813 ft. (10,916 m)!

In 2014, Canadian filmmaker James Cameron went down into the Mariana Trench too, aboard the *Deepsea Challenger*. He reached a depth of 35,755 ft. (10,898 m).

In 2019, only five countries were equipped to explore the depths of the abysses: the United States, Japan, China, Russia, and France.

NAUTILE is the name of the French submersible.
It's operated by Ifremer, France's ocean research institute.

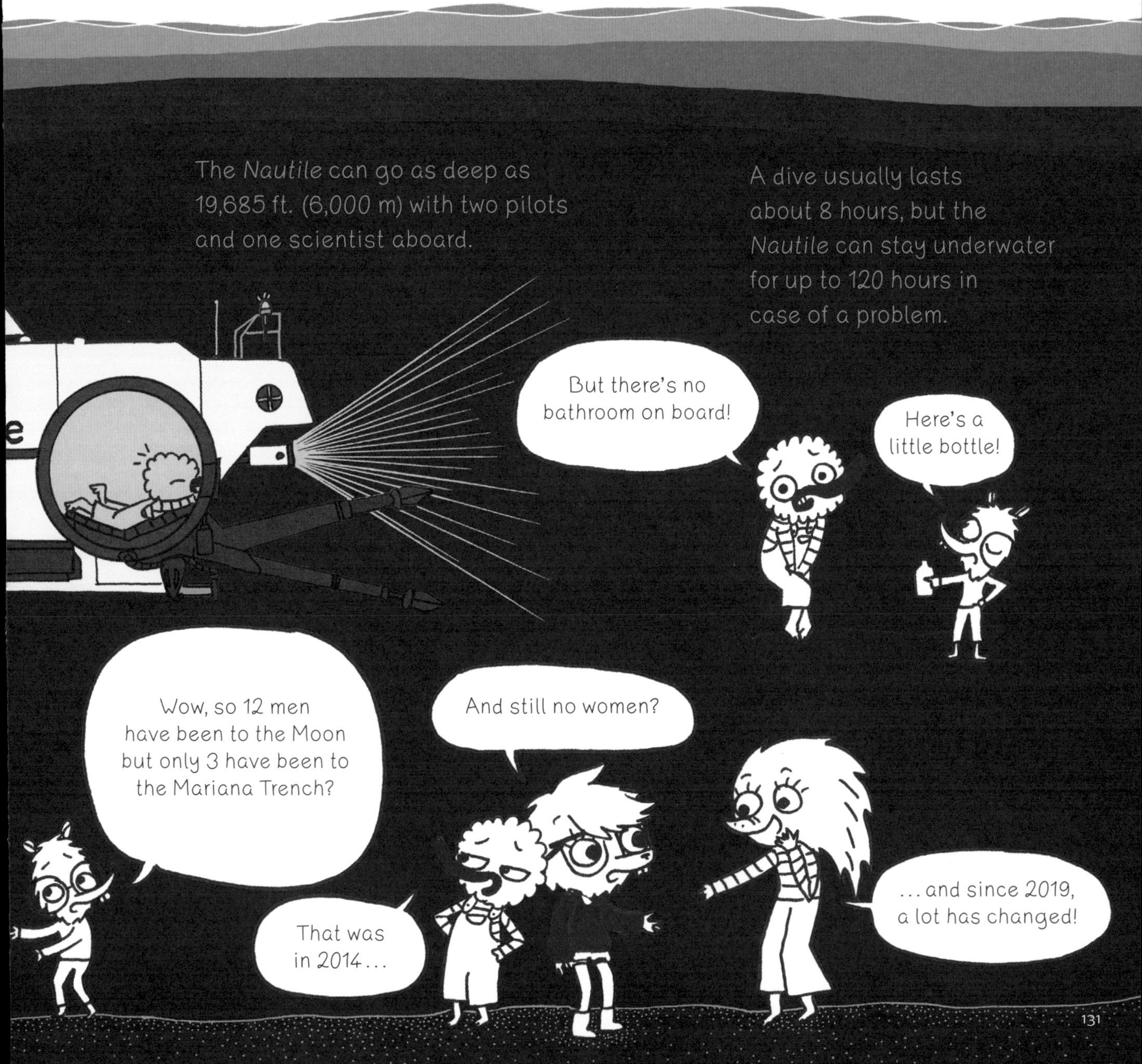

The *Nautile* can go as deep as 19,685 ft. (6,000 m) with two pilots and one scientist aboard.
A dive usually lasts about 8 hours, but the *Nautile* can stay underwater for up to 120 hours in case of a problem.
But there's no bathroom on board!
Here's a little bottle!
Wow, so 12 men have been to the Moon but only 3 have been to the Mariana Trench?
And still no women?
That was in 2014...
...and since 2019, a lot has changed!

Victor Vescevo, an American explorer, has become the first person to visit the deepest points in all five oceans.

In 2020, a Chinese dive crew sent the first live video back from the Mariana Trench.

In 2022, Dawn Wright, who specializes in mapping the seafloor, became the first Black person to dive to Challenger Deep—the deepest known point of Earth's seabed.

Some spectacular advances in underwater exploration have been made in recent years.

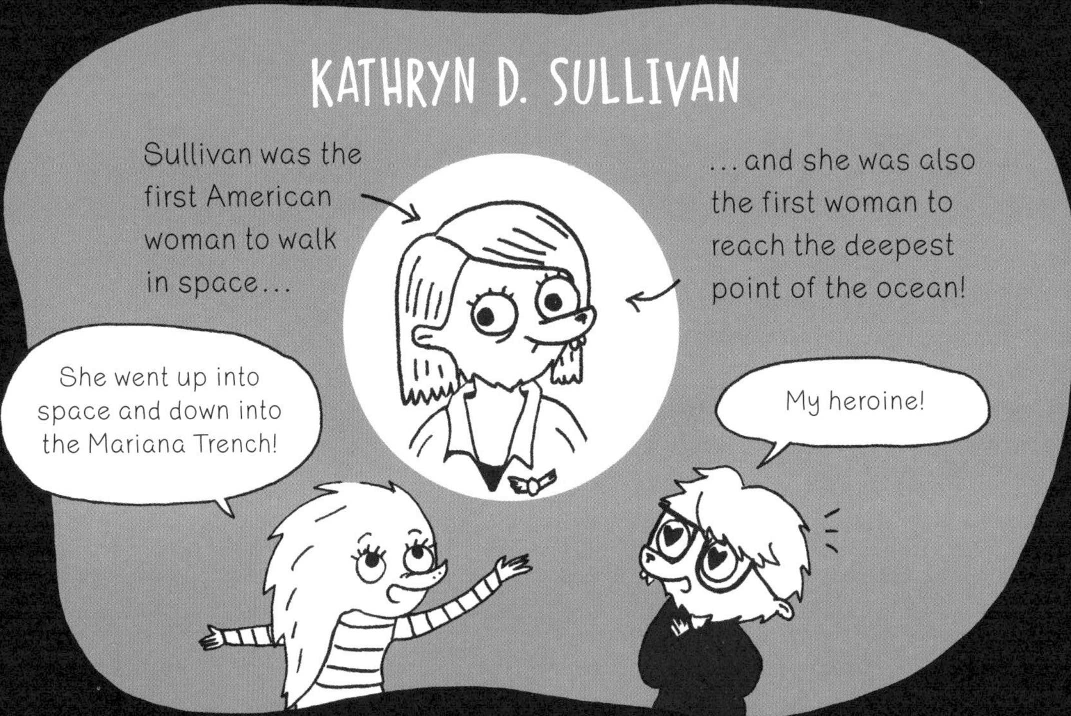
KATHRYN D. SULLIVAN
Sullivan was the first American woman to walk in space…
…and she was also the first woman to reach the deepest point of the ocean!
She went up into space and down into the Mariana Trench!
My heroine!

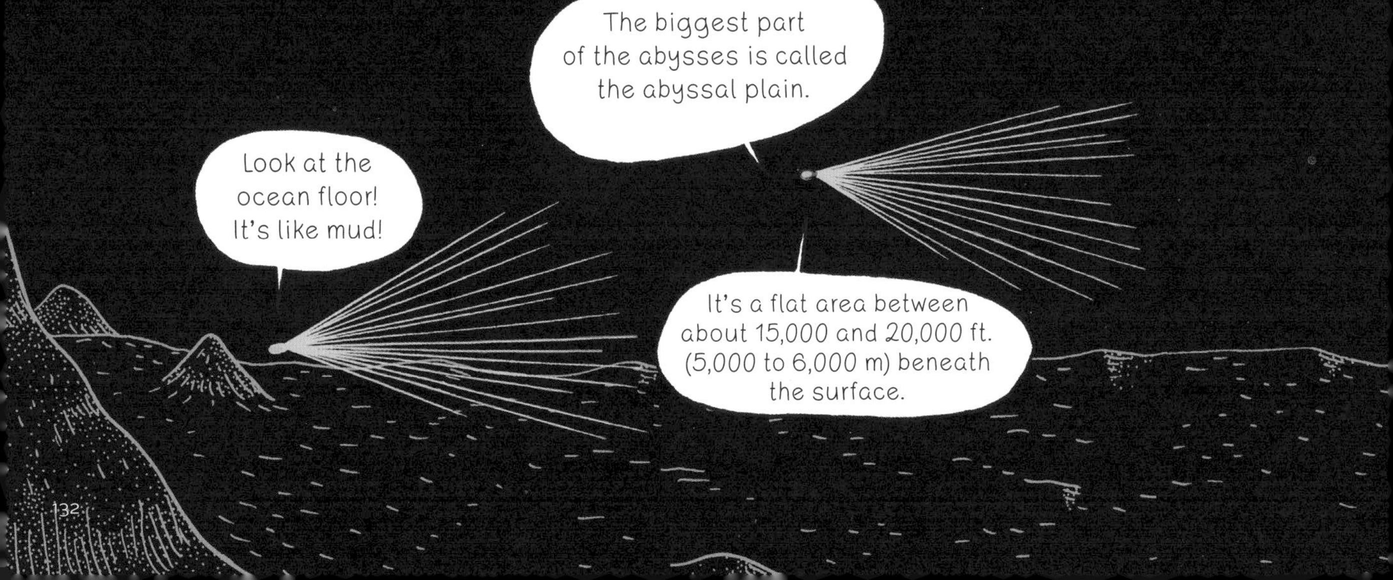
The biggest part of the abysses is called the abyssal plain.
Look at the ocean floor! It's like mud!
It's a flat area between about 15,000 and 20,000 ft. (5,000 to 6,000 m) beneath the surface.

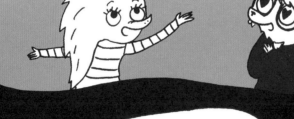

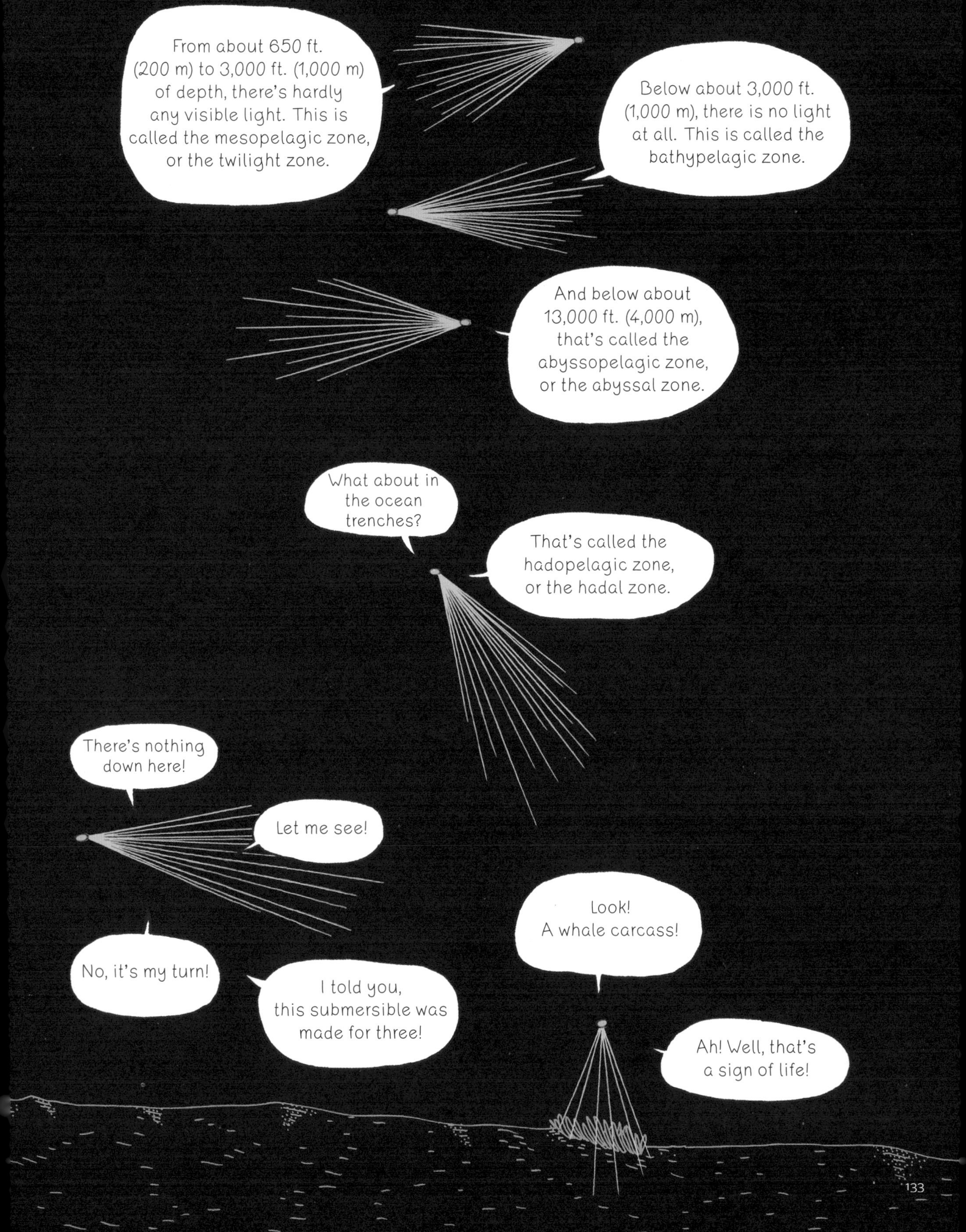
From about 650 ft. (200 m) to 3,000 ft. (1,000 m) of depth, there's hardly any visible light. This is called the mesopelagic zone, or the twilight zone.
Below about 3,000 ft. (1,000 m), there is no light at all. This is called the bathypelagic zone.
And below about 13,000 ft. (4,000 m), that's called the abyssopelagic zone, or the abyssal zone.
What about in the ocean trenches?
That's called the hadopelagic zone, or the hadal zone.
There's nothing down here!
Let me see!
No, it's my turn!
I told you, this submersible was made for three!
Look! A whale carcass!
Ah! Well, that's a sign of life!

19 IN THE ABYSSES

BASKET STARS

are huge creatures like sea stars.
They can live super deep in the ocean.

BARRELEYE FISH

have a transparent head that protects
their special tube-shaped eyes.

GRENADIER

GOBLIN SHARKS

have jaws that can shoot
forward to catch prey!

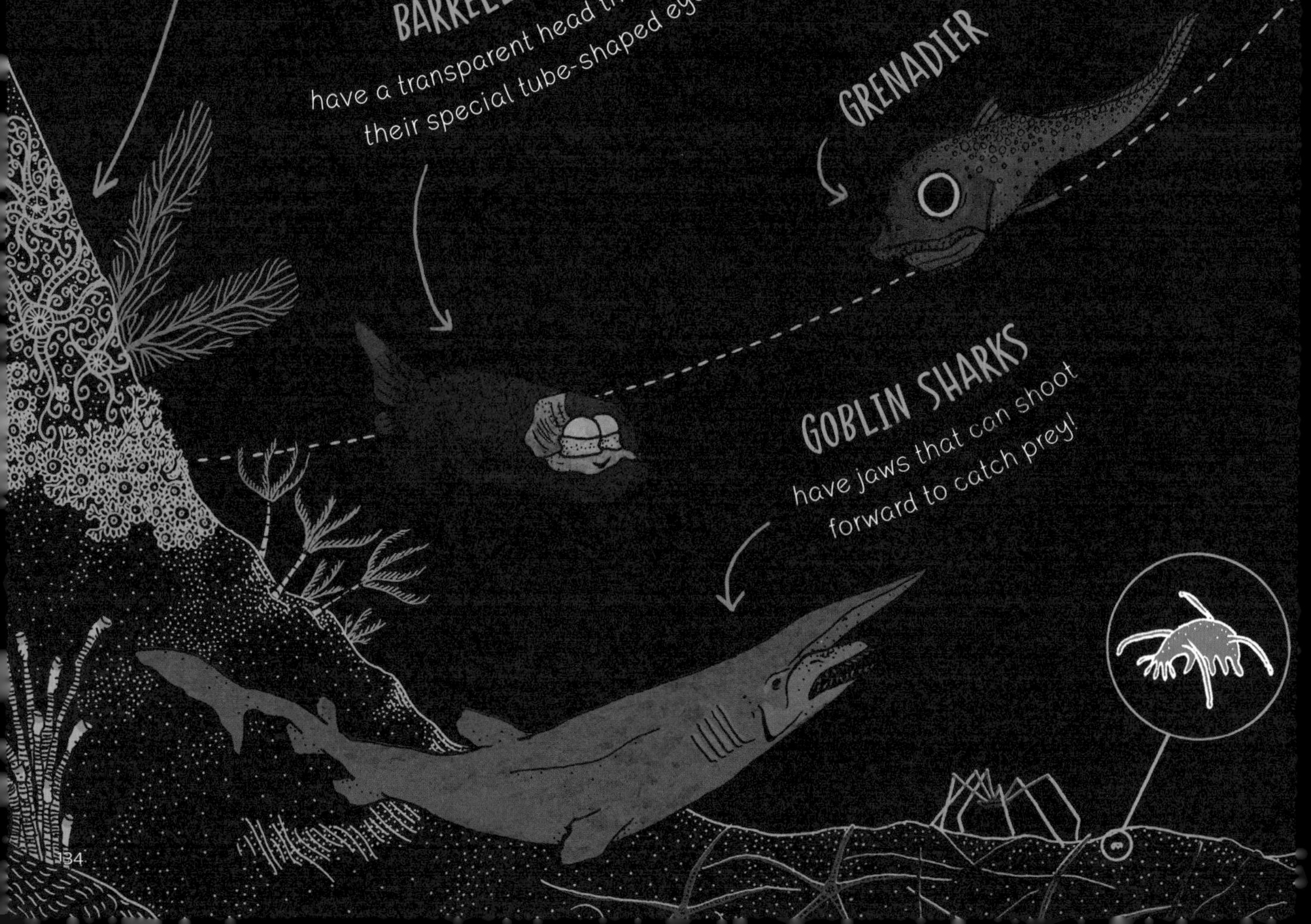

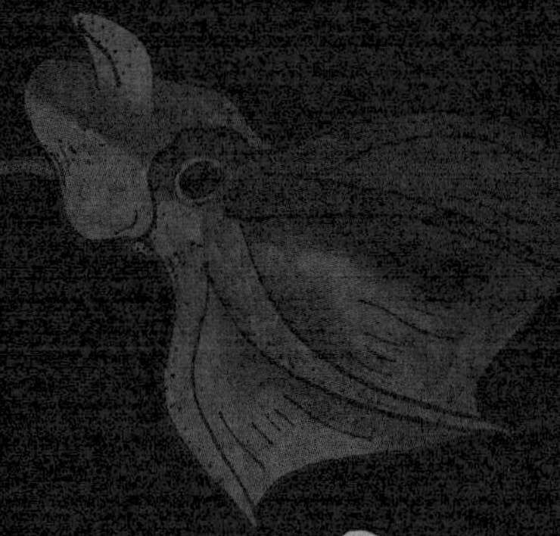

HUMPBACK ANGLERFISH

use luminous bait to attract prey.

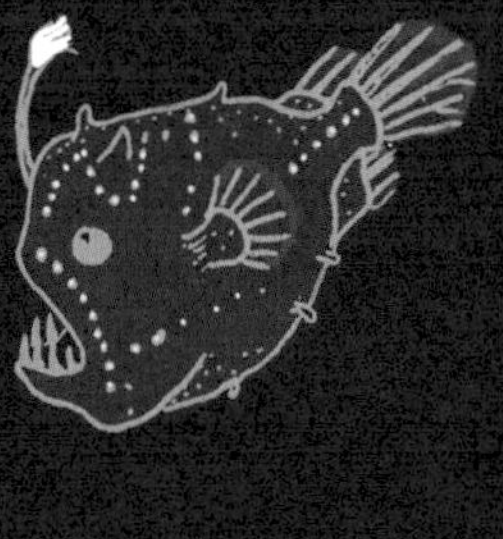

VAMPIRE SQUID

COLOSSAL SQUIDS*

are very difficult to observe alive. Photos of them have been taken at about 5,000 ft. (1,500 m) below the surface. They can grow to nearly 60 ft. (18 m) long!*

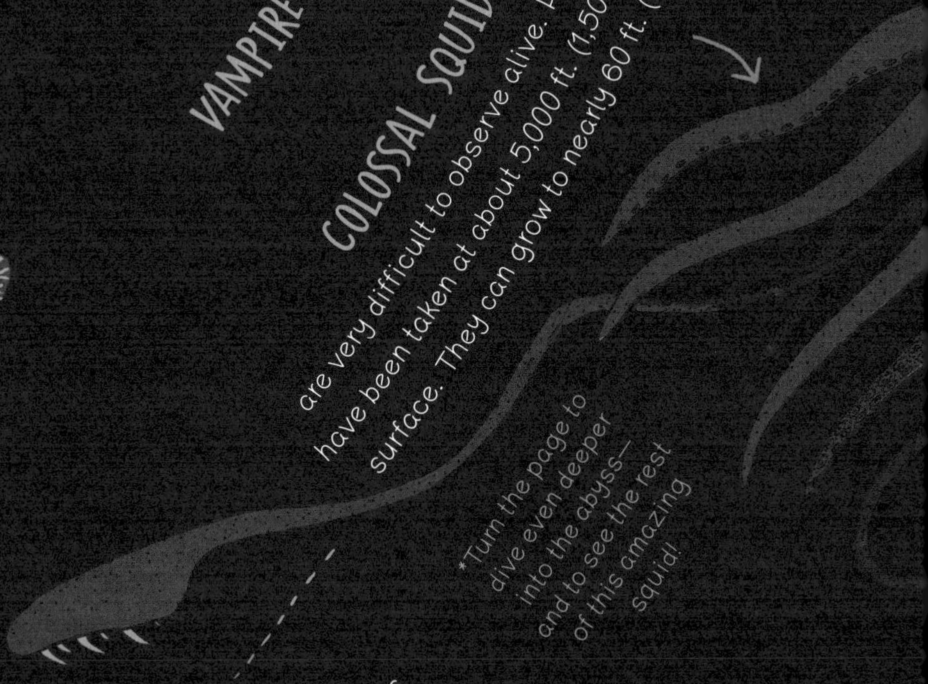

*Turn the page to dive even deeper into the abyss—and to see the rest of this amazing squid!

SEA PIGS

are transparent and live deep on the ocean floor.

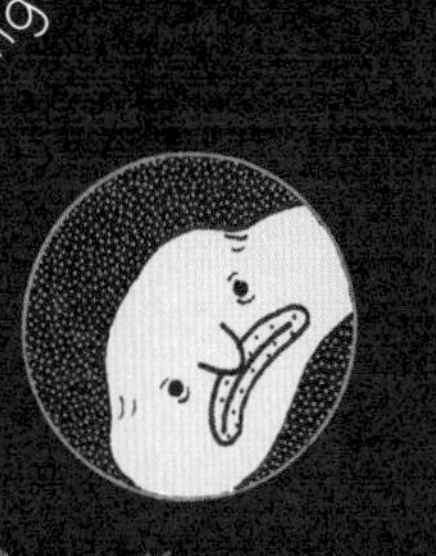

BLOBFISH

have a jellylike body that looks super squishy out of the water. That's because it's adapted for the pressure of the deep ocean. Down there, they don't look so strange!

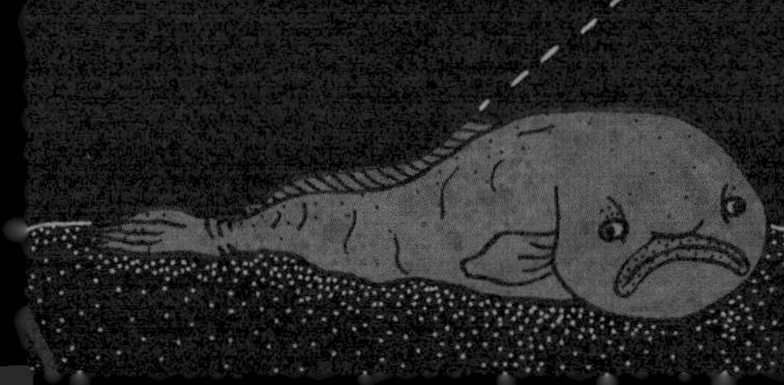

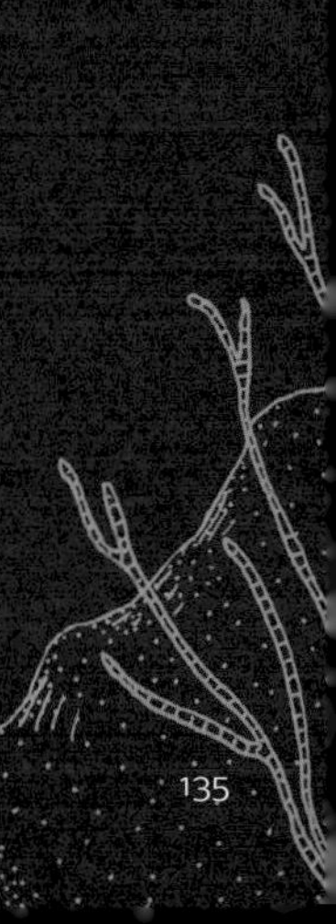

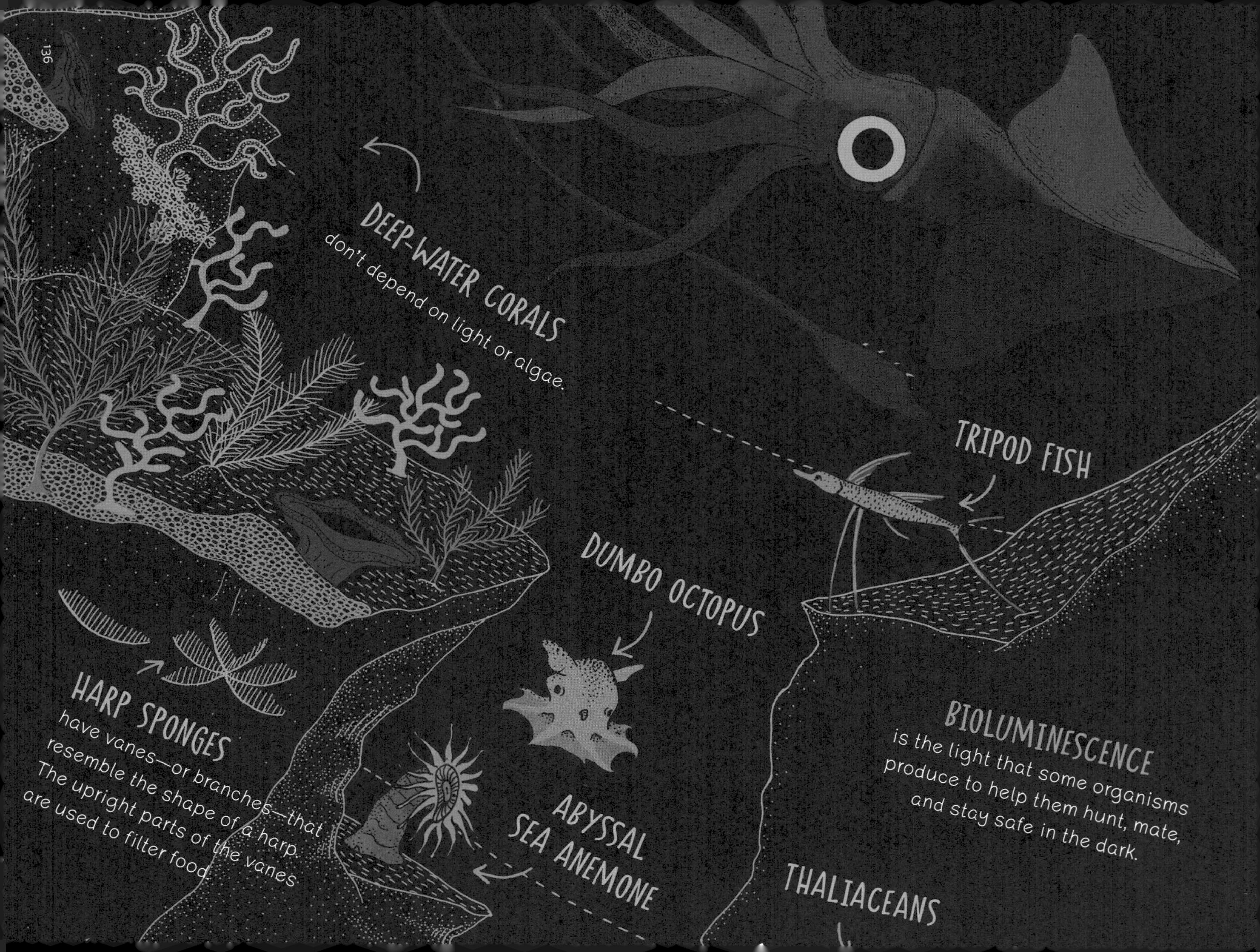
DEEP-WATER CORALS
don't depend on light or algae.
TRIPOD FISH
DUMBO OCTOPUS
HARP SPONGES
have vanes—or branches—that resemble the shape of a harp. The upright parts of the vanes are used to filter food.
ABYSSAL SEA ANEMONE
BIOLUMINESCENCE
is the light that some organisms produce to help them hunt, mate, and stay safe in the dark.
THALIACEANS

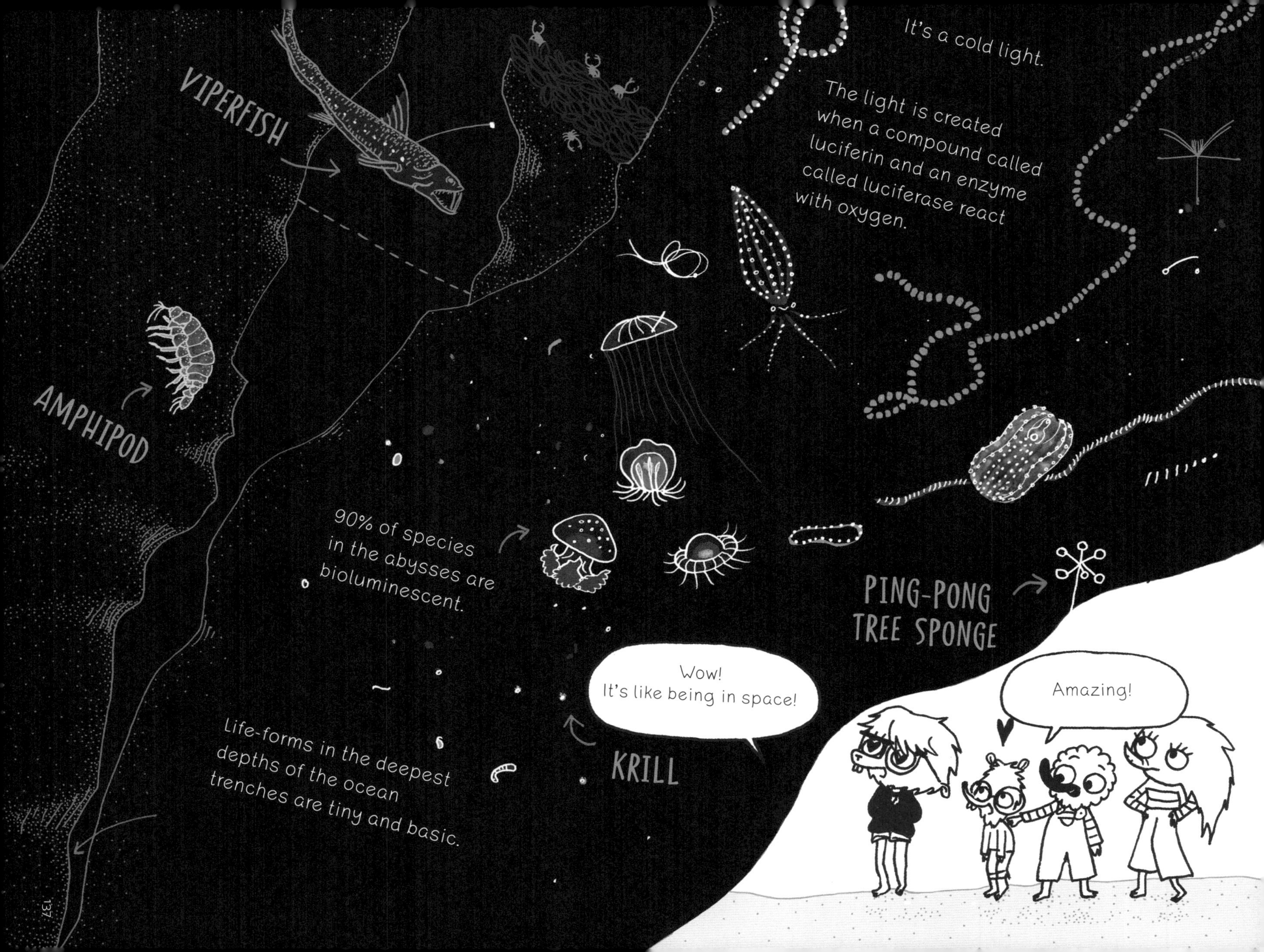
It's a cold light.
The light is created when a compound called luciferin and an enzyme called luciferase react with oxygen.
VIPERFISH
AMPHIPOD
90% of species in the abysses are bioluminescent.
PING-PONG TREE SPONGE
Wow! It's like being in space!
Amazing!
KRILL
Life-forms in the deepest depths of the ocean trenches are tiny and basic.

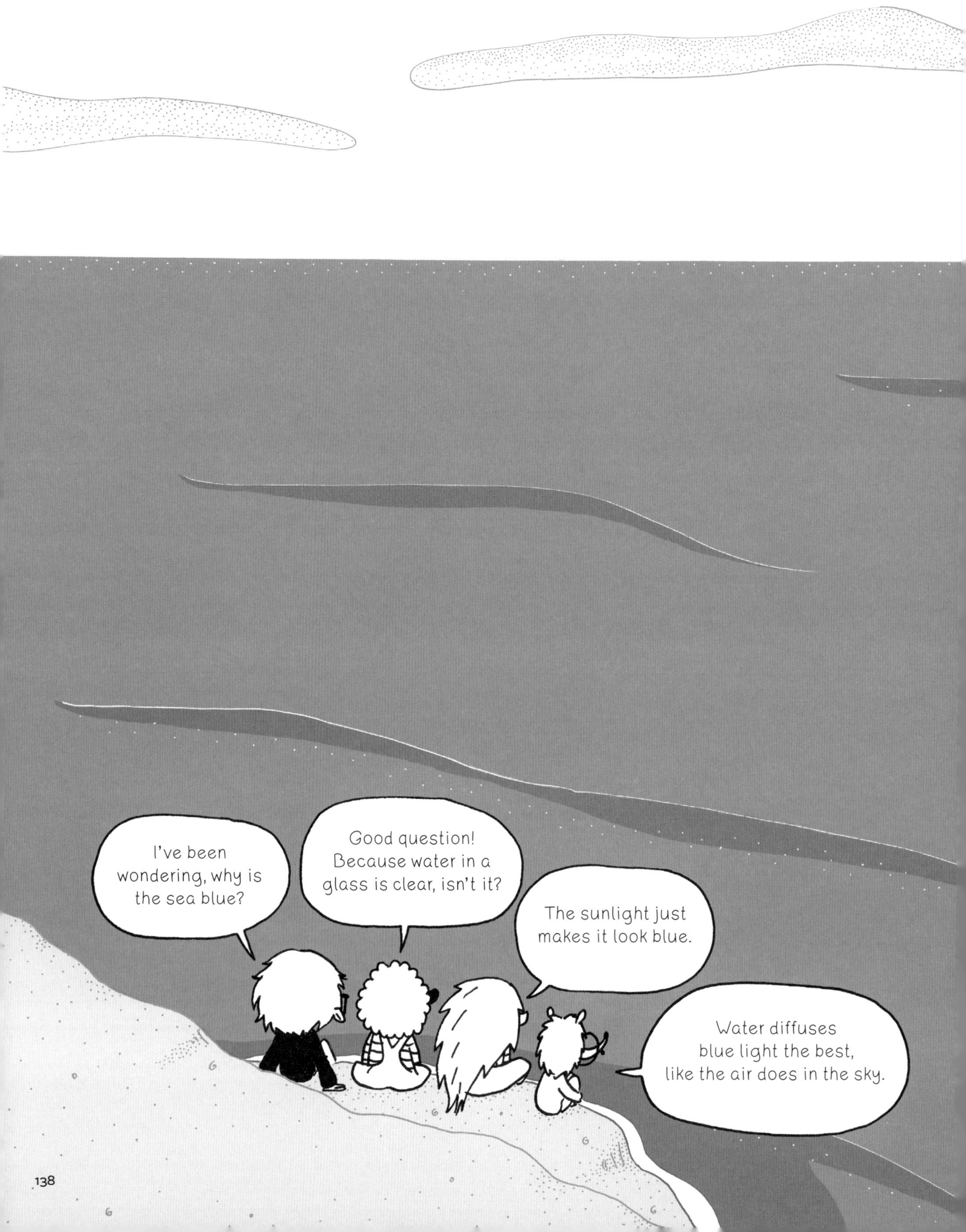
I've been wondering, why is the sea blue?
Good question! Because water in a glass is clear, isn't it?
The sunlight just makes it look blue.
Water diffuses blue light the best, like the air does in the sky.

20 LET'S TAKE THE PLUNGE!

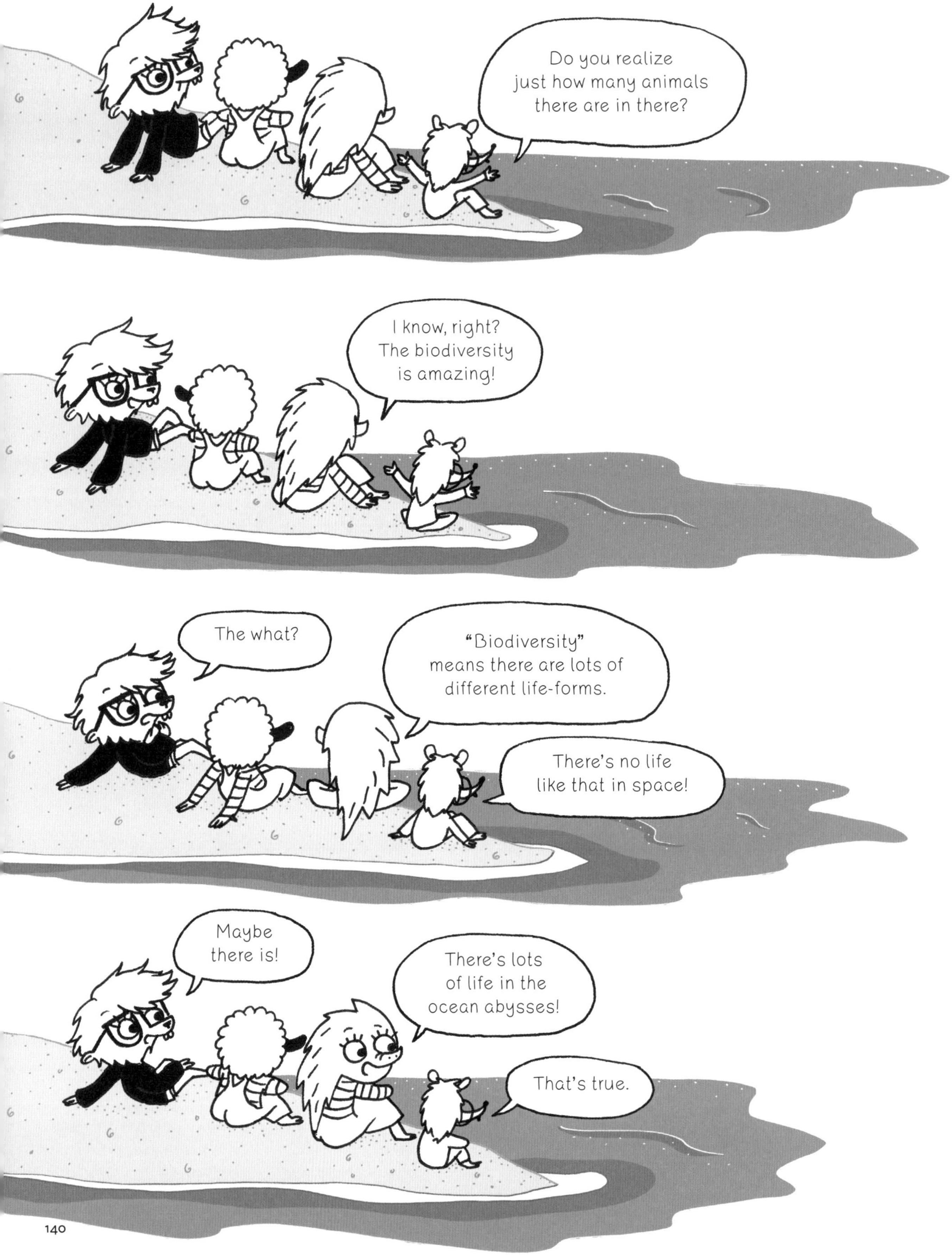
Do you realize just how many animals there are in there?
I know, right? The biodiversity is amazing!
The what?
"Biodiversity" means there are lots of different life-forms.
There's no life like that in space!
Maybe there is!
There's lots of life in the ocean abysses!
That's true.

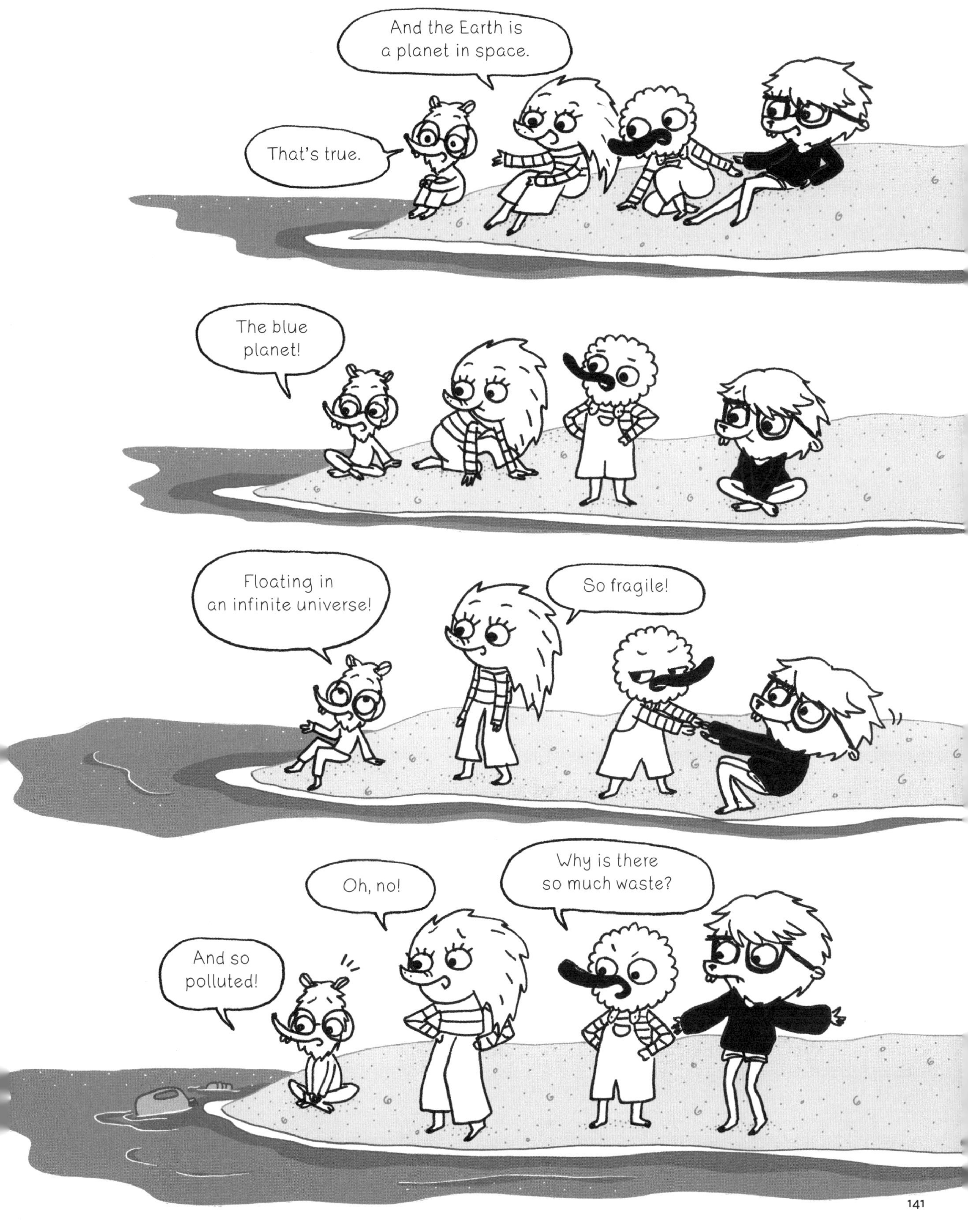

And the Earth is a planet in space.
That's true.
The blue planet!
Floating in an infinite universe!
So fragile!
And so polluted!
Oh, no!
Why is there so much waste?

WASTE

is the stuff that humans have made and no longer have a use for. Waste can include metal, fabric, glass, plastic, and even liquids!

Some things might have been used for a long time, and others just once!

Only once?! Seriously?

There are lots of things humans only use once. Packaging, straws, and drink cans are just a few examples.

My floatie isn't waste, is it?

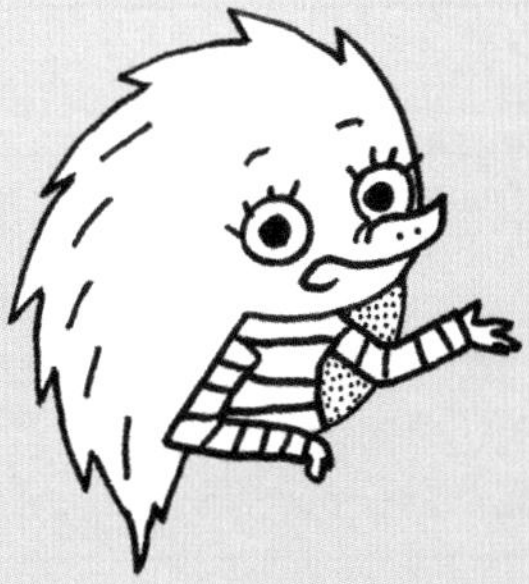

Every minute, the equivalent of a dump truck full of waste is thrown into the ocean. Plastic is the stuff we use the most. It's also the material that takes the longest to break down—between 100 and 1,000 years.

Some of this garbage floats around intact. Some of it washes up on the shore in pieces. Some pieces called microplastics are so tiny, they get everywhere.

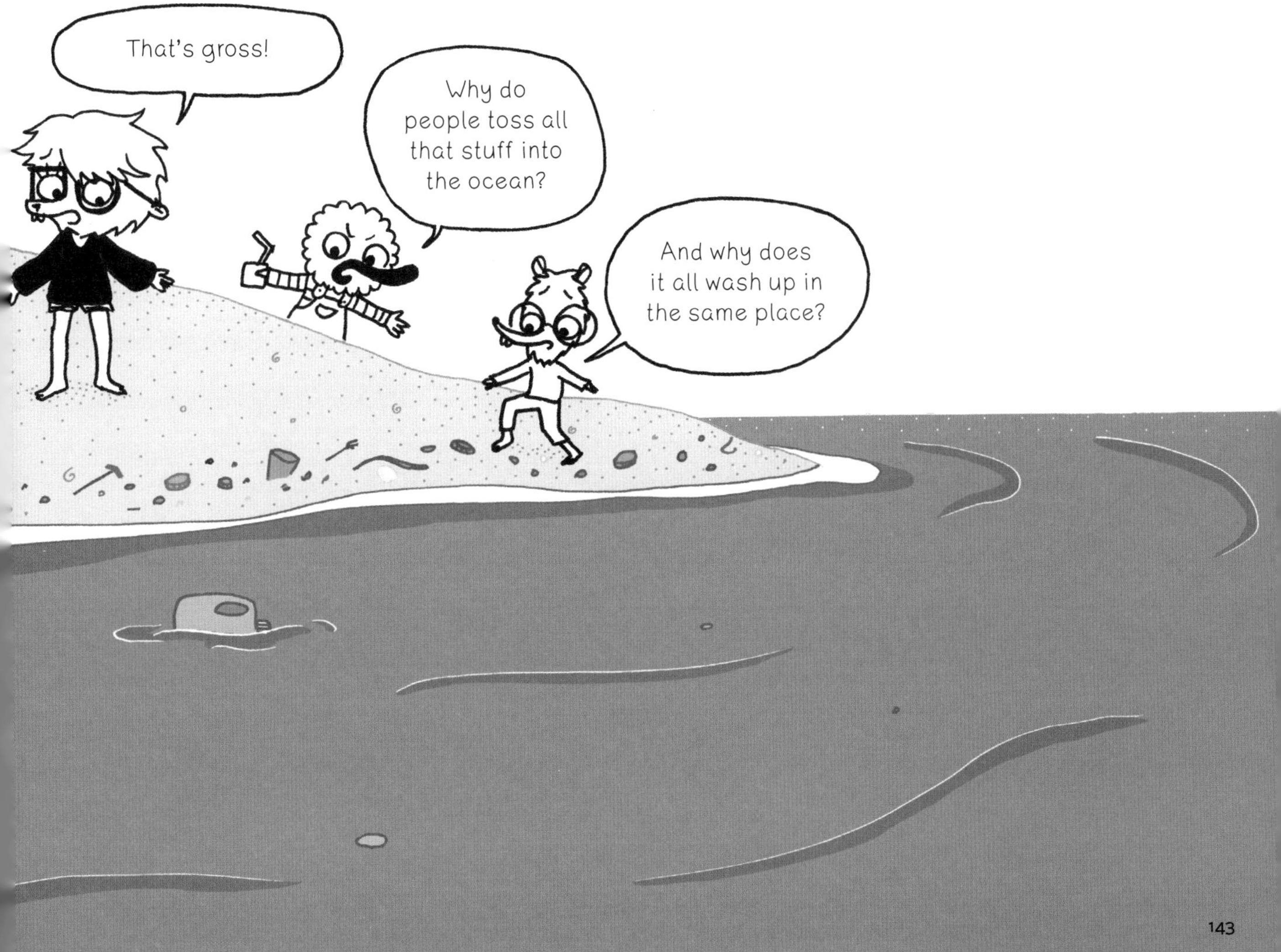
That's gross!
Why do people toss all that stuff into the ocean?
And why does it all wash up in the same place?

The waste that ends up in the ocean is called marine debris. But not all of it is thrown into the ocean.

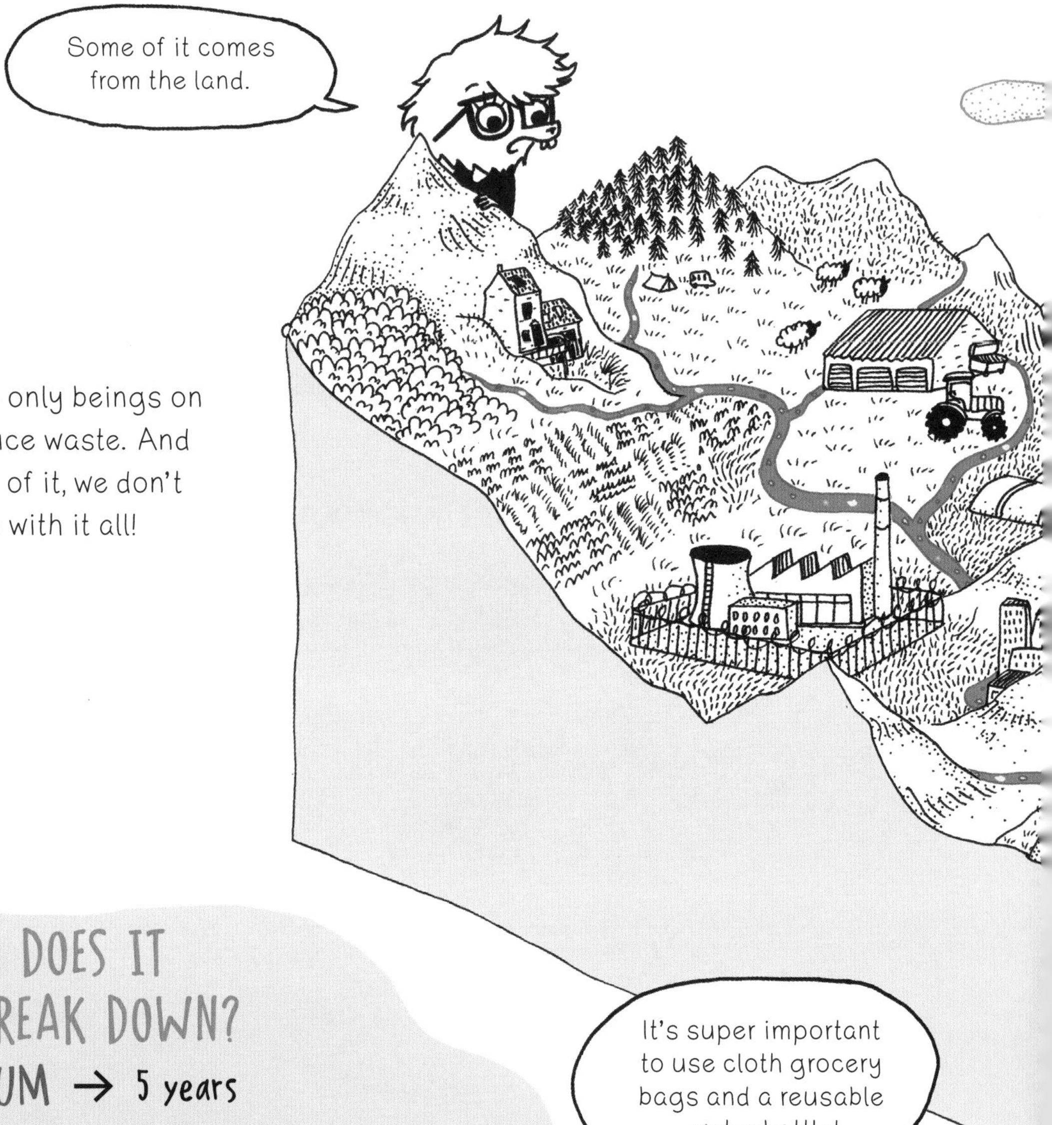
Some of it comes from the land.

Humans are the only beings on Earth who produce waste. And there's so much of it, we don't know what to do with it all!

HOW LONG DOES IT TAKE TO BREAK DOWN?

CHEWING GUM → 5 years
METAL CAN → 80 to 100 years
JUICE BOX → 100 years
PLASTIC BAG → 400 years
PLASTIC BOTTLE → 450 years
FOIL DRINK POUCHES → 400 to 1,000 years

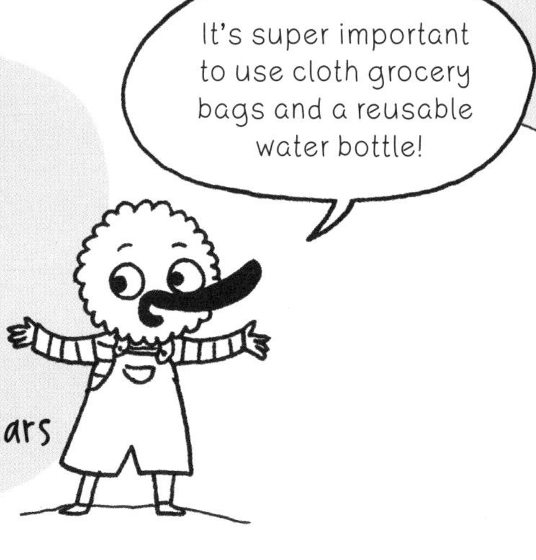
It's super important to use cloth grocery bags and a reusable water bottle!

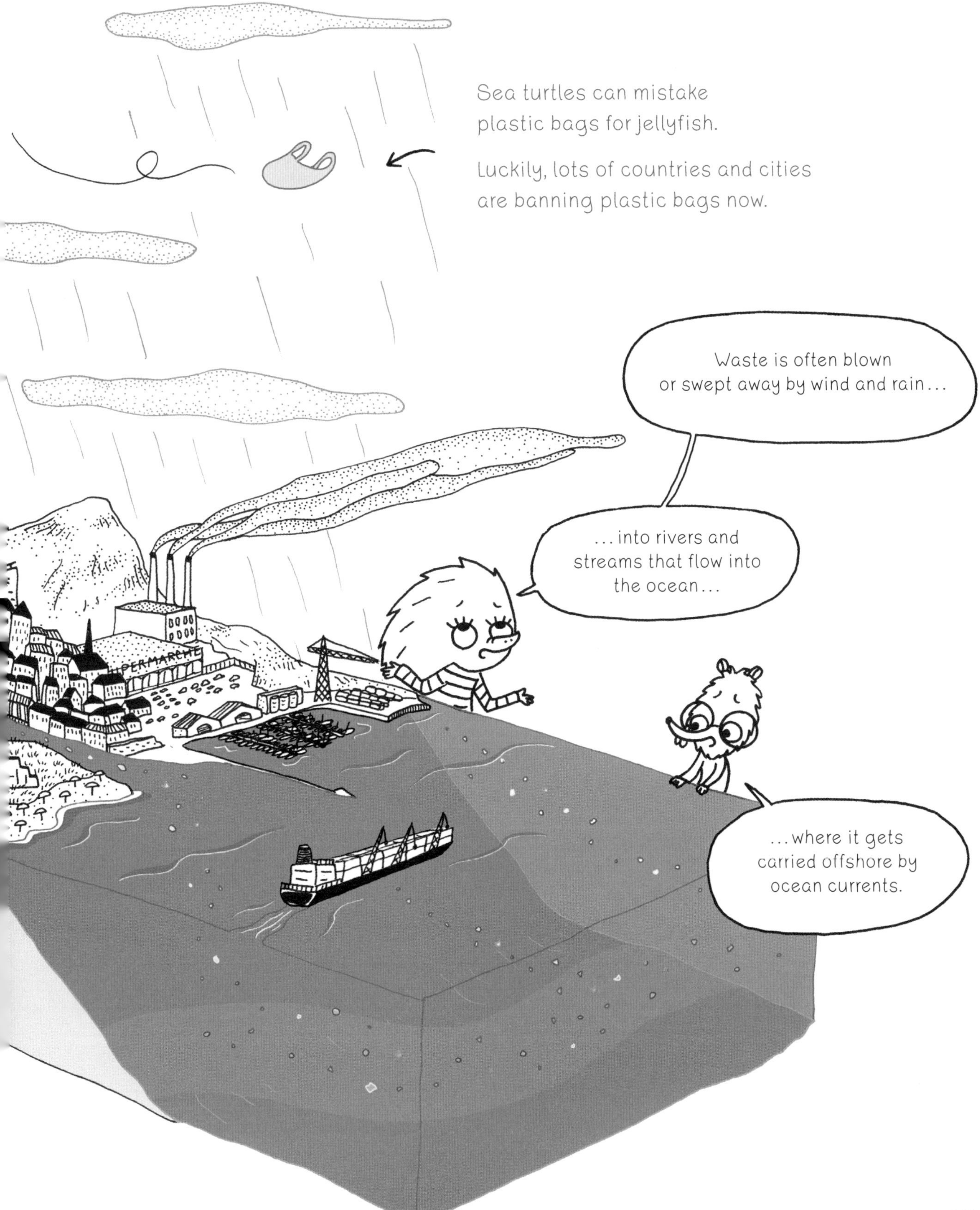
Sea turtles can mistake plastic bags for jellyfish.
Luckily, lots of countries and cities are banning plastic bags now.
Waste is often blown or swept away by wind and rain...
...into rivers and streams that flow into the ocean...
...where it gets carried offshore by ocean currents.

OCEAN GYRES

Ocean gyres are big whirlpools that collect plastic waste.

Currents carry the waste away from the shore, where it collects in big clumps.

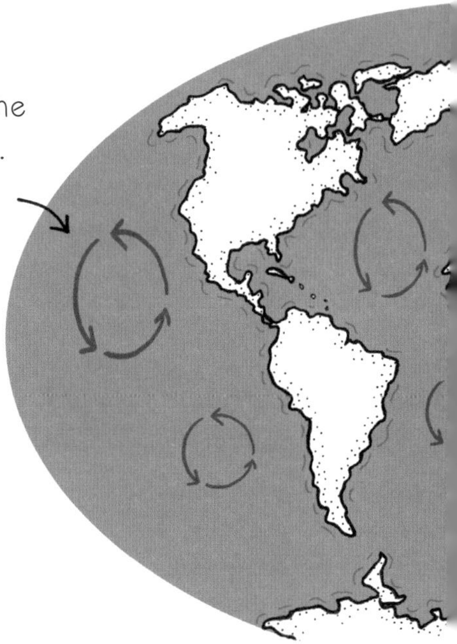

These are called plastic "continents."
The biggest one is nearly half the size of Australia!
It's called the Great Pacific Garbage Patch.

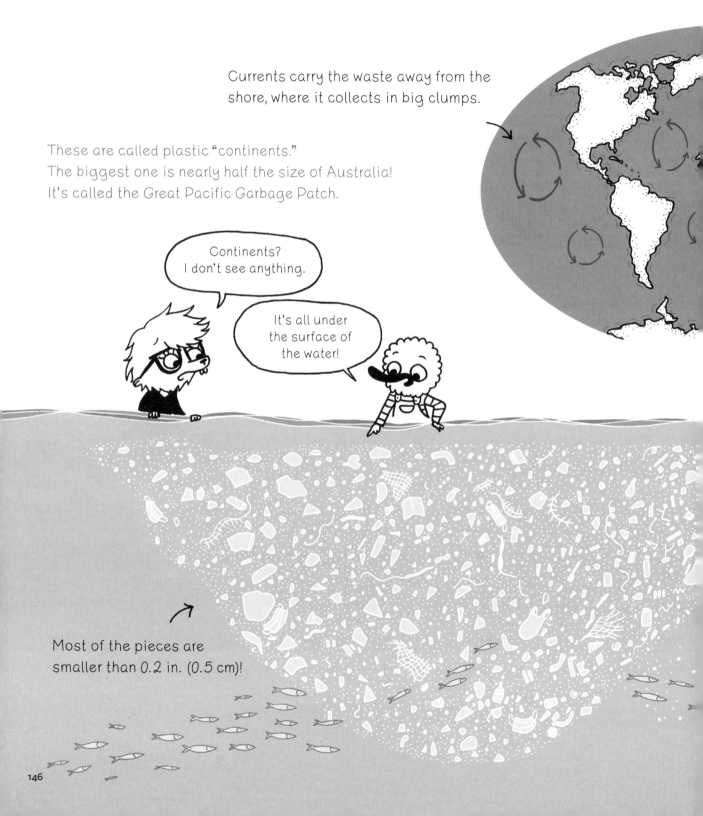

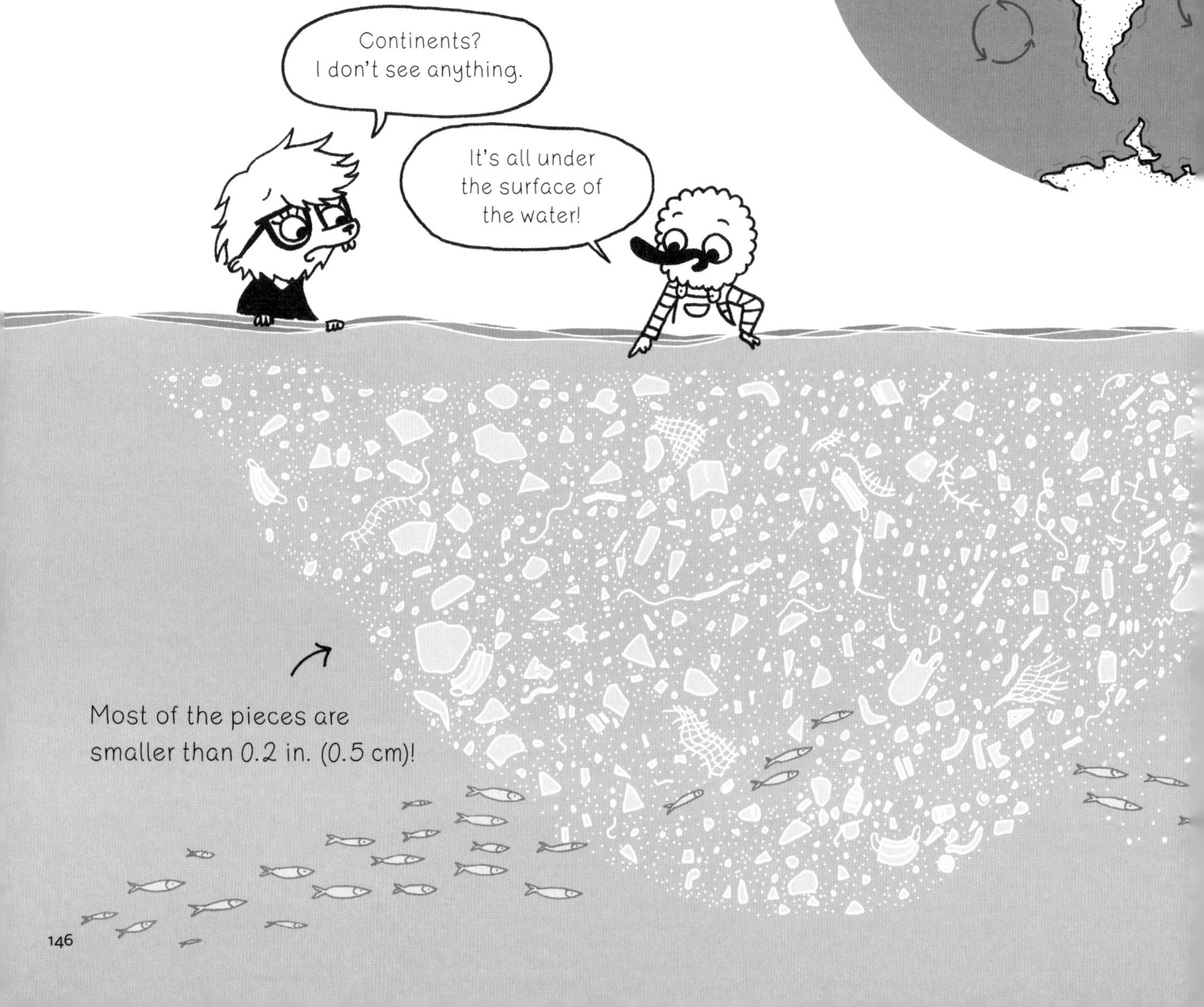
Continents? I don't see anything.
It's all under the surface of the water!
Most of the pieces are smaller than 0.2 in. (0.5 cm)!

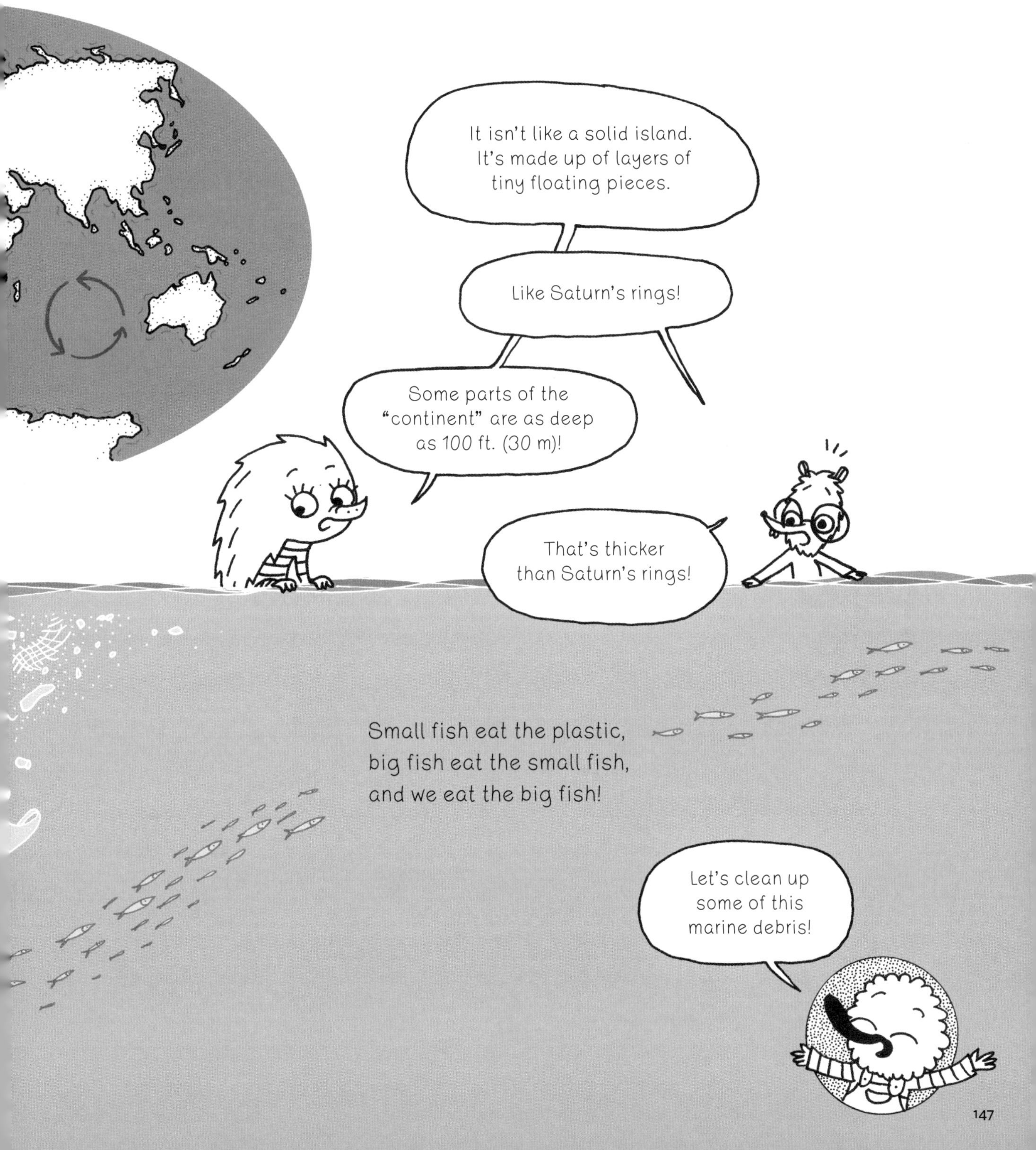
It isn't like a solid island. It's made up of layers of tiny floating pieces.
Like Saturn's rings!
Some parts of the "continent" are as deep as 100 ft. (30 m)!
That's thicker than Saturn's rings!
Small fish eat the plastic, big fish eat the small fish, and we eat the big fish!
Let's clean up some of this marine debris!

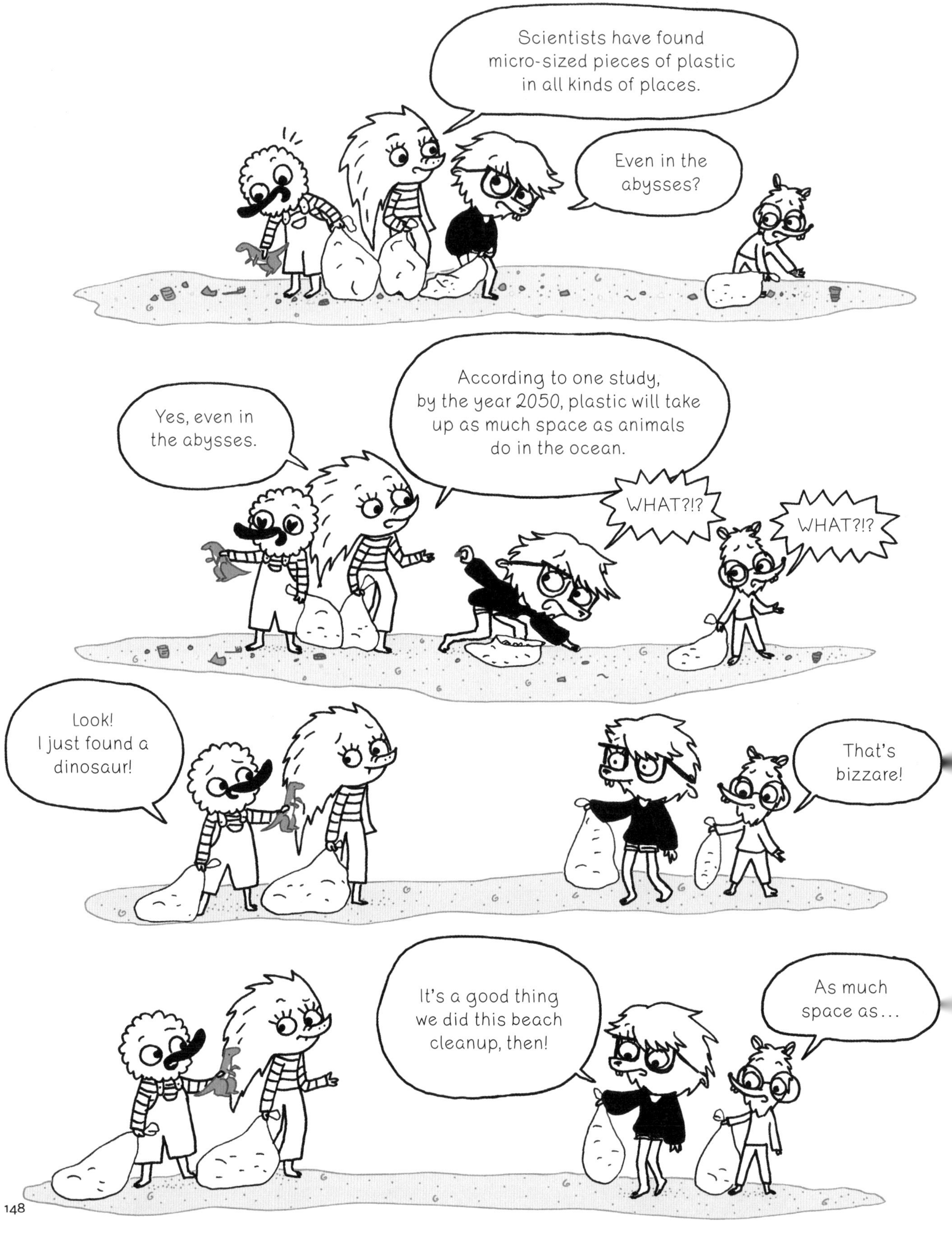
Scientists have found micro-sized pieces of plastic in all kinds of places.
Even in the abysses?
Yes, even in the abysses.
According to one study, by the year 2050, plastic will take up as much space as animals do in the ocean.
WHAT?!?
WHAT?!?
Look! I just found a dinosaur!
That's bizzare!
It's a good thing we did this beach cleanup, then!
As much space as…

CONCLUSION

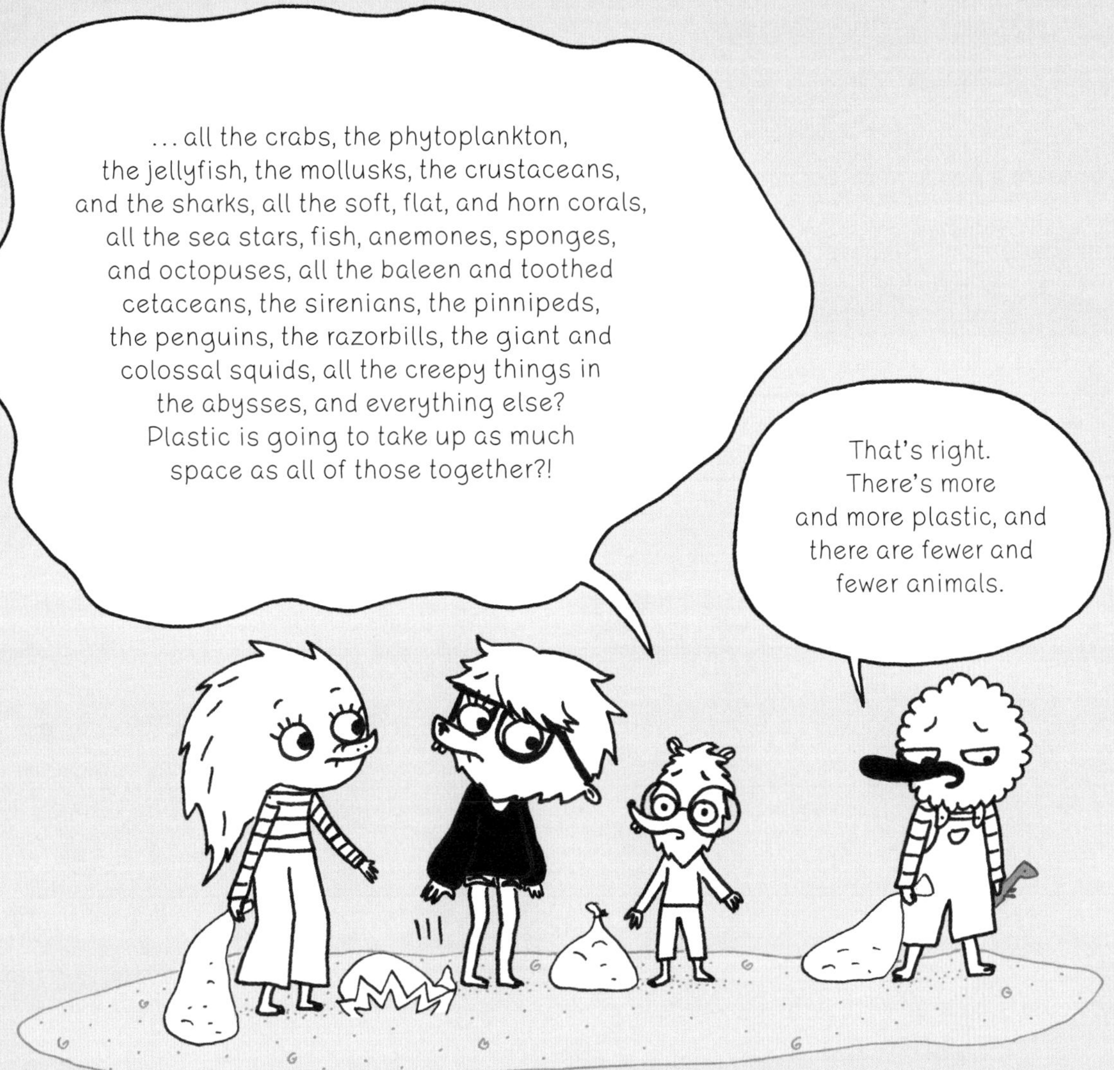

... all the crabs, the phytoplankton, the jellyfish, the mollusks, the crustaceans, and the sharks, all the soft, flat, and horn corals, all the sea stars, fish, anemones, sponges, and octopuses, all the baleen and toothed cetaceans, the sirenians, the pinnipeds, the penguins, the razorbills, the giant and colossal squids, all the creepy things in the abysses, and everything else? Plastic is going to take up as much space as all of those together?!
That's right. There's more and more plastic, and there are fewer and fewer animals.

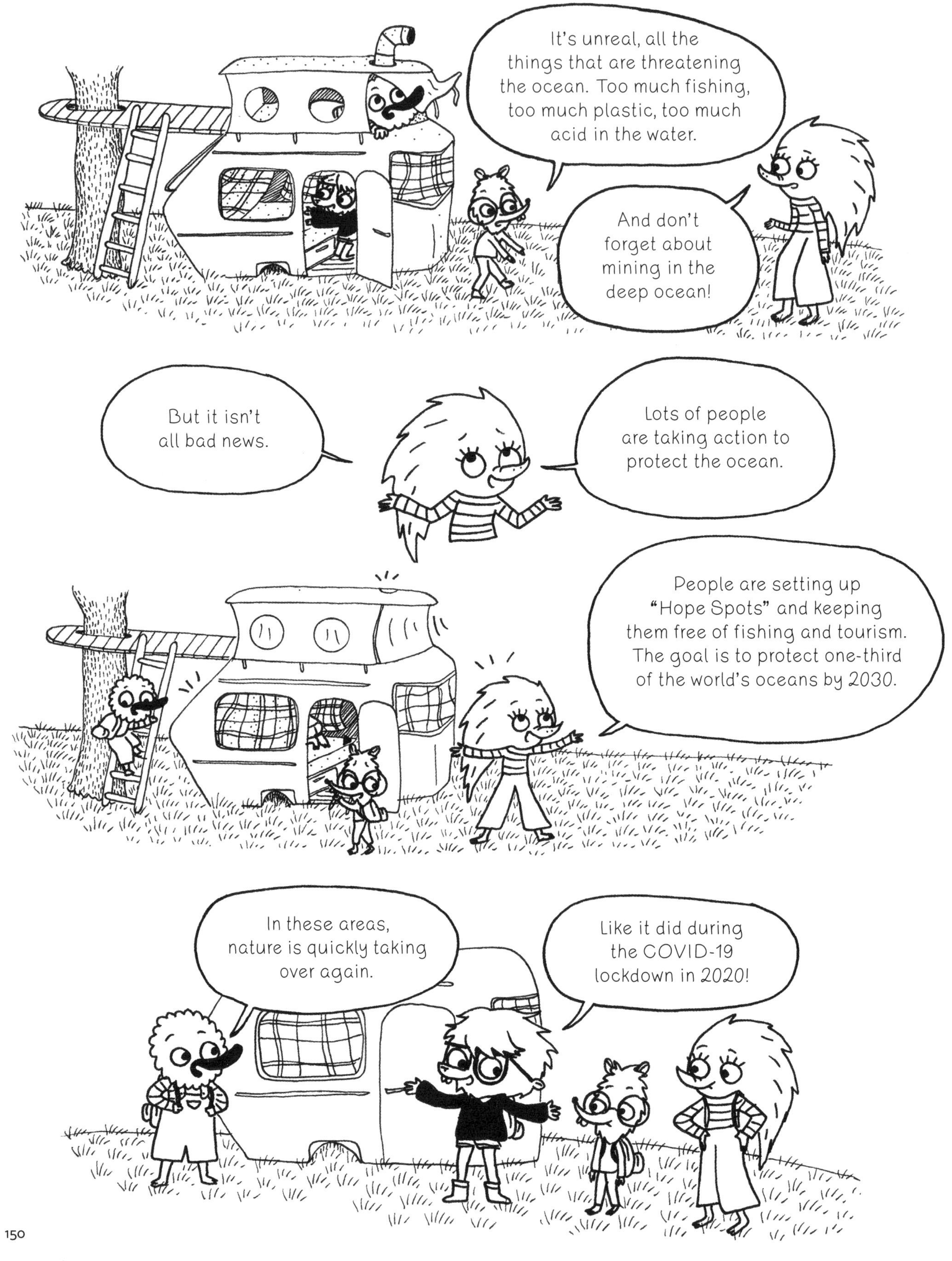
It's unreal, all the things that are threatening the ocean. Too much fishing, too much plastic, too much acid in the water.
And don't forget about mining in the deep ocean!
But it isn't all bad news.
Lots of people are taking action to protect the ocean.
People are setting up "Hope Spots" and keeping them free of fishing and tourism. The goal is to protect one-third of the world's oceans by 2030.
In these areas, nature is quickly taking over again.
Like it did during the COVID-19 lockdown in 2020!

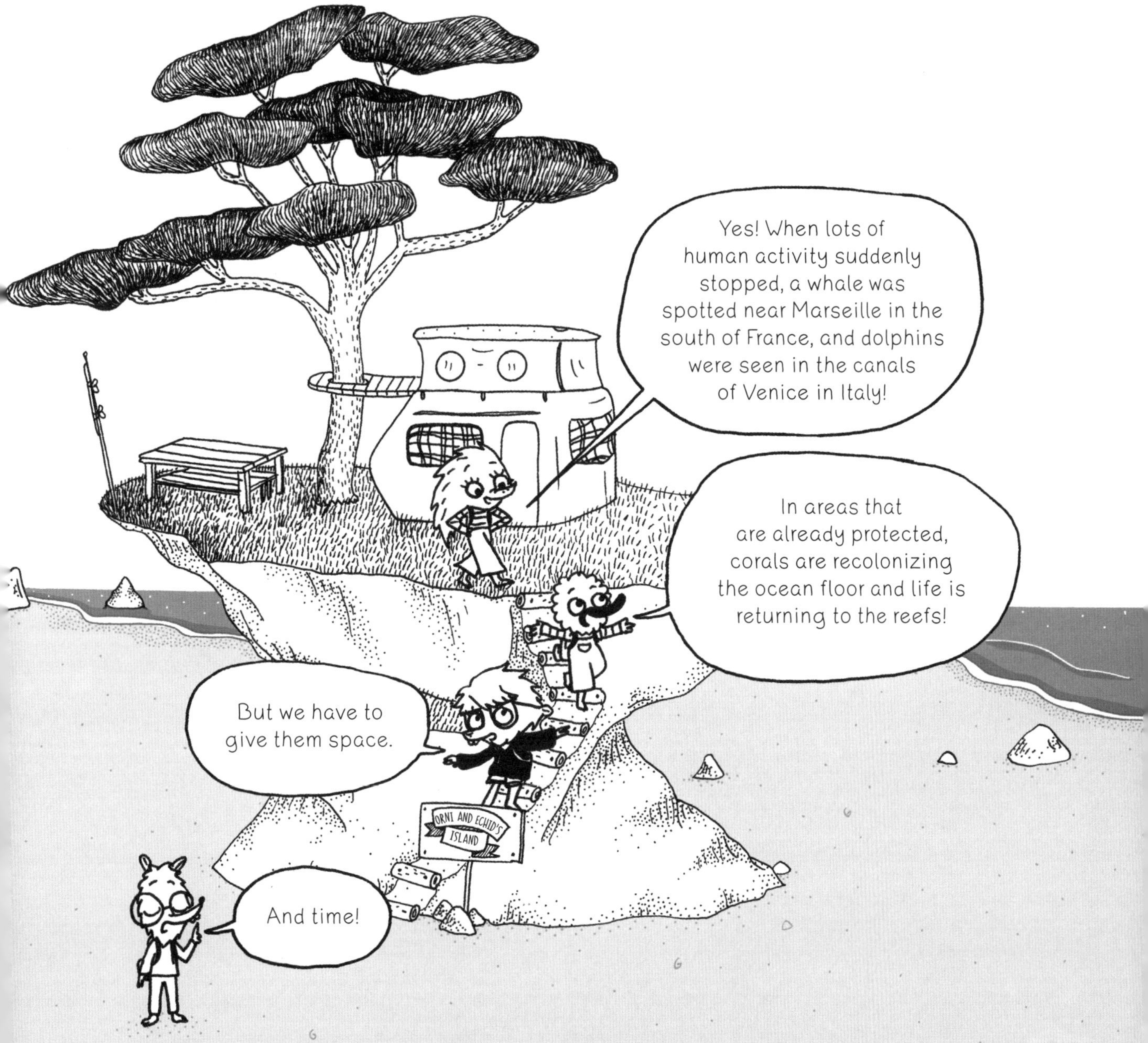
Yes! When lots of human activity suddenly stopped, a whale was spotted near Marseille in the south of France, and dolphins were seen in the canals of Venice in Italy!
In areas that are already protected, corals are recolonizing the ocean floor and life is returning to the reefs!
But we have to give them space.
ORNI AND ECHID'S ISLAND
And time!

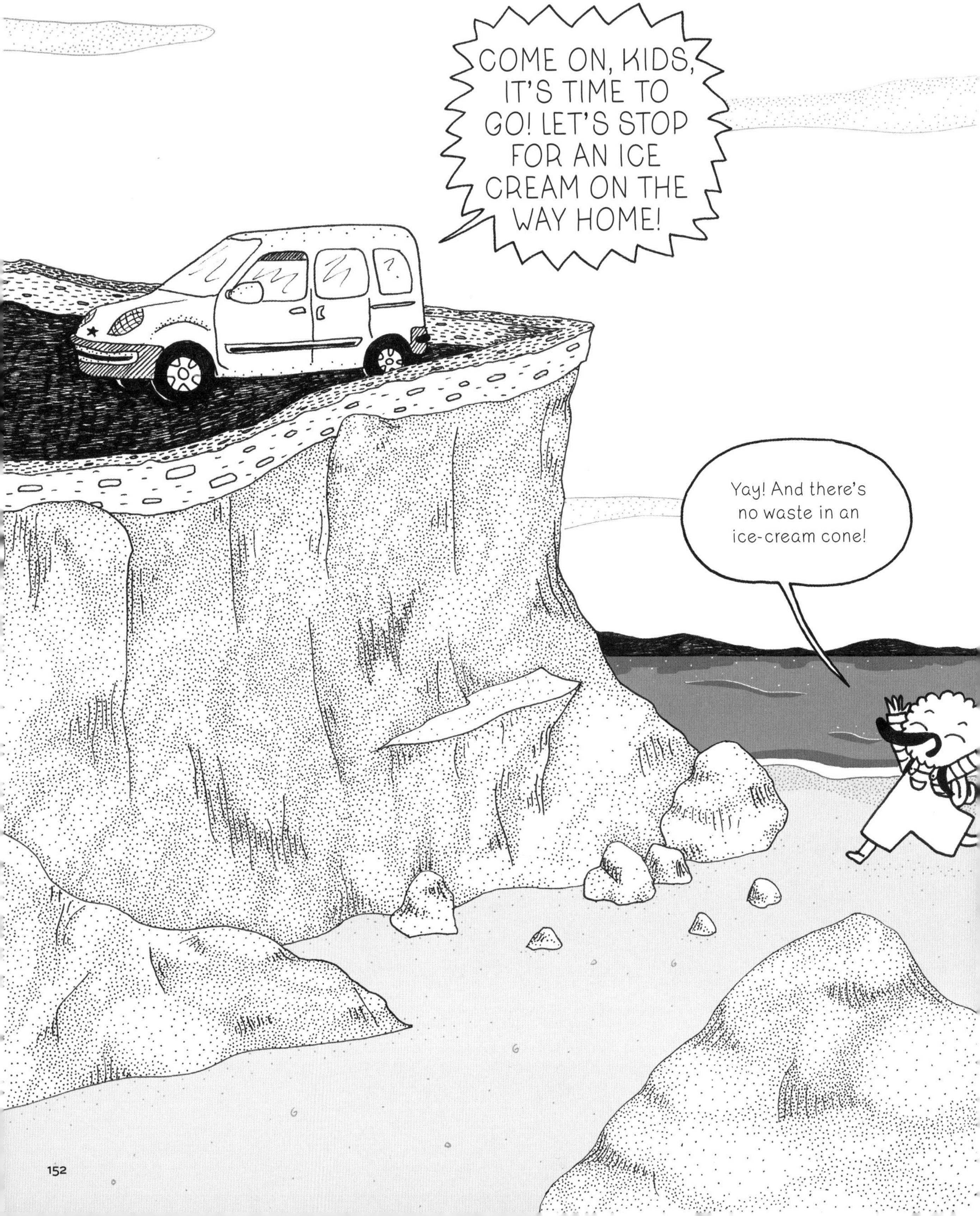
COME ON, KIDS, IT'S TIME TO GO! LET'S STOP FOR AN ICE CREAM ON THE WAY HOME!
Yay! And there's no waste in an ice-cream cone!

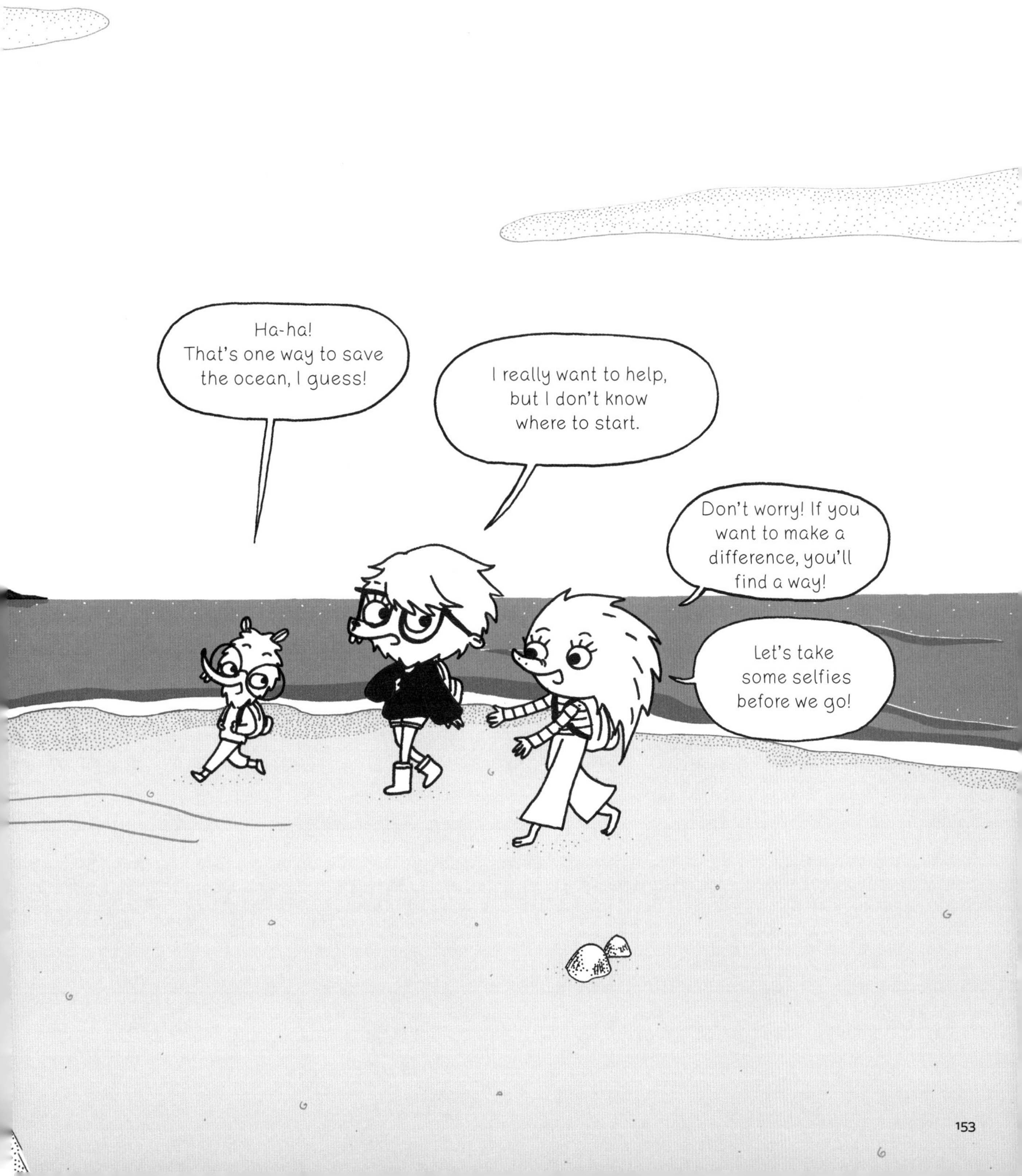
Ha-ha! That's one way to save the ocean, I guess!
I really want to help, but I don't know where to start.
Don't worry! If you want to make a difference, you'll find a way!
Let's take some selfies before we go!

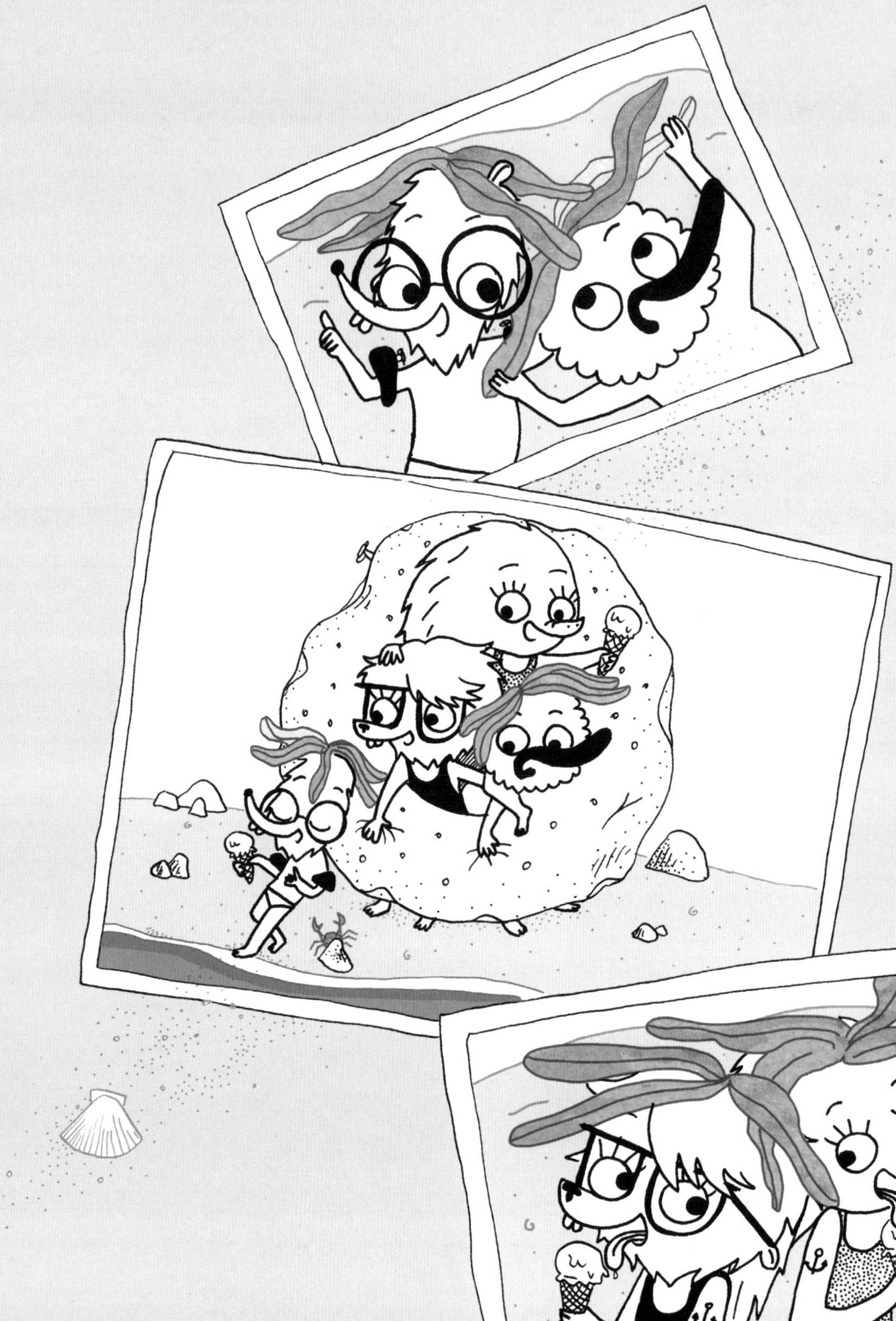

DO YOU WANT TO HELP THE OCEAN?

LET'S FIND YOUR STYLE!

How do you feel after reading this book?

SUPER SENSITIVE

You're like Castor! All of this news is kind of overwhelming and makes you feel a little sad. You want to help, but it all seems so complicated and you don't know where to start. It's okay to feel sad. This is an important issue! Just remember, every small gesture makes a difference.

Everything seems easier when you take things one step at a time!
Even just wanting to help is a good thing!
We're all different and take things at our own pace.
Ask other people what they're doing to help and what they started with.
Take a deep breath!

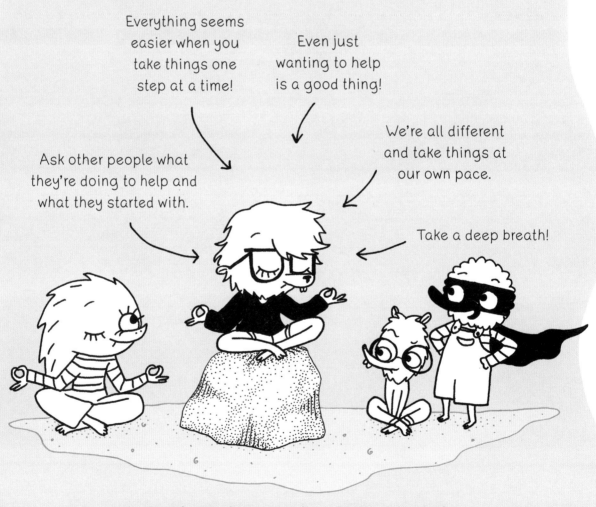

KEEP CALM AND YOU'LL FIND A WAY!

SUPER ACTIVE

You're like Orni! You love animals and you want to save the world, but you tend to go off in all directions. Go for it! Try lots of things and you'll see what works best for you.

Bring your own water bottle when you go out, and pick up any waste you find.
Learn how to sort waste and recycle.
Ride your bike or walk whenever you can.
Eat ice cream in a cone.
Say NO to plastic utensils and wrapping paper when it's your birthday.
Build a composter with your family.

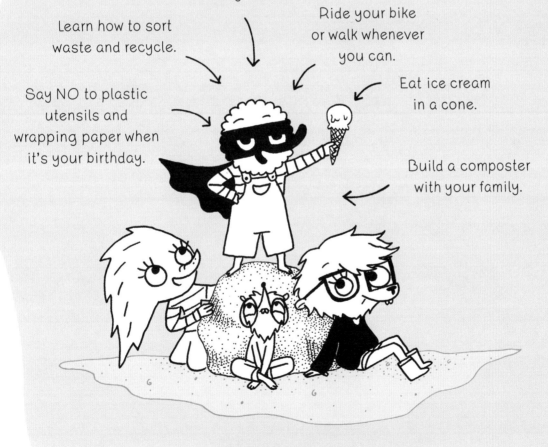

SUPERHEROES RIDE A BIKE!

SUPER COMMITTED

You're like Echid! You've carried a reusable water bottle for ages, you're an expert at recycling and sorting waste at home, and your superpower is saying "NO, THANKS. I DON'T NEED A BAG!" Maybe you've even started shopping for clothes and toys at thrift stores and garage sales. That's awesome! Keep up the good work!

Did you know there are places where you can learn how to make your own soap and even make your own bags for buying stuff without packaging?

You're already doing the right thing and setting an example for others. That's more than enough!

Always remember to bring your own cloth bag.

Everyone does things at their own pace, so be patient with the people around you.

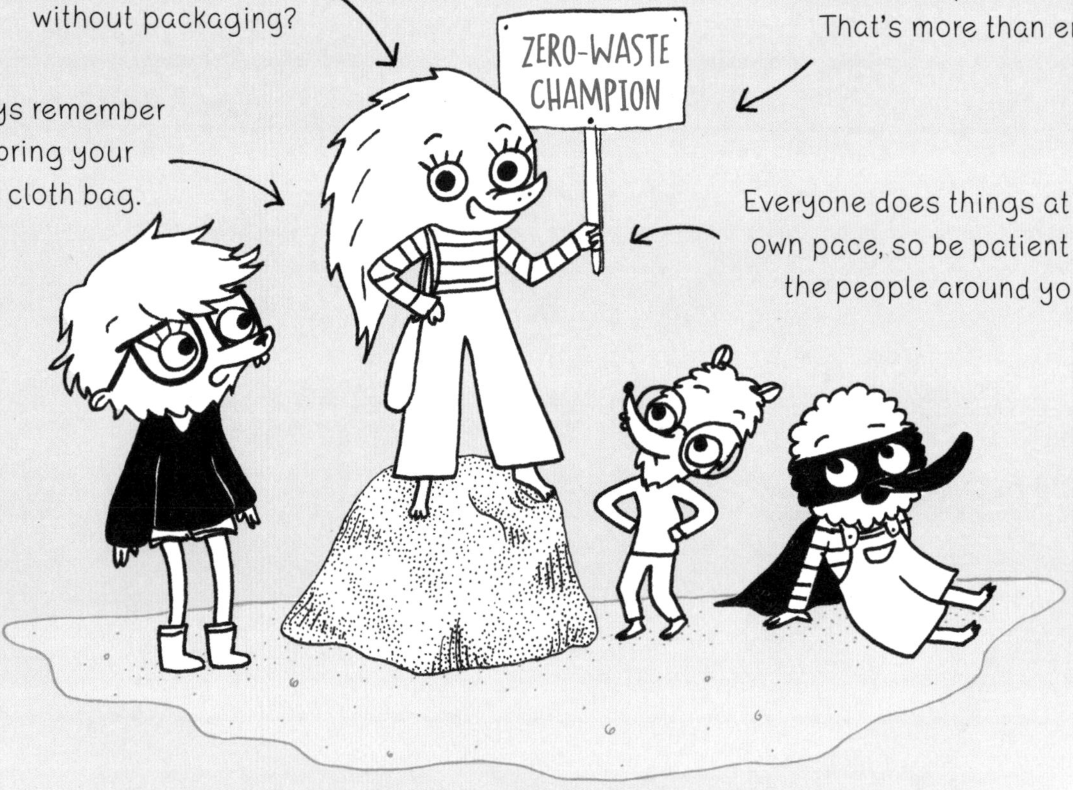

ZERO-WASTE CHAMPION

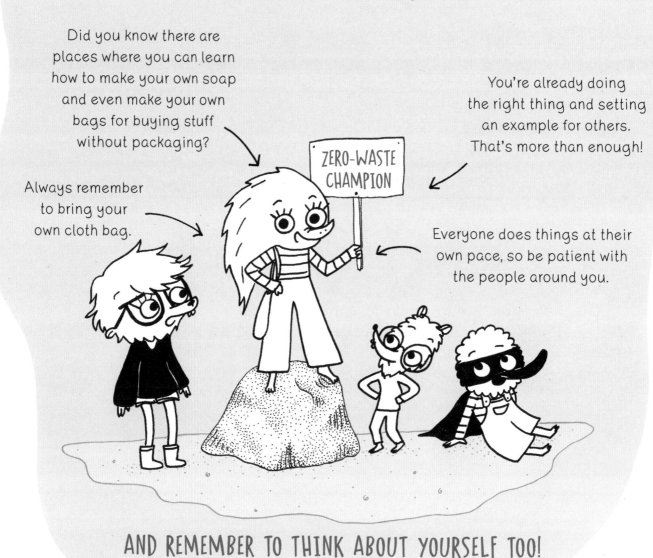

AND REMEMBER TO THINK ABOUT YOURSELF TOO!

SUPER CURIOUS

You're like Squeak! This is all new for you. You have a lot of questions and need to learn more to figure out how all this works. That's great! Go right ahead!

Don't believe everything you read or hear. Keep your eyes open, think carefully, and do your research.

And share what you've learned with your friends.

Read, look things up, ask questions at home and at school, and go to an aquarium or a natural science museum to learn more.

When you're ready to help, maybe you'll do what feels right to you!

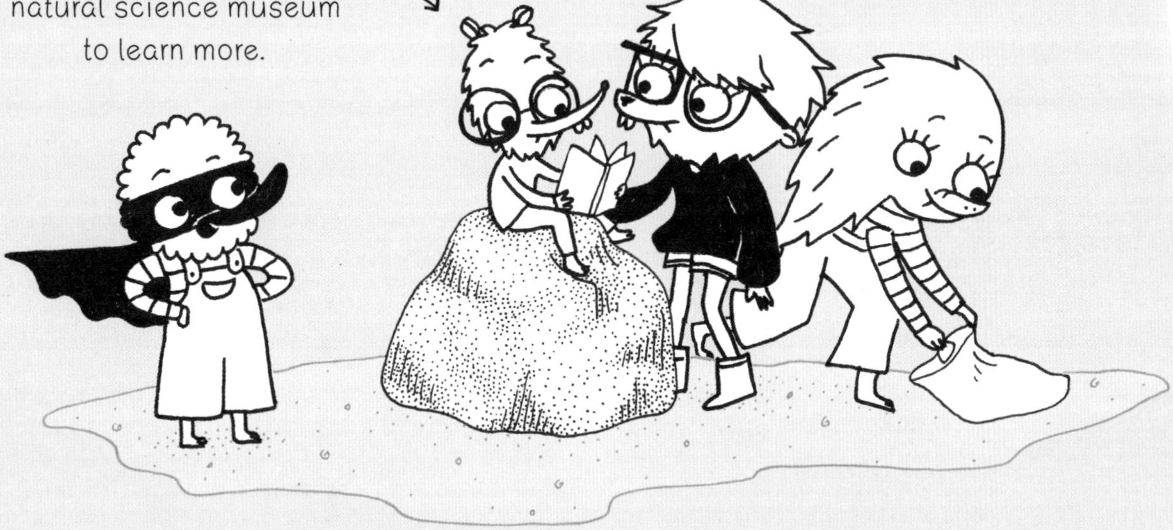

CURIOSITY IS A SUPERPOWER TOO!

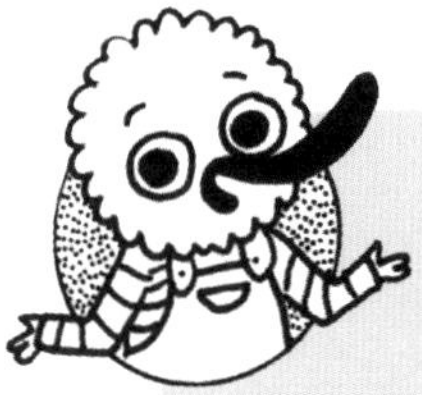

DID YOU FIND ALL THE HIDDEN ANIMALS IN THE CAMOUFLAGE AND CONFUSION SECTION?

PAGE 84: You can spot a ray above Echid, some clown fish in the anemone, and a moray eel just below. At the bottom, there's an octopus by Orni's foot, and there are some razorfish and a green fish in the coral beside the gorgonian.

PAGE 85: At the bottom, in the coral, you can spot a stonefish, a weever, a sand eel, and a flatfish (but only its eyes!). In the seaweed beside Squeak, there's a seahorse. And another one (with polka dots) is hiding in the coral above Castor. And above the cuttlefish, there's one more seahorse. This one looks like a leaf.

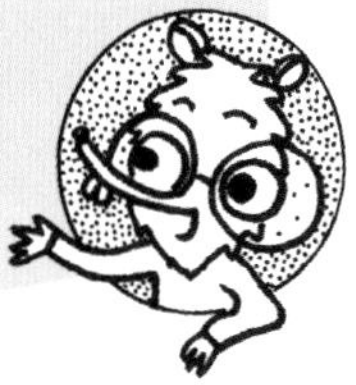

THE DIFFERENT TYPES OF MARINE CREATURES

There are so many different species on Earth, scientists have grouped them by what they have in common.

Here are the groups they've put marine creatures into.

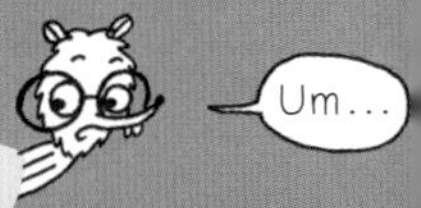

Um...

ANNELIDS

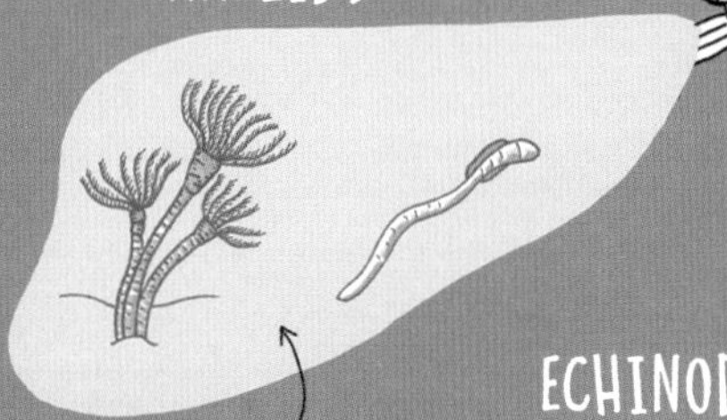

Fanworms, bristle worms...

SPONGES

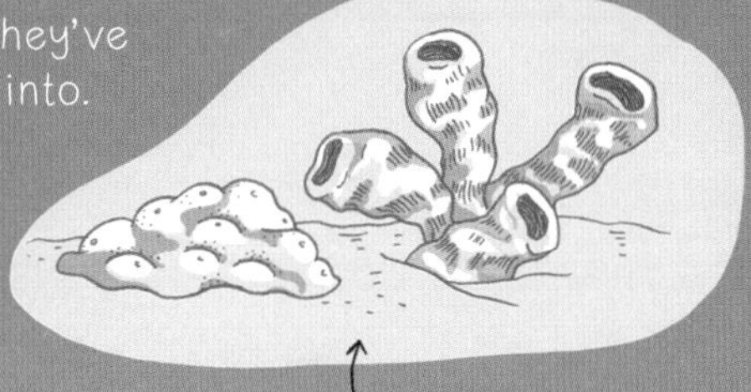

Sea sponges

ECHINODERMS

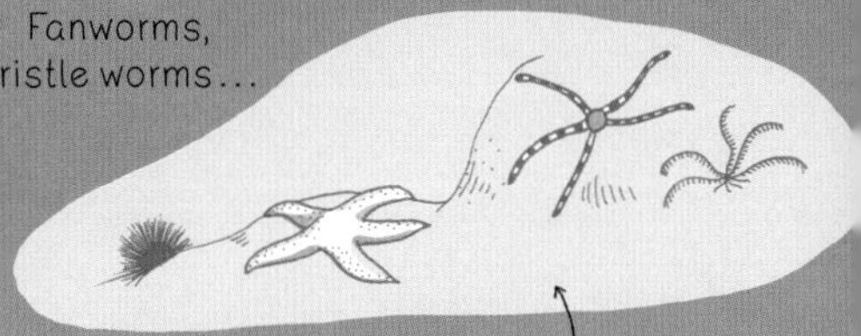

Urchins, sea stars, brittle stars, crinoids...

CNIDARIANS

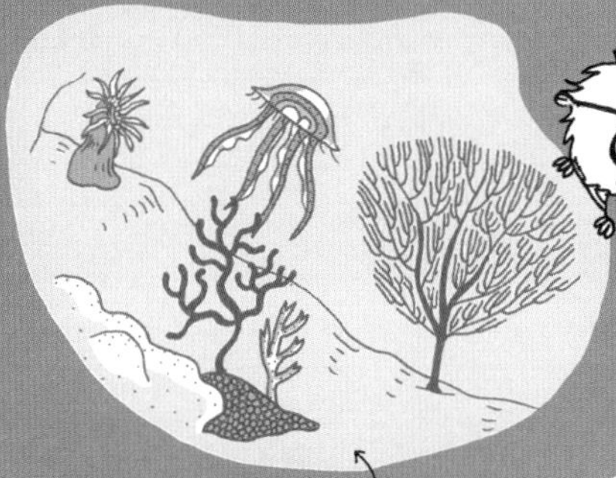

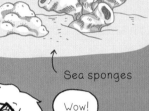

Jellyfish, anemones, corals...

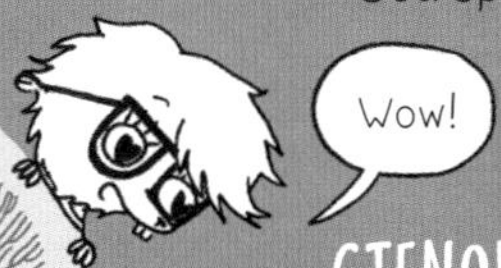

Wow!

ARTHROPODS

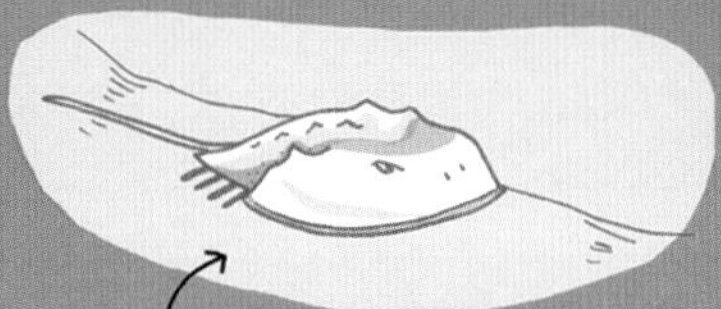

Horseshoe crabs, crustaceans...

TUNICATES

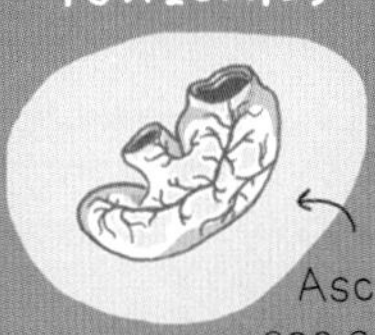

Ascidians, sea squirts

CTENOPHORA (COMB JELLIES)

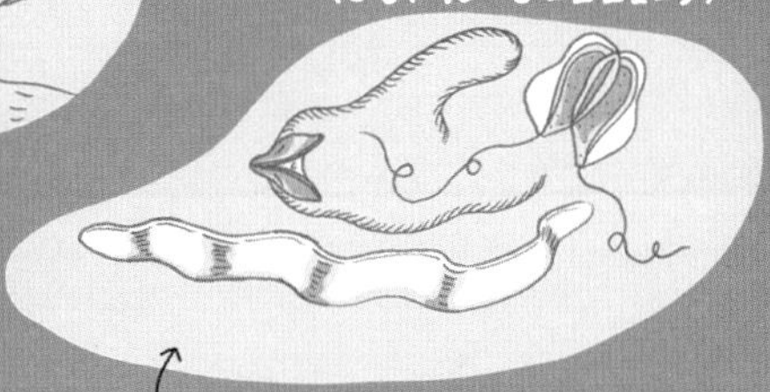

Venus girdles, which look like belts, are just one type of ctenophore.

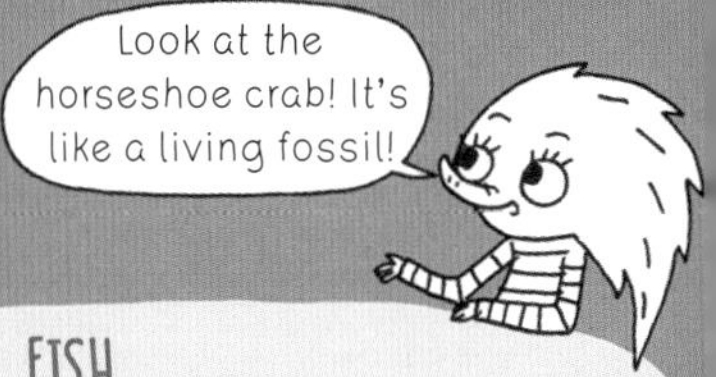

Look at the horseshoe crab! It's like a living fossil!

MOLLUSKS

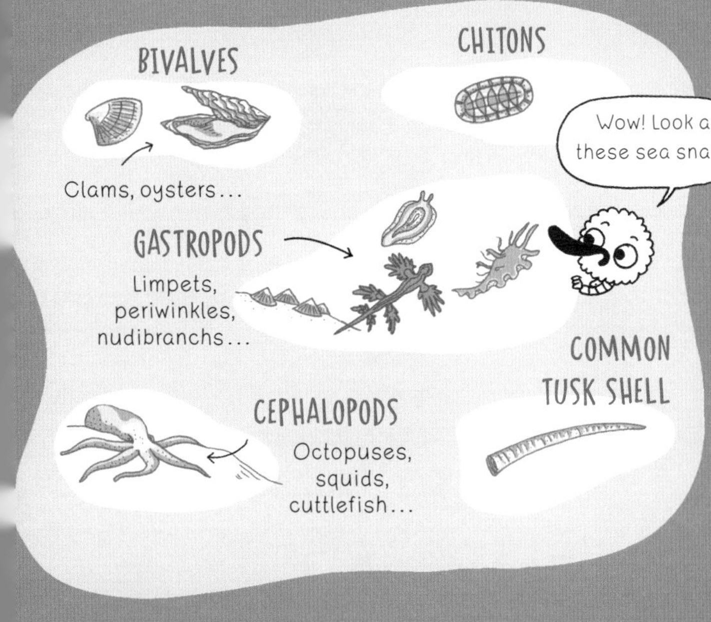

Wow! Look at these sea snails!

BIVALVES

Clams, oysters...

CHITONS

GASTROPODS

Limpets, periwinkles, nudibranchs...

COMMON TUSK SHELL

CEPHALOPODS

Octopuses, squids, cuttlefish...

VERTEBRATES

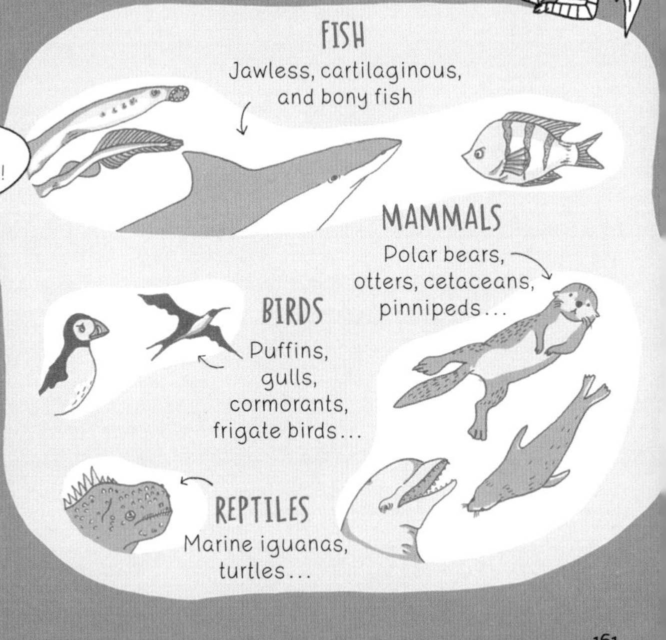

FISH

Jawless, cartilaginous, and bony fish

MAMMALS

Polar bears, otters, cetaceans, pinnipeds...

BIRDS

Puffins, gulls, cormorants, frigate birds...

REPTILES

Marine iguanas, turtles...

A NOTE FROM THE AUTHOR

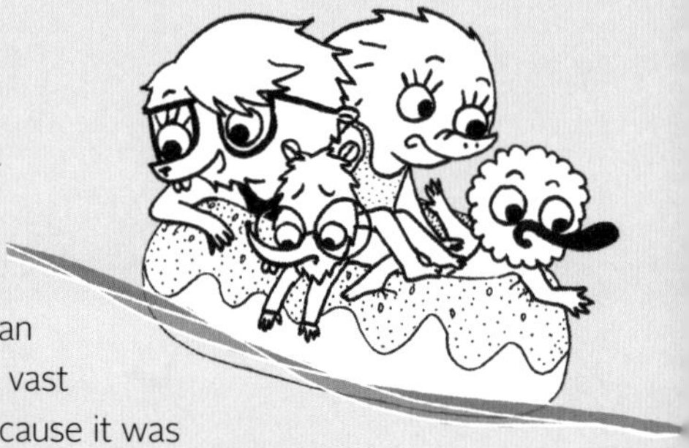

WHEN I STARTED writing this book, I didn't think it would have such a big impact on my life and the way I see things. I have never been super passionate about the ocean or about sailing. I'm not a diver, either. Unlike Orni and Echid, I've never had the opportunity to try diving.

I had a lot to learn. For a very long time, I used to get really freaked out by anything that looked remotely like a fish. When I watched TV, and even when I read a book, I used to close my eyes at the slightest sign of anything underwater, just in case… The very thought of visiting an aquarium or going for a swim somewhere I might see fish swimming was too much for me.

Determined to get over my fear, I started to read some books, I watched some documentaries, and I tried to understand how the ocean worked and how marine animals lived. Underwater images eventually became a part of my life. I started drawing scenes of the ocean floor, of corals, anemones, otters, and even fish. And my phobia gradually went away. I was already super passionate about space, and now I was discovering a whole new world, like another planet where the laws of physics were not the same as on dry land. I came to see the surface of the water as a frontier leading to another universe inhabited by creatures each as surprising and intriguing as the last, some of them looking just the way I thought aliens might look.

To me, the ocean seemed almost as vast as outer space, because it was a whole new environment to dive into, and that environment was so vibrant. I never imagined I would discover such a huge diversity of animal and plant life.

In other words, the things I fit into every one of these pages could easily have each filled a whole book. But I wanted to draw an overall picture of the ocean and the life it supports, and I wanted to show all the riches of the marine environment and its biodiversity.

Beauty and wonderment are the things that drive my curiosity and make me want to learn more about something. I believe that if we see and show beautiful things and understand how everything is connected, the inspiration for us to make a difference will come naturally. Because even though I knew when I started creating this book that the ocean and marine life were endangered, I didn't think I could do much to help. But then I realized that just by changing a few of my habits, and by sharing what I learned, I could contribute in my own way to protecting the ocean and these creatures I used to be so afraid of.

GAËLLE ALMÉRAS

SIZE (KIND OF) MATTERS!

I WISH I could have drawn all these creatures and backgrounds to the correct scale, but I soon realized that was an impossible mission. When we watch a documentary about the ocean, it's difficult to get a sense of how big things are because there's not much down there for us to compare them to. Sometimes, in shallow waters, we might see a diver on the screen to give us an idea of size, but in the deep ocean everything is as mysterious as outer space! Often I've been surprised to learn the size of creatures I thought I knew. I encourage you to go look up how big they are. You can pick up a book, look on the internet, or visit an aquarium and see for yourself! Here's one example. I figured the humpback anglerfish was about the size of a basketball, but then I found out that the males were about as small as a golf ball! The females are bigger, but even they would still fit in a human hand.

I realized that if I wanted to draw everything to scale, even if I drew the characters 0.2 in. (0.5 cm) high, I would need more than 108 ft. (33 m) of paper to illustrate the bottom of the Mariana Trench!

I know I ask a lot of my editors and publishers, but that would have been a super tall order!

THANK YOU

THANK YOU AGAIN to Marjolaine Matabos (whom I still haven't had the chance to meet but who so kindly answered all my questions and took the time to explain things to me) for being super helpful and excited about *Super Ocean Weekend* right from the start! And thank you to Christine David-Beausire, Sandra Fuchs, Camille Mellin, Ewan Pelleter, Gauthier Schaal, and Bruno Ferron for their feedback, advice, clarifications, and explanations!

Thank you to everyone at the Vaulx-en-Velin Planetarium. I'm sure it was a big job explaining to me how tides, climate, albedo, and ocean currents work! Thank you to Jérôme Mourin, director of the Lyon Aquarium, for showing me around. Thank you to Gérald Andres, specialist in traditional marine illustration at the Lyon Library Archives, for showing me his hand-painted treasures. Thank you to Claude Doumet-Pincet, curator of the *Under the Ocean* exhibition at the Cité des Sciences museum in Paris, for showing me around. Thank you to Cédric Audibert at the Musée des Confluences for introducing me to nudibranchs and spending 3 hours telling me all about mollusks, all for just one page in the book!

Thank you to everyone I've met at book fairs and in libraries who loved *Super Space Weekend* and told me they couldn't wait for the *Super Ocean Weekend* sequel! Thank you to Nathalie Beaufort-Lamy for her coaching and the incredible welcome in Le Havre. She gave me the strength to plunge into the ocean depths! (It took me a while, but I did it!)

Thank you to the 101s for listening to me whine all these years and encouraging me when I couldn't do that ***** water thing! Thank you to Chouchou and Marinovion for their advice. Thank you to Benj for his book about the abysses. Now I can finally give it back! Thank you to Pierrot for the important rereads. Thank you to Clairou for her excellent book about seaweed that really inspired me.

Thank you to Frédéric Basset for his amazing advice and super photoengraving!

Thank you to Anne and Anne Bé, my editors. We're not always on the same page, but you always encourage me to do my best and tell me if I'm going the wrong way, and you still give me the freedom I need to keep going.

Thank you once more to the Centre National du Livre for supporting this latest adventure for Squeak, Castor, Orni, my French publisher Maison Georges, and me!

And thank you, most of all, to Régis for being a curious and conscientious reader and reviser, for getting me to check what the foreshore was really like, and for coping with my ups and my downs, my doubts and my fears, and my color tests!

163

To my mom and my grandma, for all the great times we've had by the ocean! —GA

GAËLLE ALMÉRAS loves art and science, particularly astronomy and nature, and is a very active author and illustrator. In 2015, she started writing a series of popular science columns that then became *Super Space Weekend* (*Le Super week-end de l'espace*), awarded with the Prix André Brahic as best astronomy picture book for children in 2019, and a finalist of the Montreuil Book Fair Pépites as well as France's Ministry of Higher Education's Prix le goût des sciences. She lives in Dompierre-les-Ormes, France.

DAVID WARRINER grew up in the UK with a passion for French and lived in France and Quebec before deciding to call beautiful British Columbia home. He's been a professional translator for nearly half his life and has translated a range of fiction, nonfiction, and children's books for publishers on both sides of the Atlantic—including *Super Space Weekend*, the first book in the Science Adventure Club series.

DAVID SUZUKI INSTITUTE

THE DAVID SUZUKI INSTITUTE is a companion organization to the David Suzuki Foundation, with a focus on promoting and publishing on important environmental issues in partnership with Greystone Books.

We invite you to support the activities of the Institute. For more information, please contact us at:

David Suzuki Institute
219 – 2211 West 4th Avenue
Vancouver, BC, Canada V6K 4S2
info@davidsuzukiinstitute.org
604-742-2899
davidsuzukiinstitute.org

Checks can be made payable to The David Suzuki Institute.

First published in English by Greystone Books in 2024
Originally published in French in 2022 as *Le Super Week-end de l'océan* by Maison Georges. This edition was published by arrangement with The Picture Book Agency, France. All rights reserved.
Text and illustrations copyright © 2022 by Maison Georges
English translation copyright © 2024 by David Warriner
Foreword copyright © 2024 by Marjolaine Matabos

24 25 26 27 28   5 4 3 2 1

Greystone Kids / Greystone Books Ltd.
greystonebooks.com

David Suzuki Institute
davidsuzukiinstitute.org

Cataloguing data available from Library and Archives Canada
ISBN 978-1-77840-068-1 (cloth)
ISBN 978-1-77840-208-1 (pbk.)
ISBN 978-1-77840-069-8 (epub)

Editing by Linda Pruessen
Copy editing by Tracy Bordian
Proofreading by Alison Strobel
Cover design by Fiona Siu and Jessica Sullivan
Interior typesetting by Fiona Siu
The illustrations in this book were rendered in mixed media (felt-tip pen, watercolor, and ink), scanned, and digitized.

SCIENTIFIC REVIEW BY:

Marjolaine Matabos, deep-sea ecology researcher at the Ifremer Biology and Ecology of Deep Marine Ecosystems Laboratory

Christine David-Beausire, deputy director of the French Polar Institute Paul-Émile Victor

Bruno Ferron, physicist and oceanographer with the Physical and Spatial Oceanography Laboratory at the French National Center for Scientific Research (CNRS)

Sandra Fuchs, biological engineer at Ifremer

Camille Mellin, marine biology researcher at the School of Biological Sciences in the Faculty of Sciences, Engineering and Technology, University of Adelaide, Australia

Ewan Pelleter, marine geosciences researcher with the Ifremer Geo-Ocean unit

Gauthier Schaal, lecturer at the Université de Bretagne Occidentale, France

Jack Barth, executive director of the Marine Studies Initiative at the College of Earth, Ocean, and Atmospheric Sciences, Oregon State University

Marie Noël, marine biologist

Printed and bound in China on FSC® certified paper at Shenzhen Reliance Printing. The FSC® label means that materials used for the product have been responsibly sourced.

Greystone Books thanks the Canada Council for the Arts, the British Columbia Arts Council, the Province of British Columbia through the Book Publishing Tax Credit, and the Government of Canada for supporting our publishing activities.

Published with the support of the Embassy of France in Canada.

Greystone Books gratefully acknowledges the xʷməθkʷəy̓əm (Musqueam), Sḵwx̱wú7mesh (Squamish), and səl̓ilwətaɬ (Tsleil-Waututh) peoples on whose land our Vancouver head office is located.

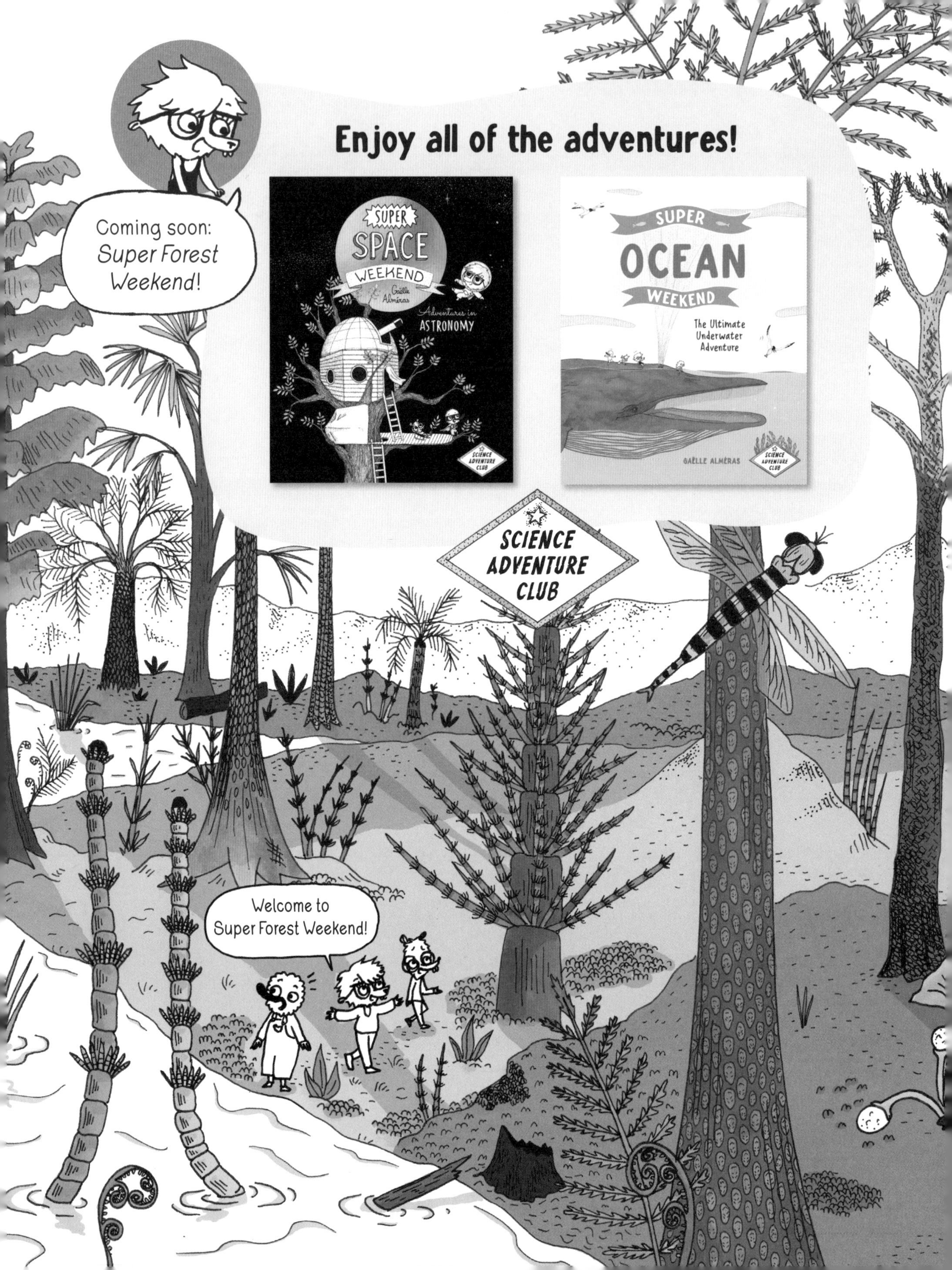
Enjoy all of the adventures!
Coming soon: Super Forest Weekend!
SUPER SPACE WEEKEND
Gaëlle Alméras
Adventures in ASTRONOMY
SCIENCE ADVENTURE CLUB
SUPER OCEAN WEEKEND
The Ultimate Underwater Adventure
GAËLLE ALMÉRAS
SCIENCE ADVENTURE CLUB
SCIENCE ADVENTURE CLUB
Welcome to Super Forest Weekend!